Advance Praise

The result of intense and committed fieldwork into the transitions and transformations of agricultural and rural capitalism, of gendered work, of production and exchange, of feudal rents and relations and of local and global capitalist markets, this rich evocation of the flatland society of a mountain state is certain to inspire comparative research, debate and reflections far and wide in agrarian studies.

Barbara Harriss-White, University of Oxford

A bold and brilliant work by Fraser Sugden. Based on the ethnography of modes of production and compelling analysis of the complex and multilinear process of agrarian change in the Nepal Tarai, the book offers a fresh look at pre-capitalist formations in the age of globalisation in one of the world's peripheral economies. This book, for its unconventional approach, is a rare contribution to the study of Nepal's political economy.

Suresh Dhakal, Tribhuvan University

Land, Labour and Agrarian Change in Nepal's Tarai-Madhesh

This book offers a historically grounded and multi-scalar analysis of agrarian change in Nepal's far-eastern Tarai. It shows how this region has since the 1700s evolved from a forested frontier home to relatively autonomous Adivasi (indigenous) cultivators to a feudal economy grounded in landlord–tenant relations, which has persisted alongside a rapidly expanding industrial and commercial sector. The book explores the changing land ownership patterns and distribution of surplus, the flow of labour between agriculture and industry, and more complex interactions with global capitalism. It thus offers unique insights into both the reproduction and transformations of class, ethnic and labour relations in Nepal during a period of rapid political transformation. It also offers deeper insights into how capitalism expands into regions on the periphery of the global economy and interacts with older economic formations.

Fraser Sugden is an Associate Professor in Human Geography at the University of Birmingham specialising in the political economy of agrarian and environmental change. He has written extensively on shifting class, gender and generational relations in agriculture globally, and their interaction with contemporary environmental, political and economic stresses. He has conducted intensive rural fieldwork across South and East Asia, with a focus on Nepal and the Eastern Gangetic Plains and, prior to joining the University of Birmingham, was based at the International Water Management Institute in Kathmandu, where he led a range of research projects on agricultural intensification, irrigation and land tenure.

Land, Labour and Agrarian Change in Nepal's Tarai-Madhesh

Fraser Sugden

CAMBRIDGE
UNIVERSITY PRESS

CAMBRIDGE
UNIVERSITY PRESS

Shaftesbury Road, Cambridge CB2 8EA, United Kingdom

One Liberty Plaza, 20th Floor, New York, NY 10006, USA

477 Williamstown Road, Port Melbourne, VIC 3207, Australia

314–321, 3rd Floor, Plot 3, Splendor Forum, Jasola District Centre, New Delhi – 110025, India

103 Penang Road, #05–06/07, Visioncrest Commercial, Singapore 238467

Cambridge University Press is part of Cambridge University Press & Assessment, a department of the University of Cambridge.

We share the University's mission to contribute to society through the pursuit of education, learning and research at the highest international levels of excellence.

www.cambridge.org
Information on this title: www.cambridge.org/9781009555593

First published 2025

Printed in India by Thomson Press India Ltd.

A catalogue record for this publication is available from the British Library

ISBN 978-1-009-55559-3 Hardback

Contents

Tables

Figures

Acknowledgements

I am exceptionally grateful for all of the invaluable assistance that was given to me from the residents of Jhorahat, Bhaudaha and Thalaha and the surrounding villages who welcomed me warmly into their communities. I would like to especially thank my host Bijay Chaudhary and family and his father, the late Hari Narayan Chaudhary, whose kind words of support and company during fieldwork will always be remembered. I am also grateful for the support of Dukha Ram Mandal, Sanju, Sunita and Yaman Sardar, and Sangita Bishwakarma. In particular, I offer my sincerest gratitude to Sagar Mudvari, Sachin Ghimire, and Pushpa Hamal, who provided research assistance and worked together with me during my original PhD fieldwork in 2007–2008. A particular thanks goes to Upendra Khawas who worked with me during the PhD fieldwork and in many later phases of research, whose local knowledge was invaluable. Without the invaluable help of this team in the early stages of this study, the research would have been impossible. I extend my thanks also to research collaborators with whom I worked on later projects in the region which contributed directly and indirectly to this study, including Niki Maskey, Ashok Rai, Brady Mccarl, Shalini Gupta and Arjun Kharel. I am also grateful for the academic inspiration offered by a range of scholars, including my then PhD supervisors Andrea Nightingale and John Cameron, as well as David Seddon, Simon Chilvers, Kumar Sanjay Singh, Rajendra Uprety, Suresh Dhakal, Hari Dhungana, Jagannath Adhikari, Ganesh Gurung, Purna Nepali, Magnus Hatlebakk, Katharine Rankin and Tula Narayan Sah.

The research was funded by a range of sources. These included the Graduate Organisation for the School of Geosciences at the University of Edinburgh, the Slawson Award for Field Studies from the Royal Geographical Society and the Richard Stapley Educational Trust for the first phase of research. Further data was collected using internal funds from the University of Birmingham School of Geography, Earth and Environmental Sciences, as well as through a number of separate projects, including two studies funded by the CGIAR Programme on Climate Change and Food Security (CCAFS) and the International Water Management Institute (IWMI). Some of the data used was also connected with the ACIAR project Improving Dry Season Irrigation for Marginal and Tenant Farmers in the Eastern Gangetic Plains; and the Horizon 2020–funded project Leaving Something Behind – Migration Governance and Agricultural and Rural Change in 'Home' Communities: Comparative Experience from Europe, Africa and Asia (grant agreement No. 822730).

1

Introduction

Revisiting the 'Pre-capitalist'

The global peasantry today is at an important crossroads. With much of the world well into a fourth decade of economic liberalisation, there are few localities left which are outside of the reach of globalised capitalist commodity or labour markets. Unprecedented improvements in transport and communication over recent decades have intensified this process of integration into the world economy. While capitalist industrialisation across the periphery is highly uneven, urban areas are experiencing a more dynamic trajectory of growth, with a surging service sector and the rise of a consumerist middle class. However, for the countryside, the expansion of capitalism has left in its wake a wave of monetisation, enclosure of land, rising costs of living and intensified inequalities (see Levien et al., 2018). These are paralleled by a cultural transformation, which includes a rising ambivalence towards the peasant 'way of life' (White, 2012). This is evident particularly amongst young people, who are increasingly in touch with the aspirations of globalised youth via the vastly improved telecommunications networks of recent decades and the social media revolution.

These economic and cultural transformations for the farming population converge with the rising ecological stresses associated with climate change. With spiralling costs of farm inputs and a depleted natural resource base, some of the gains of the 'Green Revolution' years are being reversed (Vaidyanathan, 2006). Agrarian stress, alongside cultural change amongst youth, has consolidated cyclical labour in the capitalist sector as a major feature of rural life (Shah and Lerche, 2020; Singh, 2007; Sugden, 2019; Zhan and Scully, 2018) – either via long-distance migration or 'commuting' to local towns. This applies particularly to the rural land-poor majority, who lack the ability or opportunity to 'accumulate' wealth in a liberalised economy – and follow the success of their urban middle-class counterparts. In this context, precarious wage labour in the capitalist sector is increasingly supplementing fragile agrarian livelihoods at home.

Unfortunately, these transformations have coincided with a decline in many of the radical peasant movements which emerged in the post-colonial era, and this has been most pronounced over the last decade. Some movements have lost momentum as a new generation aspires to opportunities beyond the farm, while others have been co-opted by or have lost support to the global wave of right-wing populism (Scoones et al., 2018), which has cynically capitalised on the changes brought about by neoliberal globalisation (see, for example, Akhtar, 2022).

The transformations wrought by expanding capitalist markets have been felt particularly acutely by countries and regions on the very periphery of the world economy, with agrarian-dominated economies, a long history of import dependence and a skewed pattern of industrialisation. In the South Asian context, this includes Nepal, but also large parts of eastern India and Bangladesh. While these regions frequently have relatively low levels of capitalist production on the ground in terms of industry or large-scale commercial farming, the last few decades in particular have brought about intensified articulations with the global capitalist economy. They have become important captive markets for imported goods from regional centres of accumulation, breaking down age-old barter systems and cottage industries (Blaikie et al., 2001) – while also emerging as pools of surplus labour for capitalism, particularly via migrant labour (Sunam, 2020; De Haan, 2002; Singh, 2007; Sugden, 2019).

However, if one is to scrutinise these changes and chart a new path for progressive peasant politics for the twenty-first century in these peripheral regions, a part of the puzzle is missing. While the transformations to rural life brought about by capitalist expansion for the peasantry have been unprecedented, they have not taken place in a vacuum. All of these peripheral regions are home to complex pre-existing economic formations and class relations, many of which predate capitalism in its current form, and have a fundamental impact on agrarian livelihoods, food security and well-being. These old relations were once the subject of fierce academic debate, particularly in South Asia, when debates over whether India was 'feudal' or 'capitalist' reverberated within Indian academia in the 1970s and 1980s – controversies which had critical political implications regarding the role of the peasantry in the struggle for socialism (Thorner, 1982). While there have been some promising attempts to revive these debates (Kar, 2018), the details of these controversies have now largely slipped into academic obscurity. However, the economic, social and political structures which drove them – most notably those associated with landlordism and its relationship with the state – were not dissolved overnight as South Asia was plunged into the neoliberal project. Likewise, the unceremonious end to the communist era, and the cultural turn in global academia (which precipitated a growing disinterest in the class politics that once made these debates so contentious), does not mean that the material struggles of the vast South Asian peasantry, who still sit between the pre-capitalist and capitalist, have lost their political resonance.

Now is a crucial juncture in which to understand how 'pre-capitalist' social relations have adapted to the changed economic, political and cultural reality. Important questions include whether older class relations are withering in favour of a new balance of power, potentially uplifting the livelihoods and political power of marginalised groups. Conversely, could the latest wave of capitalist expansion allow older economic formations, such as landlordism, to adapt and accommodate economic changes associated with expanding markets? Finally, could these changes bring about new class alliances, just like those which were forged in the deep history of empire when British colonial capitalism extended into the Gangetic Plains two centuries earlier, converging with the centralised feudalism of the Mughals? These are some of the questions addressed in this book – which seeks to chart the political economy of agrarian change on the plains of southeastern Nepal in the context of cultural, political, environmental and economic change.

The book offers broader lessons on the complex mechanisms through which capitalism expands into peripheral regions long associated with 'non-capitalist' forms of social and political organisation. It also sheds light on the larger debates in human geography and agrarian studies around the multilinear processes of agrarian change in the periphery of the world economy. However, it diverges from much recent scholarship through its explicit focus on the pre-capitalist. In doing so, it offers an acknowledgement of how older agrarian relations – in particular, South Asian landlordism, associated often with 'feudal' economic formations – can persist, adapt and even be reinforced in an era of globalisation. It shows how this takes place through a complex interplay of political, economic and cultural phenomena within spheres of both production and circulation. This is contrary to a lot of research on the topic, which implies landlordism is a 'relic' of limited relevance in an era of neoliberal globalisation.

The 'Capitalist' and the 'Pre-capitalist' on the Eastern Sub-Himalayan Frontier

The far eastern Tarai-Madhesh (lowlands) of Nepal forms the historic region of Morang, a frontier belt which encompasses the fertile plains between the Koshi river and the eastern border with India (see Figures 1.1 and 1.2). It is part of a much larger cultural and ecological zone which stretches deep into North Bengal and Assam, skirting the foot of the eastern Himalaya. The agrarian context within this zone epitomises many of the contradictions associated with the convergence of old and new modes of production. Not only was this formerly a forested belt at the interface between hill- and plains-based kingdoms, it also has, throughout the last three centuries, been at the intersection of capitalist, feudal and tribal or 'Adivasi' social formations. The relative isolation, its dense *sal* (Shorea robusta) forests and high prevalence of malaria supported the emergence of complex Adivasi civilisations, who lived separately from erstwhile hill- or plains-based feudal states and whose

Figure 1.1 Nepal's Morang plains are part of a highly fertile belt home predominantly to Adivasi communities which extends across the eastern sub-Himalayan lowlands

Source: Author.

livelihoods were grounded primarily in shifting cultivation, or *jhum* (Rai, 2015; Ray, 2013; Chaudhuri, 1995).

These older economic systems, however, experienced a wave of subordination to feudalism following the conquest by centralised state formations in the eighteenth and nineteenth centuries. These state formations sought the region for its plentiful fertile land, high rainfall and rich reserves of timber. In the North Bengal Tarai, this included first the Bhutanese in the eighteenth century and then the British empire in the nineteenth century, including tributary kingdoms such as the Cooch Behar princely state. Over the Nepal border in Morang, where this study is focused, the Gorkhali empire (of present-day central Nepal) conquered the region in the seventeenth century. This conquest would go on to have an unprecedented impact on agrarian relations in the decades to come. The land of the plains was a significant source of tax revenue for the rulers of the new kingdom of Nepal, who encouraged the clearing of the region's vast forests – particularly in the southern part of Morang. This entailed the implementation of a rigorous tax collection hierarchy which created stratification within the Adivasi social structure, encouraging the accumulation of surplus and the emergence of an Adivasi landed class. At the same time, the distribution of tax-free land grants, particularly on the Nepal side of the border, supported the emergence of an absentee landed class. These processes collectively precipitated the gradual contraction of the forest frontier and move from shifting cultivation to sedentary tenant farming.

While the late nineteenth century saw early inroads for capitalism in the region, this did little to undermine the dominant feudal agrarian relations, which were now entrenched. By the 1960s, the mode of production in southern Morang was dominated by landlord–tenant relations. The failed land reforms of the 1960s consolidated the absentee landlords, mostly of hill origin, as the primary landed class. Feudal agrarian relations in South Asia, as described during the earlier 'mode of production debate', entailed concentration of land amongst an upper-caste locally resident landlord class and subordinated through an interlinkage of land and usury (Prasad, 1973). However, most of these studies were from the caste Hindu heartlands of Bihar and southern Bengal, which had a much longer history of sedentary farming and landlord–tenant relations. The Morang region, like much of the eastern sub-Himalayan lowlands, differed somewhat due to the relatively recent clearing of the forest frontier and the subordination of a largely Adivasi peasantry who made up the tenant class. A majority of big landlords were absentee owners of large estates (who had received grants of uncultivated land by the state or who were appointed to settle forest land), rather than being locally based landlords whose tenants had been bonded to them for generations through debt and caste authority. Furthermore, while most of the landlords in southern Morang were upper castes from the hills, the peasantry was predominantly Adivasi, and thus the role of caste in reproducing the feudal system via *jajmani* and other ritualised ties of dependence was limited.

Nevertheless, the differences with the caste Hindu heartlands do not diminish the exploitative nature of feudalism in this belt, and it was no coincidence that the eastern sub-Himalayan lowlands had by the late 1960s become the heartland of anti-feudal struggle, when the Naxalbari revolt took hold just over the border in North Bengal. The Naxalbari region was like Morang, home to a largely Adivasi peasantry, with a mix of local Adivasi landlords and absentee landlords from other castes at the apex of the agrarian structure (Mukherji, 1987). Also of significance was the fact that both Morang and the Naxalbari region were by no means part of a 'closed' feudal economy, and were experiencing intensified integration into capitalist markets. North Bengal had emerged as a centre for tea production, while Morang's strategic location, high rainfall and rich agricultural lands made it a prime location for commercial jute production, Nepal's early industrial endeavours and commercial timber extraction. Biratnagar emerged as a centre of commerce for eastern Nepal, as well as an important administrative outpost for Kathmandu in the east, with a large 'bureaucratic' class. This, in turn, also contributed to the further concentration of land.

The agrarian trajectory of the North Bengal region diverged following successful land reforms in the 1970s, which leaves the Morang region of Nepal, with its juxtaposition of a feudal landlord and capitalist economy, as an outstanding case study to understand how older economic systems adapt to the expansion of capitalism in the periphery. It also offers insights into the mediating role of a state which has long been associated with a pre-capitalist feudal social order at home and semi-colonial relations externally, as well as older ideologies rooted in caste and ethnic hierarchy. This book seeks to explore the relationship between the capitalist and pre-capitalist across the socio-political and agroecological landscape of southern Morang. In doing so, it will offer richer understandings of landlord–tenant relations in the twenty-first century and associated forms of surplus appropriation – while examining the character of the two-way relationship between the capitalist and pre-capitalist – with lessons which extend far beyond South Asia.

Situating This Research within Agrarian Transition Scholarship

There are two primary bodies of scholarship upon which this study builds. The first, which the book is most strongly grounded in, is the long tradition within Peasant Studies on the political economy of agrarian change – which mobilises extensive empirical data, including farm surveys, combined with a Marxian conceptual framework, to understand changing class relations in agriculture and transition between modes of production – in particular, in the context of transition towards capitalism. This is a tradition with a long history, starting with seminal empirical works such as Lenin's *Development of Capitalism in Russia* (Lenin, 1960 [1899]). Marxian scholarship on agrarian transition later included a number of major historical studies, including the debate over the European transition from feudalism to capitalism (Hilton and Hill, 1953; Takahashi and Mins, 1952; Sweezy and Dobb, 1950) and the mode of production debate in South Asia. It is the latter which is particularly important for this book. This debate initially sought to determine whether South Asian (although, in particular, Indian) agriculture was 'semi-feudal' (see Bhaduri, 1973; Bhaduri, 1977; Prasad, 1973; Chandra, 1974; Sau, 1975) or capitalist (see Rudra, 1974) and went on to inform a number of classic Marxist analyses of Indian agriculture throughout the 1980s until the early 1990s. This scholarship, which will be explored in much greater detail in Chapter 2, engages directly with questions of the pre-capitalist versus capitalist – themes of crucial relevance to this book.

However, unfortunately, this tradition of scholarship in South Asia has been on the decline since the 2000s – although relevant studies do appear periodically in outlets such as the *Journal of Peasant Studies*, the *Journal of Agrarian Change* or the *Economic and Political Weekly* (see Lerche et al., 2013, as well as Rodgers and Rodgers, 2001; Shah and Harriss-White, 2011). Furthermore, there has long been an 'India bias' to this work – and while the study region of this book is part of a contiguous cultural-ecological belt which spans the Nepal–India border, the different state formations and histories of both regions mean that the lack of agrarian political economy research on Nepal represents a notable gap in the literature. There has been some work on Pakistan (Niazi, 2004; Alavi, 1976) and Bangladesh (Ito, 2002; Wood, 1981; Mahapatro and Ullah, 2014), although empirically grounded agrarian transition research on Nepal has historically been limited.

There are some recent examples from Nepal, including Laya Uprety's (2021) review book, which offers a valuable national overview of the status of Nepal's peasantry under globalisation, and Uprety, Dhakal and Basnet's edited volume (see Dhakal, 2020) on the peasantry. However, most of the large-scale empirical studies on agrarian transition were based upon data from the 1960s–1970s. These include the extensive (mostly historical) work of Mahesh Chandra Regmi, including seminal manuscripts such as *Land Ownership in Nepal* (1976), Blaikie, Cameron and Seddon's *Nepal in Crisis* (Blaikie et al., 2001) and follow-on studies (Blaikie et al., 2002), as well as erstwhile Maoist leader Baburam Bhattarai's classic thesis on the political economy of Nepal's underdevelopment (Bhattarai, 2003). Other isolated examples include Feldman and Fournier's (1976) study of agrarian class relations in the Tarai.

The second body of scholarship upon which this study builds is a long-established body of ethnographic research, largely from the field of anthropology. While the former (agrarian political economy scholarship) is focused on India, in the case of Nepal, the anthropology scholarship is particularly rich. Most of these take the form of classic 'village ethnography', and while they generally have a specific focus (for example, religion, natural resource management, identity, gender relations), they are generally focused on a single community and entail a broad overview of different aspects of social, economic and political life. Such studies are relatively well spread across Nepal and include, but are by no means limited to, ethnographies of Tamang communities of the central hills (Holmberg et al., 1999), Gurung (Macfarlane, 1976) and Magar (Gurung, 1996; Hitchcock, 1974; Hitchcock, 1966) communities of the western hills, the caste Hindu communities of the far western hills (Cameron, 1998), Kirat communities of the eastern hills (Gaenszle, 2000; Caplan, 1970; McDougal, 1973; Dahal, 1981), and Newar communities of the Kathmandu valley (Gellner, 1992). Work on the Tarai is more limited, albeit with the exception of a body of research on the Chitwan and western Tarai Tharu communities (Krauskopff, 1989; Guneratne, 2002; Muller-Boker, 1999; Rajaure, 1981).

This book fills a niche between the aforementioned two bodies of scholarship. Nepal's many 'ethnographies' significantly enrich our empirical understanding of the country's diverse communities. However, political economy or rural class relations, while usually touched upon, are rarely the main focus of the research. Existing ethnographic research in Nepal only occasionally offers an understanding of the mode of production and how it fits within the larger national or global capitalist economy. At the same time, a weakness of the South Asian agrarian political economy scholarship, as well as its India bias, was its failure to explain processes of change via ethnographic insight – this indeed was one of the reasons why debates over whether South Asia was 'feudal' or 'capitalist' ended in stalemate, as I indicate in Chapter 2. This is because the tradition has largely been dominated by agricultural economics – grounded empirically in large farm surveys, with limited qualitative insight or analysis of cultural and political processes at the grassroots.

Relatively few studies have successfully engaged explicitly with political economy and mobilised Marxian tools of analysis while also maintaining an ethnographic focus – and these represent a valuable contribution to the field. Examples include Athreya et al.'s (1990) study of agrarian change in Tamil Nadu (and the much earlier study, Djurfeldt and Lindberg, 1975), Shah's (2013) and Kunnath's (2012) ethnographies of Adivasi and Dalit communities respectively in the context of India's Maoist movement and Singh's (2007) classic analysis of the political economy of religious proselytisation amongst the Bhil of Madhya Pradesh. Research which spans both elements of Marxian political economy and anthropology in Nepal is even more limited. There are, however, examples of economic anthropology in Nepal, some of which integrate Marxian elements, which are crucial contributions to the field. These include Dahal's (1981) ethnography of the indigenous peasant economy of the Athpahariya Rai in the eastern hills, Rai's (2013, 2015) fascinating study of land and social change within the Dhimal of the eastern Tarai and Fitzpatrick's (2011) study of cardamom production and agrarian commercialisation amongst Limbu communities of the eastern hills.[1] Also of relevance is Rankin's (2004) analysis of peri-urban economic and cultural change in the 1990s Kathmandu valley.

This book takes inspiration from the aforementioned bodies of work which take elements of a Marxian approach to ethnography, yet also uphold a long tradition of agrarian class analysis which utilises farm surveys and large datasets and systematic effort to identify pre-capitalist 'modes of production' and their co-existence and articulation with capitalism. It also seeks to situate local-level change within a much broader set of regional political and economic processes spanning multiple scales. The book is also heavily influenced by the 'radical anthropology' tradition (Meillassoux, 1980; Dupré and Rey, 1979), which places a particular emphasis on the analysis of the articulation between pre-capitalist and capitalist modes of production – an approach that, with few exceptions (for example, Singh, 2007), has not been applied in South Asia.

All four empirical chapters draw upon both ethnographic and survey data spanning 17 years, yet this combination of approaches does require some compromises. Firstly, many of the early farm surveys covered a large geographical region, such as an entire state or district. This is not possible for this study, as collecting representative ethnographic data would be challenging. I have therefore compromised by focusing on a cluster of villages spread out over an area of approximately 50 square kilometres in southern Morang, which captures more of the diversity in different social relations than would be achieved via a classic 'village ethnography'. Second, it is not possible to gather the depth of ethnographic data as one would expect in a single village study, which would entail in-depth immersion into a single rural community. As the data is spread over a large number of villages, the book does not achieve the same level of detail with regard to local social relations, cultural practices and micro-politics as the classic anthropological literature on Nepal.

A final commentary with regard to the purpose of this book is that fieldwork which spanned 17 years (2006–2023) encompassed a time of considerable political change in Nepal. This included the transitional period at the end of the People's War, which led to some renewed debate around the peasantry and land reform, three rounds of ethnic mobilisation in the plains, the promulgation of a new constitution, the creation of a federal system and the restructuring of local units of governance. While the book touches upon political change, a changing governance landscape and political identities, these are not the focus of this manuscript. There is a vast body of existing scholarship already on issues such as ethnic politics (Gellner et al., 1997; Dahal, 2008; Hachhethu, 2007; Pandey, 2017), Nepal's recent post-war transition (Jha, 2014; Adhikari, 2014), the Maoist People's War (Ismail and Shah, 2015; Paudel, 2019; Zharkevich, 2019) and longer histories of peasant conflict, including the novel historical analysis by Raj (2010) and the volume by Seddon et al. (2020). Given the limits to what can be achieved in a single book, and the pre-existing scholarship, political transition, shifting political identities and the various party 'positions' on class and the peasantry in Nepal's fluid electoral landscape are only touched upon so long as they are relevant to the analysis of agrarian change and the mode of production on the ground.

About the Study Site and the Research

This book will provide an in-depth analysis of agrarian change in southern Morang, the shifting balance of class relations throughout this era of great flux, and the implications for fragile peasant livelihoods, with a focus on a core field site, made up of seven case study villages. These communities vary in terms of their history of landlordism, levels of integration into the market and ethnic makeup. They lie to the northeast of Biratnagar, the largest city in eastern Nepal with a population of 244,750. While Biratnagar city is diverse, a large share of the professional and civil servant residents are from Nepali-speaking castes whose ancestors migrated from the hills. There is also a small yet economically powerful Marwari business community associated with the large business houses, which control a notable share of the industrial sector. By contrast, however, the countryside east and northeast of town in what is Nepal's most multicultural district is home mostly to the indigenous communities of the eastern sub-Himalayan lowland belt, including Tharu, Rajbanshi, Bantar and Gangai, which surprisingly form just 5 per cent of the Biratnagar urban population (Central Bureau of Statistics, 2011).

The core field site reflects this ethnic diversity and is situated in the belt with a long history of settlement which experienced the transition from an Adivasi to feudal mode of production under Gorkha and Rana rule – processes which will be described in Chapter 3. While there are some settlers from the hills, the vast majority of the population in the core site are Adivasi. The seven villages lie 15–17 kilometres to the south of the main 'settler belt' of the Tarai, which is home to prosperous villages of owner cultivators who migrated from the hills in the 1960s and thus were free from the tax subordination and landlordism which characterised the Rana era further south.

The seven villages are spread along an east–west transect covering the three village development committees (VDCs) of Jhorahat, Bhaudaha and Thalaha (see Figure 1.2). These three VDCs were during the period of research merged into two larger administrative units, Gramthan and the Katahari rural municipality. Nevertheless, I will continue to refer to the original VDCs in this book given that they informed the original sampling. The sampled villages in Jhorahat VDC include Jhorahat Bazaar, a new settlement with a cluster of settlers from the hills, which makes up the main market in the area, the historic Tharu village of Pidarbobi and the Munda village of Jhagarahi. The sampled villages in the poorer and more peripheral Bhaudaha VDC include the Rajbanshi village of Sitpur and Bantar village of Bhaudaha. The sampled villages of the remote neighbouring Thalaha VDC include the mixed Bantar, Tharu and Munda village of Thalaha and the Bantar village of Hurhuriya. The full details of these villages are discussed in Chapter 4.

The research draws upon longitudinal data collected from these seven villages over 17 years to chart the evolution of rural livelihoods and agrarian relations since the late eighteenth century when the region was annexed into the Gorkha empire. It focuses broadly on the convergence between expanding capitalist markets, wage labour and migration on the one hand and older

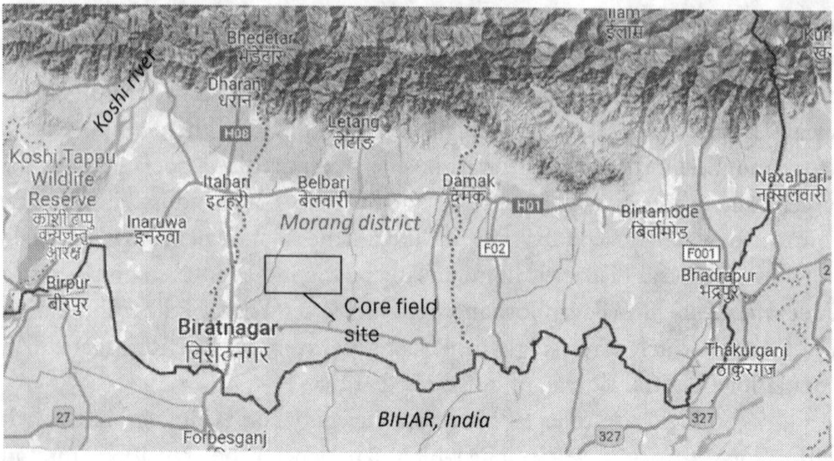

Figure 1.2 Map of far-eastern Tarai-Madhesh and location of Morang district* and the study site

Source: Author.

Notes: * The historic region of Morang includes Sunsari and Jhapa districts also.
Map not to scale and does not represent authentic international boundaries.

social and political relations oriented around a landlord and money-lending economy on the other. This is set against a larger backdrop of shifting ethnic or caste relations and political transition in Nepal.

While the insights from this site are particularly relevant to the Nepal Tarai and the larger eastern sub-Himalayan lowlands, which extend into Assam and North Bengal, most of them are also equally applicable to the larger Eastern Gangetic Plains region. This belt, which encompasses the Indian states of Bihar, West Bengal and the eastern Tarai-Madhesh of Nepal, is home to 203.3 million people as of 2011,[2] representing around 15 per cent of the combined population of Nepal and India and close to 3 per cent of the world's population. Within the Eastern Gangetic Plains, landlord–tenant relations remain a central feature of rural life despite localised variations, and thus the lessons of this case study resonate across the region as well as in other parts of the world experiencing pre-capitalist forms of inequality.

Ethnography of 'Modes of Production'

Understanding the constituent parts of multiple modes of production by its very nature cannot rely on farm surveys alone, as was the case during much of the earlier research on the topic in South Asia, and thus I pursued a methodology combining surveys with participant observation, interviews (including oral history) and archival analysis. This ethnography was also longitudinal, spanning 17 years, to capture processes of change in social relations as they happen.

Data collection began in 2006 in what could be considered a pilot study, east of Biratnagar in Katahari and Sisabani Jahada. However, these villages were close to the town and were found to be unrepresentative of the larger region, and thus after visiting sites across Morang district, the core 17 villages were selected along an east–west transect, which was designed to capture the different ethnic groups of the region,[3] as well as settlements of varying distance from the main north–south road and irrigation canals. Fieldwork in these villages commenced in the summer of 2007 and ran until late 2008.

For much of this period, I resided in the community of Pidarboni near Jhorahat and used the village as a base from which to travel out to the surrounding villages such as Bhaudaha and Thalaha by bicycle. A large part of the fieldwork involved participating in day-to-day activities such as agricultural training programmes, community events or joining farmers on the land or on their travels to the market, as well as long spells at village tea shops and meeting places – which supported frequent social exchange. Several days were also spent observing transactions with a grain merchant, or *katawala*, in the market of Naya Bazaar. The first 'formal' data collection task was a farm survey of 20 per cent of the population across the seven villages[4] (see Table 1.1). This covered a range of topics relating to land ownership, tenure, market participation, livelihoods and cropping systems. An additional survey was carried out with all but 2[5] of the 38 grain traders in the bazaars

Table 1.1 Formal interviews and focus groups carried out

Data source	2007–2008	2012–2013	2019–2023
Quantitative survey	176	100 (but not used for this study)	145
Qualitative farmer interviews	30	26	7
Other (landlords, merchants, development workers, government staff, farmer leaders)	11	0	7
Focus group discussions	4	2	2

Source: Author.

which served the field area – Katahari, Naya Bazaar, Tetariya and Jhorahat. Follow-up interviews were carried out with selected participants several months later, and topics covered included relationships with landlords, bargaining and decision-making regarding labour and resource allocation. Added to this were several oral history interviews with selected elders, particularly in Pidarboni, to capture changing land relations. Additional stakeholder interviews included staff from the land revenue office, development workers, land policy specialists and government staff. Four focus groups were also arranged with women farmers to discuss changing gender relations in agriculture.

For the interviews and surveys, I worked with four different research assistants, and their input was invaluable and hugely contributed to the shaping of this study. The longest serving of these researchers was from a neighbouring village and was conversant in local dialects and deeply knowledgeable of local agricultural issues. In between these formal data collection phases I worked independently. All interviews and informal interactions were carried out in Nepali or the local Morang Tharu dialect, which was widely spoken across ethnic groups.

Following this first round of fieldwork, I continued to be based in South Asia for much of the subsequent decade, and through various ongoing research projects, I visited the field site at least once or twice a year, for visits of up to a week at a time, up until 2023. During all visits, I took notes of changes and major events in the community. However, these visits also integrated two rounds of 'structured' data collection. A series of interviews and focus groups were carried out from 2012–2013 as part of a larger cross-border study focusing on the impact of climate change and migration on agrarian change,[6] which included the seven original villages, plus some other settlements to the north and south. Furthermore, an additional round of structured data collection took place between 2019 and 2023. This involved a series of interviews and focus groups across the seven original villages focused on economic change over the last decade. Participants included farmers, merchants, local credit institutions, a Biratnagar industrialist and peasant federation leaders in Kathmandu.[7] Furthermore, out of the original 176 households surveyed in 2007–2008, 145 were located[8] in 2019 for a follow-up survey to track longitudinal change.

Extensive secondary data was also consulted to piece together the historical and contemporary political-economy of the larger Morang region, including online resources available on government portals and a large number of publications and datasets I collected from government offices in Biratnagar and the NARC[9] library in Kathmandu. Historical sources were also reviewed. These included, most notably, the outstanding archive created by the late historian Mahesh Chandra Regmi, colonial Gazeteers from the neighbouring districts of India and the Hodgson collection in the British Library (and associated published texts).

Data collection was not without challenges. The 17 years within which fieldwork took place coincided with a period of major political change in Nepal. This encompassed the aftermath of the 10-year People's War, three Tarai-Madhesh regionalist uprisings, the drafting of the new constitution, its promulgation (and associated ethnic unrest) and the first elections under the new statute. While this made the research topically more important, it also brought up some practical and ethical challenges. There were frequent *bandh*s (general strikes), which created challenges in getting around and visiting offices and markets. Furthermore, fieldwork needed to be paused for several weeks during the first constituent assembly election in 2008 and the 2008 Madhesh Andolan (Madhesh movement), whereby there was a rise in inter-ethnic tensions.

Given the increasing influence of the then Communist Party of Nepal (Maoist) in the post-conflict state after their 2008 election victory, the spectre of land reforms at the time of research is worth mentioning. The vast majority of farmers were happy to talk about land-related issues, as it was a politically important topic. The fact that most landlords were absentee reduced proximate local sensitivities associated with the topic. Nevertheless, there was occasionally some hesitancy in responses from more prosperous farmers to discuss their economic status with outsiders.[10] This was, however, a more limited concern in later rounds of data collection, when policy discussion around land reform had fizzled out. However, the unease that respondents felt does raise ethical questions.

A further set of ethical and practical challenges related to the influence of the aid industry in Nepal. As a researcher from Europe (albeit one who was living in Nepal for much of the fieldwork period), my relationship with respondents was complex. To some respondents, particularly in the more isolated settlements, there was some indifference to my presence, where I was regarded as a generalised outsider, rather than specifically a 'western' researcher. In Jhorahat in particular, which is well connected to Biratnagar, there was an assumption by some respondents initially that I was associated with the western development 'industry'.[11] This may have shaped interactions with farmers, dilemmas discussed in Pigg[12] (1996), but also sometimes extended to a perception that I was planning some kind of development project. False expectations are a common challenge for domestic and international researchers in Nepal and a significant ethical dilemma in development research more broadly (Pratt and Loizoz, 1992; Sultana, 2007).

To address the aforementioned ethical and practical challenges, extreme care was taken during the early research to explain my respective position during the three phases of fieldwork, whereby I was initially an independent researcher and PhD candidate, then a representative of a Nepal-based agricultural research institute and finally a university-affiliated researcher. I also spent around six weeks in the community before starting formal data collection, to develop rapport and relationships locally. For all data collection phases, I had prepared a letter using university/institutional-headed paper in Nepali describing the research and its purpose, emphasising the confidentiality of any results. Courtesy visits were also made to local authorities at district and village levesl. This (along with a visiting card) helped considerably in gaining trust. The same procedures were followed when working with merchants who were traditionally a close-knit business community.[13] I also identified ways to keep a lower profile, such as travelling to the village by bicycle and later by motorbike.

It is worth finally noting that farm surveys and interviews, if poorly executed, can be extractive in character. Measures were thus taken to mitigate these unequal power relations. I sought throughout the research to make dialogues with farmers an informal and enjoyable social interaction. Some surveys and qualitative interviews even catalysed friendships, which I maintain to this day. Interviews often switched around towards the end, where I would be asked lengthy questions from subjects ranging from lifestyles and weather in Europe to my family background or to global politics. At later phases in the research, I sought feedback on the findings via a short summary in Nepali which was circulated amongst government agencies in Morang and within the village (in a focus group setting) to facilitate debate and cross-learning. This included graphs with the survey data tabulated in an accessible manner.

Importantly, it is worth noting that farm surveys and associated studies of the peasantry have formed a central basis of political debate in South Asia between the 1960s and 1980s, as noted earlier, and my research was similarly embedded in a larger commitment to social and redistributive justice (see Scheper-Hughes, 1995). In conversations, respondents frequently made requests to escalate their concerns to the government and those with political power. Dissemination of the research therefore – other than via this book and associated publications – took place via multiple forums, which included politically oriented workshops with scholar-activists as well as more policy-oriented spaces, such as a programme organised with the Ministry of Land Reform Management. The 2012 study was itself part of a larger project on migration, climate and agrarian change and involved an extensive series of impact-oriented activities and events with various government and civil society stakeholders.

Structure of the Book

Chapter 2 reviews the broader literature on agrarian transition, and outlines where this book fits within this framework. This includes larger epistemological questions over Marxian approaches, which highlight why this study is important. It proceeds to outline how the data was collected for this book, including site selection and methodology.

Chapter 3 is an extended analysis of the agrarian and industrial history of the Morang region in Nepal's far-eastern Tarai-Madhesh between the seventeenth and late twentieth centuries, set against Nepal's evolving political-economy at a national level. It will look at the historical settlement of this frontier region and shifting ethnic and caste relations to shed light on the subordination of the Adivasi of southern Morang to feudalism, and the origins of the absentee landlord economy which dominates this belt today. This is set in contrast with the more prosperous hill settler belt to the north. This chapter also looks at the parallel process of economic change, whereby southern Morang has emerged as an outpost for capitalist industrial development in Nepal. It demonstrates, however, that the skewed pattern of industrialisation echoes that of Nepal as a whole in the context of a 'semi-colonial' economy, and, thus, the emergence of industry by no means undermines the feudal economy of the countryside.

Having established the national and local historical context, Chapters 4 to 6 will provide an in-depth analysis of the rural class relations in the actual case study communities. The focus will be on understanding the livelihoods of the peasantry in a part of the country where absentee landlords remain at the apex of the agrarian structure. Chapter 4 introduces the field site and reviews the land ownership structure today. Chapter 5 looks at mechanisms of surplus appropriation by landlords via rent, and by merchant capital via interest on loans and 'distress commerce'. Chapter 6 considers what this surplus appropriation means for food security and livelihoods more broadly.

Chapter 7 goes on to analyse how recent external stresses are both reproducing while also transforming particular configurations of agrarian relations. It explores how climate change and expanding markets are aggravating the pressures marginal and tenant farmers already face due to landlordism and exploitation by merchant capital and, combined with changing cultural aspirations, are intensifying articulations with the capitalist sector. This takes place through labour migration and engagement in low-wage labour markets in local industries and the urban informal sector. Chapter 8 returns to the larger theoretical issue of agrarian transition under globalisation. It addresses the fundamental question as to whether, in light of these changes, feudal agrarian relations are under stress. It argues that there is limited potential for capitalist relations to emerge from within the peasant economy, with demand for rented land remaining high. It notes also that while migration and off-farm labour offer an alternative livelihood opportunity, it only serves to offset rising cash needs, and both feudal landlordism and capitalist wage labour persist side by side. The chapter ends by analysing what this means in terms of political alliances and mobilisation.

Notes

1. There is also a body of scholarship which is not explicitly Marxian, yet still combines anthropological insight with analyses of larger political-economic processes. This includes Sunam's (2020) analysis of overseas migration and agrarian change, and Adhikari's study on food security in the Karnali (Adhikari, 2008).
2. This is according to the census of Nepal (Central Bureau of Statistics, 2011) and India (Office of the Registrar General & Census Commissioner, 2011).
3. Census data and site visits ensured the villages selected were broadly representative of the caste makeup of the region.
4. The smallest local administrative unit, the ward, was used as the sampling frame, and eight wards were selected, which corresponded with the seven selected case study villages. The mismatch between number of wards and number of villages is because some communities spanned two wards and other wards included more than one village. Due to the non-availability of a reliable list of residents (for example, voter registration data excludes those without citizenship), a map was created of each ward, households were numbered, and then a sample of 20 per cent was selected for the survey using a random number table. Out of a selected sample size of 181, surveys were carried out with all but 4 of the sampled households (see Table 2.1).
5. Two traders opted out of the study.
6. While I led the research team, this also involved the support of researchers from the International Water Management Institute in Kathmandu (see Sugden et al., 2014, for more on this study).
7. This was part of another study on migration and agrarian change.
8. The remainder were unavailable, could not be traced or had left the area.
9. National Agricultural Research Council.

10. This may have contributed to deliberate misreporting from wealthier farmers around the size of their holdings, although in most cases farm sizes of different households were well known in the community.
11. The early stage of fieldwork coincided with a huge wave of donor-funded development in Nepal as the country emerged from the civil war and underwent several cycles of internationally observed elections and 'peacebuilding' initiatives. United Nations Mission in Nepal (UNMIN) had a large and highly conspicuous presence in Biratnagar where they had a regional headquarters, including a large number of employees from various parts of the world.
12. In Pigg's research on faith healers, she notes how local people adapted their responses in ways that would represent them as being modern, in line with ideologies of *bikas*, or 'development' – an identity which is sought for symbolic and status reasons.
13. While most merchants were happy to talk about their trade practices, which were well known locally, they were particularly sensitive to questions around asset ownership, which, unlike farmers' land ownership, is easier to conceal. It was for this reason that I avoided questions relating to asset ownership when assessing scale of enterprise and instead focused on the quantities of grain bought and sold.

References

Adhikari, Aditya. 2014. *The Bullet and the Ballot Box: The Story of Nepal's Maoist Revolution*. Verso Trade.

Adhikari, Jagannath. 2008. *Food Crisis in Karnali*. Martin Chautari.

Akhtar, Rakib. 2022. Protests, neoliberalism and right-wing populism amongst farmers in India. *Journal of Peasant Studies* 50 (6): 1–21.

Alavi, Hamza. 1976. The rural elite and agricultural development in Pakistan. *Pakistan Economic and Social Review* 14 (1/4): 173–210.

Athreya, Venkatesh B., Djurfeldt, Göran and Lindberg, Staffan. 1990. *Barriers Broken: Production Relations and Agrarian Change in Tamil Nadu*. Sage Publications India Pvt Ltd.

Bhaduri, A. 1973. A study in agricultural backwardness under semi-feudalism. *Economic Journal* 83 (329): 120–137.

———. 1977. On the formation of usurious interest rates in backward agriculture. *Cambridge Journal of Economics* 1 (4): 341–352.

Bhattarai, B. 2003. *The Nature of Underdevelopment and Regional Structure of Nepal: A Marxist Analysis*. Adroit Publishers.

Blaikie, P., Cameron, J. and Seddon, D. 2001. *Nepal in Crisis: Growth and Stagnation at the Periphery*, revised and enlarged edition. Adroit Publishers.

———. 2002. Understanding 20 years of change in West-Central Nepal: Continuity and change in lives and ideas. *World Development* 30 (7): 1255–1270.

Cameron, M. 1998. *On the Edge of the Auspicious: Gender and Caste in Nepal.* Kathmandu Mandala Publications and University of Illinois Press.

Caplan, L. 1970. *Land and Social Change in East Nepal: A Study of Hindu-tribal Relations*. University of California Press.

Central Bureau of Statistics. 2011. *Nepal Population Census 2011*. Government of Nepal.

Chandra, Nirmal K. 1974. Farm efficiency under semi-feudalism: A critique of marginalist theories and some Marxist formulations. *Economic and Political Weekly* 10 (13): 1309–1332.

Chaudhuri, A. 1995. *Enclaves in a Peasant Society: Political Economy of Tea in Western Dooars and Northern Bengal.* Peoples Publishing House.

Dahal, Dilli R. 1981. The concept of economy in a peasant society: A case study of the Athpahariya Rais in east Nepal. *Contributions to Nepalese Studies* 8 (2): 55–71.

———. 2008. The 'Madheshi' people: Issues and challenges of democracy. In *Local Democracy in South Asia: Micro-processes of Democratisation in Nepal and Its Neigbours*, edited by Hachhethu, K. and Gellner, D. SAGE.

De Haan, Arjan. 2002. Migration and livelihoods in historical perspective: A case study of Bihar, India. *Journal of Development Studies* 38 (5): 115–142.

Dhakal, S. 2020. Peasant as an anthropological category and ethnographic subject. In *Peasant Studies in Nepal*, edited by Uprety, L. P., Dhakal, S. and Basnet, J. Vajra Books.

Djurfeldt, Göran and Lindberg, Staffan. 1975. *Behind Poverty: The Social Formation in a Tamil Village*. Studentlitteratur AB.

Dupré, G. and Rey, P. P. 1979. Reflections on the relevance of a theory of the history of exchange. In *Relations of Production: Marxist Approaches to Economic Anthropology*, edited by Seddon, D. and Lackner, H. Frank Cass and Company Ltd.

Feldman, D. and Fournier, A. 1976. Social relations and agricultural production in Nepal's Terai. *Journal of Peasant Studies* 3 (4): 447–464.

Gaenszle, Martin. 2000. *Origins and Migrations: Kinship, Mythology and Ethnic Identity among the Mewahang Rai of East Nepal*. Mandala Book Point.

Gellner, D. N. J., Pfaff-Czarnecka, J. and Whelpton, J. 1997. *Nationalism and Ethnicity in a Hindu Kingdom: The Politics of Culture in Contemporary Nepal, J. G. Carrier, Studies in Anthropology and History*. Routledge.

Gellner, David N. 1992. *Monk, Householder, and Tantric Priest: Newar Buddhism and Its Hierarchy of Ritual*. Cambridge University Press.

Guneratne, A. 2002. *Many Tougues, One People: The Making of Tharu Identity in Nepal*. Cornell University Press.

Gurung, Om Prasad. 1996. Customary systems of natural resource management among Tarami Magars of western Nepal. PhD thesis, Cornell University.

Hachhethu, Krishna. 2007. Madheshi nationalism and restructuring the Nepali state: A seminar on Constitutionalism and Diversity in Nepal, organized by Centre for Nepal and Asian Studies. Tribhuvan University, Kathmandu.

Hilton, Rodney H. and Hill, Christopher. 1953. The transition from feudalism to capitalism. *Science and Society*: 340–351.

Hitchcock, John. 1966. *The Magars of Banyan Hill*. Holt, Rinehart & Winston.

———. 1974. Himalayan ecology and family religious variation. In *Family in India: A Regional View*, edited by Kurien, G. Mouton.

Holmberg, David, March, Kathryn and Tamang, Suryaman. 1999. Local production/local knowledge: Forced labour from below. *Studies in Nepali History and Society* 4 (1): 5–64.

Ismail, Feyzi and Shah, Alpa. 2015. Class struggle, the Maoists and the Indigenous question in Nepal and India. *Economic and Political Weekly* 50 (35): 112–123.

Ito, S. 2002. From rice to prawns: Economic transformation and agrarian structure in rural Bangladesh. *Journal of Peasant Studies* 29 (2): 47–70.

Jha, Prashant. 2014. *Battles of the New Republic: A Contemporary History of Nepal*. Oxford University Press.

Kitching, G. 2002. Marxism and reflexivity. In *Marx and Wittgenstein: Knowledge, Morality and Politics*, edited by Kitching, G. and Pleasants, N. Routledge.

Krauskopff, G. 1989. *Maîtres et possédés: les rites et l'ordre social chez les Tharu*.

Kunnath, George, J. 2012. *Rebels from the Mud Houses: Dalits and the Making of the Maoist Revolution in Bihar*. Routledge.

Lenin, V. I. 1960 [1899]. The development of capitalism in Russia. In *Collected Works: Volume 3*, edited by Lenin, V. I. Progress Publishers.

Lerche, Jens, Shah, Alpa and Harriss-White, Barbara. 2013. Introduction: Agrarian questions and left politics in India. *Journal of Agrarian Change* 13: 337–350.

Levien, Michael, Watts, Michael and Yan, Hairong. 2018. *Agrarian Marxism*. Taylor & Francis.

Macfarlane, Alan. 1976. *Resources and Population: A Study of the Gurungs of Nepal*. Cambridge University Press.

Mahapatro, Mausumi and Ullah, Mahbub. 2014. An impasse in capitalist transition? Resurvey of two villages in Bangladesh. *Economic and Political Weekly* 49 (2): 46–55.

McDougal, Charles. 1973. Structure and division in Kulunge Rai society. *Kailash* 1: 205–224.

Meillassoux, C. 1980. From reproduction to production: A Marxist approach to economic anthropology. In *The Articulation of Modes of Production: Essays from Economy and Society*, edited by Wolpe, H. Routledge and Kegan Paul.

Mukherji, Partha. 1987. Study of social conflicts: Case of Naxalbari peasant movement. *Economic and Political Weekly* 22 (38): 1607–1617.

Muller-Boker, Ulrike. 1999. *The Chitwan Tharus in Southern Nepal: An Ethnological Approach*. Franz Steiner Verlag.

Niazi, T. 2004. Rural poverty and the green revolution: Lessons from Pakistan. *Journal of Peasant Studies* 31 (2): 242–260.

Office of the Registrar General & Census Commissioner. 2011 Census Data. Government of India, New Delhi.

Pandey, Krishna. 2017. Politicising ethnicity: Tharu contestation of Madheshi identity in Nepal's Tarai. *South Asianist Journal* 5 (1): 304–322.

Paudel, Dinesh. 2019. Prismatic village: The margin at the center in the Nepali Maoist revolution. *Critical Sociology* 45 (4–5): 729–743.

Pigg, S. 1996. The credible and the credulous: The questions of 'villagers' beliefs' in Nepal. *Cultural Anthropology* 11 (2): 160–201.

Prasad, Pradhan, H. 1973. Production relations: Achilles' heel of Indian planning. *Economic and Political Weekly* 8 (19): 869–872.

Pratt, B. and Loizoz, P. 1992. *Choosing Research Methods: Data Collection for Development Workers*. Oxfam.

Rai, Janak. 2015. Owning land was so much of Dukha in the past: Land and the State–Adivasi relations in the Tarai. *Nepal Studies in Nepali History and Society* 20 (1): 69–98.

Raj, Yogesh. 2010. *History as Mindscapes: A Memory of the Peasants' Movement of Nepal*. Martin Chautari

Rajaure, D. 1981. *The Tharu Women of Sukhrwar*. Centre for Economic Development and Administration.

Rankin, K. N. 2004. *The Cultural Politics of Markets*. London: Pluto Press.

Ray, Subhajyoti. 2013. *Transformations on the Bengal Frontier: Jalpaiguri 1765–1948*. Routledge.

Rodgers, G. and Rodgers, J. 2001. A leap across time: When semi-feudalism met the market in rural Purnia. *Economic and Political Weekly* 36 (22): 2–8.

Rudra, Ashok. 1974. Semi-feudalism, usury capital, etcetera. *Economic and Political Weekly* 9 (48): 1996–1997.

Sau, R. 1975. Farm efficiency under semi-feudalism: A critique of marginalist theories and some Marxist formulations: A comment. *Economic and Political Weekly* 10: 18–21.

Scheper-Hughes, N. 1995. The primacy of the ethical: Propositions for a militant anthropology. *Current Anthropology* 36 (3): 409–440.

Scoones, Ian, Edelman, Marc, Borras Jr., Saturnino M., Hall, Ruth, Wolford, Wendy and White, Ben. 2018. Emancipatory rural politics: Confronting authoritarian populism. *Journal of Peasant Studies* 45 (1): 1–20.

Seddon, D., Dhakal, S. and Basnet, J. 2020. *Rural Unrest in Nepal, Delhi and Kathmandu*. Adroit.

Shah, Alpa. 2013. The agrarian question in a Maoist guerrilla zone: Land, labour and capital in the forests and hills of Jharkhand, India. *Journal of Agrarian Change* 13 (3): 424–450.

Shah, Alpa and Harriss-White, Barbara. 2011. Resurrecting scholarship on agrarian transformations. *Economic and Political Weekly* 36 (22): 13–18.

Shah, Alpa and Lerche, Jens. 2020. Migration and the invisible economies of care: production, social reproduction and seasonal migrant labour in India. *Transactions of the Institute of British Geographers* 45 (4): 719–734.

Singh, K. S. 2007. Problematising proselytisation: A case study from West Nirmar. *Social Science Probings* 19 (1): 105–148.

Sugden, F. 2019. Labour migration, capitalist accumulation and feudal reproduction: A historical analysis from the Eastern Gangetic Plains. *Antipode* 51 (5): 1600–1639.

Sugden, Fraser, Maskey, Niki, Clement, Floriane, Ramesh, Vidya, Philip, Anil and Rai, Ashok. 2014. Agrarian stress and climate change in the Eastern Gangetic Plains: Gendered vulnerability in a stratified social formation. *Global Environmental Change* 29 (November): 258–269.

Sultana, F. 2007. Reflexivity, positionality and participatory ethics: Negotiating fieldwork dilemmas in international research. *ACME* 6 (3): 374–385.

Sunam, Ramesh. 2020. *Transnational Labour Migration, Livelihoods and Agrarian Change in Nepal: The Remittance Village*. Routledge.

Sweezy, Paul M. and Dobb, Maurice. 1950. The transition from feudalism to capitalism. *Science and Society* 14 (2): 134–167.

Takahashi, H. Kohachiro and Mins, Henry F. 1952. The transition from feudalism to capitalism: A contribution to the Sweezy-Dobb Controversy. *Science and Society* 16 (4): 313–345.

Thorner, A. 1982. Semi-Feudalism or capitalism? Contemporary debate on classes and modes of production in India. *Economic and Political Weekly* 17 (51): 2061–2066.

Uprety, L. P. 2021. *Peasantry under Capitalism in Contemporary Nepal: Macro and Micro Narratives*. Bina Khatiwada (Uprety).

Vaidyanathan, A. 2006. Farmers' suicides and the agrarian crisis. *Economic and Political Weekly* 16 (4): 4009–4013.

White, Ben. 2012. Agriculture and the generation problem: Rural youth, employment and the future of farming. *IDS Bulletin* 43 (6): 9–19.

Wood, Geoffrey D. 1981. Rural class formation in Bangladesh, 1940–1980. *Bulletin of Concerned Asian Scholars* 13 (4): 2–17.

Zhan, Shaohua and Scully, Ben. 2018. From South Africa to China: Land, migrant labor and the semi-proletarian thesis revisited. *Journal of Peasant Studies* 45 (5–6): 1018–1038.

Zharkevich, Ina. 2019. *Maoist People's War and the Revolution of Everyday Life in Nepal*. Cambridge University Press.

2

Feudalism, Capitalism and the Mode(s) of Production

Reconceptualising Agrarian Transition

Capitalism is a unique economic system, and its emergence is arguably the most important turning point in the history of humanity, transforming how societies function and the physical environment in unprecedented ways. Nevertheless, it is critical to acknowledge that far from emerging onto a blank slate, capitalism has been built upon the foundations of much older economic systems which date back thousands of years. The purpose of this chapter is to review the well-established literature on the transition to capitalism within the context of an agrarian society while emphasising the need to acknowledge the 'pre-capitalist', as both an impediment to the expansion of capitalism and a mediating factor, which shapes how transition is taking place. In doing so, the conceptual framework for the book is introduced – in particular, the key concept of the mode of production.

The origins of capitalism date back to the early modern period – developing in the context of a crisis within feudalism in early modern Europe (Dobb, 1948). However, if one is to understand what lies inside of capitalism and what lies outside, it is useful to clearly define what this system actually entails. How we define capitalism has always been open to debate (see, for instance, recent contributions by Hodgson, 2016; Harris and Delanty, 2023), although Marx (1974), in the volumes of *Capital*, still gives by far the most comprehensive characterisation of the system, key features of which are still fundamental today. The first and foremost feature of capitalism is the monopolisation of the means of production (for example, land or machinery) by a capitalist class or the bourgeoisie, a process which goes side by side with the dispossession of the worker. The second feature is the payment of wages to these workers at rates which are below the value of the product they produce – allowing the capitalist to generate a profit. In this context, the artisans or farmers – rather than owning the means of their subsistence and retaining the product of their labour alongside any surplus – works for the capitalist in a much larger unit of production and subsists through the wage they earn. While separation of workers from the means of production is, of course, a feature of many other economic systems (including feudalism, which we discuss later), what is unique to capitalism is the drive to reinvest profit, to either expand production horizontally or, most importantly, to improve productivity through investment in technology. Combined with open and free markets, capitalism is a system with an unparalleled propensity for growth (Marx, 1974).

It is the colonial period which is broadly acknowledged to coincide with the intensified global spread of capitalism. This saw the emergence in the world economy of a distinct 'core', where much of the capitalist manufacturing took place with high development of the productive forces, and a 'periphery', where the production of primary goods took place, all existing within a larger global capitalist economy (Bettelheim, 1972). Following decolonisation, many peripheral states which were outside of the communist block continued to support the expansion of capitalism through the development of infrastructure and policies, arguably in an attempt to 'catch up' with the core through developing their own manufacturing capacity (Warren, 1973).

A central message of this book, however, is that the spread of capitalism within these states has long been uneven. There were large rural tracts of the periphery even during the colonial era which were only nominally integrated into the global capitalist system (see six 'transitions' reviewed in Tilzey and Sugden, 2023), including national social formations dominated by pre-capitalist modes of production (Bettelheim, 1972). This was particularly pertinent in countries such as Nepal, whereby the expansion of capitalism during the nineteenth and early twentieth centuries was slowed by the rugged topography in the uplands and dense forest in the plains, not to mention the fact that the territory was integrated into a localised 'feudal', rather than a global colonial capitalist empire – an important theme which will be explored later on. While Nepal as a country was not isolated from trade routes, at a village scale, studies from the hills (Macfarlane, 1976; Dahal, 1981) and plains (Rai, 2015) suggest that communities across large tracts of land operated with relative autonomy from the capitalist system in some locales, even up until the 1960s.

Nevertheless, a turning point for the expansion of capitalism globally was the late 1980s and 1990s, which saw the firm establishment of a neoliberal agenda throughout the periphery, driven by the imperialist agenda of the International Monetary Fund (IMF) and the World Bank. This saw a shift in the trajectory of capitalist development, whereby many countries, including much of South Asia, retracted post-colonial policies to support capitalist manufacturing, instead reorienting their economies towards the production of primary goods or the provision of low-cost ancillary services to the core. This also entailed simultaneously opening their borders to foreign capital and imported goods, generating new sources of surplus value for international capitalist firms (Tilzey et al., 2023). Surplus value has been extracted not only via low-wage labour but also via the exploitation of resources and in recent years via the use of the periphery as an 'ecological sink' in the context of a growing climate emergency[1] (Tilzey and Sugden, 2023).

A significant further change over the last three decades has been the emergence of an increasingly multipolar global economy (Wade, 2011). In the wake of the first wave of economic liberalisation, we have seen the emergence of a 'sub-imperium', most notable of which are the BRICS[2] states such as China and to a lesser extent India (Tilzey et al., 2023). Such states are actively engaged in the export of capital overseas (particularly to lower income economies) – while simultaneously being a source of surplus value for the core (Carchedi and Roberts, 2021), most notably through the internationalisation of capitalist production, as core economies seek to lower costs of production and take advantage of low-wage 'semi-proletarian' labour (Tilzey et al., 2023). Also of growing significance (particularly to South Asia) are more localised centres of accumulation, such as the petro-economies of the Gulf states, which are core nodes of the global economy, yet also extract substantial profits through low-wage labour of the peripheral economies in their vicinity (Hanieh, 2016).

This latest phase of capitalist expansion has arguably intensified the infiltration of capitalist labour and product markets into peripheral 'low-income' economies such as Nepal, including locales within these countries which had previously experienced relative economic autonomy. These countries, in turn, offer a growing pool of surplus labour, new avenues for foreign direct investment and a captive market for commodities from the not just the core but also increasingly from the sub-imperium. The spread of capitalism in low-income economies, however, has been accelerated by so-called development aid and financing. Not only were organisations such as the World Bank and regional neoliberal financiers such as the Asian Development Bank key agents in the process of structural adjustment, but from the 1990s onwards they have also invested in the physical infrastructure to support capitalist expansion, such as electrification, power generation and communications infrastructure and roads. As we move into a multipolar worldwide capitalist economy, the sources of aid or development finance are diversifying. Of note are the Chinese investments and soft loans under the One Belt One Road (OBOR or BRI) initiative (Tsui et al., 2017; Zhang, 2017). New infrastructure has brought with it access to new markets for imported goods (particularly from China) and exports of raw materials and primary products (Zhang, 2017). OBOR has been matched with further competing infrastructural initiatives by the United States, with its Millennium Challenge Corporation (MCC) (Roka, 2022), while regional powers within the periphery, such as India, have launched their own investments – which often align with their national strategic objectives (Adhikari, 2014).

In terms of grassroots development aid, there have been several shifts over the last two to three decades, which have also intensified the integration of peripheral locales into capitalist markets, even if national-level industrial development remains limited. World Bank and IMF-imposed structural adjustment programmes which were unleashed in the 1990s were in the 2000s repackaged in ways which made them amenable to the global development industry and associated 'inclusion' narratives (Carroll, 2010). While these entailed cosmetic adjustments to economic policy via Poverty Reduction Strategy Papers and a so-called pro-poor agenda, the overall commitment to the expansion of capitalist markets and neoliberal transformation has remained unchanged. What was instead unleashed was an ideology of neoliberalism from below, packaged in the language of entrepreneurship. This included, for example, the drive by development institutions and governments to promote enterprise development through the informal sector, catalysed by an explosion of rural microfinance institutions (Rankin and Shakya, 2007; Muhammad, 2015). Alongside this there was a rising emphasis placed on the integration of small farms into the market, particularly in the context of the 2008 *World Development Report*, which re-envisaged agriculture as a driver of growth in low- and middle-income countries (Akram-Lodhi, 2008; Sugden, 2009).

The important question to ask in this context is: while the infrastructure and institutions are now in place to maximise the integration of peripheral regions into the capitalist economy, what does this mean for the peasantry? While it is increasingly acknowledged that the peasantry is not simply 'dissolved' by capitalist expansion, as occurred in Europe during industrialisation, the assumption that the peasantry is 'subordinate' to capitalism tends to persist, and the role of older economic formations in generating a counterweight to the capitalist onslaught has received less research.[3] The remainder of this chapter will review the literature on agrarian transition, with a particular focus on the 'pre-capitalist' and its interaction with capitalism. A central theme is that while capitalism is infiltrating peripheral regions in new and unprecedented ways, particularly with the expansion of markets, for the peasantry, economic formations which predate capitalism are instrumental in shaping the trajectory of agrarian change, and this may include complex alliances with imperialism.

This chapter thus provides the conceptual background for a central tenet of this book – that feudal landlordism in South Asia, rather than being simply a relic that will die out over time, is instead a dynamic mode of production that is 'in flux' (Sugden, 2017), interacting with capitalism on an economic, political and cultural level. The chapter will review the Althusserian position and its utility in better understanding the pre-capitalist and its articulation with capitalism, before going on to explore the multiple understandings of feudalism from the time of Marx to India's seminal mode of production debate in the 1980s. The chapter will conclude with some reflections on the methodology of the study.

Transition to Capitalism and the Peasantry

If one looks at the global history of agriculture prior to the advent of capitalism, one can observe a spectrum of diverse forms of economic and political organisation. However, perhaps the most ubiquitous 'pre-capitalist' economic formation is that of the 'peasant' unit of production, defined as the subsistence-oriented family farm utilising primarily household labour (Shanin, 1973). This formation may exist as a mode of production in its own right, comprising independent farms with their own land that control their own surplus. Alternatively, the peasant farm may simply represent a unit of production within a larger system. This may include feudalism, where peasant surplus is appropriated by an overlord, or even capitalism itself, whereby surplus is extracted via the market. While these nuances will be debated later, what is apparent in the meantime is that the small family farm remains the backbone of the rural economy throughout the periphery and globally. Farms of less than 1 hectare are estimated by the Food and Agriculture Organisation (FAO) (as of 2014) to account for 72 per cent of farms in the world today (FAO, 2014). Over 90 per cent rely predominantly on family labour, and such farms are estimated to produce 80 per cent of the world's food – they are, in effect, the 'global peasantry'.

The future of the peasantry when set against the onslaught of capitalism has been a significant question for political economists both today and since the time of Marx.[4] There has been a tendency to assume the inevitable victory of capitalism over older forms of economic organisation. To Marx, the inevitable demise of the peasantry is summed up as an almost apocalyptic prophesy in Volume 1 of *Capital* where he stresses:

> It must be annihilated; it is annihilated. Its annihilation, transformation of the individualized and scattered means of production into socially concentrated ones, of the pigmy property of the many into the huge property of the few, the expropriation of the great mass of the people from the soil, from the means of subsistence, and from the means of labour, this fearful and painful expropriation of the mass of the people forms the prelude to the history of capital. (Marx, 1974, 762)

Indeed, Marx's most in-depth empirical analysis was of capitalist transition in England, which experienced a violent process of primitive accumulation whereby capitalism was 'forced' upon the peasantry through dispossession and enclosure. Close to the English experience described by Marx was what Lenin called the Junker Road, named after the landed nobility in Prussia. Lenin (1977) noted how feudal estates of the Junkers were transformed into capitalist farms as the landlords responded to the opportunities posed by expanding industry and global markets. Tenants who provided rent and corvée labour gradually became wageworkers, with surplus tenants being evicted, while the feudal landlords gradually emerged into profit-maximising capitalist farmers.

Both Marx and Lenin, however, acknowledge that there were in reality multiple mechanisms through which capitalist agriculture could be established (see Akram-Lodhi and Kay, 2010). Lenin (1977), for example, pointed to an alternative transition[5] in parts of Russia outside of the reach of serfdom, where there was a 'free' peasantry, yet over time the larger farmers would edge out the smaller farmers, with the former becoming an agrarian bourgeoisie and the latter a proletariat. However, this path also assumes the inevitable demise of the peasantry. Over the last few decades, a breadth of agrarian scholarship has charted the emergence of capitalist agriculture in the contemporary periphery whereby small peasants are separated from their means of production and emerge as a proletarian labour force. For example, Byres' (1981) classic study of class formation in parts of the north Indian plains undergoing the Green Revolution has parallels with Lenin's 'farmer road'. Smaller landholders who lack capital to invest in new technologies are compelled to sell their land to an emergent capitalist farming class. The partial proletarianisation opened avenues for new forms of class mobilisation.

Differentiation has been an important theme in more recent scholarship (see, for instance, review by Cousins, 2022), particularly in the context of post-1990s economic liberalisation, with cuts in subsidies and price supports, the deregulation of land markets, commodification of seeds, rising dependence on high-cost chemical inputs, and export-oriented production (Akram-Lodhi, 2007; Akram-Lodhi, 2008; Bernstein, 2003). Oya (2001), for example, demonstrated how the impact of agricultural market liberalisation amongst Senegal's commercial groundnut producers intensified the differentiation between larger profit-oriented and smaller producers. A region of the world where there is widespread differentiation are the post-socialist states where an initial equitable distribution of holdings after de-collectivisation in the early 1990s has been undermined following integration into capitalist markets, as demonstrated in Vietnam (Akram-Lodhi, 2005) and China (Zhang, 2015). While the state controls distribution of land, accumulation takes place by leasing land and investment in productive assets.

A second body of research on the development of capitalist social relations has focused not on gradual differentiation, but on a more direct transition to capitalism whereby the drive by capital from more developed regions to avert crises and locate 'super-profits' requires differentiation by 'extra-economic' means, often amounting to full proletarianisation. Akram-Lodhi (2007) terms this process of forcible separation 'neo-liberal enclosure', akin to Harvey's (2003) popularly coined 'accumulation by dispossession'. Examples include the expansion of palm oil cultivation in Southeast Asia and dispossession of the peasantry (Li, 2014). Also significant are the growing land concessions in the periphery for large-scale grain production (McMichael, 2012).[6] This wave of proletarianisation has also been shown to release of a 'reserve army' of low-wage, often migrant labour engaged in highly precarious low-wage employment (Bernstein, 2004; Walker, 2008; Araghi, 2003; Araghi, 2012). This is argued to be functional to capitalism, which is in search of a 'spatial fix' to avert the crisis associated with falling rates of profit (Harvey, 2001).

These analyses are not without critique. Hall (2013), for example, problematises assumptions which place episodes of 'accumulation by dispossession' or 'land grabs' as part of a linear model of capitalist development. Similarly, Li (2010) warns against postulations that there is a functional relationship between the processes causing dispossession and the mechanisms through which the resultant 'surplus' labour is mobilised to generate profit. For instance, heavily mechanised plantations may displace peasants and benefit from access to land, but not from the cheap labour pool which is released (Li, 2010).

The critique of these dispossession narratives highlights that the expansion of capitalism in the periphery is selective and multifaceted, with multiple class interests at play. In a similar vein, it is increasingly evident that separation from the means of production through either gradual differentiation or coercive enclosure is not necessarily a given – particularly when one considers that the peasant farm is *still* the backbone of agriculture in the periphery. The pathways to transition described by Lenin and Marx were representative of a particular conjuncture in European history, rather than being a globally applicable model. This book thus works on the premise that contemporary economic liberalisation, expanding markets, and the drive by capital for new sources of profit do not necessarily require that older economic formations or 'modes of production' be 'dissolved'. There is in this context a wide range of scholarship suggesting that surplus value can be extracted from the peasantry by capitalism *without* the need to separate them from the means of production.

A first set of literature has shown how household units of production can be functionally articulated to supply surplus to the capitalist sector through petty commodity production, even while they farm their own land (Banaji, 1977; Bernstein, 1977; de Janvry, 1981). In such contexts, peasant farmers create a surplus, which is extracted by the buyer of their crops, where they receive prices well below the value of labour used to produce them (Banaji, 1977; Bernstein, 1977), making them 'disguised proletarians' (Bernstein, 1977, 69). This is most notable through contract farming, where smallholders are linked through contracts to larger enterprises who appropriate surplus via depressed product prices and inflated input costs (White, 1997; Araghi, 2012).[7] Harriss-White's (2016) four-decade longitudinal analysis in Tamil Nadu has further expanded the concept of 'petty commodity production' through the analysis of rice commodity chains. Large-scale producers, who are more akin to capitalist farms, have consolidated their control over land at the expense of smaller producers. However, they farm in parallel to a subsector of petty commodity producers on marginal, water-scarce farms. The latter participate on the market on much more unequal terms, are unable to accumulate, and are in perpetual debt – yet survive due to self-exploitation and state interventions such as subsidised loans and procurement practices, which make commodity production viable (yet precarious) as a livelihood strategy.

A second and highly significant body of literature has explored how capitalism can extract surplus from the peasantry without them losing their land, via the employment of peasant labour (Bernstein, 2001; de Janvry, 1981; Glassman,

2006). Returning to classical debates, both Lenin (1960 [1899]) and Kautsky (1988) observed the tendency for peasants to engage in labour outside while also working on their own land. This allows capitalist enterprises to pay them less, as farming meets the 'reproduction' costs of labour for capitalism – a phenomenon of critical importance that will be revisited throughout the book. The presence of these 'allotment holding wage workers' prolongs the life of subsistence agriculture under capitalism (Lenin, 1960, 177).[8] While Lenin identified this sub-class of the peasantry in late nineteenth-century Russia, other historical examples from the same time include the crofting economy of Scotland, whereby peasants dispossessed from clan lands were offered smallholdings to provide a captive labour for coastal industries (MacKinnon, 2018). This phenomenon whereby capitalism temporarily allows the persistence of the peasantry during the process of accumulation was described in great detail in the Latin American context in de Janvry (1981), who referred to the phenomenon as 'functional dualism'. Workers in casualised employment in the capitalist sector maintain a strong link to the land in their home communities, allowing wages to remain suppressed (Janvry, 1981)). This appropriation of surplus from the peasantry via wage labour can exist side by side with the process outlined earlier with extraction of surplus from commodity-producing peasants via the market, as Harriss-White (2016) demonstrates with regard to Tamil Nadu.

The two bodies of scholarship discussed here suggest that capitalism can exist without full proletarianisation of labour. While helping to deconstruct a 'linear' narrative of capitalist transition, there is often an implication that farmers who are not dispossessed are still an integral part of capitalism, rather than being part of a non-capitalist mode of production with its own dynamics – particularly with the use of terms such as de Janvry's 'functional dualism' or Bernstein's 'disguised proletarians'. Social relations may be 'outside' the sphere of capitalist *production*, even if they are situated within a larger capitalist economy. The discussion will now turn to exploring the significance of 'pre-capitalist' formations, their persistence, and their role in mediating the transition (or lack of transition) to capitalism.

Mobilising the Althusserian Tradition to Understand the 'Pre-capitalist'

Possibly the most nuanced analyses of pre-capitalist economic formations were from the Althusserian tradition, which sought to reformulate Marxian political economy to counter critiques of economism and essentialism.

Before exploring how this approach can shed light on agrarian transition, it is worth reviewing the core theoretical tenets of the approach. A key conceptual foundation is the conceptualisation of the 'mode of production' itself, which was elaborated in Althusser and Balibar's (1968) *Reading Capital*. To Althusser and Balibar (1968, 215), the mode of production is a core conceptual concept. It is made up of three functional 'elements'. These are (*a*) the means of production, (*b*) the labourer and (*c*) the appropriator of surplus labour. These three elements are in turn structured by two 'connections': (*a*) the relation between the labourer and the means of production, or the *forces of production*, and (*b*) the property relation which defines how the surplus is appropriated and what happens to this surplus – known as the *relations of production* (Althusser and Balibar, 1968, 212–216).

Importantly, it is asserted that modes of production never exist in isolation, but coexist and articulate with others at specific historical junctures. These may exist in a larger entity known as a "social formation'. While as a concept, the social formation was theorised by Marx himself, Althusser and Balibar highlighted the utility of the concept (Burns, 2024). It is defined as a matrix of 'instances' which can be economic, political or ideological and are connected structurally with varying levels of functionality or autonomy. Within a social formation, there may be several *coexisting* modes of production. One is normally 'dominant', although, crucially, this can be either capitalist *or* pre-capitalist (Althusser and Balibar, 1968, 212–215). More simply, the social formation is considered by Tilley (1982) as a structural equivalent to the sociological concept of 'society'. How it overlaps with particular spatial configurations is less clear. Santos and Slaner (1977, 5) suggest that space gives the social formation its concrete form through the localised convergence of not just economic processes such as different modes of production, but also political and ideological processes such as those associated with particular state formations. In the context of this study, for example, the country of Nepal (a political entity) can itself be considered a social formation, although the concept can also be applied to the geographically and culturally unique Tarai-Madhesh. In terms of the global context, Bettelheim (1972) argues that there is a complex hierarchy of 'national' social formations aligning with state boundaries, in which capitalist *or* pre-capitalist systems may be dominant, although all are situated within a broader 'worldwide capitalist mode of production'.

The concept of a social formation is of important theoretical relevance for the themes of this book, as even if a national or sub-national social formation is 'dominated' by capitalism via integration into the capitalist world economy, this does not mean that modes of production on the ground are 'capitalist'. This premise sheds light on controversies such as Andre Gunder Frank's problematic assertion that peripheral economies such as Latin America and India were 'capitalist' since the colonial era because they were integrated into the global economy through mercantile capitalism. As noted by Stuart Hall (1996), Frank over-emphasises the relations of exchange (and merchant capital) rather than the relations of *production* on the ground, which may well be pre-capitalist. This ahistorical approach departs from Marx himself, who acknowledged the importance of pre-capitalist modes of production in mediating the infiltration of capitalism into peripheral locales such as colonial India (Gupta, 1977; Lin, 1980).

The processes through which more than one mode of production interact can be better understood through the concept of 'overdetermination'. To Althusser, this refers to the ways through which multiple processes in the social whole are constituted by each other. Althusser (1969, 106) stresses that within a given social formation, any given contradiction (such as that between labour and capital) can be understood only with reference to its relation to the multiple forms of the superstructure (such as the state or its ideology) and its embeddedness within specific spatial contexts. The latter may include localised culture or struggles on the one hand and a particular 'world context' on the other (that is, relations of subordination between nations). Althusser, however, diverges from some more dogmatic interpretations of Marxism to emphasise that the superstructure is not a necessary condition of the base and has its own essence and logic (Althusser, 1969).

Althusser and Balibar's approach is of significant utility for the study of agrarian transition. While it is interested in 'periodisation', the ways in which historical successions of structures are organised, it is approached in a radically different way from developmentalist (largely Stalinist) interpretations of Marxism. It must be emphasised that their approach does not intend to classify societies into a pre-ordained set of modes of production or arrange them into an evolutionary set of 'stages' (Raatgever, 1985). Instead, it seeks to examine the dominant mode of production in a social formation at a given historical conjuncture and understand the processes through which it is preserved or undermined – including the interplay between economic, political and cultural-ideological processes. To Resch (1992, 84), '[t]he problem addressed by the concept of mode of production is one of producing knowledge rather than classifying data'.

Modes of Production and Radical Anthropology

An important body of scholarship which drew heavily from the Althusserian tradition was the largely Francophone radical anthropology of the 1970s and 1980s. Mobilising ethnographic research, primarily from the West and Central African context, they sought to understand the dynamics through which capitalist and non-capitalist modes of production coexist, and the associated interaction between economic, political and ideological processes (Dupré and Rey, 1979; Meillassoux, 1973; Meillassoux, 1980; Meillassoux, 1981; van der Klei, 1985). Later iterations of this approach have been replicated in South Asia (Singh, 2007; Djurfeldt et al., 2008; Djurfeldt and Lindberg, 1975). What was unique about this body of scholarship was its use of ethnography instead of farm surveys to answer questions over the mode of production. A challenge for the analysis of modes of production is that these are theoretical constructs which facilitate understanding particular structural relations but cannot actually be 'observed' on the ground (van Binsbergen and Geschiere, 1985b) or uncovered via quantitative surveys. However, through in-depth localised ethnography, the radical anthropology was able to understand the unique internal dynamics of pre-capitalist modes of production, and the mechanisms through which the set of relations it constitutes achieve stability (Raatgever, 1985; van Binsbergen and Geschiere, 1985b).

There were several important phenomena which this approach uncovered (see Hall, 1996, and Breckenridge, 2021, for review of this scholarship). The first was the tendency for pre-capitalist modes of production to 'resist' the expansion of capitalism. van Binsbergen and Geschiere (1985a) argue that older economic formations in peripheral regions are not necessarily dissolved when they come into contact with expanding capitalist markets. While there may still be loose articulations, with flows of surplus between modes of production and alliances between pre-capitalist and capitalist dominant classes (for example, for exchange of 'prestige goods' within the elite), one cannot assume the older economic formation is 'subordinate' or functional to capitalism. Dupré and Rey's (1979) fieldwork in Congo-Brazzaville, for instance, noted how the pre-colonial lineage[9] mode of production would supply goods from capitalist markets on early contact with European traders. However, there was little interest in accumulation as exchange relations within the clan were for symbolic rather than productive purposes. This emerged as an obstacle for capitalism in its drive to yield surplus value via labour or commodities. Rey notes that it was only the *coercive* economic and political interventions of colonialism that broke these internal systems. The end result was that these modes of production were restructured and subordinated to supply surplus to capitalism (cited from Resch, 1992).

The second phenomena that this scholarship uncovered were the mechanisms through which pre-capitalist modes of production could persist while supplying surplus to capitalism. As noted earlier, Marx, Lenin and later scholars were aware of the phenomena whereby wage workers retain plots of land, which can support the suppression of wages. The radical anthropology tradition addressed this issue, but rather than viewing it as a 'transitionary' phase, whereby the persistence of the peasantry is functional to capital, or viewing such farmers as semi-proletarians (that is, wage workers who have some land), they recognised that pre-capitalist modes of production can retain stability and partial autonomy, yet simultaneously be 'restructured' to supply surplus to capitalism.

A crucial concept is that of labour reproduction. In his article 'Wage Labour and Capital' Marx (2008 [1933], 36) notes that wages in capitalism cover two elements – (*a*) the cost of the maintenance of the labourer and (*b*) the cost of *reproducing* the labour force. As he notes: 'In the same manner, the cost of production of simple labor-power must include the cost of propagation, by means of which the race of workers is enabled to multiply itself, and to replace worn-out workers with new ones.' Meillassoux (1981, 107–137) built upon this argument, noting how during Europe's industrialisation, the dissolution of the peasantry created a stable proletariat which was part of a relatively closed system. The labour power of these workers would be produced, maintained and reproduced *within* the domestic capitalist economy. This stands in contrast to the case study he provides from West Africa (Mali and Senegal). The pre-capitalist lineage mode of production was not 'dissolved' by capitalism like in industrialisation-era Europe. Instead, the older mode of production was (as also argued by Dupré and Rey) restructured via taxation or other coercive mechanisms to force the peasantry into the capitalist labour force for part – but not all – of their livelihood. As livelihoods were split between the capitalist *and* pre-capitalist modes of production (which remained intact), wages for peasants needed to only cover the cost of the labourer alone, and not the reproduction of labour. The latter was provided by the pre-capitalist economy, thus offering exceptional profits for capitalist employers (Meillassoux 1981).

Meillassoux (1981) elaborated this point in detail with the case study of migrants from West Africa to post-war France. Labour contracts dictated that they migrated without families and initially came on a temporary basis. As a result, they maintained a strong link to their home communities, where they would return periodically. They were, however, paid a wage which covered only their *minimum* subsistence needs. It would fall to the pre-capitalist lineage mode of production in their place of origin to cover the living cost of the migrant during periods spent at home, or when they were unproductive due to illness, and on their retirement. The pre-capitalist sector also covered longer-term costs of both bringing up and educating children in the place of origin (that is, creating a new generation of workers) and their 'retirement', including networks of social support to sustain them after their return. These are costs which in advanced capitalism may be borne by higher wages or the welfare state, a point also noted by Breman (2009) and Sehgal (2005). By contrast, in peripheral countries, they are provided by the pre-capitalist sector as a 'rent' for capitalism (Meillassoux, 1981).

Similar arguments were made by Wolpe (1979) with regard to the Apartheid era black 'reserves' or 'Bantustans', whereby the pre-capitalist kinship-based units of production in the reserves were actively protected by the state to cover the *reproduction* needs of labour power for capitalism, which would be supplied through cyclical labour migration, to work in sectors such as mining. This articulation was reproduced through the political apparatus of the state and its racial ideologies (see full review of these arguments by Stuart Hall, 1996).

There has been less interest in these approaches in recent years with regard to Africa (Breckenridge, 2021), although there are a few exceptions in the case of South Asia. In an outstanding study from Madhya Pradesh in India, Singh (2007, 2023) applies the Althusserian concept of articulation to Adivasi or 'tribal' social formations which are supplying labour to capitalism via cyclical migration, where there were some parallels with the communitarian African tribal societies discussed by Meillassoux. With reference to the Bhil of Madhya Pradesh, he notes how coercive mechanisms such as taxation undermined redistributive and communal elements of the relations of production, restructuring it so that it supplied workers to the capitalist sector yet continued to reproduce the labour force – a process he refers to as breaking the 'autarky' of the Adivasi social formation (Singh, 2023). This research also analyses how the process of religious proselytisation has gone alongside the growing subordination of the Adivasi social formation to capitalism (Singh, 2007).

While stopping short of mobilising the Althusserian method, some other studies have acknowledged the role of the peasantry in covering the reproduction cost of capitalist labour. Shah and Lerche (2020), using case studies from across India, reiterate (like Singh, 2007) that a significant share of migrant workers in the burgeoning capitalist sector in cities retain a strong link with their home community. They point out how an invisible rural economy of care, which looks after the migrant during parts of the year while supporting his/her extended family, is provided to capitalism, yet is not borne into the remuneration of the migrant for their labour. There is also literature in China which has explored how the pre-capitalist peasant sector is preserved to supply cover for the reproductive cost of urban labour, also via migration (Alexander and Chan, 2004; Zhan and Scully, 2018). This occurs through the *hukou* system, which regulated internal mobility by obliging farmers to access services such as education and pensions in their home. This encouraged migrant workers' dependent family members to stay in the village. The family members would be thus supported by the farm, while the workers would be sustained by agriculture during childhood, gaps in employment and retirement. This mechanism was incidentally very profitable for capitalism (Alexander and Chan, 2004). Even with the relaxation of the *hukou* system on a political level, the economic imperatives amongst workers to retain their link to the land have grown with spiralling costs of living in cities in a precarious neoliberal labour market (Zhan and Scully, 2018).

As the Chinese case suggests, the dependence upon domestic and community economic and cultural systems to reproduce labour power is becoming even more important in the context of neoliberal globalisation. This can be set against a broader shift outlined by Fraser (2018), who notes that neoliberal capitalism is increasingly dependent upon labour in the periphery. This is because colonial legacies and racialised ideology there have obstructed the development of the class compromise and legal frameworks which meet the interests of workers in the core. The latter includes the process through which the employers and the state cover labour reproduction costs through higher wages and welfare – which is a less common feature of peripheral capitalism.

Critique (and Defence) of the Althusserian Position

Althusser's approach to articulation was influential in the 1970s and 1980s, but in later years, while scholars continued to develop the ideas associated with this tradition, it also faced growing critique. A notable example is the so-called post-structuralist Marxian tradition (Gibson-Graham et al., 2001) which sought to reconsider the idea of a 'hierarchy' of modes of production subordinate to an all-powerful capitalism. It instead developed Althusser's concept of 'overdetermination' to represent the economy as a 'decentered totality' made up of multiple different forms of capitalism as well as non-capitalist formations (Gibson-Graham, 1996, 23). In this context, class structures were reframed as any 'processes' through which surplus labour would be appropriated. However, it was emphasised that these are diverse, fluid and ever-changing (Gibson-Graham et al., 2001; Gibson-Graham, 1996; Resnick and Wolff, 1989). This approach has been applied to South Asian agrarian transition by Chakrabarti and Cullenberg (2003).

As argued elsewhere (Sugden, 2019), this book agrees with the need to deconstruct the vision of an all-powerful capitalism and acknowledges that individuals can simultaneously hold multiple class positions. Nevertheless, it diverges from the implication in 'post-structural Marxism' that no process in the social world (economic, political or ideological) and no particular economic formation (capitalist or otherwise) can be considered more important than any other as a driver of change. It thus follows Glassman's critique (2003), which stresses that it is helpful to maintain a concept of structural power, particularly if one is to identify the dominant contradiction against which political struggles can be directed. The book thus, like Glassman, acknowledges that there is value in acknowledging that certain structural forces (such as articulation of modes of production) do have causal efficacy. However, like Althusser, the book recognises the book recognises that these structures are present in particular historical-empirical conjunctures, rather than being embedded in any predetermined evolutionary theory. While class structures can be understood as 'processes', in certain contexts, they also represent a form of 'crystallized power' based upon deeply embedded relations between dominant and subordinate classes, which persist over time and space (Glassman, 2003).

This argument actually parallels a much earlier defence of the structuralist Althusserian position by Stuart Hall in the face of emerging post-structural critique. He notes the capacity of the approach to acknowledge difference, while also recognising the unity which binds this diversity together: '… we have to characterize Althusser's advance, not in terms of his insistence on "difference" alone – the rallying cry of Derridean deconstruction – but instead in terms of the necessity of thinking unity and difference; difference in complex unity, without this becoming a hostage to the privileging of difference as such' (1985, 93). In another well-known essay, Hall (1996) further reaffirms the intrinsic value of the concept of the articulation of modes of production to understand the 'complex unity' of social formations. In the process he makes a strong defence of the utility of the African case studies analysed by scholars such as Wolpe and Meillassoux, as in this book (see also discussion in Karayiannides, 2023). However, in Hall's constructive critique of Wolpe's South African research, he substitutes the Althusserian notion of ideology with Gramsci's "hegemony' to understand how the ideological levels of social formations (in this context associated with race) interact with the economic (Hall, 1985).

The 'Mode of Production' Debate and the Pre-capitalist in South Asia

While the last section has set out the theoretical framework which largely inspired this book and has charted how it can be mobilised to understand the pre-capitalist, it is now time to apply this to understand contemporary agrarian transition in South Asia and the relationship between older modes of production and a nascent capitalism.

Perhaps the most well-known engagement with the pre-capitalist in South Asia was the mode of production debate in the 1970s and 1980s – mentioned in the last chapter. This debate sought to determine whether Indian agriculture was capitalist (see Rudra, 1974) or pre-capitalist, or more specifically 'semi-feudal' (see Bhaduri, 1973; Bhaduri, 1977; Prasad, 1973). This was a debate of critical political significance, as it established the trajectory that class struggle was to follow and the relevant role of the peasantry versus a capitalist proletariat. Analysis of semi-feudalism was pursued by Chandra (1974) with reference to 1960s/1970s surveys from West Bengal and Prasad (1973) with reference to Bihar. The foundation of semi-feudalism was the presence of landlords controlling large estates farmed by sharecropping peasants. The coercive appropriation of surplus remained important, although rather than occurring through political-ideological means, the emphasis was on economic processes such as the interlinkage of land, credit and produce markets. This had important implications for agrarian transition due to what Thorner called a built-in 'depressor' in Indian agriculture, whereby the appropriation of surplus via rent, usury and forced commerce impedes technological change and investment on the land (Harriss, 2013). This was captured in a classic model of semi-feudalism in rural Bengal by Bhaduri (1973) whereby land-poor peasants are bonded to landlords through the interlinkage of land ownership and usury. Innovations to increase yields were withheld by landlords as they would lower the tenants' indebtedness and undermine the power and authority of the landowners. Closely connected with the concept of semi-feudalism was that of the 'semi-colonial' social formation. Under the latter, the capitalist sector has been distorted by imperialism, and thus does not have the capacity to end the rural poor's dependence on landlords. In this context, 'semi-feudalism' survives in rural areas (Chandra, 1974; Sau, 1975).

While lacking the conceptual or empirical sophistication of the Althusserian-inspired radical anthropology, the semi-feudalism debate does represent a critical juncture in the analysis of the pre-capitalist in South Asia and cast doubt on the idea that an all-powerful capitalism will inevitably dissolve the peasantry. Nevertheless, the concept was controversial. Other than the counter-narratives of the debate such as Rudra (1974), who identified evidence of capital formation in agriculture in the same parts of India claimed to be semi-feudal,[10] the concept was critiqued on a theoretical level – and at times this was justified. Unlike the radical anthropology tradition, research on semi-feudalism during these debates remained largely economistic. Brass (2002) problematises the concept in lieu of its ambiguous definition and the implication that it is part of a 'linear' interpretation of history. He notes how semi-feudalism tends to be defined by the presence of unfree agrarian relationships alone. These are interpreted as historical relics, when in fact such relationships are widespread under capitalism. Brass also critiques the term 'semi-' which suggests an ambiguity in systems which are otherwise defined clearly in Marxism. For the same reason, this book also prefers to simply refer to feudalism rather than semi-feudalism.

The research on interlinked contracts, which was central to the semi-feudal models described by Bhaduri, was critiqued by Hart (1986), who noted that conditions of un-freedom can appear in the context of productive reinvestment as well as so-called backward agrarian contexts. Hart asserts that unfree relationships can instead be viewed as a means through which dominant classes exercise social control, rather than being somehow emblematic of semi-feudalism or a transitional stage in the development of agrarian capitalism. Chakrabarty and Cullenberg (2003) critique the implied passivity of the subordinate class; the assumption that there is no incentive for landlords to develop the productive forces; the reduction of class power to ownership of the means of production; and the primacy given to surplus appropriation via the sphere of circulation (that is, usury) rather than production.

This book still asserts the utility of concepts of feudalism. However, rather than simply re-applying old models, it asserts the need for a more anthropological analysis of feudal agrarian relations – in the same way that the French radical anthropology analysed the lineage mode of production. It seeks a more nuanced understanding of what feudalism is, while accepting that the mode of production, like capitalism itself, is dynamic and subject to flux, taking on different forms at particular historical conjunctures, in line with changes on a cultural-ideological, political as well as economic level. Importantly, it seeks to better understand how feudalism relates to capitalism. Rather than implying feudal relations are a 'relic', this book seeks to show how they can maintain a dynamic – and not necessarily functional or subordinate – relationship with capitalism. This includes an analysis of how surplus can be transferred between capitalist and feudal formations in the region, a process which has thus far received limited attention in the context of South Asian feudalism.

Feudalism: In Pursuit of a Definition

One reason that there has been so much controversy over the concept of feudalism (or semi-feudalism) is the lack of a clear and broad-based definition. The mode of production debate tended to focus on extra-economic coercion and interlinked contracts, and while this at times constitutes an example of a 'feudal' relationship, this is by no means the only feature. Paradoxically, while academic definitions have often been very narrow, actual leftist political parties in Nepal and South Asia more widely have frequently used the term 'feudalism', or *samantibad* in Nepali/Hindi, relatively broadly,[11] usually referring to the presence of landlordism, yet often lacking a standard, agreed definition of what makes feudal land ownership different from capitalist.[12]

It is thus useful to go back to Marx's original interpretations. Marx refers to feudalism in a number of writings, and while there is no single systematic definition, the mode of production is discussed largely as part of his analysis of the transition to capitalism. A careful reading of these extracts thus offers insights into the key elements of feudalism, albeit in the European context. As well as extra-economic coercion, key features include the concentration of land by an overlord, appropriation of surplus through corvée labour and absolute ground rent, and the diversion of surplus into consumption rather than productive purposes.

The first feature entails the concentration of land and extra-economic coercion. In the German Ideology, Marx describes the emergence of feudalism as a new form of landed property emerging in the context of falling agricultural output, and the contraction in trade and population following the collapse of the Roman empire (Marx, 1947, 45–46). It was based around community units, like the communal or state-owned property which preceded it, yet was headed by a nobility with military power and control over land, with the primary subordinate class being the small peasantry. The economics of European feudalism is dealt with in more detail in the section entitled 'Rent of Land' from the *Economic and Philosophical Manuscripts* (Marx, 1959). In this passage he characterises feudalism as the original form of private property, where there is control over the means of production by a small land-owning aristocracy – what he calls an 'immovable monopoly'.

Marx does make reference to extra-economic coercion as a mechanism to maximise surplus appropriation. However, this focuses not on interlinked contracts (which more recent debates dwelled on), but instead on the ideological power which binds tenants to landlords. Marx points to an individualised relationship between the landlord and his land, often tied to one's political position, matched by a similarly individualised relationship between the serfs and landlords, with the former bound by what Marx terms 'respect, allegiance, and duty' (Marx, 1959).

The second feature of feudalism relates to the form of surplus appropriation. To understand how control over land and ideological power translate into different forms of exploitation, it is helpful to review a wider range of texts. The two primary mechanisms of surplus appropriation under feudal relations of production to Marx include a labour rent and ground rent. In Volume 1 of *Capital* Marx discusses corvée labour in the Danubian Principalities whereby the peasant works for part of the week on his own plot and part on the land of the lord. However, it is ground rent which is most significant in the South Asian context today, and this is dealt with in more detail in Volume 3 of *Capital*, where Marx clearly differentiated feudal ground rent from its counterpart under capitalism. To Ricardo, the primary form of ground rent under capitalism was known as 'differential rent'. This theory states that under capitalist conditions, the owner of property can appropriate a differential rent if, due to natural endowments, a parcel of land can yield a profit above the average rate of profit for the society as a whole (cited from Patnaik, 1983). In these contexts, the Marxian 'prices of production' for commodities produced on a parcel of land are less than the society-wide price of production.[13] The landlord can therefore appropriate the surplus profit as a rent, while the capitalist operator continues to receive average rates of profit (Marx, 1967, 641).

However, Marx builds upon Ricardo's theory to develop a new concept, that of *absolute rent*. Ricardo's theory of differential rent assumed the worst land does not yield rent, while in reality, all land owned by a given landlord can be subject to rent. Marx notes that where there is a class monopoly over landed property, rent can be extracted *regardless* of differences in the fertility of the land (Marx, 1967). In the context of capitalist agriculture, the demand by landlords for an absolute rent, even from the most marginal land, can result in a rise in the market price of commodities above their 'price of production' as the farmers must pay a rent while still yielding an average profit comparable with non-agricultural activities. In other words, landed property itself, rather than natural endowment, actually 'creates' rent (Marx, 1967). Absolute ground rent to Marx therefore 'forms a portion of the value, or more specifically, surplus value, of commodities, and instead of falling into the lap of the capitalists, who have extracted it from the labourers, it falls to the share of the landlords, who extract it from the capitalists' (Marx, 1967, 771). Supply and demand determine whether rent constitutes the entire profit or only part of the profit (Marx, 1967).[14]

Importantly, absolute ground rent is the *predominant* form of ground rent under *pre-capitalist* conditions. The difference is that under capitalism, rent represents the surplus which remains for the landowner after a producer has yielded an average rate of profit, whereas under pre-capitalist or 'feudal' conditions, it represents the surplus over subsistence needs and necessary production costs of the tenants (Marx, 1967, 795). It may even absorb part of some producers' subsistence requirements. In pre-capitalist situations where there is low development of the productive forces, Marx emphasises that subsistence is the aim of producers, rather than achieving an average rate of profit, and farmers often continue to cultivate the land when subsistence has been forced down to a bare physical minimum (Marx, 1967).

In other words, under capitalist 'tenant' agriculture,[15] rent is simply an 'excess' of the surplus value (extracted from workers) over that which is retained by the farmer as profit, which is distributed to the landowner (Marx, 1967, 800). By contrast, under feudal agriculture, rent represents the *primary* mechanism through which the product of surplus labour is appropriated. Rent therefore falls under the relations of production, rather than simply representing a distribution of already produced surplus. It may be appropriated by a territorial overlord or a centralised state (Patnaik, 1983). The former represents the predominant form of rent in contemporary South Asia as discussed in the mode of production debate, and the latter represents the centralised feudalism of the mid-eighteenth to mid-twentieth centuries such as under India's Mughal rule or Nepal's Gorkhali and Rana regimes.

Marx notes that pre-capitalist absolute ground rent acts as a considerable barrier to capitalist development, stating that it '... may assume dimensions which seriously imperil the reproduction of the conditions of labour, the means of production themselves, rendering the expansion of production more or less impossible and reducing the direct producers to the physical minimum of means of subsistence' (Marx, 1967, 796). Rather than profit representing the limit of rent, rent represents the limit of profit (Marx, 1967).

A final feature of feudalism, which Marx refers to yet is often overlooked, is the use of surplus for *consumption* rather than productive reinvestment. This is in contrast to the drive to invest to develop the productive forces under capitalism. In the *Economic and Political Manuscripts* Marx notes that 'the feudal lord does not try to extract the utmost advantage from his land. Rather, he consumes what is there and calmly leaves the worry of producing to the serfs and the tenants' (Marx, 1932). This point is taken further in *Grundrisse*, where he asserts that the feudal lord consumes the product of the land rather than investing it as capital to maximise productivity. Even if the surplus is sold, generating 'value', it is used for 'luxury consumption' (Marx, 1973, 469). This represents a fundamental difference between feudal and capitalist agricultural land ownership, although a shift towards profit orientation and expanded reproduction by landlords may pave the way for Lenin's so-called Junker path to capitalism in the future.

Applying Marx's Vision of Feudalism to South Asia

A long-standing challenge of applying Marxian concepts to other parts of the world is the extent to which his models, which draw from the European context, are applicable elsewhere. Nevertheless, R. S. Sharma's (1985) definition of medieval Indian feudalism generally echoes that of Marx, noting similarities as well as subtle differences between historical Europe and India. He refers to an agrarian system where the peasantry is subjugated to overlords who mobilise extra-economic power to control land and extract surplus. These extra-economic elements include social, political and religious subjugation. It also includes 'ideological power' alone, whereby peasants believe they are duty-bound to pay rent or other tribute. However, Sharma emphasised that feudal social relations vary across historical and geographical contexts. The character of the land-owning class in medieval India was highly variable, as were the political-ideological mechanisms used to coerce the peasantry. Surplus was also appropriated through forced labour, taxation as well as rent and different hierarchies of exploitation were present, including sub-infeudation and simultaneous exploitation by centralised feudal states as well as local functionaries (Sharma, 1985). This echoes the situation in Nepal, particularly as recognised by Mahesh Chandra Regmi. Regmi (1976) documents a transition from a centralised state to a more decentred set of relationships we see today between landlords and tenants, which built upon the foundations of these older state formations. While Regmi refers to this as 'state landlordism' rather than feudalism, it parallels the system described by Sharma.

This book will therefore *loosely* utilise Marx's definition of feudalism – namely the concentration of landed property, surplus appropriation through absolute ground rent and/or labour tax via extra-economic coercion, and use of surplus for consumption rather than productive reinvestment. It will, however, like Sharma, be flexible in identifying the component parts of feudalism, which vary according to particular temporal and spatial junctures. The three features that I have drawn from Marx are not necessarily out of line with domestic understandings of feudalism in Nepali political discourse. For instance, while, as noted earlier, they do not give a systematic definition, the Nepal Communist Party's first manifesto (1949), in its broad description of 'feudal production' or *saamanti utpaadan*, does acknowledge the presence of various phenomena such as concentration of land amongst the landlord and Rana class, surplus appropriation from the peasantry by sharecropping, and diversion of the surplus for personal use.

The Disintegration of Feudalism in South Asia?

A remaining question is the current status of academic debates on feudalism in South Asia. Most of the earlier discussion around modes of production in the region took place between the 1960s and 1980s. However, there have been astronomical changes in the global capitalist economy in the last 40 years in the wake of neoliberal globalisation. While there has been some resurgence of interest in South Asian 'modes of production', particularly in the context of economic change (see Lerche et al., 2013), there is a tendency to assume that feudalism is of limited relevance in the twenty-first century.

Scholars such as Patnaik (2006) have, like Bernstein (2006), moved away from the traditional 'agrarian question' and mode of production debates entirely. Arguing from the Indian context, Patnaik suggests that scale-backs of state support and the drive towards commercial farming have left farmers vulnerable to falling prices, exploitation by global agribusiness through contract farming, and outright dispossession due to corporate land grabs. This, Patnaik argues, has impeded the development of capitalism within agriculture. The primary antagonism in this context is not between landlords and tenants, or between marginal producers and emerging capitalist farmers, but between farmers across the land ownership spectrum and the corporate food regime. Agriculture and industry meanwhile are increasingly disarticulated, so the development of capitalist agriculture is no longer necessary to support an emerging industrial base (Patnaik, 2006). While many of these assertions relating to agrarian stress under liberalisation may be relevant in highly commercialised locales, there is an implication that there is a nascent capitalism in agriculture which has been 'blocked' by imperialism. This conceptualisation is also of less relevance in many peripheral regions of South Asia with low levels of commercial farming and limited infiltration of corporate agribusiness. This includes large parts of eastern India, which were the focus of the 1960s–1970s semi-feudalism debate, as well as Nepal.

There have, however, been a range of studies which have more explicitly engaged with the question of whether semi-feudalism persists in Indian agriculture or is indeed a relic of limited contemporary relevance. With some exceptions (for example, Kar, 2018), most scholarship has implied that there is a decline in what may be termed 'feudal' agrarian relations under expanding neoliberal markets and labour migration (Harriss, 2013; Basu and Das, 2013; Rodgers and Rodgers, 2001; Datta et al., 2014). While there is an acknowledgement that inequality persists and the majority of farms remain marginal, it is argued that the disproportionate economic control by landlords has dissipated (Gupta, 2005). Harris (2013), for example, points to the reduction in the leased area, fragmentation of estates, and the declining importance of land for political control, with landlords seeking new sources of political or economic dominance outside of agriculture. Paralleling this are the new sources of off-farm income for subordinated castes, most notably through migration, which has broken ties of bondage to landlords (Datta et al., 2014). Basu and Das (2013, 379) argue that 'the landlord-dominated semi-feudal economy of the 1940s and 1950s has given way to an agrarian economic structure marked by a preponderance of small-scale farms, non-farm petty production and a ceaseless circulation of footloose labour.' While not all scholarship goes on to characterise agriculture in South Asia as capitalist, there is a strong implication that the concept of 'semi-feudalism' or 'feudalism' is of reduced relevance. In fact, certain relations such as bonded labour in agriculture have also been reinterpreted as 'capitalist' in character (Guérin, 2013).

The aforementioned studies do offer insights into trajectories of change in what is a complex and economically diverse region. However, this book stops short of dismissing the concept of feudalism. What it instead argues is that landlordism persists, albeit in a rapidly changing form, while still retaining a character which is *closer* to feudalism than capitalism. At the foundation of this research is the more flexible definition of feudalism outlined earlier, which moves beyond simplistic criteria such as the presence of interlinked contracts, and instead seeks to understand how various 'feudal' relations have evolved in line with a changing external political-economic context. The book also does not claim that empirical research on the 'dissolution' of feudal landlordism is incorrect, either from South Asia or beyond – given that in some regions, landlord control over the means of production has reduced considerably (see Sugden, 2017, for instance, with a comparison between different parts of Nepal and Bihar). The book instead traces a more complex process of transition in one locality within the Nepal Tarai-Madhesh – the southern part of Morang district. This trajectory – which is relevant in many other parts of the region – accepts the presence of *both* feudalism and capitalism. Instead of asking whether or not one or the other is present, the focus is on how they interact and articulate in a complex unity, and undergo change, at a time of unprecedented economic, cultural and political transformation. The approach is in tune with the most critical epistemological break of the Althusserian tradition – the importance of identifying historical individualities of given social formations rather than attempting to 'fit' what is observed into an evolutionary framework drawn from a priori theory.[16]

Contemporary Feudal and Capitalist Relations in the Eastern Gangetic Plains: Situating the Study Site

It is worth touching upon where the case study site of southern Morang fits within the larger region. This locality, along with much of the Nepal Tarai-Madhesh, falls within a much larger socio-cultural and agro-ecological region – the Eastern Gangetic Plains. This is an important region for South Asian agrarian studies, as many of the classical studies on South Asian semi-feudalism (Chandra, 1974; Sau, 1975; Bhaduri, 1973) were from within this belt. This stems in part from the legacy of the zamindari system of land tenure from the colonial period (Bandyopadhyay, 1993) and the similar *jimidari* system from Rana-era Nepal (Regmi, 1976).

There have arguably been many changes in the Eastern Gangetic Plains since the early studies of semi-feudalism in the 1970s and 1980s. Relatively successful land reforms in West Bengal in the late 1970s, particularly Operation Barga, mean that landlordism in that part of the plains is far less significant today than in adjoining regions (Banerjee et al., 2002; Bakshi, 2008). Areas which experienced reforms include the Naxalbari region, which was the heartland of the Maoist-inspired anti-feudal revolt in the 1960s (Banerjee, 2006). In Bihar and the Nepal Tarai-Madhesh, however, past land reforms have had limited success in undermining landlordism (Adhikari, 2006; Regmi, 1976; Rorabacher, 2016) – yet there are other changes of note, most notably the significant rise in labour migration, economic liberalisation and a rapid expansion of markets (Sugden et al., 2016; Sunam, 2015). In fact, the Eastern Gangetic Plains represent a good example of a region which was never central to colonial-era accumulation and commercial activity and was a stronghold of pre-capitalist agrarian formations, yet today finds itself at the 'frontier' of expanding capitalist markets for commodities and the export of surplus labour.

While feudal relations have undergone flux, it is important to also note that there is considerable geographical diversity in the character of feudalism and the trajectory of change – and this played an important role in choosing the location for this study, which was one of several carried out by the author across the region. There are several distinct belts within the Gangetic plains. The region west of the Koshi river on both sides of the Nepal–Bihar border is known historically as Mithilanchal. This region has a rigid caste structure, a history of economic marginalisation with negligible industry or off-farm capitalist production, and a long history of subordination to hierarchical state formations. Research linked to this study suggests that in Mithilanchal, the mode of production is still undeniably feudal in character, yet is looser in terms of the monopoly of economic power held by the landed elite, in a relationship which varies according to local political and economic histories (Sugden, 2017). In some pockets such as the Janakpur region of Nepal, landlords have sold off much land, and it has made a transition towards an agrarian formation dominated by large farmers (Sugden, 2019), while migrant remittances have allowed some formerly landless households to get a foothold on the land market, undermining their dependence on the old landed elite (Rinck, 2024).

In other locales such as the Koshi floodplains of Nepal and Madhubani of Bihar, landlords retain considerable economic and political power and maintain a monopoly over land. While farmers are no longer bonded to single landlords through usury, they remain indebted to more than one money lender (Sugden, 2016). Importantly, these linked studies suggest that despite the moderate expansion of markets and articulations with capitalism through labour migration, there is no evidence of capitalist social relations emerging *within* agriculture, either through internal differentiation or subordination to the market through petty commodity production. Sharecropping is the primary mechanism of surplus appropriation, although corvée labour persists in some localities (Sugden, 2016), and most surplus is consumed locally and not 'reinvested' on the land. In fact, these past studies suggest that growing linkages with capitalism through emerging markets and labour migration are actually bolstering the power of landlords and money lenders, with usury in particular growing in influence with rising economic stress and monetisation (Sugden, 2017; Sugden, 2019; Sugden et al., 2014).

The wetter, more fertile region east of the Koshi river, where the southern Morang case study for this book is located, represents a quite different political-economic context. This was one of the primary reasons the region was chosen. The Morang region has even more severe land inequalities than Mithilanchal (Sugden, 2017). This stems from the history of 'land grants' in this region to elites from the hills, and its historic importance to the feudal Gorkha and Rana regimes. However, another difference which sets the Morang region apart from Mithilanchal is with regard to the levels of articulation with capitalism. While Mithilanchal has very limited capitalist production, even off the farm, with negligible levels of industrial development, the more fertile plains east of the Koshi have over the last three decades forged relatively strong links with the global capitalist economy through some cash crop production and industry. This includes not only the Morang region covered in this book, but also the Purnea region of Bihar (see Rodgers and Rodgers, 2001) to the south and the North Bengal plains to the east. Morang itself has limited cash crop production today, yet maintains a sizeable industrial belt, high labour migration, and good transport and market infrastructure which has integrated rural communities into global and regional markets for consumer goods to a far greater extent than Mithilanchal. The juxtaposition of particularly high levels of landlordism alongside deepening articulations with capitalism makes it an excellent case study to understand how older pre-capitalist inequalities interact with an expanding capitalism. It allows one to understand the complex mechanisms through which capitalism expands into parts of the world economy long associated with 'non-capitalist' forms of social and political organisation.

In doing so it will explore how this process is mediated by political, cultural and environmental change, and what this means for the future of the peasantry in the Eastern Gangetic Plains.

Notes

1. This may, for instance, include land grabs for carbon offsetting or biofuel production.
2. BRICS stands for Brazil, Russia, India, China and South Africa.
3. See discussion in chapter 1 of Tilzey and Sugden (2023) for a review of these themes
4. Central to this debate was the Agrarian Question, which was concerned with the creation of a proletariat, a class who was separated from ownership of the means of production, yet was free to sell their labour power, who in turn could eradicate class society (Akram-Lodhi and Kay, 2010). The peasantry created a conundrum, as they embodied both characteristics of the proletariat (ability to sell labour) and bourgeoisie tendencies, notably in their ownership of land.
5. Drawing a parallel with the North American context, whereby capitalism emerged spontaneously from within the settler peasantry in the absence of a landlord class, Lenin termed this model the 'American path'. It entailed a peasantry composed of large, commercialised farmers, a middle peasantry of small land owners, and land-poor households who were predominantly farm workers. The middle peasants lacked the technology or assets to produce a large saleable surplus, and being heavily in debt and vulnerable, they would over time be compelled to sell their assets to emerging capitalist farmers, thus entering the proletariat. The middle segment of the peasantry would thus disappear, paving the way for a capitalist mode of production dominated by large, accumulating commercial farms and a large landless proletariat. This was close to the model he described much earlier in 'The Development of Capitalism in Russia' (Lenin, 1960 [1899]) where he charts the dissolution of the small-scale family farm, whereby the large farms of the more competitive *kulak*s emerge into an agrarian bourgeoisie.
6. McMichael (2012) associates this with a shift towards a new global food regime after the 2008 food crisis, which saw a shift in emphasis from production of niche cash crops in the periphery towards production of cheap wage foods destined for the core (a reversal of the earlier practice of dumping cheap grain from large-scale farms in the core).
7. It is asserted that even when crop and input prices erode these households' subsistence needs, peasant farms may already be dependent on commodity production and trapped in cycles of debt. Their ability to continue cultivation

is possible by using their labour more intensively, thus yielding absolute surplus value for capitalist firms, a process termed by Bernstein (1977) as the 'simple reproductive squeeze'. This echoes Kautsky (1988), who suggests that competition from capitalist producers will not necessarily cause the dissolution of small farms but may cause them to persist in the short term through the overwork and under-consumption.

8. Lenin considered this as a temporary phase in the much longer-term process of transition to full capitalist social relations, with the implication that these would inevitably be sold off to nascent capitalist farmers – as implied in 'The Development of Capitalism in Russia' (Lenin, 1960 [1899]). In reality, however, this has been found to have persisted long after the full development of capitalism.
9. By this they referred to a mode of production whereby the clan or lineage, rather than individual peasant household, was the primary unit of economic and political organisation – and while some accumulation may have taken place, surplus would be largely be redistributed within the clan.
10. Rudra noted that 'landlords' in Bengal were increasingly making investments in irrigation infrastructure, high yielding varieties of seeds and other improved inputs while providing tenants with their irrigation costs, part of the fertiliser cost and interest-free loans.
11. For instance, in the first manifesto of the Communist Party of Nepal (1949), *samantibadi* (feudalism) or *samanti* (feudal) is mentioned 22 times. The term was also used frequently throughout the 1996–2006 People's War.
12. This is not to say that parties do not have a 'position' on the topic – yet the definitions used in political writings are often relatively broad. While the 'feudalism' position is often associated with Maoist parties (not least in Nepal), Mao himself, in his analysis of classes in Chinese society (Mao, 1960), discusses the concept, but the relations of production (in terms of the nature of land ownership, role of coercion, mechanisms of surplus appropriation and how it is put to use) are not elaborated in detail. More concrete definitions by leftist political actors may, nevertheless, have been used in less well-known political writings.
13. *Prices of production* constitute the price at which commodities should exchange under ideal market conditions. It is defined by the formula $k+p$, whereby k is the cost of production, determined by the value of labour power (value of necessary labour) plus the value of the means of production, while p is determined by an *average* rate of profit across the economy (Marx, 1967, 165). Increases in productivity can increase the price of production above the 'value' of the product, yielding a surplus profit.
14. Kautsky (1988, 81), however, notes that in the context of an open economy, competition from other regions would set a limit on the levels of absolute rent, leading to a trend for absolute rent to fall in the long term. Cheaper commodities would restrict the influence of rent on commodity prices.

The landowner can, however, still control the price by controlling output. They will only lease out their land if the market price of the product has risen above the price of production to the point that a surplus profit is made to cover the cost of rent and yield an average profit (Kautsky, 1988, 80).

15. This likely has resonance in areas such as the United Kingdom where the legacy of feudal landed property means that many capitalist farms are in fact rented from the old feudal landlord class (see Tilzey et al., 2023).
16. See the intervention by Bois (1978) in the debate with Brenner over the divergent paths of French and English feudalism.

References

Adhikari, J. 2006. *Land Reform in Nepal: Problems and Prospects.* Nepal Institute of Development Studies.

Adhikari, Monalisa 2014. Politics and perceptions of Indian aid to Nepal. *Strategic Analysis* 38 (3): 325–340.

Akram-Lodhi, H. 2005. Vietnam's agriculture: Process of rich peasant accumulation and mechanisms of social differentiation. *Journal of Agrarian Change* 5 (1): 73–116.

———. 2007. Land, markets and neo-liberal enclosure: An agrarian political economy perspective. *Third World Quarterly* 28 (8): 1437–1456.

———. 2008. (Re)imagining agrarian relations? The World Development Report 2008: Agriculture for Development. *Development and Change* 39 (6): 1145–1161.

Akram-Lodhi, A. Haroon and Kay, Cristobal. 2010. Surveying the agrarian question (part 1): Unearthing foundations, exploring diversity. *Journal of Peasant Studies* 37 (1): 177–202.

Alexander, Peter and Chan, Anita. 2004. Does China have an apartheid pass system? *Journal of Ethnic and Migration Studies* 30 (4): 609–629.

Althusser, L. 1969. *For Marx.* Verso.

Althusser, L. and Balibar, E. 1968. *Reading Capital.* Redwood Burn Ltd.

Araghi, F. 2003. Food regimes and the production of value: Some methodological issues. *Journal of Peasant Studies* 30 (2): 41–70.

———. 2012. The invisible hand and the visible foot: Peasants, dispossession and globalization. In *Peasants and Globalization: Political Economy, Rural Transformation and the Agrarian Question*, edited by Akram-Lodhi, A. H. and Kay, C. Routledge.

Bernstein, Henry. 2006. Is there an agrarian question in the 21st century? *Canadian Journal of Development Studies/Revue canadienne d'études du développement* 27 (4): 449–460.

Bettelheim, C. 1972. Theoretical comments. In *Unequal Exchange: A Study of the Imperialism of Trade*, edited by Emmanuel, A. Monthly Review Press.

Bhaduri, A. 1973. A study in agricultural backwardness under semi-feudalism. *Economic Journal* 83 (329): 120–137.

———. 1977. On the formation of usurious interest rates in backward agriculture. *Cambridge Journal of Economics* 1 (4): 341–352.
Bois, Guy. 1978. Against the neo-Malthusian orthodoxy. *Past and Present* 69 (4): 60–69.
Brass, Tom. 2002. Rural labour in agrarian transitions: The semi-feudal thesis revisited. *Journal of Contemporary Asia* 32 (4): 456–473.
Breckenridge, Keith. 2021. What happened to the theory of African capitalism? *Economy and Society* 50 (1): 9–35.
Breman, Jan. 2009. The great transformation in the setting of Asia. Public lecture to accept honorary doctorate (International Institute of Social Studies, The Hague).
Burns, Tony. 2024. Marx and the concept of a social formation. *Historical Materialism* 1: 1–30.
Byres, Terence J. 1981. The new technology, class formation and class action in the Indian countryside. *Journal of Peasant Studies* 8 (4): 405–454.
Carchedi, Guglielmo and Roberts, Michael. 2021. The economics of modern imperialism. *Historical Materialism* 29 (4): 23–69.
Carroll, Toby. 2010. *Delusions of Development: The World Bank and the Post-Washington Consensus in Southeast Asia*. Springer.
Chakrabarti, A. and Cullenberg, S. 2003. *Transition and Development in India*. Routledge.
Chandra, Nirmal K. 1974. Farm efficiency under semi-feudalism: A critique of marginalist theories and some Marxist formulations. *Economic and Political Weekly* 9 (32/34): 1309–1332.
Communist Party of Nepal. 1949. *Nepal kamyunist partiko pahilo ghoshanapatra (purnapatha)*. https://www.cpnmc.org.
Cousins, Ben. 2022. Social differentiation of the peasantry (Marxist). *Journal of Peasant Studies* 49 (7): 1387–1398.
Dahal, Dilli, R. 1981. The concept of economy in a peasant society: A case study of the Athpahariya Rais in east Nepal. *Contributions to Nepalese Studies* 8 (2): 55–71.
Datta, Amrita, Rodgers, Gerry, Rodgers, Janine and Singh, B. K. N. 2014. Contrasts in development in Bihar: A tale of two villages. *Journal of Development Studies* 50 (9): 1197–1208.
de Janvry, A. 1981. *The Agrarian Question and Reformism in Latin America*. John Hopkins University Press.
Djurfeldt, Göran, Athreya, Venkatesh, Jayakumar, N., Lindberg, Staffan, Rajagopal, A and Vidyasagar, R. 2008. Agrarian change and social mobility in Tamil Nadu. *Economic and Political Weekly* 43 (45): 50–61.
Djurfeldt, Göran and Lindberg, Staffan. 1975. *Behind Poverty: The Social Formation in a Tamil Village*. Studentlitteratur AB.
Dobb, Maurice. 1948. *Studies in the Development of Capitalism*. Routledge.

Dupré, G. and Rey, P. P. 1979. Reflections on the relevance of a theory of the history of exchange. In *Relations of Production: Marxist Approaches to Economic Anthropology*, edited by Seddon, D. and Lackner, H. Frank Cass and Company Ltd.

FAO. 2014. *The State of Food and Agriculture 2014*. Food and Agriculture Organisation. http://www.fao.org/3/a-i4036e.pdf (accessed June 2023).

Fraser, Nancy. 2018. Roepke lecture in economic geography: From exploitation to expropriation – Historic geographies of racialized capitalism. *Economic Geography* 94: 1–17.

Gibson-Graham, G. K., Resnick, S and Wolff, R. D. 2001. Towards a poststructuralist political economy. In *Re/Presenting Class: Essays in Post-modern Marxism*, edited by Gibson-Graham, G. K., Resnick, S. and Wolff, R. D. Duke University Press.

Gibson-Graham, J. K. 1996. *The End of Capitalism (As We Knew It)*. Blackwell.

Glassman, J. 2003. Rethinking overdetermination, structural power, and social change: A critique of Gibson-Graham, Resnick and Wolff. *Antipode* 35 (4): 678–698.

———. 2006. Primitive accumulation, accumulation by dispossession, accumulation by 'extra-economic' means. *Progress in Human Geography* 30 (5): 608–625.

Guérin, Isabelle. 2013. Bonded labour, agrarian changes and capitalism: emerging patterns in South India. *Journal of Agrarian Change* 13 (3): 405–423.

Gupta, Dipankar. 2005. Whither the Indian village? Culture and agriculture in 'rural' India. *Review of Development and Change* 10 (1): 1–20.

Gupta, N. Sen. 1977. Further on the mode of production in agriculture. *Economic and Political Weekly* 12 (26): A55–A63.

Hall, Derek. 2013. Primitive accumulation, accumulation by dispossession and the global land grab. *Third World Quarterly* 34 (9): 1582–1604.

Hall, Stuart. 1985. Signification, representation, ideology: Althusser and the post-structuralist debates. *Critical Studies in Media Communication* 2 (2): 91–114.

———. 1996. Race, articulation, and societies structured in dominance. In *Black British Cultural Studies: A Reader*, edited by Baker, Houston A., Jr., Diawara, Manthia and Lindeborg, Ruth H., 16–60. University of Chicago Press.

Hanieh, Adam. 2016. *Capitalism and Class in the Gulf Arab States*. Springer.

Harris, Neal and Delanty, Gerard. 2023. What is capitalism? Toward a working definition. *Social Science Information* 62 (3): 323–344.

Harriss-White, Barbara. 2016. From analysing 'Filieres Vivrieres' to understanding capital and petty production in rural south India. *Journal of Agrarian Change* 16 (3): 478–500.

Harriss, John. 2013. Does 'landlordism' still matter? Reflections on agrarian change in India. *Journal of Agrarian Change* 13 (3): 351–364.

Hart, Gillian. 1986. Interlocking transactions: Obstacles, precursors or instruments of agrarian capitalism? *Journal of Development Economics* 23 (1): 177–203.

Harvey, David. 2001. Globalization and the spatial fix. *Geographische Revue* 2 (2): 23–31.

———. 2003. *The New Imperialism.* Oxford University Press.

Hodgson, Geoffrey, M. 2016. Conceptualizing capitalism: A summary. *Competition and Change* 20 (1): 37–52.

Kar, Guruprasad. 2018. The enduring prevalence of semi-feudal agrarian relations in India. *Journal of Labor and Society* 21 (2): 193–213.

Karayiannides, Efthimios. 2023. Stuart Hall, development theory, and Thatcher's Britain. *Modern Intellectual History* 20 (4): 1273–1296.

Kautsky, K. 1988. *The Agrarian Question.* Zwan Publications.

Lenin, V. I. 1960 [1899]. The development of capitalism in Russia. In *Collected Works: Volume 3*, edited by Lenin. V. I. Progress Publishers.

———. 1977. *The Agrarian Programme of Social-Democracy in the First Russian Revolution, 1905–1907.* Progress Publishers.

Lerche, Jens, Shah, Alpa and Harriss-White, Barbara. 2013. Introduction: Agrarian questions and left politics in India. *Journal of Agrarian Change* 13 (4): 337–350.

Li, Tania Murray. 2010. To make live or let die? Rural dispossession and the protection of surplus populations. *Antipode* 41 (1): 66–93.

———. 2014. What is land? Assembling a resource for global investment. *Transactions of the Institute of British Geographers* 39 (4): 589–602.

Lin, Sharat G. 1980. Theory of a dual mode of production in post-colonial India. *Economic and Political Weekly* 15 (10): 516–529.

Macfarlane, Alan. 1976. *Resources and Population: A Study of the Gurungs of Nepal.* Cambridge University Press

MacKinnon, Iain. 2018. 'Decommonising the mind': Historical impacts of British imperialism on indigenous tenure systems and self-understanding in the Highlands and Islands of Scotland. *International Journal of the Commons* 12 (1): 278–300.

Mao, Tse-Tung. 1960. Analysis of the classes in Chinese society. In *Selected Works of Mao Tse-tung.* Foreign Languages Press, Peking.

Marx, K. 1932. *Economic and Political Manuscripts.* Progress Publishers.

———. 1947. *The German Ideology.* International Publishers.

———. 1967. *Capital: A Critique of Political Economy (Volume 3).* Progress Publishers.

———. 1973. *Grundrisse: Foundations of the Critique of Political Economy.* Penguin.

———. 1974. *Capital: A Critical Analysis of Capitalist Production (Volume 1).* Progress Publishers.

———. 2008 [1933]. *Wage Labour and Capital.* Wilside Press.

———. 1959. *Economic and Philosophic Manuscripts of 1844.* Foreign Languages Publishing House.

McMichael, Philip. 2012. The land grab and corporate food regime restructuring. *Journal of Peasant Studies* 39 (3–4): 681–701.

Meillassoux, C. 1973. The social organisation of the peasantry: The economic basis of kinship. *Journal of Peasant Studies* 1 (1): 81–90.

———. 1980. From reproduction to production: A Marxist approach to economic anthropology. In *The Articulation of Modes of Production: Essays from Economy and Society*, edited by Wolpe, H. Routledge and Kegan Paul.

———. 1981. *Maidens, Meal and Money: Capitalism and the Domestic Community.* Cambridge University Press.

Muhammad, Anu. 2015. Bangladesh – A model of neoliberalism: The case of microfinance and NGOs. *Monthly Review* 66 (10): 35.

Oya, C. 2001. Large- and middle-scale farmers in the groundnut sector in Senegal in the context of liberalization and structural adjustment. *Journal of Agrarian Change* 1 (1): 124–163.

Patnaik, U. 1983. Classical theories of rent and its application to India: Some preliminary thoughts on sharecropping. In *Sharecroppers and Sharecropping*, edited by Byres, T. J. Frank Cass and Co.

———. 2006. The agrarian crisis and importance of peasant resistance. *People's Democracy* 30 (5).

Prasad, Pradhan, H. 1973. Production relations: Achilles' heel of Indian planning. *Economic and Political Weekly* 8 (19): 869–872.

Raatgever, R. 1985. Analytic tools, intellectual weapons: The discussions among French Marxist anthropologists about the identification of modes of production in Africa. In *Old Modes of Production and Capitalist Encroachment: Anthropological Explorations in Africa*, edited by Van Binsbergen, W. and Geschiere, P. KPI Limited.

Rai, Janak. 2015. Owning land was so much of Dukha in the past: Land and the State–Adivasi relations in the Tarai, Nepal. *Studies in Nepali History and Society* 20 (1): 69–98.

Rankin, K. N. and Shakya, Y. B. 2007. Neoliberalizing the grassroots? Microfinance and the politics of development in Nepal. In *Neoliberalization: Networks, States and Peoples*, edited by Kim England and Kevin Ward. Blackwell.

Regmi, M. 1976. *Landownership in Nepal.* Adroit Publishers.

Resch, R. P. 1992. *Althusser and the Renewal of Marxist Theory.* University of California Press.

Resnick, S. A. and Wolff, R. D. 1989. *Knowledge and Class.* University of Chicago Press.

Rinck, Jacob, 2024. Marxist past to speculative futures: migration, land markets, and political storytelling in Nepal's Tarai. *Journal of Peasant Studies*: 1–21.

Rodgers, G. and Rodgers, J. 2001. A leap across time: When semi-feudalism met the market in rural Purnia. *Economic and Political Weekly* 36 (22): 2–8.

Roka, Hari. 2022. Why oppose the millennium challenge corporation in Nepal? *World Review of Political Economy* 13 (3): 401–413.

Rorabacher, J. A. 2016. *Bihar and Mithila: The Historical Roots of Backwardness.* Manohar.

Rudra, Ashok. 1974. Semi-feudalism, usury capital, etcetera. *Economic and Political Weekly* 9 (48): 1996–1997.

Santos, Milton and Slaner, Stephan. 1977. Society and space: Social formation as theory and method. *Antipode* 9 (1): 3–13.

Sau, R. 1975. Farm efficiency under semi-feudalism: A critique of marginalist theories and some Marxist formulations – A comment. *Economic and Political Weekly* 10 (13): 18–21.

Sehgal, Rakhi. 2005. Social reproduction of Third World labour in the era of globalisation: State, market and the household. *Economic and Political Weekly* 40 (22/23): 2286–2294.

Shah, Alpa and Lerche, Jens. 2020. Migration and the invisible economies of care: production, social reproduction and seasonal migrant labour in India. *Transactions of the Institute of British Geographers* 45 (4): 719–734.

Sharma, R. S. 1985. How feudal was Indian feudalism? *Journal of Peasant Studies* 12 (2–3): 19–43.

Singh, K. S. 2007. Problematising proselytisation: A case study from West Nirmar. *Social Science Probings* 19 (1): 105–148.

———. 2023. Moribund capital in tribal societies. *Seminar* 265: 47–51.

Sugden, F. 2009. Neo-liberalism, markets and class structures on the Nepali lowlands: The political economy of agrarian change. *Geoforum* 40 (4): 634–644.

———. 2016. Improving dry season irrigation for marginal and tenant farmers in the Eastern Gangetic Plains: Baseline socio-economic report. Unpublished project report, International Water Management Institute.

———. 2017. A mode of production flux: The transformation and reproduction of rural class relations in lowland Nepal and North Bihar. *Dialectical Anthropology* 41 (2): 129–161.

———. 2019. Labour migration, capitalist accumulation and feudal reproduction: A historical analysis from the Eastern Gangetic Plains. *Antipode* 51 (5): 1600–1639.

Sugden, F., Saikia, P., Maskey, N. and Pokharel, P. 2016. Gender, agricultural investment and productivity in an era of out-migration: A case study from Nepal and Bihar. In *The Ganges River Basin: Status and Challenges in Water, Environment and Livelihoods*, edited by Bharati, L., Sharma, B. R., Makhtin, V. and Mandal, A. S. Earthscan.

Sugden, Fraser, Lata, Shrestha, Bharati, Luna, Pabitra, Gurung, Laxmi, Maharjan, Janmaat, J, Price, J. I., Sherpa, Tashi Yang Chung, Utsav, Bhattarai and Shishir, Koirala. 2014. *Climate Change, Out-migration and Agrarian Stress: The Potential for Upscaling Small-scale Water Storage in Nepal.* IWMI Research Report. International Water Management Institute.

Sunam, Ramesh. 2015. The significance of foreign labour migration and land for poverty reduction in Nepal. In *Poverty Reduction Policies and Practices in*

Developing Asia, edited by Heshmati, Almas, Maasoumi, Esfandiar and Wan, Guanghua. Springer.

Tilley, Christopher. 1982. Social formation, social structures and social change. In *Symbolic and Structural Archaeology*, edited by Hodder, I. Cambridge University Press.

Tilzey, Mark and Sugden, Fraser. 2023. *Peasants, Capitalism, and Imperialism in an Age of Politico-Ecological Crisis*. Taylor & Francis.

Tilzey, Mark, Sugden, Fraser and Seddon, David. 2023. *Peasants, Capitalism, and the Work of Eric R. Wolf: Reviving Critical Agrarian Studies*. Taylor & Francis.

Tsui, Sit, Erebus, Wong, Lau, Kin Chi and Tiejun, Wen. 2017. One belt, one road: China's strategy for a new global financial order. *Monthly Review* 68 (8): 36–45.

van Binsbergen, W. and Geschiere, P. 1985a. Introduction. In *Old Modes of Production and Capitalist Encroachment*, edited by Van Binsbergen, W. and Geschiere, P. KPI Limited.

———. 1985b. Marxist theory and anthropological practice: The application of French Marxist anthropology in fieldwork. In *Old Modes of Production and Capitalist Encroachment*, edited by Van Binsbergen, W. and Geschiere, P. KPI Limited.

van der Klei, J. S. 1985. Articulation of modes of production and the beginning of labour migration among the Diola of Senegal. In *Old Modes of Production and Capitalist Encroachment: Anthropological Explorations in Africa*, edited by Van Binsbergen, W. and Geschiere, P. KPI Limited.

Wade, Robert H. 2011. Emerging world order? From multipolarity to multilateralism in the G20, the World Bank, and the IMF. *Politics and Society* 39 (3): 347–378.

Walker, K. L. 2008. Neoliberalism on the ground in rural India: Predatory growth, agrarian crisis, internal colonization, and the intensification of class struggle. *Journal of Peasant Studies* 35 (4): 557–620.

Warren, Bill. 1973. Imperialism and capitalist industrialization. *New Left Review* 81 (1): 3–44.

White, B. 1997. Agroindustry and contract farmers in upland West Java. *Journal of Peasant Studies* 24 (3): 100–136.

Wolpe, H. 1979. Capitalism and cheap labour-power in South Africa: From segregation to apartheid. *Economy and Society* 1: 425–456.

Zhan, Shaohua and Scully, Ben. 2018. From South Africa to China: Land, migrant labor and the semi-proletarian thesis revisited. *Journal of Peasant Studies* 45 (5–6): 1018–1038.

Zhang, Qian Forrest. 2015. Class differentiation in rural China: Dynamics of accumulation, commodification and state intervention. *Journal of Agrarian Change* 15 (3): 338–365.

Zhang, Xin. 2017. Chinese capitalism and the maritime silk road: A world-systems perspective. *Geopolitics* 22 (2): 310–331.

3

An Agrarian and Industrial History of the Morang Region

The historic region of Morang has made a remarkable transition over 200 years from a forested frontier at the fringes of the Mughal empire to a breadbasket and source of natural resources for the emerging state of Nepal. This chapter reviews this historical transformation. It begins by exploring the subordination of the 'Adivasi mode of production' to feudalism, particularly following its annexation into the centralised Gorkhali state. Interconnected processes include the imposition of agrarian taxation, stratification within the indigenous peasantry, the clearing of the forest frontier and the distribution of land grants – the precursor to the absentee landlordism of today. The analysis goes on to look at the emergence of imperialism, and how the persistence of rural feudalism went alongside the distorted and uneven development of capitalism, particularly of industry. The final section explores the changes in the rural economy following the downfall of the Rana regime and rise of the monarchical Panchayat system. As the king pursued a developmentalist agenda in the 1960s, the agrarian relations on the ground remained similar, yet the relationship between caste, class and ethnicity shifted – particularly in the wake of the 1960s land reforms. In particular, the chapter charts the declining wealth of the indigenous Tharu landed elite, and the emerging dominance of absentee landlords at the apex of the agrarian structure with close ties to the state. The final part of the chapter charts the emerging articulations with capitalism following the establishment of manufacturing industry in the Morang region and the perpetuation of semi-colonial trade relations. It explores the further stresses on industry following economic liberalisation, the rise in the service sector, and the growing political, economic and ethnic tensions that shaped the 2000s and beyond – which sets the context for the more detailed empirical case studies of later chapters.

Adivasi Mode of Production on the Forest Frontier

While Morang is itself a modern administrative unit (see Figure 1.2), as noted in Chapter 2, it was historically a much larger region which included much of the Tarai belt east of the Koshi, and today includes not only Morang but also Sunsari and Jhapa districts. This chapter is largely focused on the contemporary political district of Morang – where much of the data collection took place, although some primary data as well as archival sources were also compiled from Sunsari, which was split from Morang in the 1960s and has a very similar history. Some data and archival resources were also consulted from the easternmost district of Jhapa which split from Morang in the 1950s, although there are some differences in Jhapa in the trajectory of change which will be touched upon later – and thus, the conclusions of this chapter largerly refer to modern day Morang and Sunsari.

The historic region of Morang was for centuries a forested frontier between the spheres of influence of the state formations of the Gangetic plains to the southwest, hill chieftaincies to the north, and the Brahmaputra valley to the east. In the sixteenth and seventeenth centuries while large parts of the subcontinent were under Mughal influence, this belt is known to have fallen under the influence of successive state formations. The first was a kingdom centred in Vijayapur (present-day Dharan). It was believed to have been possibly ruled by the 'Kotche' kings, who had migrated from the Cooch Behar region of North Bengal (Subedi, 2005). They ruled in conjunction with Kirat chieftains in the hills who were appointed as ministers. The Morang region was conquered by the Sen dynasty of central Nepal in the seventeenth century (Subedi, 2005)[1] a lineage of kings, possibly of Rajput descent (Stiller, 1975; Hamilton, 2007 [1819]). Following a split within the dynasty, a new Sen kingdom was formed with a capital also in Vijayapur (Acharya, 1973).[2] The borders of the Tarai tract stretched as far as the Mahananda river near present-day Siliguri, bordering on to the powerful Mughal tributary Koch state of Kamatapur centred on Cooch Behar (Nath, 1989; Debnath, 2010).

The population of Morang between the sixteenth and eighteenth centuries was likely sparse and fell within a heavily forested and culturally fluid belt home to a number of indigenous communities who reside across the sub-Himalayan lowlands from Nepal into North Bengal and Assam. The expansion and contraction of various loose state formations as well as semi-nomadic livelihoods is likely to have paved the way for the ethnic diversity one sees today. Colonial sources from shortly after the fall of the Sen kingdom in the late eighteenth and early nineteenth centuries suggest the population of the forested lowlands between the Koshi and Tista rivers included Adivasi (indigenous) groups such as the Rajbanshi, as well as the Tharu, Bantar, Dhimal, Meche and Gangai (Grunning, 2008 [1911]; Hamilton, 2007 [1819]) – who continue to make up a large share of the indigenous population today.

While these are distinct communities, they share historical and cultural links. Communities such as the Tharu of Morang (also known as Morangiya or Lampucchwa Tharu) have links with other Tharu groups further west within Nepal and share a common identity in spite of the cultural differences (Guneratne, 2002). Meanwhile, the Tharu of Morang also have strong cultural-linguistic links with other indigenous groups such as the Bantar, Gangai and Rajbanshi. The latter reside across the sub-Himalayan lowlands, with the Rajbanshi heartland lying in Cooch Behar of North Bengal. Smaller indigenous groups such as the Meche (known in Assam as Bodo) also extend from Jhapa in the Nepal Tarai into the lower Brahmaputra valley of Assam, a state where they today form a sizeable minority.

The history of the Tarai and wider sub-Himalayan lowlands is intricately intertwined with that of the region's Adivasi communities, who have long pursued livelihoods connected to the region's forests. In spite of the expansion and contraction of various state formations, it is likely that most lived in relative autonomy, as shown in multiple studies from across this belt (Krauskopff, 1989; Rai, 2015; Müller-Böker, 1999; Ray, 2002).

Reconstructing the Adivasi 'mode of production' in this region prior to the establishment of feudalism is, however, challenging, and there were likely to have been significant divergences depending on the cultural group, their livelihood practices, and different degrees of isolation. While there is limited historical research on the Tharu, Rajbanshi and Bantar who make up the core population in this book's case study, literature from across this cross-border cultural belt can provide some insights into key features of the historic agrarian formation. Two key elements have been identified.

First, it is likely that the mode of production entailed collective rather than individualised or 'private' relationship with the means of production. To better understand this relationship, one must consider the form of agriculture. Literature from across the region suggests that cultivation was not carried out on fixed plots. Shifting cultivation or swidden farming has instead been recorded as the primary historical agricultural system amongst the Tharu across the Nepal Tarai (McDonnaugh, 1989; A. B. Gurung, 2003; Müller-Böker, 1991) and in its natural continuation into the North Bengal Doors (Ray, 2002). With regard to the Dooars, which has cultural similarities with the Morang region, Ray (2002) suggests that the indigenous Meche and Garo communities lived in small settlements, led by a *mandal*, or headman, and periodic migration was central to livelihoods. After cultivating a plot for three years, farmers would leave it fallow for several years, and settlements themselves would be relocated every seven–eight years. As one moved further south though, agriculture became more sedentary, with cultivation in forest clearings of paddy, tobacco and mustard and fixed villages.

Historical sources on Morang itself are sparse, although accounts from shortly after the fall of the Sen kingdom in the early nineteenth century appear to confirm that the indigenous peoples of the region east of the Koshi, specifically the Rajbanshi and Gangai (who reside across the primary field site of southern Morang today), carried out a form of slash and burn agriculture with the use of a hoe rather than plough, and regular movement of fields (Hamilton, 2007 [1819]). Rai's (2015) in-depth historical ethnography of the Dhimal community, who traditionally inhabited the forested belt of Morang to the north of the core study area,[3] also points to a semi-nomadic form of agriculture in the dense forests up until the nineteenth century. As well as shifting cultivation, the Dhimal subsisted through foraging, hunting and fishing. Rai (2013, 2015) suggests that the risk of wild animals (who would destroy crops) and frequent epidemics of malaria and cholera would discourage permanent settlement in one location. The cultural memory of shifting cultivation persists in the vernacular amongst the Dhimal today. Rai (2015), for instance, points out the term *jaya kheraka*, which refers to the clearing of bushes to plant wild millet, reflects the swidden agriculture of the past.

In terms of the ownership of the means of production, it is likely that in the Tarai the land was de facto common property. While in the hills, some indigenous communities recognised forms of customary tenure linked to a clan over a fixed geographically bounded territory (Caplan, 1970; H. Gurung, 1996); this appeared less common in the lowlands, where the forests were extensive and population was sparse. Ray (2002), for instance, with regard to the North Bengal forests, suggests that the uncultivated forest lands were extensive (see Figure 3.1) and thus the means of production was considered common property rather than being linked to individual households or lineages. Rai (2013), with reference to the Dhimal, suggested that rather than a legal relationship with a particular tract of farmland, they had a more culturally embedded relationship with the land – which met their subsistence needs through shifting cultivation, foraging, fishing and hunting. This is exemplified by the fact that deities associated with the forest and riverine

Figure 3.1 Sub-Himalayan *sal* forests. Landscapes such as this (pictured in the Dooars of North Bengal) were once characteristic of most of the sub-Himalayan lowlands in Nepal and India, yet were gradually cleared from the south in a northward direction up until the mid-twentieth century.

Source: Author.

ecosystems, which provided their subsistence, were honoured during rituals (Rai, 2013).

A second element of the Adivasi mode of production relates to how surplus was distributed and how labour was managed. According to K. S. Singh (2007), in his historic analysis of the Bhil of Madhya Pradesh in India, South Asia's Adivasi social formations historically produce little surplus product. They are driven by the need to meet the survival of its members rather than to accumulate wealth, and all labour is thus in Marxian terms 'socially necessary' rather than 'surplus' labour. Any potential accumulation which does take place is undermined by redistributive systems, which represent the 'reproductive mechanism' of this economic formation.[4] A strong cultural ethos of exchange and reciprocity was also observed in Rai's (2015) study of the Dhimal of Morang. Though the Dhimal had a customary leader known as a *majhi*, this was not a 'vertically ranked' social position. It was instead rooted in a moral economy based upon strong kinship ties and mutual support. Even as the Adivasi mode of production was gradually dissolved, the *majhi* continued to play a role in redistributing food and resources to those who needed it (Rai, 2013). K. S. Singh (2007) also points to lateral rather than vertically segmented use of labour for production, and a younger working-age population would engage in labour often on a collective basis. While communal labour regimes have been well documented amongst hill Adivasi groups (Macfarlane, 1976; B. Campbell, 2018), there is less research in the plains. Nevertheless, oral histories in Morang pointed to earlier collective labour systems.

It is also worth noting that the forests of Morang were unlikely to have been entirely isolated from external markets. North–south trade routes passed through the region, and writing in the early nineteenth century, Hamilton reports the seasonal migration of herders from Purnea to the south into Morang with their cattle, where they could graze on comparably rich forest land (Hamilton, cited in Regmi, 1969). Similar reports were present in the case of the North Bengal Dooars, whereby seasonal herders or *moisal*s resided in temporary forest settlements known as *bathan*s, where they sold milk and ghee to local people (Ray, 2002). This suggests there may have been low-level monetary exchange and possibly some 'accumulation'. Rai (2015) also suggests that the Dhimal of northern Morang traded extensively with populations to the north and south, in spite of their relatively isolated forest-based livelihoods up until the mid-nineteenth century. Some market engagement was likely part of the cropping system by forest-based shifting cultivators. The former British resident in Kathmandu, Brian Hodgson (1880 [1847]), writing as of the mid-1880s with reference to the Dhimal, suggests that while grain staples included dry rice (*ghaiya dhan*), millet, maize and pulses alongside a range of vegetables and roots that were produced as subsistence crops, they also produced marketable commodities such as cotton. Later correspondences with the British resident also point to the presence of opium cultivation in Morang (A. Campbell, 1841). Hodgson (1880 [1847]) suggests the Dhimal would use the cash from cotton to procure rice to make up for production shortfalls, suggesting that even within the Adivasi mode of production, there was some cash circulating. However, it is likely that the growing tax burden in later years would accelerate this trend.

Centralised States and the Transition to Feudalism: 1774–1950

While it is likely that much of the Morang region was forested in the past and dominated by some form of Adivasi mode of production, as outlined earlier, this had transformed by the early twentieth century. While the northern belt, which was home to the Dhimal, remained heavily forested, the southern half, which was home to Tharu, Rajbanshi, Gangai and other Adivasi groups, had seen widespread clearing of the forest frontier. Agriculture was sedentary, and the mode of production was hierarchical and feudal in character. Central to explaining this change is the expansion of more powerful centralised state formations from the late seventeenth to early twentieth centuries. As noted earlier with regard to the pre-capitalist mode of production in West Africa (Meillassoux, 1981; Dupré and Rey, 1979), externally imposed interventions by the European colonial state were necessary to subordinate these modes of production and open them up to supply surplus to capitalism. In the Nepal case it differs, in that prior to any articulations with capitalism, the Adivasi modes of production were first subordinated to supply surplus to a centralised feudal mode of production by the non-capitalist land-based empire of the Gorkhas. Nevertheless, there are similarities with regard to how an external state was able to break the autonomy of indigenous modes of production. There were three associated changes, which will be described in subsequent pages.

Charting the Dissolution of the Adivasi Mode of Production

The appropriation of surplus, primarily through taxation, has in South Asian history frequently been the first process through which the autonomy of Adivasi economic formations is undermined (K. S. Singh, 2023). In Morang, it is probable that extraction of tax from the indigenous clan-based units undercut the redistributive mechanisms which were once central to the Adivasi modes of production (see K. S. Singh, 2007). Alongside taxation was the associated process of enforcing titles for land to support tax administration, breaking the looser customary and collectivised rights that farmers enjoyed to land while it was still under forest. A second process that was likely to have been present in Morang was the creation of an indigenous functionary class in the taxation hierarchy. There is evidence that this broke down egalitarian social relations within Adivasi society and supported the accumulation of surplus amongst the elite. A third process was the consistent effort by the hill-based rulers to expand cultivation to maximise tax revenue and state control, and clear the forest frontier, pushing farmers out of shifting cultivation and onto fixed taxable plots.

There is limited evidence of exactly *when* this process of subordination started, although it is likely to have occurred unevenly across the region between the seventeenth and nineteenth centuries. The forest frontier was gradually cleared in a south to north direction, as has occurred across the Nepal and North Bengal plains (Nath, 1989; Gaige, 1976),[5] and the subjugation of the indigenous population to feudalism in all probability followed this trajectory as well, with the southern border regions being the first to experience it. Historical studies of the Sen state from the early eighteenth century contain some of the earliest recorded evidence of an administration system with feudal tax appropriation capabilities (Regmi, 1970; Hamilton, 2007 [1819], although this may have existed earlier. According to early colonial sources, the Vijayapur-based Sen kingdom had introduced a taxation system based upon that used by the Pathan rulers in northern India prior to the rise of the Mughal empire (Regmi, 1970). While tax was appropriated from the peasantry by the Sen rulers, a tribute was paid to the *nawab*s of Bengal to the south (Acharya, 1973).

Nevertheless, the taxation of the Tarai peasantry was likely hindered by the dense forest and 'frontier' nature of this belt. The Sens, along with other hill principalities, were reluctant to actively encourage the clearing of the forest given the natural barrier it offered them against invasion from the south. Nevertheless, this did not mean that tax was not appropriated from the forest-dwelling population. In North Bengal Dooars, which was under Bhutanese rule in the mid-eighteenth century, Ray (2002) suggests that the forest-dwelling Meche population was subject to taxation on forest produce by the Bhutanese state. Indigenous shifting cultivators would exchange local cotton for cash, then transfer revenue to officials (Ray, 2002). Other forms of taxation included labour service such as portering for government officials, as well as levies for residing in the forest, trading and plying boats, and operating weaving looms (Grunning, 2008 [1911]). In the adjacent Darjeeling Tarai, Hodgson (1988 [1848]) also observed much later in the nineteenth century how the Dhimal and Meche living within the forest would offer corvee labour to the Sikkim *raja* (who controlled this portion of the plains) for portering and other activities, while also giving 1 rupee per agricultural implement in cash, which was a relatively small share. Such looser mechanisms of revenue generation were likely to have been in place in the communities residing deep within the forest of Morang prior to the Gorkha conquest, and they were unlikely to have significantly impacted the indigenous agrarian formation.

Nevertheless, this was likely not uniform. A description of the Vijayapur kingdom's administration in Morang through records compiled by Regmi

(1970) from the eighteenth century points to a relatively complex, hierarchical and monetised system of tax administration. While the Sen state most likely had greater control over its hill territories and there was even the presence of landlordism (Hamilton, 2007 [1819]), it would be unsurprising if sedentary agriculture, even under feudal conditions, had not already been established in some locales of the plains, particularly when rulers were known to have distributed Tarai land grants to members of the hill nobility (K. Pradhan, 2009). By contrast, Rai's (2015) paper observes that as late as the twentieth century in the north of Morang and Jhapa, the Dhimal were not official title holders to any land. Many even actively avoided legally registering their plots and continued, as much as possible, a forest-based livelihood, which temporarily allowed them to minimise the tax burden that would be placed upon them had they been fixed titleholders. It is likely therefore that some communities retained relative economic and political autonomy from the state for a longer period.

Regardless of the actual chronology of change throughout the last 300 years, a key turning point was likely the conquest of the far-eastern Tarai-Madhesh by the Gorkhali empire in the late eighteenth century. Gorkha was a hill principality[6] west of contemporary Kathmandu ruled by the Shah dynasty. The Shahs themselves were Khas people, an ethnic group living across the central Himalayan foothills who spoke an Indo-European language which was to become recognised as Nepali today (K. Pradhan, 2009), and following waves of migration from the south paved the way for Sanskritisation and adoption of Brahmin or Kshatriya (Chettri) identity (Sharma, 1977). The Gorkha rulers themselves were Thakuri, a Chettri sub-caste which claims Rajput descent. Jointly, these Nepali-speaking upper castes were to emerge in later years as the most politically powerful social groups in Nepal.

It is following the Gorkha conquest that the three stages of subordination to feudalism really took root across much of Morang. A hierarchy of new revenue collection roles appears to have been imposed or adapted from the Sen-era hierarchies, and this had a profound impact on the mode of production on the ground.

We start with a consideration of the appropriation of surplus through tax. The bureaucracy in the far-eastern Tarai-Madhesh region expanded considerably following the Sen king's eventual overthrow in 1774 when the Gorkhali empire took control (Regmi, 1969), and it became, in effect, a colony of Kathmandu, which was to become the capital of the new kingdom of Nepal. The indigenous cultivators of the plains were over time eventually compelled to give a significant portion of their crop directly to the state. This was sanctioned by the attempts to bring all land, including forest, under a legal tenure known as *raikar*, which allows individual households to independently operate personal plots on payment of tax, while the state remained the ultimate landlord (Regmi, 1978b). With peasants being allocated fixed plots, this undermined pre-existing production relations whereby farmers practised shifting cultivation on land which was not held in anyone's name. Taxation itself absorbed a large portion of the physical surplus of the peasantry, and undermined the internal self-sufficiency of the Adivasi economic formation – contributing to rising debt and demand for cash. Tax rates in the Tarai were variable depending on local conditions, but Karky (1981) estimates that they varied from around a third to 40 per cent of the crop. In Morang, they were calculated in cash, with the rate adjusted according to the crop (Hamilton, 2007 [1819]).[7] It is probable that for non-cash crops payment was made in kind.

Across Nepal, the state also reserved the right to extract compulsory labour service, or *jhara*, for work such as construction and defence (Regmi, 1976), although this was more common in the hills than lowlands.

Aside from the sale of elephants and timber to the British colonial regime in India, taxation of the Tarai-Madhesh peasantry was of huge economic importance to Kathmandu. As of 1851 it was reportedly contributing to 76 per cent of total tax revenue (Regmi, 1988). Morang in particular was prized for its revenue generation potential (Mørch, 2023), likely due to its high rainfall and agricultural prospects. The enforcement of *raikar* tenure and taxation was backed up by the political, legal and military authority of the Kathmandu rulers, a spatial relation of power which would persist until the present day. It appears that taxation was imposed successfully in large parts of southern Morang early in Gorkha rule, particularly given that many locales were already being taxed by the Sen administrative system. However, as noted earlier, there was resistance to state control in remoter domains of the north. Rai (2015) suggests that attempts by the state to enforce land registration on the Dhimal resulted in some even migrating to forest regions over the border in India. This paralleled similar eastward migration of the Meche, who migrated into Assam to escape subordination by British colonialism in North Bengal.[8]

We now move on to the second process of subordination to feudalism – the creation of an indigenous functionary class. The expansion of the tax collection hierarchy discussed earlier required an administrative class to oversee the collection of revenue. While some kind of agrarian bureaucracy was likely already present in areas of Morang with a longer history of settlement, such as along the southern border, the Gorkhas established a more elaborate tax administration hierarchy and extended this into more isolated domains alongside the clearing of the forest frontier. Morang (which then included present-day Sunsari and Jhapa districts) as of the early nineteenth century was led by a *subah*, yet was divided into three *taluk*s, or districts, and for each, a deputy collector, or *fouzdar*, was appointed to administer revenue collection (Hamilton, 2007 [1819]). Such top-level posts were generally taken by powerful members of the Gorkha elite (Regmi, 1971a; Stiller, 1975).

Under each *taluk* were several *parganna*s (eight in total across the three *taluk*s) (Hamilton, 2007 [1819]). This was the local-level revenue collection unit, which comprised of a cluster of villages. A *chaudhari* was placed in charge of extracting tax from the peasantry (Hamilton, 2007 [1819]). Unlike top-level posts, however, the *chaudhari* were generally a customary leader from the Tharu community (Regmi, 1988; Regmi, 1970), although it appears from conversations in the field site that functionary roles extended to other communities such as the Rajbanshi. Below the *chaudhari* were a number of subordinate roles. These included the *mandal*, a village-level functionary who would assist in the collection of revenue, and the *qanungoe* (or *kanugoya*), who would maintain records of *parganna*-level revenue rates. The *patuwari* was a clerk who would keep records of accounts (Regmi, 1970).

Stratification increased within Adivasi society as functionaries accumulated resources. Functionaries were granted land assignments, salaries or tax concessions for their services (Regmi, 1970, 1971a). For instance, a *qanungoe* was entitled to cultivate 5 per cent of the land in the village without paying tax, while the *patuwari* would receive a smaller share. Lower-level positions such as the *gorayit*, or messenger, would receive a consignment of grain. It is likely that functionaries were also entitled to extract 'labour rents' from the peasants under their jurisdiction. Documents on taxation from Mahottari, further west note how the *mokkadam*, or village-level revenue administrator, was entitled to one labour day of a ploughman and field worker per year from every family.[9] A similar system was observed amongst the Tharu of Dang (Krauskopff, 1989). It is probable that there was similar 'tribute' in labour paid by the Adivasi population of Morang.

Oral histories from Pidarboni village reported that over the generations, the Tharu functionaries developed into a locally powerful Adivasi landlord class with large personal holdings, which included both taxable and non-taxable lands. Many of these holdings would then be sublet to cultivators with less land or who had lost their allocated plots (often due to failure to pay rent), causing them to be subject to dual surplus appropriation by both state and landlord.

It is likely that this expanding stratification and accumulation of surplus amongst an indigenous landed class, not to mention the additional appropriation of surplus from the central state, will have played a role in undermining the redistributive mechanisms within the Adivasi mode of production. K. S. Singh (2023), with reference to the subordination of the Bhil in Madhya Pradesh, equates this with a strengthening of vertical (hierarchical) relationships and a weakening of horizontal (often reciprocal) relations.

In Morang, this would have been a gradual process, as suggested by Rai's (2015) description of the Dhimal's relationship with the state. In the north of Morang, like their Tharu and Rajbanshi neighbours further south, the Dhimal customary leaders, or *majhi*s, were tasked with revenue collection. Rai, however, notes that while the *majhi*s were tasked with tax collection and were granted large personal holdings, there was some reluctance on their part to take on these lands in their names due to the practical challenges of managing the tax revenue for the fields under their jurisdiction. Furthermore, the *majhi*s themselves had an important customary position in an economic formation that had been grounded in reciprocity and exchange, and this persisted even after their co-option by the state (Rai, 2015). They depended upon the support of tenants to meet tax obligations, and thus the landlord–tenant relationship which was imposed by the state was relatively egalitarian initially, and they would, for example, help tenants out at times of need by providing them food or cash (Rai, 2013). For this reason, many households preferred to rent land from the *majhi*'s personal holdings rather than register plots in their own names (Rai, 2013, 2015).

This transitional period whereby relationships between indigenous landlords and tenants were less exploitative may also have been present in the Tharu and Rajbanshi domains further south, although oral histories suggest that by the nineteenth century, a much more hierarchical relationship between Tharu or Rajbanshi landlords and their tenants had emerged, with the latter being subject to surplus appropriation through taxation as well as via rent and interest on loans. Nevertheless, given that both landlords and tenants were from the Adivasi community, the nature of this relationship was likely different from in the caste heartland of Mithila further west, whereby lower-caste tenants farmed the land of upper-caste landlords. Relations would have been characterised by strong patron–client bonds, backed up ideologically by shared ethnicity or lineage. Mukherji (1987), with reference to landlord–tenant relations in Naxalbari of North Bengal prior to the 1960s revolt, describes the relationship between tenants and landlords within the Rajbanshi community as 'patrimonial-feudal', as they were both often from the same ethnic community, unlike in other parts of the plains where one's position in the semi-feudal agrarian structure aligned to caste divisions.[10]

A final process of feudal subordination that we now explore is the efforts by both states to expand the cultivable area and encourage settlement. Unlike the Sen kingdom, for the Gorkhas, the clearing and settlement of the Tarai was a priority – particularly as the demand for tax, and land to give out to the nobility intensified (Stiller, 1975). *Chaudhari*s and associated functionaries in the eastern Tarai-Madhesh were therefore encouraged to clear tracts of forests and distribute land to tenants, who would pay tribute to the state (Regmi, 1978a). Across the Tarai, the forests were cleared in a gradual process from the Indian border in a northwards direction (Gaige, 1976). This south-to-north contraction of the forest frontier has been paralleled across the eastern sub-Himalayan lowlands (and is described also in North Bengal; see, for instance, Ray, 2002). A decree issued in 1798 to local land revenue functionaries[11] in Morang (alongside Saptari, Mahottari, Rautahat, Bara and Parsa) encourages the clearing of land (Regmi, 1978a), with subsidies and reduced tax being offered to encourage settlers from elsewhere (Dahal, 1983). Once forests were cleared, while many Adivasi who resided in these domains became tenants on the new estates, there was by no means sufficient labour, and thus functionaries also brought in new cultivators from non-taxable *jagir* and *birta* lands or from India (Dahal, 1983). Migrants from India were particularly encouraged, as bringing settlers from within Nepal would potentially result in a loss of revenue from existing holdings (Ojha, 1983).

It is within this context that southern Morang emerged into a region with a rich ethnic diversity, including not only the original forest-dwelling communities, but also Maithili-speaking lower and middle castes from contemporary Bihar, who settled particularly along the Nepal–India border, and Adivasi groups from elsewhere, who settled alongside local indigenous groups. The latter included the Munda and Santhal from central India. This latter migration has not been formally documented. However, Rai and Oraon (2014) suggest that another community from central India, the Oraon, migrated there following the collapse of an older Oraon kingdom before the Gorkha conquest. This was part of a larger wave of northwards migration of Indian Adivasi groups in the nineteenth century. Populations of Santhals,

Oraons and Musahar, for instance, settled over the border in Purnea of Bihar, where they were 'invited' to clear new lands from the jungles and marshlands by the local zamindars and they later became sharecroppers (Mitra and Vijayendra, 1982).[12] Oral histories suggested that they were valued as tenants on new estates due to their skills at clearing the forest. The Musahar represents an interesting case – as they were thought to be also an Adivasi group, which had migrated from central India's Chotanagpur plateau in the twelfth century to the north Indian plains (where their subordinate relationship with upper castes resulted in them being integrated into the caste hierarchy as Dalit) (Giri, 2012). Many also migrated onwards to Nepal in the nineteenth century, and Giri (2012) suggests they were employed as labourers to clear the forest.

Another means through which forest lands were colonised – and an important feature of land policy in this era – was the distribution of land grants through a tenure known as *birta.* They were a means through which to win the loyalty of local nobility. The distribution of *birta* grants had started during the Sen dynasty. For instance, Regmi (1989a) records that *birta* grants were distributed to Maithili Brahmins in the Mahottari-Dhanusha region by the Sen kings. These bestowments were reconfirmed by the Gorkha king Rana Bahadur Shah in 1794,[13] a practice widespread across Nepal as the new rulers sought to win the loyalty of local nobles (Stiller, 1975). However, the distribution of *birta* grants expanded considerably under the Gorkha rulers, with vast grants of forest land being distributed, primarily to members of the hill bureaucratic elites and former nobility (Regmi, 1989a, 1976). *Jagir* grants, which were lands bestowed in lieu of salary to military generals, were also distributed in synergy with *birta* and were critical for the growth of the empire (Mørch, 2023; Stiller, 1975), although how widespread these were in Morang is not known.

The new estates deriving from these land grants were likely settled in the same way as *raikar* lands (with local Adivasi and settlers from India), yet operated as independent feudal vassals with settlement oriented to maximising rent for the owner rather than revenue for the state. Smaller *birta* grants were, however, also distributed as an incentive for wealthy individuals to clear the forest with revenue generation in mind, whereby part of the newly settled land would be under standard *raikar* tenure and part would be bestowed as personal tax-free *birta* holdings (Regmi, 1989a).

These state interventions combined to drive the contraction of the forest frontier. The groups for whom this expansion of cultivation affected the most were the Adivasi communities who had once depended on the region's vast forests. This played a key role in interrupting the long-established pattern of nomadic shifting cultivation in the locales where it persisted, compelling the Adivasi peasantry to make a transition towards cultivating fixed plots as tax-paying *raikar* landholders, or sub-tenants for local landlords, thus generating revenue for the regime. It is important to note though that this clearing of the region's forests was not a single event, but took place gradually over many decades.

The Anglo-Nepal War of 1814–1816 with the British colonial empire to the south, and the Suguali treaty which followed, resulted in the Gorkha empire ceding at least a third of its territory to Britain, consolidating the borders of what would become the Kingdom of Nepal. Nevertheless, this would have had limited impact on the mode of production on the ground in southern Morang – which was now arguably feudal in character. Unlike classical feudalism, it was the central state that was the ultimate landowner. The state had more power than the local nobility and much of the agricultural surplus was channelled to the centre. Nevertheless, the presence of a local landlord class who were leasing out their surplus land (including *birta* recipients of tax-free land or functionaries with titles for large taxable estates) meant that local-level landlord–tenant relations with surplus appropriation by rent persisted side by side with the direct payment of tribute to the state. The peasantry were thus divided into two groups – those who were farming under the centralised feudalism of the state, with surplus being appropriated via taxation, and a second who were renting land from intermediary landlords, with surplus appropriated via rent.

The acclaimed economic historian of Nepal, Mahesh Chandra Regmi termed the overall mode of production in the nineteenth century Tarai-Madhesh as 'state landlordism' (Regmi, 1976). Nevertheless, I will continue to refer to this formation as a form of feudalism. Sharma (1985: 21), with reference to early medieval India, makes the point that even when producers experience a 'double servility' to the state and local-level landlords, this is just one amongst many mechanisms through which the peasantry are subjugated under feudalism. In line with the definition of feudalism given in this book, the Gorkhali state sought to impose a mode of production grounded in control over land by a minority class and the appropriation of surplus through extra-economic means, facilitated by a powerful local administrative apparatus, and diversion of surplus for elite consumption rather than productive reinvestment.

With regard to the latter point, government directives from the late eighteenth century[14] indicate how surplus was used in the early Gorkha period. The Morang *subba*, or district administrator, lists the expenditures made with agrarian revenue, including gifts for distribution within royal networks, wedding and medical expenses for the royal family and salaries for artisans to maintain palaces. A later directive indicates expenses such as providing hospitality for visiting 'Englishmen, Nawabs and Rajas and Wakils' (Regmi, 1988, 1). A further set of directives from 1804 to 1805 recorded in Regmi (1973) point to military uses of revenue. These include the use of tax revenue from Morang to purchase steel from Calcutta (present-day Kolkata) for the manufacture of munitions.

Towards a 'Disciplined' Revenue Bureaucracy and Expansion of the Landlord Class

Following the ascendancy of the Rana rulers[15] in 1846, the economic importance of the Tarai-Madhesh to fund the regime grew (Guneratne, 2002), and Jang Bahadur Rana in 1861 sought to reform the revenue collection system. The revenue collection unit of the pre-Rana era, the *pargana*, was deemed to be too large for the existing functionary, the *chaudhari*, to administer tax (Regmi 1978:78–79). It was therefore sub-divided into smaller *mauja*s, made up of a village or cluster of villages, with a new position known as *jimidar* being appointed at the *mauja* level and replacing the *chaudhari* as the primary tax collector. As under the earlier system of administration, each *jimidār* was supported by several *patuwari*s, or clerks – functionaries to assist in the collection of taxes and maintenance of accounts and records (Regmi, 1978b) – and a village-level administrator, or *mokkadam* (Regmi, 1978c, Regmi, 1978b) (see Figures 3.2 and 3.4).

These changes served to strengthen tax collection discipline and the reach of the state into more peripheral regions – while also accelerating the colonisation of the forest frontier. A *jimidar* was responsible for collecting tax in an existing settlement, yet was also under pressure to clear land in the vicinity to create new *mauja*s (Regmi, 1978c; Regmi, 1978b). Where this was not possible by existing *jimidar*s, individuals with capital were incentivised to come from elsewhere and create new *mauja*s. They would be rewarded with the offer of large personal holdings and would be appointed *jimidar* in the case of estates over 100 *bigha*s (Government of Nepal, 1974 [1923]). While the majority of tenants in Morang were still drawn from the existing indigenous population, the cultural diversity of the region continued to grow throughout the Rana era.

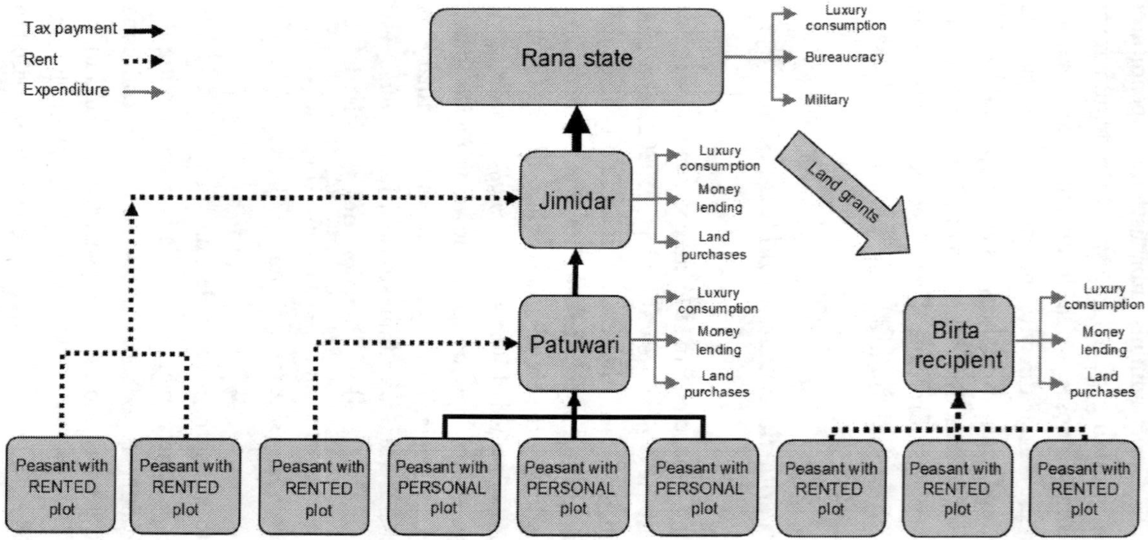

Figure 3.2 Simplified model of the distribution of the agricultural surplus during the Rana years in the far-eastern Tarai-Madhesh

Source: Author.

As part of the state-building process, the regime initially sought to encourage settlers from the hills, as they were believed to pose a lesser threat to the hill-based regime than indigenous cultivators, who had a very different culture and language from the ruling class. However, most of the upland communities preferred to migrate eastwards into the hilly regions of Darjeeling and Sikkim (Lal, 2002; Shrestha and Velu, 1993). The regime continued therefore to look to the south, where peasants pauperised by early colonial land tenure policies were enticed to take up new lands in Nepal. Provisions in Nepal's first legal code allowed foreign nationals to purchase titles to *raikar* land to facilitate settlement (Kansakar, 1985). Furthermore, a notification from the 1920s in the government newspaper *Gorkhapatra* called upon hill people who had migrated to India to return and clear forest land set aside for the purpose in Morang district.

Many of the original *chaudhari*s were converted into either *jimidar*s or *patuwari*s under the new system (Regmi, 1978b, 1988). However, the Ranas now also favoured filling the new posts with elites from the hills with strong connections to the bureaucracy, usually from the dominant Brahmin and Chettri castes (Guneratne, 2002; Regmi, 1988). The state believed that bringing in outsiders with links to the bureaucracy supported fiscal discipline, as rather than being local leaders with customary authority, they were de facto employees of the state and could be dismissed if they failed to perform their duties (Regmi, 1988). In some circumstances *jimidar*s from the hills could not be found, opening the door for Hindu castes of Indian descent to be given the positions (Regmi, 1982). It is not, however, clear how widespread this was in the Morang region. Unlike the *jimidar*s, it was required that other positions, such as that of the *patuwari*, would be drawn from the local community under their jurisdiction, and thus an indigenous elite retained some power (Regmi, 1978b).

As in the pre-Rana era, *birta* grants continued to be used to provide an incentive for individuals to settle forest lands. Records from the early twentieth century show evidence of land being cleared by General Bhim Shumshere J. B. Rana in Morang, and the tenure was changed to *birta* after the establishment of the settlement (Regmi, 1989b). Regmi (1978) notes how these grants were particularly sought after by top-ranking members of the army and bureaucracy for whom a *birta* grant was considered to offer greater security of tenure than the temporary *jagir* holdings many of these individuals possessed. Jang Bahadur Rana also distributed *birta* grants in the plains to compensate those affected by an earlier confiscation of estates by Bhimsen Thapa in 1808 (Nepal, 1998), often giving out grants of forest land (Regmi, 1976).

The expansion of *birta* distribution combined with the new *jimidari* system consolidated the rise of a local landlord class (Regmi, 1976). While the *birtawalas* (recipients of *birta* lands) operated their own independent vassals with a large number of tenants, *jimidars* and even lower-level functionaries were also able to accumulate significant lands. First, *jimidars* were allowed to retain a percentage of the taxes in compensation for their collection activities which they could use to purchase holdings, as land markets took hold (see discussion on the market for land later in this chapter) (Regmi, 1976). Second, they could extract additional unauthorised payments from the peasantry or appropriate the land of tax-defaulting peasants. Third, *jimidars* who cleared the forest and promoted settlement would often receive a bestowment of land as payment. This included, for instance, 10 years' tax exemption and a tenth of the reclaimed land as a personal tax-free *birta*, which could be let out to tenants (Regmi, 1978c; Yadav, 1984). Some were also entitled to additional grants of lands known as *jirayat* which did not include full property rights and were taxable. Nevertheless, these could be sublet to new immigrants or local farmers to yield rent, as long as taxes were paid (Regmi, 1976). Subordinate functionaries were also able to access land through their appointments (see Figure 3.3).

Figure 3.3 Ruins of the *malpot* office where farmers would once deposit grain as tax for the Rana regime

Source: Author.

For example, a *mokkadam* would receive a small share of land in their jurisdiction free of tax, while *patuwari*s would receive a share of the revenue (Regmi, 1976). Oral histories in Morang suggested that the surplus appropriated by these functionary-landlords through rent and usury was invested in an extravagant lifestyle. Landlords reportedly kept elephants as status symbols and for transport. Similar histories testifying to the wealth of the Tharu *jimidar*s, including the keeping of elephants, were collected in Dang (Krauskopff, 1989).

It was the Rana era which likely completed the dissolution of the Adivasi mode of production, particularly in the core field site. Oral histories reported that during this period, hunting-gathering and shifting cultivation had entirely lost their significance as a form of subsistence. With the exception of the small Adivasi elite, most of the indigenous population had become rent- or tax-paying sedentary farmers and labourers under the predominant feudal mode of production. While there were still large areas of forest along the foot of the hills in the north and to the east (particularly in the region which would later become Jhapa district), most of the southern half of present-day Morang and Sunsari districts had been converted to permanent agricultural fields. (see Figure 3.4).

Figure 3.4 Jalthal, a remnant forest in Jhapa district. While forest still spans the north near the foot of the hills, this is the only area of untouched forest in the southern part of the far-eastern plains. The felling of the jungles intensified during the Rana years, with most remaining southern forests cleared by the 1960s.

Source: Author.

It is worth noting though that Morang's Adivasi elite maintained economic and political power locally in the Rana years only for the pragmatic purpose of revenue generation – the central Rana bureaucracy was composed almost entirely of Nepali-speaking Brahmins and Chettris (Mørch, 2023). The majority of the Adivasi in rural Morang, as across the Tarai, were marginal tenant producers. Meanwhile, the Rana era also saw the consolidation of ideological institutions which reproduced the subordinate status of the Adivasi small peasantry and strengthened the control of upper castes over the bureaucracy. This includes most notably the 1854 Muluki Ain, or civil code, which institutionalised the relations between Nepal's diverse communities at a state level, placing Nepali-speaking Brahmins and Chettris at the top of the institutionalised hierarchy (Höfer, 1979). Maithili-speaking occupational castes who had migrated from India alongside their Nepali-speaking counterparts in the hills were placed at the bottom, again based upon their position in the classical *varna* hierarchy, and were divided into 'touchable' and 'untouchable' (or Dalit) categories (Höfer, 1979).

Despite the fact that the Adivasi of Nepal were not even part of the classical hierarchy, some communities were granted a position in the state sanctioned code. Nepal's indigenous groups were ranked, being placed above the touchable or untouchable occupational castes but below the Chettri. The Tharu were placed at the bottom of this category[16] (Höfer, 1979), cementing their subordinate position within the state apparatus – in spite of their revenue collection role. Perhaps more significant though is the fact that caste increasingly fused with ethnicity towards the latter part of the Rana era – changes which would become far more significant in later decades. Not only were upper-caste Nepali-speaking castes of the hills given priority for government administrative posts, but lowland indigenous groups along with those who had migrated from India were lumped together as quasi-foreigners within Nepal and even needed a passport to visit Kathmandu. Nationality was purely based upon ethno-linguistic markers, which differentiated the Adivasi and settler population of the plains from the Nepali-speaking castes who controlled the central government (Gaige, 1976). The institutionalisation of caste and ethnicity set the stage for the ethnic exclusion that would mark future generations.

Imperialism and Internal Feudal Transformation

The culmination of the Rana and pre-Rana land settlement and tax generation policies resulted in an entrenched centralised feudal mode of production in rural Morang by the early twentieth century. Land was controlled by both the state and local landlords, who were either *birta* recipients or functionaries with large tracts of *raikar* land. Surplus was divided between the Kathmandu bureaucracy and ruling families on the one hand and the local nobility on the other. At the base of the agrarian structure was a large class of indigenous, middle- and low-caste labourers, tenants and marginal landowners. At its apex was a politically powerful class of usually high caste but also indigenous landlords and intermediaries who extracted surplus through rent, interest on loans and tax, a large portion of which was sent to the state (Sugden, 2013; Regmi, 1976).

It is during this period that capitalist formations began expanding across the sub-Himalayan lowlands in neighbouring India in the wake of British imperialism – and before looking at Morang itself, it is helpful to review the changes across the larger eastern sub-Himalayan frontier. While Purnea to the south has been under colonial control for several decades and was the site of notable cash crop production (Chaudhury, 1965), the Darjeeling Tarai and North Bengal Dooars (the natural eastwards extension of the Morang and Jhapa plains into Indian territory) fell to the British empire in 1850 and 1846 respectively. This region had been subject to a similar feudal regime under the Sikkimese and Bhutanese states (Ray, 2002). While the existing feudal social structure was maintained to facilitate administration, the colonial overlords were quick to see the economic potential of the plains for the production of cash crops and tea. The establishment of plantations, commercial forestry and communication infrastructure thus facilitated the early emergence of capitalist production (in parallel with various pre-capitalist formations), which simultaneously drew labour from the local peasantry (Ray, 2002; Chaudhuri, 1995).

In the Nepal Tarai, however, a more complex relationship with capitalism was emerging at the turn of the century. While the region was by no means unaffected by the expanding colonial social formation to the east, imperialism did not seek direct articulations with the Tarai's older modes of production through labour as was occurring in the plantation economy in North Bengal. At a country level, nominally independent Nepal offered the colonialists not labour, but a source of raw materials and an untapped market for manufactured commodities, including both luxuries for the ruling class and daily consumption goods (Blaikie et al., 2001). The Communist Party of Nepal, on its founding in the 1940s, referred to Nepal as a 'semi-colony', or *ardha-upanivesh*, described by Lenin as a country which is formally independent but which in reality is subordinate to colonial powers, often via financial dependence[17] (Lenin,

1987). Blaikie et al. (2001) suggest that Nepal was a semi-colony of the British empire from at least the mid-nineteenth century onwards.

In spite of the memory of the Anglo-Gorkha war, by the time of the Rana regime, Nepal was a committed ally of the British empire. The British guaranteed Nepal's formal independence so long as they opened their borders to imports and allowed them access to resources such as timber (Blaikie et al., 2001). The development of railways as far as the southern border with Nepal from 1895 to 1898 was instrumental in further entrenching this unequal relationship. This included a railway from Jogbani to the south of Biratnagar to the main Indian rail network in Katihar, which was built between 1887 and 1909.[18] These railheads maximised outflows of raw materials while facilitating the import of commodities (Blaikie et al. 2001), which included cloth and hardware from British manufacturing centres (N. S. Singh, 1997), although in later years these would be produced within colonial India itself.

While Nepal maintained a favourable trade balance initially due to the plentiful raw materials (particularly timber and agricultural produce) it had at its disposal (N. S. Singh, 1997),[19] in the longer term, the import of consumer goods served to impede the development of domestic industry in the Tarai or indeed anywhere else in Nepal (Blaikie et al., 2001). Most notably, cheaper factory-made imports contributed to the decline in the cottage industries such as brassware, woodwork and textiles which Regmi (1977) suggests had flourished in Nepal prior to the Rana era in spite of the country's relative isolation. The Anglo-Nepal treaty of 1923 dealt a further blow to these industries through facilitating an unrestricted import of manufactured goods from the British empire (B. P. Shrestha, 1967). The Ranas even went as far as discouraging certain industries such as *bidi*s (local cigarettes) as that would undermine tax revenue on imported cigarettes (B. P. Shrestha, 1967). By the late 1920s, a trade deficit had emerged, and the value of merchandise exported from Nepal was NPR 27,943,000 while imports were valued at NPR 58,200,000 (N. S. Singh, 1997).

During this period, the first towns emerged on the Tarai, including Rangeli, then the district capital of Morang district. This was later shifted to Biratnagar, which emerged into the larger urban centre. However, rather than being centres of capitalist accumulation drawing peasants from the countryside, they were frontier outposts for the Kathmandu regime. Government officials would be stationed there, and agrarian revenue would be collected, while the towns would also be nodes for the export of timber and other primary products. Government documents compiled by Mahesh Chandra Regmi suggest that there was extensive export of agrarian produce from the Morang region during the nineteenth century (Regmi, 1977), suggesting that a large portion of the agrarian revenue collected in kind was exported to India from these outposts, with the revenue being transferred to Kathmandu in money form.

In terms of actual cash crops, which were sold directly by farmers, this limited predominantly to sugarcane and jute (Aubriot and Buslé, 2023). The latter was arguably the most significant, being well suited to the high rainfall climate of Morang and neighbouring Jhapa. This was largely cultivated by local farmers from the late nineteenth century onwards (Regmi, 1988), with an estimated 60,000 acres being cultivated as of the 1930s (Regmi, 1977). Whether these cash crops were produced by commercialised owner-cultivator farmers or by tenants and marginal farmers as a form of 'distress commercialisation' is not clear. With reference to the subordination of Bhil farmers in Madhya Pradesh, K. S. Singh (2023) demonstrates how taxation had created debt, which was used to encourage Adivasi peasants to produce cotton to generate cash. With oral histories suggesting that debt had become a lived reality by the late Rana era with growing monetisation, a similar trend may have been present in Morang.

Other articulations with capitalism, however, were via the emerging industries in the Tarai – and this would become far more significant in future decades. While cottage industries were being undermined, there were some efforts by the 1930s to support large-scale industries – although these were restricted to agro-processing. There was therefore some limited capitalist development in the 1930s with the establishment of early factories in Biratnagar (Karan and Ishil, 1996; Regmi, 1977a). This included Biratnagar Jute Mill, established in 1936 with government investment, and two private cotton mills (one in Biratnagar and another in Birgunj), which were established in the 1940s (B. P. Shrestha, 1967). These industries had some short-term success due to high demand during the Second World War – but rapidly lost profitability after the return of normal market conditions, and the Birgunj factory closed in 1947. A number of other joint stock companies were established with domestic and Indian capital (B. P. Shrestha, 1967). However, many of these early factories were speculative in character, employment was scarce, and profits were often repatriated to India (Regmi, 1977a). Mismanagement and fraud were widespread and out of the remaining 46 joint stock companies in 1951, 21 of them subsequently closed due to heavy losses (B. P. Shrestha,

1967). Only 6 of the 19 rice and oil mills established in the late Rana era were still operating by the 1960s (B. P. Shrestha, 1967).

Under the Ranas, there was little evidence of a significant emerging domestic capitalist class in Nepal, or 'national bourgeoisie', to challenge the ruling elite on a political level (Blaikie et al., 2001; Mishra, 2007). The anglophile Rana nobility represented a classic comprador class who benefited from the unequal relation between two social formations. They were enriched from the imposition of taxes on the import of manufactured goods from the British empire to the south and the export of raw materials such as timber, which were invested in an extravagant lifestyle (Bhattarai, 2003a; Blaikie et al., 2001, 2002). Revenues were used to import luxury commodities from the British empire for the ruling elite (Seddon, 1987).

Up until the mid-twentieth century therefore, the feudal elite was primarily 'extractive', collecting taxes and maintaining law and order rather than being 'productive', with a commitment to support industry and development (Blaikie et al., 2001, 2002; R. S. Pradhan, 1984), beyond the few tokenistic agro-processing investments. Most capital which could potentially be mobilised remained in the hands of the aristocracy and was primarily invested in land (see later on emerging property rights), and there were few incentives to generate other forms of wealth (Karan and Ishil, 1996). Although there was a growing merchant capitalist class, they were not involved in production but in the import–export business (Regmi, 1977), a sector in which many of the Rana elite also had stakes (Seddon, 1987).

On the ground in the Morang plains, the comprador–colonial alliance impeded the emergence of alternative livelihood options for a pauperised peasantry, while on a political level it strengthened the wealth and power of the class with primary control over land, the Ranas. There were, however, internal transformations within the feudal mode of production, brought about by state interventions in the context of expanding market relations. These saw changes in the distribution of surplus without actually changing the relations between tenants and landlords.

The first intervention which changed the distribution of surplus was the development of property rights for *raikar* land, allowing cultivators to buy or sell their state-owned holdings so long as tax was still paid. While the revenue settlement between 1854 and 1868 at the onset of Rana rule secured peasant cultivators or landlords de facto tenure to a plot of land, it was still officially state property with restrictions on the buying and selling of plots (Regmi, 1976). However, the right to buy or sell *raikar* land was finally legalised formally in 1921 – consolidating private property rights. Under these new rules, anyone could buy, sell or mortgage land so long as taxes were paid (Regmi, 1976). Meanwhile, cadastral surveys (see Tamrakar, 2012) which took place during the late Rana era likely served to further consolidate the property rights of existing landed elites wherever there was ambiguity over the title holder for existing *raikar* lands. Research from the Dang valley by Krauskopff (1989) suggests that many Tharu households, which even included landlord-functionaries, lost their estates to upper-caste hill-origin *jimidar*s not only due to debt, but also due to deception during cadastral surveys and the ability to more easily buy and sell holdings. Whether this process was replicated amongst the Tharu of Morang is not known, although it may have been a precursor to the decline of the Tharu landlord class, which is described in the next section.

The second intervention that changed the distribution of surplus was the devaluation of land tax. By the first half of the twentieth century, government revenue had diversified, meaning they were less dependent upon land tax alone. With the rising import of manufactured consumer goods upheld by the burgeoning comprador class and the export of timber and cash crops, the value of trade had risen from NPR 9.8 million in 1879–1890 to NPR 87.9 million by 1920–1921 (Mishra, 1987). At the same time, land tax from the peasantry was gradually declining in importance, and monetised tax rates were kept static, despite rapidly rising commodity prices (Regmi, 1976). In Mahottari district, for example, Regmi (1976) notes how paddy prices increased ninefold between 1940 and 1961 despite static monetary tax rates. This parallels a similar shift in India (Habib, 2002). For instance, land tax formed 70 per cent of government revenue in India in 1839–1840, yet had declined to just 16 per cent by 1938–1939 and a meagre 6 per cent by 1948–1949 (Joseph, 1960). In the case of Nepal, this decline in the value of land tax meant that the *raikar* landowner needed a smaller amount of grain to meet tax obligations. This made it more desirable for landlords to rent out excess holdings, because, after paying tribute to the state, rents could be increased while still allowing tenants to meet their minimum subsistence needs (Regmi, 1976).

The outcome of the aforementioned two processes was that they encouraged *jimidar*s to further expand their holdings while also providing an incentive for other individuals with capital to buy land, worsening the concentration in land ownership. For those working as tenants on plots of *jimidar*s or *birtawala*s (owners of *birta* estates), there would have been little material change to their livelihoods other than the fact that much of the surplus appropriated as rent would be retained by the landlords themselves rather than being paid as tax. Another outcome, however, was that peasants with their own plots of *raikar* land were now emerging as an independent cultivator class who could retain much of their surplus. This can be considered an 'independent peasant' mode of production based upon the owner-cultivation of private plots which emerged as a consequence of *internal* feudal transformation. However, this group was small in number, and growing indebtedness to moneylenders following the monetisation of tax (and the wider economy) resulted in many peasant landowners falling back into the grasp of feudal tenancy as they lost their property to the landed classes. Elders in the study communities noted how *jimidar*s themselves used to appropriate land from those unable to meet tax or debt repayment obligations. Regmi (1976, 118) cites a government survey in 1948 noting that while some *jimidar*s in Morang district owned up to 22,000 *bigha*s; 23 per cent of cultivating households owned less than 1 *bigha* each.

In sum, devaluation of tax, monetisation and the rising concentration in landed property which accompanied it consolidated ground rent to landlords as the primary form of surplus appropriation. This was backed up by the power of the state and is the origin of the predominant form of landlordism in today's Tarai-Madhesh.

Land Reforms and Feudal Reproduction: 1951–1990

Land Reforms, Nationalism and the Modernisation Agenda

In the wake of Indian independence to the south, a pro-democracy movement in the late 1950s successfully unseated the Rana regime, and Nepal saw the formation of its first, albeit short-lived, democratically elected government. However, it is unlikely that there were any immediate significant changes to the mode of production on the ground in rural Morang – with a large share of the agricultural surplus being appropriated as rent. However, the second half of the twentieth century was also an era of land reforms across the world, as newly independent states sought to break the unequal agricultural structures generated by colonialism, while the rising imperialist power of the United States of America sought to curtail the growth of communism (Kapstein, 2017). Land reform was thus a major agenda for all the emerging new political parties, and a Royal Land Reform Commission was established in 1952 (Dhakal, 2020). With vast tracts of land still under tax-free *birta* tenure and in the hands of powerful landlords, abolishing this system in particular was a priority for the monarchy and the emerging political parties to demonstrate their commitment to change. There was of course reluctance from landlords with whom the monarchy was sympathetic and even from some leaders within the new political parties (Gill, 2009). However, in 1959 the Birta Abolition Act was finally pushed through.

The act classified *birta* land into two categories. Type A lands (which included tracts of uncultivated forest) were those whereby the owner was receiving income only equivalent to the land tax on adjoining *raikar* lands. Type B lands, by contrast, were those where the owner was yielding rents from tenants or cultivating them independently. Class A lands were taken back under government control, while class B lands were simply converted into *raikar* tenure and thus became taxable. The abolition of *birta* therefore did not culminate in any actual redistribution of cultivated holdings or lead to any change in landlord–tenant relations (Gill, 2009). Much of the former *birta* land under tenancy appears to have remained with the owners but under *raikar* tenure and rents therefore continued to be appropriated in the same way as before. As taxation was a modest share of the surplus, this would have been a small burden for landlords (Gill, 2009).

Other measures during the 1950s included the Tenancy Rights Acquisition Act (TRAA), which sought to give tenants titles to land they had cultivated for generations. However, as taxes and rents collected were usually registered under the name of landlords (rather than the tenants), this act paradoxically strengthened landlords' control over their property (Sugden and Gurung, 2012). Another legislation was introduced in 1957, purportedly to protect tenants' rights. Rent was set at 50 per cent of the crop, and tenants who had cultivated a plot for over a year were entitled to tenancy rights and could not be evicted. However, Gill (2009) notes that the implementation was weak as the government lacked systematic records on landlords or tenants.

Multiparty democracy ended following the royal coup of 1960 by the Shah monarchy, which imposed the authoritarian party-less Panchayat system. However, across Nepal, the population could no longer be shielded from progressive emancipatory ideologies. In this context, new measures were necessary to garner popular support. The Panchayat regime sought authority on an ideological level through reactionary ethnic nationalism on the one hand and a 'developmentalist' agenda on the other, which included a continued 'commitment' to land reform. Both processes are significant in understanding the later evolution of agrarian relations.

With regard to the nationalist agenda – this was grounded in the culture of the dominant ethnic group, the Brahmin and Chettri, Khas castes of the hills, and their language, Nepali, while the king was the figurehead. A Panchayat slogan was: *ek bhasha, ek bhesh, ek desh* (literally: one language, one style of dress, one country). Central to the nationalist vision was a fierce cultural differentiation of Nepal from India to the south (Gaige, 1976; Caddell, 2007). While there was very limited change in the semi-colonial relationship between the two countries, and the regime continued to prosper from this relationship of dependence, as will be discussed subsequently, aggressive cultural nationalism was a valuable diversion to seek legitimacy amongst its increasingly politically aware populous.

The nationalist Panchayat-era vision needed to be combined with a rhetoric of development, in line with the state-led modernisation agenda of the 1960s and 1970s (Gaige, 1976), particularly as the new regime sought to distance itself from the 'extractive' image which shaped the Rana era. There was a substantial expansion of the bureaucracy and state apparatus (Blaikie et al. 2001). This included the establishment of a plethora of government offices in district centres across the country – in sectors such as agriculture, land revenue, banking, as well as the police and army. Blaikie et al. (2001) note that the expenditure on establishing these offices in towns and paying salaries to the newly appointed staff was disproportionate to what was actually spent on rural development in the countryside in terms of infrastructure and basic services – and was emblematic of the continued concentration of state revenue within the bureaucracy.

In Morang, the district headquarters shifted from Rangeli to Biratnagar, and the city emerged as an important administrative centre for a large part of eastern Nepal as well as being a border trade and industrial hub. Urbanisation was driven in part by the expansion of the bureaucracy in the city. The latter remained largely dominated not by local Tharu, Rajbanshi or Maithili-speaking plains castes (known collectively as Madheshis) of the rural hinterland, but by Nepali-speaking Brahmin and Chettri, many of whom had settled in the city from the eastern hills – a trend echoed across the Tarai-Madhesh (Jha, 2014). This paved the way in Morang for a process described later, whereby the rural-oriented agrarian bureaucracy of the Rana era, in which the Tharu and other indigenous groups had a position, was replaced by a more urban-centric state apparatus focused on Biratnagar, which was dominated by hill castes.

Associated with the king's promise of development, or *bikas*, and in collusion with the emerging 'international development' industry and its associated geopolitical interests, much of the Tarai-Madhesh experienced a drive to settle the remaining forest frontier, implement land 'reforms' and develop infrastructure. Despite the populist rhetoric, the outcome of this fusion of ethnic nationalism with an economic modernisation drive was a further dispossession of the land-poor and tenant-farming majority in Morang and many other parts of the Tarai, and a further marginalisation along the lines of caste and ethnicity – and it is to these processes we now turn.

The first 'development' initiative of interest implemented by this expanded bureaucracy was a continuation of the 1950s land reform programme. The most important ruling in Nepal was the 1964 Lands Act (Gaige, 1976). A significant shift from earlier legislations were the efforts to actually *redistribute* land. A maximum ceiling of 10 *bigha*s of agricultural land was set for the Tarai-Madhesh (Government of Nepal 1964). Lands which were above the ceiling were acquired by the government after payment of compensation. This was fixed at ten times the annual tax for farmland (five times for non-agricultural lands). This surplus land was then meant to be redistributed to the tillers or landless people (Regmi, 1976). The 1964 act also set agricultural rents at a maximum ceiling of 50 per cent of the crop, and registered tenants were offered the opportunity to claim half of the cultivated land after five years, during which landlords were also prohibited from selling the land (J. Adhikari, 2006), although this only applied to registered tenants.

Another important change was the abolition of the *jimidari* system of land revenue collection that was previously in place. The district land revenue offices and VDCs took over the collection of taxes and administration, a task overseen by the newly established Ministry of Land Reform and Management (Regmi, 1976). While this politically disenfranchised the Adivasi revenue functionaries in rural Morang, these roles were already becoming redundant as agrarian tax became a much smaller share of the overall harvest.

In spite of the tenancy rights promised in the 1960s reforms, these were weakly enforced. There were reportedly few tenants who were able to independently take up legal cases against landlords, and Gill (2009) reports that landlords even evicted tenants before the legislation came into effect.[20] A later amendment to the 1964 act in 1996 stated that tenants must provide a receipt within six months, showing the submission of a share of the produce to the landlords, and after this they would receive rights. However, J. Adhikari (2006) notes that this information was not adequately communicated with the tenants and few actually registered their tenancy. If anything, the efforts to regulate tenancy simply moved it underground (Bhandari, 2006) into the realm of informal 'word of mouth' contracts (Sugden and Gurung, 2012). Landlords actively thwarted farmers from registering their tenancies. This even went as far as attempts to block their access to citizenship papers (see later) (Mørch, 2023).

In terms of redistribution, which could have perhaps been the most significant outcome of the reforms, success was similarly limited. An often-cited figure by Regmi (1976) suggests that by 1972, the government had acquired approximately 50,000 hectares of land across Nepal, representing only 3 per cent of the cultivable area, and it was estimated that only 22,000 hectares were actually redistributed, benefiting only 10,000 households (Regmi, 1976). Zaman (1973), supported by FAO, was commissioned by the government to evaluate the land reform programme across Nepal, and an estimated 34,000 hectares were redistributed, affecting 9,000 landowners. This process was, however, slow and subject to repeated delays, with landlords having time during this period to sell off their estates or subdivide them within the family (Bhandari, 2006).

In the Morang region, the land reform programme did have a lasting impact on agrarian relations. The primary change, however, appeared to be not in the overall distribution of holdings but in the composition of the landlord class. The most powerful landlords, most of whom were of hill origin, were known to have been successful in retaining their estates, even after the reforms. As noted earlier, this region was home to a number of large *birta* estates of former forest land granted to members of the hill aristocracy during the Rana and Gorkhali era, which were converted into *raikar* tenure following *birta* abolition in the 1950s. Many of these landlords were able to avoid the seizure of their land during the reforms or use the legislation to consolidate their economic and political power locally.

A number of reasons for the failure of the reforms across Nepal have been cited. For instance, Basnet (2018) notes that land which had been seized needed to be purchased by the tillers. Prices were set at between NPR 140 and 280 per *bigha* depending on the quality. Prospective buyers for these holdings had to take government loans. However, many poorer buyers could not keep up with payments, forcing them to take loans from private lenders at high interest. A default on these private loans would mean that land would often go back into the hands of the landlords.

From oral histories compiled in Morang, however, it appears that the most significant mechanism through which large landlords such as former *birtawala*s retained their estates was through conscious avoidance of the reform process. The implementation of the reforms in phases in different parts of the country gave landlords ample opportunities to plan in advance so they could identify and take advantage of loopholes (Basnet, 2018). Morang was part of the third phase of the reforms scheduled to be implemented only in 1970, whereas Jhapa and parts of the hills were scheduled to begin in 1968 (Government of Nepal, 1964).

There were several avoidance measures or loopholes which were known to have been exploited. Some landlords, for instance, registered themselves as the official cultivator, yet continued to rent out the land to tenants unofficially (Regmi, 1976). Most commonly in such cases, land was registered in the name of different family members so their officially registered holding would appear to be within the ceiling (Basnet, 2018). During interviews, for instance, we learned of a woman in Morang who married into a powerful landed family and had inherited up to 70 *bigha*s of land. During the land reform, she made papers in the name of some of the tenants but continued to extract rent as a landowner. While the original tenants have moved on, we were told with some amusement of how the son now wants to sell some of her land, but cannot find the tenants in whose name it was originally registered. Another practice said to have been widespread in rural Morang was the registration of land in the name of different family members. It was reported how a Morang landlord who had 20 *bigha*s and lived with his son would register some in the name of the son as a separate household (10–10), even if they lived together. Sometimes the landlord could register the land in the name of the daughter even though the rent was kept themselves. There were also rumours of married couples having legal divorces so some land could be registered in the husband's name and some in the wife's name. Even high-level staff in the Morang land revenue office stated that 'officially' no landlord owns more than 5–6 *bigha*s of land, but, as it is all registered in the name of different family members, their estates are likely to be far larger, a legal loophole which is difficult to enforce, paralleling findings from Athreya et al.'s (1990) study from Tamil Nadu.

During the land reforms, a number of landlords in the region also registered their lands as commercial farms which were not subject to the same ceiling rules. Then after the reforms they would just keep the land as it is and give it out to sharecroppers. Landlords would also reportedly bribe reform officials. One farmer in Morang joked that the officials themselves are landlords, so why would they have any incentive to conduct reforms.

In terms of the registration of tenants or the share of the crop taken as rent – there was very limited progress during the reforms and subsequent years. In the remote village of Hurhuriya in Thalaha VDC, for instance, it was estimated by the local people that only around 5 per cent of the tenants are *mohi*, statutory tenants with legal documents, who may be entitled to a share of the land after five years. This is reflected in the survey data which shows that only five households had received land as *mohi* (registered tenants) between 2007–2008 and 2019, totalling a meagre 0.91 hectare. In Sitpur of Bhaudaha, respondents were not aware of anyone at all who was registered. When I enquired about this in interviews, the response by one participant was blunt: 'Land is like a hand. People are not going to cut off their hand. That is why landlords are not willing to lose their land to a mohi!' As noted earlier, the land reforms gave the landlords the incentive to 'informalise' the contracts so that they did not need to adhere to rent ceilings or allow farmers to claim a share of the land after a number of years. In Bhaudaha it was reported that landlords evicted established tenants at the time of the act and then gave out the land on an informal word-of-mouth contract to others.

The challenges of implementing land reforms in Nepal can be better understood when one remembers the importance of land to political authority over the last two centuries. Set against this context, the landlords often had the land reform officials on their side. The *birta* and *jagir* systems had incorporated the feudal lords within the state bureaucratic alliance (Mishra, 2007), and large landlords were important support bases of the king in the 1960s, often influencing implementation agencies or individuals on the ground (Khanal et al., 2005; Gill, 2009). The local state was in this context often willing to cave in to landed interests at the grassroots to ensure the continued loyalty of local elites (Joshi and Mason, 2007).

The Nepal case stands in stark contrast to relatively successful land reforms such as those in West Bengal under Operation Barga in the 1970s. The successful redistribution of land and regulation of tenancy was dependent upon a communist government at the time which was committed to land reform, and mass-scale grassroots campaigns and mobilisation (Banerjee et al., 2002). Similar successes, particularly in registering tenants, were evident in Tamil Nadu in certain villages, due to the backing of the Dravida Munnetra Kazhagam (DMK) (Athreya et al., 1990). This is not to say there were not localised 'successes' in Nepal – for instance, in the Kathmandu valley, particularly Bhaktapur district, where tenants and the tillers were relatively more successful in registering the land they were cultivating. However, here, like in West Bengal, a locally powerful communist party and active peasant movement had organised and alerted the peasants to their rights in the context of the reforms (Hachhethu, 2004). The dynamics of this struggle are described in intricate detail in Raj (2010).

Oral histories from Morang Tarai suggested that the primary losers from the land reforms in the far-eastern region were the indigenous landlord class, many of whom were part of the now obsolete revenue collection apparatus. It was recalled how the Tharu nobility, as well as former functionaries from the Rajbanshi and other Adivasi groups, did not have the same links to the bureaucracy as their high-caste counterparts and were therefore more likely to have their land confiscated. Whether this land was redistributed to smaller peasants is not known. The ethnography by Krauskopff (1989) in Dang noted that while the economic and political power of the Tharu landed class was already in decline prior to the land reforms, many Tharu also sold off their land prior to the reforms to avoid having it confiscated, only for it to be bought up by the emerging Brahmin and Chettri landlord class. Only a small number of Tharu small peasants had the means to buy up these lands.

The declining economic authority of Adivasi landlords went side by side with their dwindling political authority. Tharu and other Adivasi landlords had served their purpose as local-level intermediaries under the more centralised form of feudalism of the Rana period. Under the Panchayat system, the old *jimidari* system had been replaced by an expanding modern bureaucracy, increasingly filled by hill castes, who were migrating to the plains in rising numbers (particularly following the control of malaria – see later). The Tharu and other Adivasi elites were therefore no longer needed to manage revenue and other political affairs locally. Other than token Tharu representation in the national parliament, they had in a short period of time become politically disenfranchised (Mørch, 2023). Their weaker political position also meant it was more difficult for them to bypass land reform legislation and maintain their power as a landlord class. Furthermore, despite the expanding modern bureaucracy which replaced the older rural tax collection administration – there were limited opportunities for the Adivasi, or indeed Madheshi, of the Tarai to compete for jobs with Nepali-speaking castes (Gaige, 1976). This can be understood in the context of the aggressive hill nationalism of the Panchayat era and, in particular, the foregrounding of the Nepali language of the hills in all aspects of political and bureaucratic life, not to mention the education system. Indigenous groups such as the Tharu were increasingly junior partners in the rapidly expanding political and bureaucratic apparatus (Guneratne, 2010). Gaige's (1976) study from four Tarai districts in the 1970s suggested that 82 per cent of officers and 81 per cent of police in the district administration were of hill origin.

Dwindling Holdings, Debt and the Rise of the Absentee Landlord

As the power of the Tharu nobility declined relative to the upper-caste landed class, a significant shift was a rise in absentee landlordism. Some bigger landlords had always resided in urban centres, given that many were bureaucratic elites. This increasingly became the norm during the Panchayat era. It is important to note, however, that there was still a sizeable class of small, middle and larger farmers operating as owner-cultivators. These 'independent peasants' included farmers who retained plots of taxable *raikar* land from the Rana times or had received land redistributed in the reforms. Furthermore, they also included many of the former Tharu landlords who had lost their extensive estates and had instead become medium-to-large farmers. However, oral histories suggested that this group of independent peasants dwindled in number throughout the 1970s, 1980s and 1990s. In villages such as Bhaudaha, it was noted that most of the Bantar and Rajbanshi farmers had their own land in the early Panchayat period, but over the decades this was gradually sold off or seized, resulting in them entering the burgeoning class of sharecropping tenants, while consolidating the power of absentee landlords. There were several processes which precipitated this.

First, with rising population, the division of land amongst sons contributed to dwindling holdings amongst land-owning peasants. This appeared to be particularly severe amongst the former Adivasi landlords (Figure 3.5), who had already lost land in the reforms. Oral history interviews carried out in Pidarboni as well as in Dainiya, a Gangai village further south, found that former Rana-era land functionaries from the Tharu, Gangai and Rajbanshi communities lost a lot of land in the post-land-reform decades due to the subdivision of holdings amongst sons. Some had owned up to 50 *bigha*s in the past and now were left with just a few *bigha*s of heavily fragmented holdings. The division of holdings was a symptom of the overdependence on agriculture and relative lack of external professional opportunities for Tharu sons to move into (that is, an exit from agriculture). The absentee Brahmin and Chettri landlords by contrast were under less pressure to subdivide their holdings. They had access to better political networks and a virtual monopoly over government employment opportunities during the Panchayat era. Furthermore, they often had multiple sources of income, so not all the sons were expected to remain engaged in agricultural activities.

Figure 3.5 Village ponds such as this were often built by the old Tharu nobility. Their estates rapidly disintegrated during the Panchayat era, and these remain the last visible signs of their past prosperity.

Source: Author.

A second reason for dwindling holdings was indebtedness. A number of Rajbanshi and Tharu families interviewed in central Morang also reported how their grandparents had once owned land, but due to unpaid loans and outright deception by absentee landlords, they had lost what land had remained in their hands. Paradoxically, debt also affected the Tharu landed class. Just as they had been able to accumulate lands through moneylending in the past, they themselves had fallen into cycles of indebtedness in later years to urban-based landlords and local moneylenders.

However, as one would expect, it was the smaller landowning Adivasi farmers who were hit particularly hard by debt. These owner-cultivator farmers would take loans either from other landlords or moneylenders, often for medical or wedding expenses. Land left as collateral would be lost if debts could not be repaid. An interview with a Bantar farmer in Baijnathpur recalled how his grandfather was cheated by a notorious absentee landlord and moneylender. The grandfather could not read and signed papers for a much bigger loan than he had originally taken – culminating in the loss of his holding.

The causes of growing indebtedness amongst both poorer farmers and the old indigenous elite likely had multiple causes, although the gradual monetisation of the economy and market expansion possibly played a critical role. Even if land was not 'seized' through deception, a number of farmers sold off plots due to economic stress. One landless tenant recalled that their family land was sold to a *pahadi* (hill person) who came to the village and was going from house to house asking who was willing to sell him plots.

In his study of the Bhil communities in Madhya Pradesh, K. S. Singh (2023) suggests that rising debt in the context of market expansion arises alongside a gradual process of monetisation driven by several interlinked processes. This includes the production of commercial crops such as cotton and the associated demand for cash to buy irrigation and fertiliser. However, in Morang, in spite of lofty ambitions to increase production of cash crops by 73 per cent in the 1965–1970 Third Five Year Plan (National Planning Commission, 1970), cash crop cultivation remained limited with the exception of jute. Nevertheless, farmers were increasingly dependent upon chemical fertilisers for subsistence production. These were promoted by the government, which in the Fourth Five-Year Plan aimed to achieve 33 per cent of its increased production targets through the use of chemical fertiliser (National Planning Commission, 1970).[21] However, chemical nutrients were also becoming a necessity for farmers following the contraction of the forest frontier, which meant *gobar* (or dung) needed to be used as a fuel rather than as a source of organic nutrients. Also driving monetisation was the shift towards hybrid seeds[22] and costs of tubewell irrigation, as farmers sought to increase output and compensate for dwindling holdings in the context of a rising population and the rent burden.

In this context, merchant and moneylending capital began to make inroads into rural Morang with the rising need for cash for inputs. As well as ordinary moneylenders, a network of *katawalas*, or grain merchants, established enterprises in all of the main market settlements – particularly Naya Bazaar, where farmers would travel from distant villages to access credit to procure inputs, which could be repaid in grain – a process described at length in later chapters. This interlinkage of merchant and moneylending capital likely contributed in part to rising debt – a process also described with regard to K. S. Singh's (2023) study.

While it has been established that rising debt was driving distress sales of land, often to absentee landlords, it is useful to dig a bit deeper to understand who these landowners were. It is apparent that some of the alienated holdings were absorbed into the estates of an old landed class. This includes descendants of *birta* recipients and Brahmin and Chettri *jimidar*s, the majority of whom lived in Biratnagar or even Kathmandu. However, there was also a rise in a new class of absentee landlords – fuelled by the rising prosperity in Biratnagar and the expanding bureaucracy. As Regmi (1976) notes, land remained a profitable source of investment following the reforms, with the Lands Act maintaining rents at a level that ensured landowners continued to receive an income equivalent to what would be achieved had they invested elsewhere in the economy (Regmi, 1976). Rent was set at half of the crop, more than the third that had originally been proposed (J. Adhikari, 2011). In this context, there were rising purchases of land by town dwellers with salaried employment. Even improvements to the productive forces – most notably via the construction of irrigation systems – increased the incentives for outsiders to buy up land. The most significant intervention was the construction of the Chatra canal, which aimed to irrigate 56,500 hectares of land in Morang and Sunsari districts (National Planning Commission, 1970). This reportedly encouraged an inflation of rents while also making land investments more lucrative.

This changing composition of the landlord class echoes Regmi's (1976) observation that the emergence of de facto ownership rights in land had made 'ascriptive' rights less important, and the traditional landed elite were increasingly joined by a 'non-ascriptive' land-owning class. However, there was limited evidence of a shift in the relations of production for these new landlords, and rent was extracted in the same way in which it was on the estates of the old landed class. Land was valued by both old and new landlords for speculative purposes, but also for the grain provided by sharecroppers and additional income from the sale of the rent. Surplus extracted by landlords was generally put towards consumption of imported luxuries and speculative investment (J. Adhikari, 2011). The National Sample Census of Agriculture data for across Nepal suggested that big landlords owning more than 10 hectares owned on average 19 hectares in 1961, while by 1981 it had reached 22 hectares (Basnet, 2018). This suggests that this increasingly diverse class of landlords had continued to purchase land even after the land reforms.

While absentee landlords in the cities appeared to be consolidating their economic power throughout the 1960s and 1980s, there were other beneficiaries of the break-up of larger estates and distress sales by smaller cultivators. This was mostly further south along the Indian border, which is home to a number of Maithili-speaking middle castes such as the Kushuwaha with a tradition of commercial agriculture. It was reported in the Dainiya and Katahari region that local farmers bought up some of the land from the former indigenous nobility. Some of these included the wealthier middle-caste farmers, such as the Yadav and Kushuwaha. One Kushuwaha family reported how their forefathers owned only small plots of land, but through industrious vegetable growing, they had bought up land from cash-strapped neighbours and expanded their estate considerably.

For poorer cultivators, however, opportunities to gain a foothold on the land market were limited. This was aggravated for some households due to citizenship restrictions. Just as caste relations were institutionalised under the Ranas through the Muluki Ain, ethnic exclusion in the Tarai was institutionalised through citizenship legislation – with Nepali citizenship a primary requisite for registering land in one's name or even securing a formal tenancy agreement. For the many individuals who were unable to prove either their birth in Nepal or the citizenship of their parents, naturalisation was the route to creating one's citizenship papers. However, the 1964 Citizenship Act defined requirements for naturalisation as being able to speak and write Nepali while being of 'Nepalese origin' (Gaige, 1976). The requirements to write in Nepali was of course impossible for many illiterate tenant farmers. Meanwhile, racialised interpretations of the 'Nepalese origin' clause by some officials resulted in many people not of hill descent being denied citizenship. This included, in particular, Maithili-speaking castes as well as Adivasi groups who originate in India, such as the Santhal (UNHCRC Nepal, 2011) and Musahar (Giri, 2012). A study from Jhapa district east of Biratnagar suggested that during the 1960s land reforms, many Santhals who had actually cleared the forest in the past did not have citizenship papers to register the land they themselves had cleared – resulting in the loss of their holdings (UNHCRC Nepal, 2011). More notably, Mørch (2023) suggests that following the 1964 Lands Act, some landlords colluded with state officials to ensure that their tenants could not acquire citizenship papers, as this would make it more challenging for them to register as legal tenants, or *mohi*, which would entitle them to a share of the land.

Resettlement: A New Mode of Production on the Forest Frontier

In sum, it has been shown that in southern Morang throughout the Panchayat era, land inequality remained entrenched and short-term gains from the reforms were rapidly undermined, while rent remained the primary mechanism of surplus appropriation. However, the trajectory of change was different in the remaining, sparsely populated forested tracts. Across the far-eastern Tarai at the start of the Panchayat era, the forest frontier was generally concentrated in the northern half of the lowlands, extending south from the Himalayan foothills, although the far-eastern part of Morang and most of Jhapa district was also heavily forested at points as far south as the Indian border.

There were also some remnant forests within more settled country, including the area around present-day Jhorahat Bazaar.[23]

A critical component of the Panchayat state's nation-building project was the clearing of many of the remaining forested tracts and the settlement of these lands with migrants from the hills, not as tenants for landlords, but as owner-cultivators. While there were some resettlement schemes in the Morang region during the late Rana period, these were not as successful as planned. The often-cited causes were the presence of malaria in this belt, a disease that the local Rajbanshi and Tharu were known to have relative immunity to (A. Campbell, 1841). While this may have played a role, Ojha (1983) pointed to a more complex set of factors. These include the exodus of young men for military recruitment in the late Rana period, which absorbed a significant proportion of the labour, and the excesses of the extractive Rana state, which made reclamation of land in Assam and other regions a more favourable option.

However, continuing population pressure in the hills and technologies to eradicate malaria meant that the widespread resettlement of hill people was finally possible after the 1960s. The state had several reasons to make this a priority. While earlier efforts to colonise the forest frontier were oriented around maximising revenue, by the 1960s these efforts had a clearer political motive. First, it would help maintain social harmony in the hills, where population pressure, soil erosion, deforestation and declining agricultural yields were making it increasingly difficult for rural populations to subsist (Ojha, 1983). Second, it offered an alternative mechanism through which land-poor farmers could access plots at a time when the political will for genuine land reform was limited (N. R. Shrestha, 1990). Finally, the resettlement drive was also important for the hill nationalism of the Panchayat era whereby the state sought to expand the spread of hill culture and Nepali language across the plains, furthering the one-language, one-culture policy of the regime (Gaige, 1976). The population movements over the next 30 years across the entire Nepal Tarai led to significant demographic shifts with long-lasting consequences for the larger social formation of the region.

At a national level, the state's efforts began initially with formal resettlement programmes. This started further west in the Chitwan valley which, in collaboration with the WHO, was made possible by DDT spraying to eradicate malaria. This was a programme funded by the US government seeking to increase its Cold War influence in the country (Robertson, 2018). However, the malaria eradication campaign was gradually rolled out by the government across the Tarai to encourage settlement. In this context, the 1960s and 1970s saw significant spontaneous migration which had the active approval of the state, even though it was not part of a formal resettlement programme (Gaige, 1976). As a result, the migration was mostly unplanned, resulting in a massive decline in the remaining forest frontier, with better-resourced settlers often being able to acquire large tracts of personal land (Shrestha and Velu, 1993). While in the western Tarai, the clearing of the forest frontier was a more drawn-out affair, in the Morang region it was particularly rapid (Gaige, 1976), and all remaining forests in the southern half of contemporary Morang and Sunsari districts were cleared by the 1970s. While the unplanned nature of resettlement allowed some Tarai people (mostly Madheshi castes) to acquire land,[24] this was less common in Morang and Sunsari, with only some limited migration into northwestern Sunsari from the Mithila region. The majority of the settlers were Brahmin, Chettri, Rai and Limbu.

In terms of the mode of production, these new settlements were home to owner-cultivating peasant farmers, unlike the feudalism which was entrenched in the domains with a longer history of settlement further south. As part of an effort to formalise the process, in 1968–1969 the Department of Forests set about creating an inventory of new settlements and confirming land ownership rights (Ojha, 1983). Local farmers who were interviewed in Dainyia, for instance, east of the core field site and to the south of an area which was once under forest, recalled that a formal survey took place to identify which newly cleared land belonged to which household. This meant that settlers had secure ownership of their plots. In this context, the distribution of land was relatively more equitable than in the areas already under sedentary cultivation during the Rana era, and most farmers were able to meet their basic subsistence needs from the land. While there were inequalities between better-resourced farmers who had acquired more land and those with smaller holdings, most farmers at least had a plot of land that they were farming independently without a rent burden.

The resettlement programme had a relatively small immediate impact on the core field site of Jhorahat, Bhaudaha and Thalaha, as it was far to the south of the main settler belt. Nevertheless, there was a remnant forest around what became Jhorahat Bazaar – and this was cleared in the Panchayat period and settled by mostly Brahmin and Chettri farmers from the hills. These farmers were largely land-owning peasants, whose lands were surrounded by absentee landlord estates. In subsequent years though, they were joined by destitute migrants from the hills who arrived much later and became sharecroppers. Nevertheless, the primary forest frontier, which was cleared, started around 15 kilometres north of Jhorahat.

Economically and culturally, this contributed to a split of the Morang plains into two domains – the newly settled tracts mostly concentrated in the north home to land-owning predominantly hill settlers and some migrants from elsewhere in the Tarai, and the historically settled domains to the south which were home mostly to indigenous groups, who were heavily subordinated to absentee landlords. This geographical divide was intensified by the construction of the East–West Mahendra Highway by the Panchayat state in conjunction with foreign donors. The highway bypassed border cities such as Biratnagar and the historic trade routes and instead skirted the foot of the hills in the north of the Tarai. This alignment was read at the time by some plains-based activists as being a ploy to sideline the Adivasi groups and Madheshi castes who lived in the border belt while offsetting any geopolitical risks posed by India (Jha, 2014). Regardless of the intentions, the highway arguably shifted the gravity of economic activity away from the historically settled tract in the south while simultaneously contributing to the prosperity of the new settlements of owner-cultivating Nepali speakers in the north who experienced improved access to markets, infrastructure and services (Rankin et al., 2017). In this context, the southern tract of the lowlands became economically peripheral, with the exception of Biratnagar itself and its adjacent industrial belt.

Migration from the hills continued into the 1970s and 1980s, although it is difficult to measure the exact numbers. However, there were concerns amongst officials over the rates of deforestation as the years passed, leading to confrontations with the authorities. The most serious incident occurred at Ramailo-Jhora in northern Morang district, where more than 4,000 landless hill people resisted police attempts to burn their huts and force them out of the forest (Gaige, 1976). Confrontations also took place due to encroachment on private forest land, leading to clashes in Jhapa in the 1970s (Ojha, 1983). It was in this context that the government restricted any future clearance of the forest frontier – which was now reduced to a narrow strip in northern Morang close to the East–West Highway.

Forest, Land and Ethnic Relations

A number of politically contentious questions remain over the relationship between the hill settlers and the indigenous groups of the plains. Hachhethu (2007) notes that the primary losers from internal migration were the plains Adivasis. Indeed, Gaige's (1976) study notes that hill Brahmins and Chettris preferred to migrate to regions home to plains indigenous groups such as the western Tarai (for example, Dang, Kailali and Kanchanpur) and Morang,

Sunsari and Jhapa. He also suggests that they would avoid areas adjacent to Madheshi high castes and intermediate castes, given the greater difficulties in competing for economic resources and political power in these regions. Gaige notes that the indigenous groups of the plains were more likely to borrow money without understanding consequences, and many rapidly lost their land to the new hill settlers. Many of the Nepali-speaking upper-caste settlers, by contrast, had access to capital, higher education and knowledge of or links to the bureaucracy, making it easier for them to clear larger estates (Gaige, 1976).

This may help to explain the fact that most settlers of the Morang forests were from the hills, unlike the Mithilanchal belt of the central Tarai-Madhesh, where Gaige suggests that a majority of settlers on the forest belt were plains castes from further south. The unequal interactions between plains Adivasi (particularly the Tharu) and wealthier hill settlers have been well documented in the western Tarai and Chitwan valley (Krauskopff, 1989; Müller-Böker, 1999). The rapid clearing of the forest and migration of hill people adjacent to Tharu settlements culminated in loss of land due to debt and deception (Krauskopff, 1989) and created the environment for deeply exploitative systems such as bonded labour, or *kamaiya*, to emerge (Maycock, 2012; Dhakal, 2001).

However, in Morang, a more complex story emerges. The areas which were settled were to the north of most of the existing Adivasi population. The latter had already been heavily subordinated to the absentee landlords of the hills from the Rana era. Panchayat-era losses of land were not so much to new settlers from the hills, but to the old landlords expanding their estates or to urban dwellers buying land as an investment. Unlike in the western Tarai and Chitwan, a majority of the new settlers cleared their land from the jungle far from these long-established settlements (see Figure 3.6). There were nevertheless unequal relations between settlers and the Dhimal, a comparatively smaller indigenous group whose homeland was within the dense jungles of northern Morang and Jhapa which were cleared in the 1960s, and many experienced alienations from their land (see Rai, 2013, 2015). Similarly, unequal relations between new settlers and the more sizeable indigenous groups such as the Tharu, Rajbanshi and Gangai were evident in the villages that were on the pre-1960s forest fringe. One such example was Dhaniya, in the east of the district, which was once on the edge of the forest. Oral histories collected from Dhaniya in 2012 suggested that it was much easier for the hill settlers to secure land than the local population. Attempts by the indigenous Gangai to also clear forest land to set up new farms were often unsuccessful. Many did not know about the rules surrounding land reclamation until the hill people had already begun the resettlement, and few had the relatives or connections to the

Figure 3.6 Settlements on the forest fringe near Urlabari, north Morang. This was one of the most recent regions to have been settled from the hills, in the second half of the twentieth century. The region around Jhorahat was once similar in character before the felling of the remaining jungle.

Source: Author.

bureaucracy of their Brahmin and Chettri counterparts. In this context, they ended up working as wage labourers for the new settlers, but when they also tried to clear some land for themselves, officials would stop them, saying it was not open for settlement. Some also reported being threatened by the new settlers.

The Trajectory of Industrial Development in Morang: 1951–1990

Expansion of the Morang–Sunsari Industrial Belt

In parallel with the consolidation of feudalism with absentee landlords at the apex of the agrarian structure in southern Morang and the emergence of an owner-cultivating peasantry in northern Morang, both modes of production – although particularly the former – saw growing articulations with capitalism. From the 1950s onwards, there was a slow wave of industrial development across Nepal.

While some industries were concentrated in the Birgunj area in the central Tarai, a large number of the Tarai industries were concentrated in the Morang region, and it soon emerged as one of the main industrial belts of Nepal. There were three primary industrial areas – the first was concentrated around the Indian border at Jogbani, south of Biratnagar and close to the old industries from the Rana era, such as the Biratnagar Jute Mills. The second extended northward from Biratnagar towards Itahari in Sunsari district, to the west of the field site. The second smaller belt was north of the field site and extended eastwards from Biratnagar towards the old district capital of Rangeli. The industrial sector in Morang was slow to get off the ground. With reference to Biratnagar in the 1950s, Regmi (1977) notes how, with often outdated machinery, local manufacturers could not develop the productive forces to levels sufficient to compete with the cheaper commodities being imported from India. They were restricted by a lack of forward and backward linkages, such as an absence of appropriate sources of credit and an inability to procure spare parts (Regmi, 1977), as well as obsolete and often second-hand equipment (R. S. Pradhan, 1984; Regmi, 1977). There was a lack of adequate maintenance facilities and skills, while due to energy shortages, factories depended upon diesel and coal imported from India (Regmi, 1977). Early hydropower schemes set up in the Rana era, such as one in the hills of northern Morang itself on the Chisang river, stopped operation in the 1960s due to a landslide, and while the First Five Year Plan (1956–1961) aimed to add 20 megawatts of capacity, this failed to be met, and it was only much later in the Panchayat era that significant capacity was added (D. Adhikari, 2006).

Despite these persisting challenges, which were to signal a long-term trend of distorted growth, the number of manufacturing enterprises in the Morang region further expanded during the Panchayat era. State-run enterprises continued to be established alongside a profusion of smaller, privately owned industries focused mainly on the processing of agricultural produce. As of 1962, 72 per cent of Nepal's 1,686 privately owned smaller industries were situated in the Tarai-Madhesh (Gaige, 1976). While many were established by Indian businesses extending their investments over the border to avoid excise taxes and to be closer to raw materials, there were also notable investments by hill Brahmins and Chettris with capital, alongside the Marwari business community which was becoming well established in Biratnagar (Gaige, 1976). Business regulations, however, were tight, and often, as Shakya (2018) notes in her study of the textile sector, political connections were necessary to establish successful enterprises. Early industrial development strategy had protectionist elements in line with the dominant development thinking of the era (Khatri, 2018). In this context, efforts at establishing import-substitution manufacturing in the 1970s (including state-run enterprises) had some initial impact on the economy by facilitating an increased supply of domestic manufactured goods (FAO, 2003).

It is in this context that off-farm labour in the industrial sector became more prevalent from the Panchayat era in southern rural Morang, and represented a first concrete articulation with the capitalist mode of production via wage labour. With growing rural monetisation, rising debt and persistent landlessness and the rent burden, the Adivasi peasantry of southern Morang provided a large captive labour force for the emerging industries in the region. However, the levels of employment remained modest, and thus it had only a limited impact on the feudal mode of production within which a majority of the workers operated. A recorded 7,538 people were employed in factories in the far-eastern Tarai (which includes Sunsari, Morang and Jhapa) as of 1964–1965 (Goil, 1972). While this represented the highest level of industrial employment of all the regions in Nepal, it is still a relatively small number given the size of the population in these three districts, which as of 1971 was 762,087 (H. Gurung, 1981). The vast majority worked in agro-processing industries where work was more seasonal and unskilled, with 4,294 employees working in jute mills alone[25] as per the 1964–1965 data (Goil, 1972). Rather than drawing farmers out of agriculture, industrial employment for the peasantry could be read as a classic 'articulation' of modes of production, whereby marginal and tenant farmers would have family members working periodically in factories as well as other menial jobs in Biratnagar – a phenomena which would remain entrenched up until the present day.

Industry, Imperialism and the Semi-colony

This trajectory of industrial development in Morang, and across Nepal, which fails to draw its population out of agriculture, was typical of many social formations subordinate to imperialism. As noted earlier, Nepal has been described as a semi-colony, or *ardha-upanivesh*, in the context of the colonial era, whereby it was officially sovereign yet still subjugated to colonial relations with the British empire. This term took on a new meaning in the mid-twentieth century when peripheral states became independent, yet their economies remained structured to serve imperialism.

Before understanding what this means for Nepal, it is useful to briefly cover what independence meant for the larger economy to the south – that of India. Marxian scholars established that after India became independent, it made a transition from the status of 'colony' to that of 'semi-colony'. In the Indian context, the economy was characterised by an industrial sector lacking forward and backward linkages which was dependent on foreign capital for technical resources and capital goods (Ghosh, 1983; Lin, 1980). De Janvry (1981) described this phenomena (with regard to Latin America) as 'sectoral disarticulation' – whereby the economy is distorted by imperialism, and enterprises operate as independent units, dependent on imported machinery for production or sending products abroad for further processing.[26] In the context of India it was argued that this had blocked the organic development of capitalist industry and was closely tied with the persistence of feudalism in rural areas (Ghosh, 1983).

While it is clear that the post-independence Indian economy remained semi-colonial in character, the development of the productive forces in industry was still relatively more developed than in Nepal, with the presence of a wider range of industries beyond just agro-processing, particularly in the context of India's post-independence import-substitution policies and heavy state support (N. S. Singh, 1997). Nepal lacked forward and backward linkages to an even greater extent than the post-colonial Indian economy, and Nepali enterprises simply could not compete with the cheaper variants being imported from the south, either directly from India itself or via India from overseas (Blaikie et al., 2001; FAO, 2003; Regmi, 1977). The difficulties competing with foreign industry in this context prevented the generation of capital to develop the productive forces, further reducing their competitiveness and increasing levels of sectoral disarticulation. This was worsened by the lack of a sufficient 'home market' (Bhattarai, 2003a) and a legacy of political alliances hostile to domestic industrialisation which had put Nepal-based enterprises at a severe disadvantage in a competitive regional economy (Regmi, 1977).

Baburam Bhattarai, the former Maoist leader, extensively documented the semi-colonial structure of Nepalese economy in the Panchayat era. He observed that the organic composition of capital in Nepali manufacturing industry remained low when compared to other countries, preventing increases in the productivity of labour. It was recorded that the capital–labour ratio in manufacturing increased only by 14.1 per cent between 1965 and 1976–1977. In the same period meanwhile, there was a 5 per cent decline in the proportion of the total capital invested in machines and assets, with capital being predominantly invested in sectors such as construction (Bhattarai, 2003a). As of 1974–1975, only 9 per cent of the value added to industry was made up of metal industries, which included all of the 'capital goods' such as machinery – in stark contrast to the 53 per cent of value added that was derived from processing food crops such as rice and sugar. Niitsu et al. (1983) note that imports of machinery and transportation equipment accounted for an estimated 20 per cent of Nepal's total imports, and three quarters of the machinery and equipment investment by local industries was imported. Even a large share of raw materials had to be brought from India, representing a significant burden for newly established enterprises (Niitsu et al., 1983).

Structural dependence on imports and a lack of organic forward and backward linkages were aggravated by persistent weak energy supply, skill shortages, poor transportation infrastructure, and the absence of any tariff barriers to protect local industries (Niitsu et al., 1983). In 1974–1975, the manufacturing sector contributed to just 4.2 per cent of Nepal's gross domestic product (GDP) (Karan and Ishil, 1996). Set against this context of distorted industrial growth, the primarily agricultural-focused industries in the Morang region depended on the large pool of surplus labour in surrounding villages, but the wages and levels of employment generation were by no means sufficient to undermine the dependence of the Adivasi peasantry on landlords for their subsistence.

Economic Liberalisation and Its Implication for Agriculture and Industry: 1990s–2020s

Political Transformation and the Reproduction of Landlordism

The infiltration of capitalism into rural Morang intensified in the 1990s – a period of tremendous political change which coincided with Nepal's economic liberalisation. Following a popular uprising against the monarchy, democracy was restored in 1991. This precipitated some reconfiguration of power in Kathmandu and the emergence of some neo-elites, although the political culture and structure of the state remained hierarchical and amenable to the continued concentration of wealth. The vast majority of leaders in the newly formed political parties were from the dominant Nepali-speaking Brahmin and Chettri communities of the hills, who had held political and economic privileges during the Rana and Panchayat eras, and were disproportionately represented in the vast bureaucracy (Baral, 2012). What was particularly notable though was how political parties, like the bureaucracy itself, rapidly replicated feudal social relations, particularly through patron–client relationships which mediated access to resources (Pfaff-Czarnecka, 2008; Joshi and Mason, 2011).

This change is also reflected in terms of actual relations of production on the ground in rural Morang. The restoration of democracy had limited impact on the land ownership structure. Even though there were some new political elites who rose the economic ladder with the emergence of party politics, some of the landed classes who amassed their wealth during the Panchayat or Rana era in Morang were to become part of Nepal's emerging party politics. Biratnagar itself emerged as an important political hub in the east, and the Nepali Congress party that led Nepal for much of the 1990s and 2000s had a strong base in the region. It was noted in oral history interviews how leaders from across the political spectrum had estates in the Morang countryside of varying sizes, and their control over land at times has helped strengthen their political influence.

This process has been well documented by Joshi and Mason (2007), whereby peasants would vote for the parties favoured by their landlords, as they were dependent upon them for land and access to state resources – even if it meant that they were voting against their 'class interests'. In the case of Morang, many landlords themselves were political representatives, but there were likely other ways through which landed interests were maintained – through, for instance, landlords courting the local leaders of parties that represented their interests and encouraging the poor peasantry to vote for them. This helps explain election results after the 1990s. While mainstream communist parties such as the Communist Party of Nepal (United Marxist Leninist) advocated land reforms and formed a short-lived government in the mid-1990s, its commitment was vague and the party itself had the support of some landlords. They failed to win subsequent elections. The parties which had a more radical land reform agenda – including the forerunners to the Communist Party of Nepal (Maoist) – performed poorly in elections (Joshi and Mason, 2007).

Even leaving aside the role of political parties in perpetuating landlordism, high-ranking members of the bureaucracy still held land in the Morang countryside, some inherited from the Rana period and some purchased more recently – and this was not changed by the transition to multi-party politics.

Structural Adjustment and the 'Semi-colony'

While it appeared that feudal landlordism was not undermined by political change in the centre, a remaining question was whether the structure of

Nepal's economy and the class interests it perpetuated were still 'semi-colonial' in character. An observation of the impact of economic liberalisation that went alongside the restoration of democracy in many ways answers this question. Nepal underwent its first phase of economic reforms in 1984–1985, with a structural adjustment loan from the IMF, set against the backdrop of budget deficits and balance-of-payment problems (Khanal et al., 2005; Pyakuryal et al., 2010). Reforms continued into the 1990s under the new elected government (Blaikie et al., 2001), in line with the global neoliberal turn. In this context, Nepal had removed the few trade barriers that existed for domestic industry (Shakya, 2018), thus signalling an end to largely unsuccessful efforts at import substitution. There was meanwhile even greater emphasis on the export of primary goods such as agricultural produce (Deraniyagala et al., 2003). Alongside this was reduced public spending and encouragement for private enterprise in service provision such as healthcare and education (Deraniyagala et al., 2003).

While three decades of economic liberalisation did support an increase in the number of large (employing more than 10 individuals) manufacturing establishments across Nepal, which rose from 4,271 in 1991–1992 to 5,017 in 2018–2019 (Central Bureau of Statistics, 2022), the disarticulated structure of industry identified by Bhattarai (2003a), which was present in the 1960s and 1970s, appears to still be in place. To the political left in Nepal, economic liberalisation simply represented the latest phase of imperialist domination and an intensification of Nepal's position as a semi-colony (Tamang, 2018). While the industrial base was increasingly diverse, moving beyond agro-processing alone, production was still dominated by low-value consumer goods. As of 2006–2007, two decades after structural adjustment, the Census of Manufacturing Industries suggested consumer non-durable goods such as food, textiles and apparel represented a substantial 52 per cent of the total value of manufacturing output and 65 per cent of the value added (see Table 3.1). This had decreased to 36 per cent of the output and 33 per cent of the value added according to data in the 2019–2020 National Industrial Survey (see Table 3.2), with an increase in consumer durable goods (long-lasting finished products), which predominantly included rubber or plastic products and furniture.

Intermediate goods, which include semi-complete inputs for industry such as timber, glass and metal building materials, represented 35 per cent of the total value of output and 21 per cent of the value added – with a small increase in 2019–2020 to 37 per cent of the value of the output and

Table 3.1 Use-based classification of manufacturing industries 2006–2007

Industry type	No. of establishments	No. of employees	Gross fixed assets at year's end (000s NPR)	Value of output (000s NPR)	% total value of output	Total value added (000s NPR)	% total value added
Consumer non-durable goods	1	126,626	52,219	87,786	52%	26,668	65%
Consumer durable goods	301	4,258	699	1,430	0.009%	507	0.01%
Intermed. goods	672	28,699	10,316	58,013	35%	8,714	21%
Basic goods	207	7,729	9,688	20,586	12%	4,795	12%
Capital goods	4	No data	No data	No data	No data	No data	No data
Other	20	538	234	142	0.0008%	56	0.001%
Total	3,290	167,853	73,155	167,815	100%	40,740	100%

Source: Adapted from the Central Bureau of Statistics 2006–2007 Census of Manufacturing Establishments (Nepal Rastra Bank, 2018).

Table 3.2 Use-based classification of manufacturing industries 2019–2020

Industry type	No. of establishments	No. of employees	Gross fixed assets at end of year (000s NPR)	Value of output (000s NPR)	% total value of output	Total value added (000s NPR)	% of total value added
Consumer non-durable goods	29,274	111,655	183,310,271	433,699,580	36.11	117,426,617	33.13
Consumer durable goods	7,153	34,343	35,897,341	87,055,308	7.25	25,484,659	7.19
Intermed. goods	10,486	189,920	147,543,463	441,652,780	36.80	134,632,037	37.98
Basic goods	4,845	35,184	238,218,337	155,916,718	12.98	55,579,888	15.68
Capital goods	469	1,934	2,306,541	4,337,398	0.36	1,520,869	0.43
Other	7,956	8,642	12,225,076	78,466,050	6.53	19,835,119	5.60
Total	60,183	381,678	619,501,029	1,201,127,834	100	354,479,189	100.00

Source: Adapted from the National Industrial Survey 2019–2020.

38 per cent of the value added – likely fuelled by the expanding construction sector – a theme dealt with later in the book. As of 2019–2020, capital goods (which would increase the long-term productive capacity of the industrial sector through reduced 'sectoral disarticulation') represent a mere 0.36 per cent of the value of output and 0.43 per cent of the value added. Machinery and mechanical appliances still represent 16.3 per cent of Nepal's total imports (Central Bureau of Statistics, 2021a), representing just a small drop from the 1970s. In the Morang and neighbouring Sunsari, as of 2011–2012 (when the most recent district-level data was available), 30 per cent and 40 per cent respectively of manufacturing was composed of food, beverage and tobacco industries. Thirty-seven per cent and 23.1 per cent respectively was composed of non-durable consumer goods such as textiles, wood, paper and plastic products. Most remaining manufacturing was of intermediate goods such as construction materials and chemicals as well as furniture (Central Bureau of Statistics, 2014b). Recent data (2021) points to a similar picture for the Morang–Sunsari industrial corridor. The large industries are dominated by jute (17.57 million tonnes annual output) and food processing (218,412 tonnes), followed by packaging materials and bottles (108,412.5).[27]

The industrial sector in both Morang and Nepal more broadly remains subservient to foreign capital. A drain of profits through foreign direct investment (FDI) after liberalisation has been cited as contributing to a continued distortion of domestic industry and underdevelopment in low- and middle-income countries (see, for example, Mosala, 2021, on Kenya). However, in Nepal, foreign investment has been relatively low compared to the region, with FDI net inflows (2016) at just 2 per cent of GDP when compared to the South Asian average of 6.3 per cent (Bikas Udhyami, 2019), and only 15 per cent of FDI was invested in manufacturing as of 2018[28] (Nepal Rastra Bank, 2018). However, as Khanal et al. (2005) argues in his analysis of the post-1990s industrial structure, even when firms themselves were locally owned and established using domestic capital, inputs as well as machinery and tools were often imported, representing a drain of profits abroad, and many industries therefore were, in effect, individual units of production with relatively limited *domestic* forward and backward linkages. Furthermore, many of the business houses which have invested in industries are simultaneously engaged in the import and distribution of intermediate and capital goods as well as consumer goods for direct sale in the domestic market – a phenomenon which will be discussed later (Lamsal and Pande, 2018).

The distorted pattern of growth was aggravated by the removal of trade barriers following liberalisation, which paved the way for a surge in imported commodities and intensifying competition for local manufacturers (Khanal et al., 2005). As with before, imports from India were dominant, representing 64.95 per cent of the total imports as of 2017. Imports from China also rose considerably, three quarters of which were consumer goods, and as of 2017 represent 12.63 per cent of the total (World Bank, 2019). As one would expect, a context of rising imports and only modest growth in manufacturing has resulted in an intensifying trade deficit for Nepal throughout the last decade. Nepal had a negative trade balance of USD 2.8 billion in 2011–2012, and this had grown to USD 9.92 billion by 2017–2018 (Department of Customs, 2018), particularly driven by the imports of capital goods and construction materials (Asian Development Bank, 2019). During this period exports rose by 29 per cent , yet imports rose by a substantial 69 per cent . The national trade deficit reached 52.4 per cent of GDP in 2019, up from 28.3 per cent in 2010 (Central Bureau of Statistics, 2021a). In the Morang region itself, which is one of the main industrial regions in Nepal, the Biratnagar customs point exported USD 210 million worth of goods – representing a 30 per cent share of Nepal's exports. However, this same border crossing imported USD 1.3 billion worth of goods (Department of Customs, 2018).

Some industrial sectors actually went into decline after liberalisation. These include small-scale cottage industries (Khanal et al., 2005), but also once lager scale industries large employed large numbers of workers such as textiles. The textile industry showed a dramatic decline in the share of value added in the Nepali economy from 25.9 per cent to 3.8 per cent between 1991–1992 and 2011–2012. The decline in this sector is well documented by Shakya (2018) and demonstrates the vulnerability of the sector to shifts in global markets.[29] Some domestic manufacturing ventures also suffered during the 2000s and 2010s due to chronic power shortages – although there was some moderate recovery by 2018, with a small increase in the number of establishments, as electricity supply improved (Asian Development Bank, 2019). Nevertheless, in Morang, the decline in local industry was a common narrative which emerged in interviews between 2018 and 2023. The most notable decline was in once important agro-processing industries such as jute. Five out of 11 jute mills in Nepal had closed, the majority of which were in the Biratnagar region, and cultivation has dropped considerably.[30] An interview with an industrialist in the Morang–Sunsari industrial belt noted that while the industrial sector was not 'in decline', there was limited growth, with producers struggling with consistent competition from India and China (particularly of unregulated imports from India along the open border), the high cost of finance in Nepal, the lack of the required skills and technical knowhow, and consistent power supply problems. These challenges were also confirmed in a Morang Chamber of Industries (2021) report.[31] Also important is a shift in the centre of gravity for industry towards Birgunj in the central Tarai which is close to Kathmandu, and Butwal-Bhairahawa in the western Tarai which is closer to the more prosperous districts of Nepal and the industrially developed western states of India.

The structure of industry and the country's position in the global capitalist economy suggest that the Nepal's status as a 'semi-colonial' social formation has not changed dramatically. When one observes what this means for class relations at a national level though, and the composition of the dominant class in the urban capitalist sector, a more complex picture emerges. As has taken place globally, economic liberalisation in Nepal was associated with deepening inequalities, with rising incomes for some groups, albeit heavily concentrated in urban areas (Khanal and Bracarense, 2020). While it is beyond the scope of this book to analyse in detail who is 'accumulating' wealth in the urban capitalist sector since liberalisation, any 'national bourgeoise' in the Marxian sense is small. Baburam Bhattarai, writing in the early 2000s suggested that domestic merchant capital in Nepal, which may have (outside of a semi-colonial context) been transformed into national industrial capital, is instead developing into comprador merchant capital focused on importing commodities. He suggests that merchant capital was playing a greater role in the Nepali economy than ever before, but rather than being oriented around internal trade, it was focused on imports, capturing what little there was of a home market within Nepal for consumables (Bhattarai, 2003b).

Bhattarai also suggested that the state actively upholds the control of merchant capital over the economy – noting that as of the early 2000s, a third of the state's budget revenue came from trade, in particular tariffs on imports. When this includes sales tax also, this rises to 60 per cent, and hence he argues that the bureaucracy was itself largely dependent on merchant capital – and thus serves its interests (Bhattarai, 2003b), just as was the case during the late Rana period when trade replaced land tax as the primary source of revenue. Looking at more recent data – the structure of government revenue appears to have changed little. Revenue from income tax has risen from around 22 per cent in 2000 to just over a quarter in 2021–2022. However, tax on imports still represents a substantial 23 per cent of the government's revenue. Value added tax (VAT) (which replaced the earlier sales tax) makes up 26 per cent, and excise duty meanwhile makes up 15 per cent (UNICEF, 2021) – although Bhoosal and Byanjankar (2022) note that a large share of both these revenue streams are collected through imports. This highlights the continued importance of comprador merchant capital to the bureaucracy. Even if one moves beyond the classic Marxist literature on the 'comprador bourgeoise', it is clear that state patronage to uphold an import-oriented economy subservient to foreign capital is a widespread phenomenon in peripheral economies – as Marshall (2002), for instance, notes with regard to the Eastern Caribbean – whereby an alliance between the state and merchant capital, particularly in import trading, generates high yields for the government in taxes, while businesses benefit from political patronage for low-risk commercial investments which yield short-term gains, but little in the way of long-term growth (see also Mosala, 2021, on Kenya).

Arguably, the 'comprador' character of the dominant class in the capitalist sector has increased after liberalisation, particularly as demand for imported luxuries increases, and Nepal's trade deficit grows. In fact, there is growing diversity in the investment portfolio of the capitalist class more broadly. First, both merchant and industrial capitalists are investing in finance as well as the service sector – which is where most growth has been located following economic liberalisation. In 1980, the contributions of the service sector was just 26 per cent of GDP, but this share rose dramatically to 57.6 per cent by 2018. During the same period, the contributions of industry to GDP dropped from 16 per cent to 14.2 per cent (Asian Development Bank, 2019). The value added by manufacturing specifically, as a percentage of GDP, declined from 7.1 per cent in 2011–2012 to 6.6 per cent in 2018–2019 (Central Bureau of Statistics, 2021a). The services subsectors that have experienced growth in Nepal include transport, storage and communications (value added of 4.8 per cent of GDP) and financial intermediation (6.6 per cent), education (6.5 per cent), and health (6.6 per cent) (Central Bureau of Statistics, 2014a). The explosion of privatised healthcare (Sapkota et al., 2020) and education (Sharma Poudyal, 2017) in particular, have significantly increased the expenditure of the rural population, as will be discussed later in the book. Mid- to higher-level employees of the service sector form a burgeoning middle class in cities such as Biratnagar – and their rising incomes contribute to demand for imported consumer goods.

What is also clear from this shift is that the capitalist class is itself increasingly diverse – and there is growing overlap between industrial, financial and merchant capital. Most of the factories in the Morang–Sunsari industrial belt as well as large retail and trading companies are owned by corporate groups, usually in the form of family-run 'business houses' with close political links (Upadhaya, 2020), which increasingly include investments in multiple sectors. An illustrative example is in an analysis of sectoral investments by 30 of the top business houses in Nepal, by a private sector monthly (see Table 3.3).

Table 3.3 Sectoral investment of 30 Nepali 'business houses'

Sectoral Investments	**No. of Business Houses**
Manufacturing only	1
Manufacturing, trade,* finance	1
Manufacturing, trade, services, finance, energy	3
Manufacturing, trade, finance, energy	1
Manufacturing, trade, services, energy	1
Manufacturing, trade and services	1
Manufacturing, trade, services, finance	1
Manufacturing, trade	1
Manufacturing, trade, finance	1
Manufacturing, finance, energy	1
Manufacturing, services, finance, energy	4
Manufacturing, Services, energy	1
Manufacturing, services, finance	2
Manufacturing, services and trade	2
Manufacturing and finance	1
Manufacturing and trade	1
Services and energy	1
Services, finance and energy,	4
Trade, services, finance and energy	1
Total	29**

Source: Lamsal and Pande (2018).

Notes: *Trade refers broadly to what may fall within the category of merchant capital – that is, retail or wholesale trade, and the import of commodities.

**One of the 30 omitted due to missing data.

A deeper analysis of the data in this article shows that while there are some business houses which have traditionally been associated with manufacturing (particularly those owned by the Marwari community[32]), these companies increasingly have investments in finance as well as trade – which usually revolve around importing luxuries to supplement what cannot be produced in their own enterprises or importing capital and intermediate goods to service other industries. They have also been joined by a more diverse group of companies owned mostly by hill upper castes, with investments spread across multiple sectors – with hydropower being a common investment – and one which generates government revenue, but little by the way of employment.

The list in Table 3.3 of course just gives a small sample of companies – but it offers an insight into the trajectory of change. Thus, not only is merchant capital failing to be transformed into industrial capital as Bhattarai (2003b) had warned. But, instead, industrial capital is increasingly overlapping with merchant capital – and this appears even more understandable in light of the challenging investment environment for manufacturing. It also re-emphasises the fact that the capitalist class is increasingly diverse, yet is largely subservient to foreign capital – and retains its comprador character. Any growth in large-scale manufacturing beyond agro-processing appears highly doubtful in the years ahead.

The remaining question which will be covered at multiple points in subsequent chapters (especially Chapter 7) is: what does the evolving character of capitalism in Nepal mean for the Morang peasantry and for landlordism? What is important to emphasise at this point is that the post-liberalisation context likely supported only a moderate increase in industrial employment – and like in the Panchayat era, this by no means drew the peasantry away from agriculture.

In discussions over India's semi-colonial growth trajectory in the 1970s, it was argued that a critical outcome of sectoral disarticulation was the failure of capitalist manufacturing to absorb the rural labour force (Ghosh, 1983). In Nepal as a whole, the employment share in industry (which represents 14 per cent of contributions to GDP) is just 11.8 per cent (Asian Development Bank, 2019), and within this manufacturing forms an even smaller share. The diversification of investment into the service sector over manufacturing itself represents a further dwindling in the capacity of the Nepali social formation to generate employment. As Kar (2018) notes with regard to India, a burgeoning service sector after liberalisation does not undermine the overall semi-colonial, semi-feudal structure of the national economy. Neither services nor manufacturing has the capacity to absorb the labour of the rural poor to the level that these forms of external employment would undermine feudalism in the countryside. Employment growth in India is thus primarily for the better-educated social groups (Harriss-White and Gooptu, 2009).

In Nepal, this is also reflected in employment data. For instance, the Annual Household Survey of 2014–2015 demonstrates that the employment share of services is just 18.8 per cent, in spite of it making up 58 per cent of the contributions to GDP, unlike industry where these two figures are proportionate to each other (11.8 per cent and 14 per cent respectively). Many of the jobs in the key services subsectors such as health, education, real estate and banks require higher levels of education and are thus out of reach to large segments of the peasantry. The only area where some employment has been generated is construction, which has in part been spurred on by growth in the service sector – a change discussed in Chapter 7. While construction represented only 8.1 per cent of the national employment share as of the 2021 census (Central Bureau of Statistics, 2021b), it is of growing importance in the Morang region due to the vicinity of Biratnagar. The size of the construction industry increased by 48.1 per cent from 2011–2012 to 2018–2019 (Central Bureau of Statistics, 2021a)

Also of concern in Nepal is that much of the growth even within services is in 'non-tradable' sectors such as the rental of property (office and home space) and real estate investment, which fail to generate employment at all. Real estate represents 19.7 per cent of the gross value added among service industries in Nepal, second only to retail and wholesale which make up 23 per cent (Asian Development Bank, 2019). This has been noticeable even in the countryside around the Jhorahat field site, particularly along the road towards Biratnagar – where land (often belonging to landlords) has been set aside to sell for future residential units, a practice known locally as 'plotting'.

The shifting patterns of capital investment were evident in the case of a factory site, on the road towards Biratnagar from the core field site. There had once been a carpet factory there. It operated for 9 to 10 years, but due to poor market prices it shifted to making pashminas, and later sweaters. It eventually closed its doors due to high competition and poor market prices. The 7 *bigha*s (4.76 hectares) on which the factory was situated has now been sold to real estate speculators and is being turned into plots by four separate land brokers, with additional plots having been bought from absentee landlords who owned the adjacent land. An interview with a prominent industrialist in Biratnagar highlighted that in the context of a risky investment environment and intense competition with imported goods from India and China, many individuals in Biratnagar with capital prefer to invest their money 'non-productively' in sectors such as property or land buying and selling. In fact, the report on top business houses cited earlier indicated that many had also invested capital in housing colonies and commercial real estate (Lamsal and Pande, 2018).

Market Expansion and Failed Agricultural Commercialisation

While the articulations with capitalism in the Morang region were primarily through the supply of labour for industries, it is worth also briefly reviewing articulations between feudal and peasant modes of production through agricultural markets after economic liberalisation. A central pillar of Nepal's agricultural development strategy in the post-1990s context was the 1996–2016 Agriculture Perspective Plan (APP), which outlined a 20-year plan for rapid agricultural growth and prosperity through encouraging smallholders to shift from subsistence production to the production of high-value, market-orientated agricultural produce (APROSC, 1995). The plan sought to model Nepal's agrarian transformation on the 'success' of Punjab and Himachal Pradesh, which took advantage of each region's comparative advantage for commercial agriculture to unleash market-led growth. It was based heavily on the economist John Mellor's study of these two regions (Mellor, 1976) – whose consultancy was involved in drafting the plan.

While elements of the plan were influenced by pre-liberalisation state developmentalism (for example, emphasis on state spending on infrastructure for agricultural growth), it was largely a neoliberal strategy. The plan itself was part of a larger donor-led shift in priority in low-income countries in the 1990s and 2000s, which viewed export-led small-scale agriculture as a driver of development – rather than plantation-style agriculture which characterised the colonial era, or import-substitution industrialisation which characterised the post-colonial era. This shift towards a small-farm-led growth strategy, which Ellis and Biggs (2001) term the 'small farm paradigm', was central to the 2008 *World Development Report* mentioned in Chapter 2 (World Bank, 2008),[33] which emphasised that countries should focus on production of high-value agricultural commodities and labour-intensive agro-products as per their 'comparative advantage'. In the case of Nepal, this entailed making the most of the country's altitudinal diversity and wide range of agro-ecological niches (APROSC, 1995; Nepal National Planning Commission, 2004). Furthermore, the APP itself buys into an ideology of 'self-help' (Sugden, 2009), whereby in the context of privatisation and cutbacks in state spending, the poor are expected to find their own solutions to their livelihood needs through utilising their skills and resources to 'seize' the opportunities made available by the global economy (Rankin, 2001, 2004).

In the case of the Tarai, the focus was on the commercial production of grain for the domestic market, as well as niche cash crops such as jute in the case of Morang. The hypothesis was that commercial growth in agriculture and rising incomes would, through a multiplier effect, stimulate non-agricultural growth in employment-intensive industries, including agro-processing. The focus was on rolling out 'priority inputs', including the building of roads which would expand agricultural markets, irrigation to boost yields and rural electrification which would cheapen the use of farm equipment. Further priority inputs included 'fertiliser', with initiatives to improve the supply of quality nutrients, and 'technology', with an emphasis on improved research and extension, and provision of credit (APROSC, 1995).

The APP ended not long after the promulgation of the new constitution in 2015, and was replaced by the Agricultural Development Strategy (ADS) in 2016. Some of the APP targets were close to being met, such as those associated with transport infrastructure. However, on the whole, the transformation in the sector which the plan envisaged remained elusive (Cameron et al., 2016). The ADS in terms of its overall aims differed little from the APP – and there was considerable focus again on market-oriented production, with one of the strategic components being 'profitable commercialisation', alongside improved governance, higher productivity (through, for instance, improved inputs and climate-resilient technologies) and increased competitiveness (through, for example, building upon comparative advantage and creating an investment-friendly climate) (Ministry of Agricultural Development, 2015).

While it is too early to gauge the impact of the ADS, the limited success of the APP has been widely discussed (Cameron et al., 2016; Khanal et al., 2020). Economic liberalisation itself had paradoxically for many farmers undermined the goals of Nepal's commercialisation drive (Cameron et al., 2016a). Many of the tariffs and restrictions on imports of agricultural products had been removed, with agricultural tariffs being the lowest in South Asia in the early 2000s (Pyakuryal et al., 2010). This put farmers at considerable disadvantage when compared to their counterparts across the border in India, where the stronger developmental state in the latter offered a greater level of support for farmers, even after liberalisation (Sugden, 2009). This was particularly relevant in the case of the Morang region, where unlike in the hills with its unique agro-ecological niches, Tarai farmers lacked any 'comparative advantage' against Indian producers further south in the Gangetic plains. Added to this was a substantial drop in public spending in agriculture, from 30 per cent of state spending in the 1970s to just 4.87 per cent by 2017–2018 (Joshi and Khanal, 2020). The Morang region saw cutbacks in agricultural extension, with the number of service centres reduced by half.

A deeper problem of Nepal's agricultural growth strategy was that it made an assumption that the peasantry is made up of small, independent land-owning peasants who, with access to infrastructure and markets, could unleash their entrepreneurial potential (Sugden, 2009; Roka, 2017). This overlooks the deeply entrenched pre-capitalist forms of exploitation and the vast inequalities in the distribution of land and assets, which impedes farmers from producing any saleable surplus – a theme dealt with at length in Chapter 6. With reference to the ADS, for instance, Roka (2017) notes that the strategy ignores the structural causes of poverty, and the East Asian agricultural growth models cited in the ADS ironically were rooted in the egalitarian distribution of holdings following land reforms – interventions which in rural Morang and much of the Tarai had been unsuccessful.

While articulations with capitalism via the sale of commodities is relatively low, where these articulations are increasing across the rural far-eastern Tarai is via consumer markets. In part, this was facilitated by improved rural infrastructure. While across Nepal only 9,000 kilometres of roads were constructed between 1951 and 1993, 8,000 kilometres of road were built between 1993 and 2004 (Baral, 2012). However, rather than infrastructure stimulating rural industrial or agricultural development, it accelerated the expansion of markets for consumer goods into peripheral parts of the country (Sugden et al., 2018). Alongside a rising trend towards consumerism (Baral, 2012; Liechty, 2003), expanding availability of consumer goods has contributed to a long-established trend towards monetisation in rural areas.

In the Morang field site, there was reportedly no proper road to Biratnagar during the early Panchayat era, and farmers had to take a circuitous route, via Katahari (see Figure 3.7). To sell grain it would take one day in an ox cart, through rivers and often waterlogged paths, with farmers returning the next day. Travelling Marwaris would go from house to house to sell clothing and household goods. The improvement in infrastructure, however, in the subsequent years facilitated an expansion of markets with greater access to consumer goods from Indian and local industries. *Bazaar*s developed along the blacktopped road linking Jhorahat with Biratnagar to the south and the highway to the north (see Figure 3.8). While this made it easier for farmers to

Figure 3.7 Crossing the Lohandra river to transport grain to the market. Weak rural transport infrastructure makes it more challenging for farmers to access markets, a situation which has changed rapidly in the last few decades.

Source: Author.

Figure 3.8 The Biratnagar to Jhorahat road. The blacktopping of roads such as this in the 1990s and 2000s has made it considerably easier for farmers to travel to and from the town for work and to sell agricultural produce.

Source: Author.

access the urban labour and agricultural produce market, it also precipitated the monetisation of the rural economy and rising demand for cash and consumer goods – a topic which will be dealt with in Chapter 7.

The Remittance Economy

A notable change which coincided with economic liberalisation was a substantial rise in labour migration. This will be explored in much more detail in Chapters 7 and 8 although it is worth briefly touching upon this change now, given that it was closely connected with the rising costs of production and soaring demand for cash.

As of the 1981 census, there were 402,977 Nepalese household members classed as 'absentee' – many of whom were in India. The 1990s saw the opening-up of new opportunities for cyclical labour migration to overseas destinations. Of particular significance was the rising demand for labour from Gulf governments in the early 1990s and the aftermath of the Gulf war. These states sought a cheap workforce on temporary contracts, who were culturally separated from their own citizens. They also sought workers who were non-aligned to the political fissures of the Arab world which were perceived as a threat by the ruling monarchies, which at the time threatened the ruling elites (Chalcraft, 2010; Hanieh, 2010). The peasantry from countries such as Nepal, therefore, offered these states an ideal temporary labour force. Their labour power could be reproduced through the agrarian system at home, keeping wages depressed, while short-term contracts would ensure their mobility remains cyclical and they retain links to their home communities (Sugden, 2019). Since the 1990s, therefore, migration rose rapidly to countries such as Qatar, Saudi Arabia and Kuwait. Malaysia also emerged as an important recruiter for Nepalese labour around this period (Sharma et al., 2014) due to the demand for low-wage labour in plantations and factories. Government policy in Nepal since the 1990s has actively facilitated this cyclical overseas migration through various foreign employment acts and bilateral treaties (Sijapati and Limbu, 2012).

By the 2011 census, overseas migration had increased more than fourfold to 1,921,494, and had reached 2.1 million, or nearly 7.4 per cent of the population, by 2021, with a large share in the Gulf states and Malaysia (MoLESS, 2022). The Department of Foreign Employment (DoFE), meanwhile, has as of 2022 issued over 4.7 million new approvals for Nepali workers to take up overseas employment since 2008–2009, and has renewed over 1.8 million approvals since 2011–2012 (MoLESS, 2022). How this change has been realised in

Morang will be explored in the final chapters. For the government, migration could be considered a 'safety valve' for youth, particularly when faced with a stagnant industrial sector and civil unrest (Wickramasekara, 2016). It also represents a parallel mechanism through which the pre-capitalist mode of production in Morang and elsewhere in Nepal articulates with capitalism.

Nepal's Political Awakening: A Transformation or Reconfiguration of Class Relations?

Thus far this chapter has reviewed the agricultural and industrial history of the Morang region, set against the larger political and economic changes unravelling across Nepal. The last two centuries have been marked, first, by the subordination of an Adivasi mode of production to centralised feudalism, via the combined processes of land tax, the clearing of the forest frontier and the creation of an indigenous elite. This has had a lasting legacy on the ground and has paved the way for the landlord–tenant relations that dominate the agrarian landscape today, with a clear class division between a landless and small landholder majority made up primarily of Adivasi groups, and a mostly hill upper-caste absentee landlord class – a structure explored in the next chapter. The last two centuries have, however, also seen shifting political alliances and relationships between ethnicity and class within this largely feudal social formation. The short-term prosperity of the Tharu landed class during the Rana period, whereby they formed a rural elite alongside the Brahmin and Chettri landed nobility from the hills, was rapidly reversed in the Panchayat era. Land reforms meanwhile, far from transforming class relations, served to consolidate absentee landlords at the apex of the agrarian structure. The primary segment of the peasantry who gained during this period were the settlers from the hills who established new farms free from the yoke of landlords on the fertile forest land to the north.

In synergy with these post-1960s agrarian changes was the emergence of an industrial belt which cut straight through the feudal heartlands of southern Morang. However, the industrial trajectory has paralleled that of the country more broadly, and is emblematic of a classic 'semi-colonial' economy – with a sector dominated by low-value agro-processing and consumer goods industries, which generate some employment, yet fail to draw significant shares of the labour force out of agriculture. Morang's industrial belt is now in relative decline, being eclipsed by the service sector in the wake of economic liberalisation. Simultaneously, efforts to unleash agriculture-led growth through commercial farming have been largely unsuccessful.

The skewed pattern of capitalist development in Nepal after economic liberalisation alongside the persistence of landlordism and deep rural inequalities in districts such as Morang can shed some light on the political crises that marred the 1990s and 2000s, in spite of the restoration of democracy. Faced with a perceived failure of parliamentary democracy to address deep-seated inequalities, the Communist Party of Nepal (Maoist) launched its People's War in 1996 (Joshi and Mason, 2007). As in much of the country, Morang saw active mobilisation by the Maoists at the grassroots outside of the towns. There were reports of various forms of direct action such as crop seizures from landlords, particularly those affiliated to mainstream political parties. However, the movements' influence was arguably less powerful than in the hill districts and parts of the central and western Tarai-Madhesh – and there was little evidence of any efforts to directly change the relations of production on the ground. This was, however, likely due to the proximity of Biratnagar, a bastion of state power, rather than being due to the absence of inequalities and potential popular support on the ground.

In many ways the post-liberalisation skewed industrial development and legacy of landlordism in Morang during the 1990s and 2000s were emblematic of the larger political economic injustices at a national level against which the Maoist movement directed their struggle. Baburam Bhattarai explicitly framed the movement within the context of semi-feudal relations on the ground, alongside a weakening industrial base due to Nepal's structural position in the neoliberal global economy (Bhattarai, 2003b). The '40 point demands' included not only a redrafting of the constitution, abolition of the monarchy, and ethnic autonomy for oppressed nationalities, but also redistributive land reform, as well as measures to break the monopoly of foreign capital, protection of cottage industry, and abolition of unequal trade treaties with India (Seddon and Karki, 2003). After the Royal Massacre in 2001,[34] and the crowning of King Gyanendra, the war intensified, aided in part by state crackdown, and only ended with the signing of a peace accord in 2006, followed by the abolition of the monarchy and elections to form a Constituent Assembly tasked with drafting a new constitution.

The subsequent years were filled with hope for transformative change in rural Morang and across Nepal – particularly of land reform, and there were some positive developments in the Tarai-Madhesh such as a citizenship distribution campaign. While not successful in reaching out to all households,[35] it demonstrated commitment to address the historic injustice that had prevented many of the poorest socio-economic groups accessing land or government services. However, the optimism was perhaps short lived. The Communist Party of Nepal (Maoist) won the first Constituent Assembly election in 2008. They performed well in Morang, alongside the United Democratic Madhesi Front, a coalition of plains-based parties. The latter had been advocating greater autonomy for the Tarai-Madhesh and were instrumental in leading a mass movement in 2007–2008 to improve the representation of the Madheshi and plains Adivasi communities in the new state structure (Chamlagai, 2021) – the so-called Madhesh Andolan I. However, at a national level the Maoists lacked the majority to bring sweeping changes, and the drafting of a new constitution was marred by sustained conflict with the establishment parties such as the Nepali Congress and the mainstream 'communist' CPN-UML as well as the plains-based parties (Baral, 2012).

The first Constituent Assembly was dissolved, and the centrist Nepali Congress and CPN-UML emerged once again as the main parties in the new Constituent Assembly, with the Maoists performing poorly (Kumar, 2019). Against this context, any 'redistributive' agenda was watered down, while Nepal's neoliberal economic policies remained entrenched (Roka, 2017). Furthermore, as a reaction against the rising political mobilisation amongst Adivasi groups and the Madheshi community, there was a revanchist wave of majoritarian nationalism by the mainstream political forces. This saw many of the post-conflict promises of ethnic autonomy being reversed by the new political establishment in the constitution-drafting process, in spite of the establishment of a federal system (Rai and Shneiderman, 2019), fuelling simmering disillusionment amongst many of the plains Adivasi and Madheshi communities (Chamlagai, 2021). The new constitution was rushed through in 2015, against the backdrop of a popular uprising in the Tarai, the so-called Madhesh Andolan II. As well as a perpetuation of discriminatory citizenship laws,[36] there were disagreements over representation in government and the federal boundaries in the new statute (Hutt, 2020; Bashyal and Bashyal, 2023; Rai and Shneiderman, 2019). The truncation of the far-eastern Tarai (including Morang) from the rest of the plains in the new federal provinces appeared to renege on the long-standing demands for autonomy – sowing the seeds for future conflict. Lawoti (2019) interpreted the drafting of provincial boundaries as a form of 'gerrymandering' which has weakened the political power of marginalised groups and maintained the dominance of the Nepali-speaking hill upper castes in all but one province.[37]

Aside from the failure to address ethno-regionalist issues, the post-2015 political settlement saw redistributive land reform all but drop from the political agenda. In 2017 the former Maoists merged with the mainstream CPN-UML to form the Nepal Communist Party, and went on to win a majority in parliamentary elections. While on the surface it was framed as a 'leftist' alliance, in reality they were courting a populist wave grounded in majoritarian ethnic politics (Rai and Shneiderman, 2019), ultra-nationalism and a revival of Panchayat-era cultural symbols.[38] Since then, there have been multiple party splits, and shifting alliances, largely shaped by personal political ambitions rather than ideology. The last decade has seen the dissolution of the radical left in Nepal and a reproduction of the old political order. In spite of some positive changes with regard to decentralisation, any meaningful attempt to reverse the structure of the economy which remains semi-colonial in character, or to end feudal agrarian relations on the ground, remains elusive. The perpetuation of upper-caste hill hegemony through the new constitution meanwhile risks further perpetuating some of the unequal state–Adivasi relations that sustained feudalism at the grassroots during the Rana and Panchayat periods. It is against this backdrop that we will move to the study villages themselves to better analyse how these changes have been realised in one cluster of villages, while exploring the trajectory of change for the future.

Notes

1. Das (2014) suggests that the Sen dynasty, while having its seat in central Nepal, was related to the Senas of Bengal, and following the collapse of their empire, the descendants of its rulers created new principalities in Nepal. Burghart (2016), however, suggests that the Sen dynasty traces their ancestry to Rajasthan and were in fact Rajputs fleeing the Muslim invasions.
2. The Vijayapur-based kingdom was formed following a split within the Sen dynasty of central Nepal, which created a separate state (Acharya, 1973).
3. While Rai's scholarship focuses predominantly on the Dhimal, who live further north in the eastern plains, it is highly likely that Adivasi mechanisms of surplus redistribution in the Tharu, Bantar and Rajbanshi domains of Morang (where the study in this book is concentrated) were similar, particularly when one considers the close ties between the indigenous groups of the region. However, given that the region's subordination to an expanding feudal economy occurred much earlier than the Dhimal homelands further north, which were deforested only in the 1960s, it is more challenging to identify the specific character of the Adivasi mode of production of the past.
4. Singh argues, like Rey, that it is only taxation and other coercive measures of capitalism and/or feudalism that restructure this mode of production, as this chapter will go on to argue.

5. For example, an account of the transition from the forested Bengal Dooars into the more settled kingdom of Cooch Behar in the pre-colonial period noted how agriculture was more settled as one got further south, with cultivation in forest clearings of paddy, tobacco and mustard and villages home to sedentary farmers. This, however, was a gradual process as the *bhuyan*s, the small landlords, gradually introduced wet rice cultivation (Nath, 1989).
6. Gorkha was one of the Chaubisi Rajiya (24 principalities), which from the fifteenth to eighteenth centuries controlled much of central Nepal to the west of the Malla city states of the Kathmandu valley and the Sen domains to the south and east (Vaidya, 2020).
7. Records for the year 1811 compiled by Hamilton suggest tax was highest for cash crops such as sugarcane, tobacco and vegetables and lowest for cotton or mustard, with rice falling in the middle.
8. The Mech population in the western Dooars reportedly declined from 21,608 in 1891 to 10,777 by 1921 as they moved to Assam to escape subjugation and the tax burden of the colonial state (Debnath, 2010, 53).
9. See government papers compiled by Regmi (1971b).
10. It was only with the purchase of land by other castes and the growing antagonisms between tenants from other Adivasi groups and landlords that the revolt was triggered (Mukherji, 1987).
11. The order states, 'Continue cultivating the lands that are already under cultivation, and retain their cultivators there as usual, so that revenue may not decline. Attract settlers from birta and jagir lands, as well as from the Moglan (i.e. India), and reclaim and settle Kalabanjar [uncultivated] lands' (Regmi, 1978a).
12. In the western Dooars, the British had also turned to the Adivasi belt of central India as well as Rajbanshi and Muslim communities from neighbouring Koch Behar and Rangpur to meet the critical labour shortages associated with colonial expansion and to expand the distribution of *jote*s (cultivable plots) to enterprising farmers and their tenants (Chaudhuri, 1995; Grunning, 2008 [1911]). Unlike in Morang though, the migration of Santhal, Munda and Oraon communities was particularly oriented to the tea garden sector, whereby agents would travel to Chotanagpur and the Santhal Parganas to directly recruit labour (Grunning, 2007 [1911]).
13. Regmi (1976) notes that during the Gorkha expansion, *birta* grants given by earlier state formations were confiscated, although rulers who had collaborated were more likely to keep their estates. In 1787 efforts were made to scrutinise earlier *birta* (and *guthi*) grants, whereby many earlier grants were restored.
14. These were compiled by Regmi (1971a).

15. The Ranas were a dynasty of nobles who took power from the Shah kings to rule as hereditary prime ministers. The king was reduced to being a figurehead.
16. The exact position of the other Tarai indigenous groups such as the Rajbanshi, Bantar and Munda was not specified in the Muluki Ain. Nevertheless, there is evidence of an informal caste hierarchy within the indigenous population, which appears to have evolved in parallel to shifts in the mode of production. The Tharu, who played the most significant role as functionaries for the state and within which a land-owning class had developed, at times considered themselves 'higher' status than poorer indigenous groups such as Bantar, who were often considered 'Dalits'.
17. Examples of 'semi-colonies' given by Lenin included, for instance, Persia and China.
18. *Times of India*, 9 November 2021, 'Jogbani–Katihar line foundation stone laid', https://timesofindia.indiatimes.com/city/patna/jogbani-katihar-line-foundation-stone-laid/articleshow/1884645499.cms (accessed June 2023).
19. Nepal's exports as of 1899 were valued at NPR 20,934,621 while its imports were valued at NPR 13,744,745 (Singh, 1997).
20. In the memoir of Krishna Bhakta Caguthi, for instance, a prominent peasant leader from Bhaktapur in the Kathmandu valley, published by Raj (2010), the reluctance of landlords to give rent receipts to facilitate the registration of tenants was described in depth. It was only consistent political movement of the peasants that allowed this to take place, a level of mobilisation which was far more limited in the Morang plains.
21. The impact of rising fertiliser use is itself questionable when one observes Tarai-wide data which suggests that yields per hectare had declined between 1974–1975 and 1977–1978 from 1,755 kilograms per hectare to 1,580 kilograms per hectare (Seddon, 1987).
22. There was a notable shift towards hybrid seeds which offered notably higher yields across Nepal during the Panchayat era. For example, the Taichung variety rice was introduced in 1966, yielding potentially 6.6 to 7.9 tonnes per hectare. This was far higher than local varieties. New varieties of maize and wheat were also promoted by the government (Paudel, 2017).
23. The name for Jhorahat itself refers to settled forest land, or *jhora*, where a market, or *hat*, is situated.
24. Gaige's (1976) survey from across the Tarai showed that over half of migrants were in fact of plains origin.
25. This was Nepal-wide data, but as jute production is largely restricted to the far-eastern Tarai districts, it is highly probable that most if not all of these establishments were located there.
26. The corollary of 'sectoral disarticualtion' is 'social disarticualtion', which applies not so much to South Asia as to cash crop economies in Latin

America. In these contexts, export orientation means that workers are not consumers of the product, and thus the incentive to raise wages is low (De Janvry, 1981).

27. The next highest output after those related to food and agro-processing is construction materials (34,947.5 tonnes) and water tanks (18,000 tonnes), which are notably lower.
28. Most was invested in services, with some also invested in hydropower. Firms were initially attracted to Nepal, particularly from India, by temporary profits arising from its lower labour costs (Khanal et al., 2005). As of 2016, the paid-up capital from India was by far the highest and is estimated to be NPR 11.2 billion. This was followed by China, where it was NPR 7.3 billion (Nepal Rastra Bank, 2018).
29. In this case, the expiry of the multifibre agreement (MFA), which offered Nepali garments duty-free access to US markets, in 2005 was largely responsible for the downfall of the sector (Shakya, 2018).
30. See report in *Kathmandu Post*, 22 September 2014, 'Demand drop leaves jute industry in doldrums', and *Gorakhpatra* article, 24 August 2014, 'Jute industries in eastern region in crisis'.
31. A survey from the Morang Chamber of Industries (2021) showed that 48 per cent of industries experienced one–two power outages per day, while 37 per cent reported three–five outages.
32. This includes particularly those owned by the Marwari business community, a well-established community of industrialists that had been invited to Nepal from India by the Ranas (Shakya, 2018) and are particularly well established in Biratnagar.
33. The 2008 *World Development Report* claims that while agricultural development is crucial to poverty alleviation, it can also be the sector most central to economic development. In the context of less developed countries, it states that 'comparative advantage in the tradable sub-sectors will still lie in primary activities (agriculture and mining) and agro-processing for many years, because of resource endowments and the difficult investment climate for manufactures' (World Bank, 2008, 8).
34. The official story is that the massacre was instigated by the crown prince following a family dispute and paved the way for the eventual abolition of the monarchy (Whelpton, 2005).
35. For example, in a study of the Santhal of Jhapa, 20 per cent of eligible households did not receive citizenship in the campaign (UNHCRC Nepal, 2011b).
36. New citizenship laws were introduced in the new constitution that further restricted women's right to pass on citizenship by descent to their children (S. Shrestha, 2017). This law, which was driven by a long-standing 'conspiracy theory' of mass immigration from India, would disproportionately impact Tarai communities where cross-border marriage was common.

37. This one province is Madhesh Province, which encompass a cluster of central Tarai districts with a Madheshi majority. The formation of this province which was widely read as a 'concessionary' offering to appease regionalist sentiment, fell short of the demands of the larger Madhesh movement for at least two pan-Tarai provinces. For instance, the Tharu majority districts were all merged with the hills (Bashyal and Bashyal, 2023).
38. Examples include the restoration of the Prithvi Jayanti holiday in 2023, celebrating the birth of Prithvi Narayan Shah, the founder of the Gorkha empire, which had been earlier abolished during the republican wave of 2006.

References

Acharya, B. 1973. Annexation of the Sen kingdoms. *Regmi Research Series* 5 (5): 81–85.

Adhikari, Deepak. 2006. Hydropower development in Nepal. *NRB Economic Review* 18: 70–94.

Adhikari, J. 2006. *Land Reform in Nepal: Problems and Prospects*. Nepal Institute of Development Studies.

———. 2011. Contentions and prospects of land reform in Nepal: A historical review. *New Angle: Nepal Journal of Social Science and Public Policy* 1 (1): 17–31.

APROSC. 1995. *Agriculture Perspective Plan*. Agricultural Projects Services Centre, Kathmandu.

Asian Development Bank. 2019. *Macroeconomic Update* 7 (1): 1–25.

Athreya, Venkatesh B., Djurfeldt, Göran and Lindberg, Staffan. 1990. *Barriers Broken: Production Relations and Agrarian Change in Tamil Nadu*. Sage Publications India Pvt Ltd.

Aubriot, Olivia and Bruslé, Tristan. 2023. Agrarian changes in the Nepalese lowlands: Local actors and the state. *European Bulletin of Himalayan Research* 60: 1–23.

Banerjee, Abhijit V., Gertler, Paul J. and Ghatak, Maitreesh 2002. Empowerment and efficiency: Tenancy reform in West Bengal. *Journal of Political Economy* 110 (2): 239–280.

Baral, L. R. 2012. *Nepal: Nation State in the Wilderness*. SAGE.

Bashyal, Lalita Kaundinya and Bashyal, Keshav. 2023. The Madhesh movement in Nepal: At the crossroad. In *Migration, Regional Autonomy, and Conflicts in Eastern South Asia: Searching for a Home(land)*, edited by Ranjan, Amit and Chattoraj, Diotima. Springer.

Basnet, J. 2018. Marginalisation of tenants in Nepal. In *Peasant Studies in Nepal*, edited by Uprety, L. P., Dhakal, S. and Basnet, J. Vajra.

Bhandari, Ravi. 2006. Searching for a weapon of mass production in Nepal: Can market-assisted land reforms live up to their promise? *Journal of Developing Societies* 22 (2): 111–143.

Bhattarai, Baburam. 2003a. *The Nature of Underdevelopment and Regional Structure of Nepal: A Marxist Analysis*. Adroit Publishers.

———. 2003b. The political economy of the people's war. In *The People's War in Nepal: Left Perspectives*, edited by Karki, A. and Seddon, D. Adroit Publishers.

Bhoosal, Yam Lal and Byanjankar, Rohan. 2022. An empirical study on the determinants of government revenue in Nepal. *Economic Review* 34 (2): 30–49.

Bikas Udhyami. 2019. *Factsheet: Investment in Nepal*. Nepal in Data Initiative.

Blaikie, P., Cameron, J. and Seddon, D. 2001. *Nepal in Crisis: Growth and Stagnation at the Periphery*, revised and enlarged edition. Adroit Publishers.

———. 2002. *Peasants and Workers in Nepal*. Adroit Publishers.

Burghart, R. 2016. *The History of Janakpurdham: A Study of Asceticism and the Hindu Polity*. Himal Books.

Caddell, Martha. 2007. Education and change: A historical perspective on schooling, development and the Nepali nation-state. In *Education and Social Change in South Asia*, edited by Krishna Kumar and Joachim Oesterheld, 251–284. Orient Longman.

Cameron, John, Pandey, Phaindra and Wagle, Bimala Kafle. 2016a. Assessing the impact of the agriculture perspective plan (1995 to 2015): The Maoist insurgency on rural lives in Nepal and reflections on the current Agricultural Development Strategy. *New Angle: Nepal Journal of Social Science and Public Policy* 4: 18–43.

Campbell, A. 1841. Letter from A. Campbell to Hodgson relating to the Nepal Tarai 08-23-1841. Hodgson Collection, British Library, London, vol. 14 fol(s) 79–81.

Campbell, Ben. 2018. Moral ecologies of subsistence and labour in a migration-affected community of Nepal. *Journal of the Royal Anthropological Institute* 24 (S1): 151–165.

Central Bureau of Statistics. 2014a. *Development of Manufacturing Industries in Nepal*. Government of Nepal.

———. 2014b. *National Census of Manufacturing Establishments, 2011/12*. Government of Nepal.

———. 2021a. *National Economic Census 2018: Analytical Report – Manufacturing Industry*. Government of Nepal.

———. 2021b. *National Population and Housing Census 2021*. Government of Nepal.

———. 2022. *Nepal National Industrial Survey 2019–20*. Government of Nepal.

Chalcraft, John. 2010. Monarchy, migration and hegemony in the Arabian Peninsula. Kuwait Programme on Development, Governance and Globalisation in the Gulf States (12). London School of Economics and Political Science, London, UK.

Chamlagai, Abi. 2021. Nepal: Tarai/Madhesh movements and political elites. *Journal of Asian and African Studies* 56: 949–963.

Chaudhuri, A. 1995. *Enclaves in a Peasant Society: Political Economy of Tea in Western Dooars and Northern Bengal.* Peoples Publishing House.

Chaudhury, R. C. R. 1965. *Bihar District Gazetteers: Purnea.* The Superintendent Secretariat Press.

Dahal, Dilli, R. 1983. Economic development through indigenous means: A case of Indian migration in the Nepal Terai. *Contributions to Nepalese Studies* 11 (1): 1–20.

Das, Basudevlal. 2014. The Sena Dynasty: From Bengal to Nepal. *Academic Voices: A Multidisciplinary Journal* 4: 9–16.

De Janvry, Alain. 1981. *The Agrarian Question and Reformism in Latin America.* JHU Press.

Debnath, S. 2010. *The Dooars in Historical Transition.* S.N.L. Publishers.

Department of Customs. 2018. *Nepal Foreign Trade Statistics: Fiscal Year 2017/18 (2074/75).* Ministry of Finance, Government of Nepal.

Deraniyagala, S., Katiwada, Y., Sharma, S., Roy, R. and Deshpande, A. 2003. *Pro-Poor Macro Policies in Nepal.* UNDP, Asia-Pacific Regional Programme on Macroeconomics of Poverty Reduction.

Dhakal, S. 2001. *Issues and Experiences: Kamaiiya System, Kanar Andolan and Tharus in Bardiya.* SPACE.

———. 2020. Peasant as an anthropological category and ethnographic subject. In *Peasant Studies in Nepal*, edited by Uprety, L. P., Dhakal, S. and Basnet, J. Vajra Books.

Dupré, G. and Rey, P. P. 1979. Reflections on the relevance of a theory of the history of exchange. In *Relations of Production: Marxist Approaches to Economic Anthropology*, edited by Seddon, D. and Lackner, H. Frank Cass and Company Ltd.

Ellis, F. and Biggs, S. 2001. Evolving themes in rural development 1950s–2000s. *Development Policy Review* 19: 437–448.

Food and Agriculture Organisation (FAO). 2003. *Agricultural Policy and Strategies for Poverty Alleviation and Food Security.* Government of Nepal.

Gaige, Frederick Hughes. 1976. *Regionalism and National Unity in Nepal.* University of California Press.

Ghosh, S. K. 1983. The Indian bourgeoisie and imperialism. *Bulletin of Concerned Asian Scholars* 15: 2–17.

Gill, Peter. 2009. The politics of land reform in Nepal 1951–1964. *Studies in Nepali History and Society* 14 (2): 217–259.

Giri, Madhu. 2012. Politico economic history of marginalization and change among the Musahars of East-Central Tarai Nepal. *Identity and Inclusion* 69.

Goil, R. M. 1972. Wages in manufacturing in Nepal. *Indian Journal of Industrial Relations* 8 (1): 47–66.

Government of Nepal 1964. *The Lands Act, 2021 (1964)*. Ministry of Land Management, Cooperatives and Poverty Alleviation. https://faolex.fao.org/docs/pdf/nep6239.pdf (accessed April 2025).

Grunning, John F. 2008 [1911]. *Eastern Bengal and Assam District Gazetteers: Jalpaiguri*. N. L. Publishers.

Guneratne, Arjun. 2002. *Many Tongues, One People: The Making of Tharu Identity in Nepal*. Cornell University Press.

———. 2010. Tharu-state relations in Nepal and India. *HIMALAYA, Journal of the Association for Nepal and Himalayan Studies* 29 (2): 19–28.

Gurung, Astrid Björnsen. 2003. Insects – a mistake in God's creation? Tharu farmers' perception and knowledge of insects: A case study of Gobardiha Village Development Committee, Dang-Deukhuri, Nepal. *Agriculture and Human Values* 20: 337–370.

Gurung, Harka. 1981. Population change in Nepal (1971–1981). *Himalayan Review* 13: 1–22.

Habib, Irfan, 2002. *Essays in Indian History: Towards a Marxist Perception; With, the Economic History of Medieval India: A Survey*. Anthem Press.

Hachhethu, Krishna. 2004. Municipality leadership and governance: A case study of Bhaktapur. In *Nepal: Local Leadership and Governance*, by Baral, L. R., Hachhethu, K., Khanal, K. P., Kumar, D., and Sharma, H., 33–72. Adroit Publishers.

Hamilton, F. B. 2007 [1819]. *An Account of the Kingdom of Nepal: and of the Territories Annexed to This Dominion by the House of Gorkha*. Rupa and Co.

Hanieh, Adam. 2010. Temporary migrant labour and the spatial structuring of class in the gulf cooperation council. *Spectrum: Journal of Global Studies* 1 (1): 67–88.

Harriss-White, Barbara and Gooptu, Nandini. 2009. Mapping India's world of unorganized labour. *Socialist Register* 37: 89–118.

Hodgson, B. 1988 [1848]. From Kathmandu to Darjeeling. *Regmi Research Series* 20 (1): 2–12.

Höfer, A. 1979. *The Caste Hierarchy and the State in Nepal: A Study of the Muluki Ain of 1854*. Universitätsverlag Wagner.

Hutt, Michael. 2020. Before the dust settled: Is Nepal's 2015 settlement a seismic constitution? *Conflict, Security and Development* 20 (3): 379–400.

Jha, Prashant. 2014. *Battles of the New Republic: A Contemporary History of Nepal*. Oxford University Press.

Joseph, S. C. 1960. Land tax and land use. *Indian Journal of Agricultural Economics* 15 (1): 27–54.

Joshi, Kanchan and Khanal, Kalpana. 2020. Neoliberal globalization, migration and food security: The case of Nepal. In *Principles and Practices of Food Security: Sustainable, Sufficient, and Safe Food for Healthy Living in Nepal*, edited by

Rasali, D. P., Bhandari, P. B., Karki, U., Parajulee, M. N., Acharya, R. and Adhikari, R. Association of Nepalese Agricultural Professionals of Americas.

Joshi, Madhav and Mason, T. David. 2007. Land tenure, democracy, and insurgency in Nepal: Peasant support for insurgency versus democracy. *Asian Survey* 47 (3): 393–414.

———. 2011. Peasants, patrons, and parties: The tension between clientelism and democracy in Nepal. *International Studies Quarterly* 55 (1): 151–175.

Kansakar, Vidya Bir Singh 1985. Land resettlement policy as a population distribution strategy in Nepal. In *Population Redistribution and Development in South Asia*, edited by Kosiński, Leszek A. and Elahi, K. Maudood. Springer.

Kapstein, Ethan B. 2017. *Seeds of Stability: Land Reform and US Foreign Policy*. Cambridge University Press.

Kar, Guruprasad. 2018. The enduring prevalence of semi-feudal agrarian relations in India. *Journal of Labor and Society* 21 (2): 193–213.

Karan, P. and Ishil, H. 1996. *Nepal: A Himalayan Country in Transition*. United Nations University Press.

Karky, Jaya. 1981. A study in revenue collection system in Nepal 1846–1923. *Contributions to Nepalese Studies* 9 (1–2): 55–64.

Khanal, D. R., Rajkarnikar, P. R. and Acharya, K. 2005. *Understanding Reform: A Case Study of Nepal*. Institute for Policy Research and Development.

Khanal, Kalpana and Bracarense, Natalia. 2020. Institutional change in Nepal: Liberalization, Maoist movement, rise of political consciousness and constitutional change. *Review of Political Economy* 33 (1): 145–166.

Khanal, Narendra Raj, Nepal, Pashupati, Zhang, Yili, Nepal, Govind, Paudel, Basanta, Liu, Linshan and Rai, Raju 2020. Policy provisions for agricultural development in Nepal: A review. *Journal of Cleaner Production* 261 (10): 1–10.

Khatri, Mukti Bahadur. 2018. Industrial development in Nepal: Problems and prospects. *Economic Journal of Nepal* 41 (3–4): 25–40.

Krauskopff, G. 198. Maîtres et possédés: les rites et l'ordre social chez les Tharu.

Kumar, D. 2019. Politics in federal Nepal. In *The Politics of Change: Reflections on Contemporary Nepal*, edited by Thapa, D. Social Science Baha and Himal Books.

Lamsal, Madan and Pande, Sabin Jung. 2018. Nepal's top 30 business houses: Leading the way. *New Business Age*, April.

Lawoti, Mahendra. 2019. Constitution and conflict: Mono-ethnic federalism in a poly-ethnic Nepal. In *Identities in South Asia: Conflicts and Assertions*, edited By Sachdeva, V., Pradhan, Q. and Venugopalan, A. Routledge India.

Lenin, V. I. 1987. Imperialism, the highest stage of capitalism. *Essential Works of Lenin: 'What Is to Be Done?' and Other Writings*. Dover Publications.

Liechty, Mark. 2003. *Suitably Modern: Making Middle-class Culture in a New Consumer Society*. Princeton University Press.

Lin, Sharat, G. 1980. Theory of a dual mode of production in post-colonial India. *Economic and Political Weekly* 15 (10): 516–529.

Macfarlane, Alan. 1976. *Resources and Population: A Study of the Gurungs of Nepal.* Cambridge University Press.

Marshall, Don, D. 2002. At whose service? Caribbean state posture, merchant capital and the export services option. *Third World Quarterly* 23 (4): 725–751.

Maycock, Matthew William. 2012. *Masculinity, Modernity and Bonded Labour: Continuity and Change amongst the Kamaiya of Kailali District, Far-West Nepal.* University of East Anglia.

McDonnaugh, Christian. 1989. The mythology of the Tharu: Aspects of cultural identity in Dang, West Nepal. *Kailash* 15 (3–4): 191–206.

Meillassoux, C. 1981. *Maidens, Meal and Money: Capitalism and the Domestic Community.* Cambridge University Press.

Mellor, J. 1976. *The New Economics of Growth: A Strategy for India and the Developing World.* Cornell University Press.

Ministry of Agricultural Development. 2015. *Agriculture Development Strategy (ADS) 2015 to 2035.* Government of Nepal.

Mishra, Chaitanya. 1987. Development and underdevelopment: A preliminary sociological perspective. *Occasional Papers in Sociology and Anthropology* 1: 105–135.

———. 2007. *Essays on the Sociology of Nepal.* Fine Print Inc.

Mitra, M. and Vijayendra, T. 1982. Agricultural labourers and peasant politics: Rural proletarianisation in Purnea, Bihar. *Journal of Peasant Studies* 9 (3): 88–118.

MoLESS. 2022. *Nepal Labour Migration Report 2022.* Ministry of Labour Employment and Social Security, Government of Nepal.

Morang Chamber of Industry. 2021. *Industrial Survey 2078: Sunsari Morang Industrial Corridor.* Morang Chamber of Industry, Biratnagar.

Mørch, M. 2023. *Plains of Discontent: A Political History of Nepal's Tarai (1743–2019).* Fine Print Books.

Mosala, S. J. 2021. *The Role of the Comprador Bourgeoisies in Post-Independent Africa: The Case of South Africa and Kenya.* North-West University.

Mukherji, Partha. 1987. Study of social conflicts: Case of Naxalbari peasant movement. *Economic and Political Weekly* 22 (38): 1607–1617.

Müller-Böker, Ulrike. 1991. Knowledge and evaluation of the environment in traditional societies of Nepal. *Mountain Research and Development* 11 (2): 101–114.

———. 1999. *The Chitwan Tharus in Southern Nepal: An Ethnological Approach.* Franz Steiner Verlag.

Nath, D. 1989. *History of the Koch Kingdom: 1515 –1615.* Mittal Publications.

National Planning Commission. 1970. *Fourth Five-Year Plan (1970–75).* Government of Nepal. https://www.npc.gov.np/images/category/fourth_eng.pdf (accessed June 2023).

Nepal, G. M. 1998. *Nepalnirupan.* Nepal Rajkiya Pragya-Prathisthan.

Nepal National Planning Commission. 2004. *Progress Report on Poverty Alleviation: An assessment of the tenth Plan (PRSP) Implementation*. Government of Nepal. http://www.npc.gov.np/tenthplan/Booklet.pdf (accessed June 2023).

Nepal Rastra Bank. 2018. *A Survey Report on Foreign Direct Investment in Nepal*. Nepal Rastra Bank Research Department.

Niitsu, Kōichi, Hideshima, Keiichiro, Wachi, Yasuko and Vaidya, K. K. 1983. Capital goods sector in Nepal: Present position and prospects. ILO Working Papers 992228793402676, International Labour Organization.

Ojha, Durga, P. 1983. History of land settlement in Nepal Tarai. *Contributions to Nepalese Studies* 1.

Paudel, M. N. 2017. Green revolution: Global effects and impacts in Nepal. In *Rice Science and Technology in Nepal (A Historical, Socio-cultural and Technical Compendium)*, by Crop Development Directorate and the Agronomy Society of Nepal. Department of Agriculture, Government of Nepal.

Pfaff-Czarnecka, J. 2008. Distributional coalitions in Nepal: An essay in democratisation, capture and (lack of) confidence. In *Local Democracy in South Asia: Micro-processes of Democratisation in Nepal and Its Neighbours*, edited by Hachhethu, K. and Gellner, D. SAGE.

Pradhan, K. 2009. *The Gorkha Conquests: The Process and Consequences of the Unification of Nepal, with Particular Reference to Eastern Nepal*. Himal Books.

Pradhan, R. S. 1984. *Industrialisation in Nepal: A Macro and Micro Perspective*. NBO Publishers and Distributers.

Pyakuryal, Bishwambher, Roy, Devesh and Thapa, Y. B. 2010. Trade liberalization and food security in Nepal. *Food Policy* 35 (1): 20–31.

Rai, J. and Oraon, Bechan. 2014. *Oraon of Nepal*. Ethnographic Research Series 4. Central Department of Sociology and Anthropology, Tribhuvan University.

Rai, Janak. 2013. Malaria, Tarai Adivasi and the landlord state in the 19th century Nepal: A historical-ethnographic analysis. *Dhaulagiri Journal of Sociology and Anthropology* 7: 87–112.

———. 2015. Owning land was so much of Dukha in the past: Land and the state–Adivasi relations in the Tarai, Nepal. *Studies in Nepali History and Society* 20 (1): 69–98.

Rai, Janak and Shneiderman, Sara. 2019. Identity, society, and state: citizenship and inclusion in Nepal over time. In *The Politics of Change: Reflections on Contemporary Nepal*, edited by Thapa, D. Social Science Baha and Himal Books.

Raj, Yogesh. 2010. *History as Mindscapes: A Memory of the Peasants' Movement of Nepal*. Martin Chautari.

Rankin, K. N. 2001. Governing development: Neoliberalism, microcredit and rational economic women. *Economy and Society* 30 (1): 18–37.

———. 2004. *The Cultural Politics of Markets*. Pluto Press.

Rankin, Katharine, N., Sigdel, Tulasi S., Rai, Lagan, Kunwar, Shyam and Hamal, Pushpa. 2017. Political economies and political rationalities of road building in Nepal. *Studies in Nepali History and Society* 22 (1): 43–84.

Ray, Subhajyoti. 2002. *Transformations on the Bengal Frontier: Jalpaiguri, 1765–1948*. Routledge-Curzon.

Regmi, Mahesh C. 1969. Economic conditions in Morang district during the early 19th century. *Regmi Research Series* 1: 37–39.

———. 1970. Revenue functionaries in the Eastern Tarai districts. *Regmi Research Series* 2 (5): 107–109.

———. 1971a. Notes of the history of Morang district. *Regmi Research Series* 3 (12): 224–233.

———. 1971b. Taxation in Mahottari district, 1809. *Regmi Research Series* 3 (2): 28–30.

———. 1976. *Landownership in Nepal*. Adroit Publishers.

———. 1977. Industrial development in Nepal. *Regmi Research Series* 9 (1): 1–4, 16–21, 45–48, 61–64,74–79, 87–92, 99–106, 113–120.

———. 1978a. Land reclamation in the eastern Tarai region. *Regmi Research Series* 10 (8).

———. 1982. Chaudharis and Jimidars. *Regmi Research Series* 14 (7): 97–99.

———. 1988. *An Economic History of Nepal*. Nath Publishing House.

———. 1989a. Confirmation of Birta grants: AD 1794. *Regmi Research Series* 21 (5): 68–71.

———. 1989b. Some Bakas-Birta grants. *Regmi Research Series* 21 (7): 91–94.

———. 1978b. *Land Tenure and Taxation in Nepal*. Bibliotheca Himalaya.

———. 1978c. *Thatched Huts and Stucco Palaces: Peasants and Landlords in 19th-century Nepal*. Vikas Publishing House.

Robertson, Thomas B. 2018. DDT and the Cold War jungle: American environmental and social engineering in the Rapti Valley of Nepal. *Journal of American History* 104: 904–930.

Roka, Hari. 2017. The status of smallholder farmers in Nepal's agricultural development strategy (2015–2035). *Agrarian South: Journal of Political Economy* 6 (3): 354–372.

Sapkota, Taranath, Houkes, Inge and Bosma, Hans. 2020. Vicious cycle of chronic disease and poverty: A qualitative study in present day Nepal. *International Health* 13 (1): 30–38.

Seddon, D. 1987. *Nepal: A State of Poverty*. Vikas Publishing House.

Seddon, D. and Karki, A. 2003. *People's War in Nepal: Left Perspectives*. Adroit.

Shakya, Mallika. 2018. *Death of an Industry: The Cultural Politics of Garment Manufacturing during the Maoist Revolution in Nepal*. Cambridge University Press.

Sharma Poudyal, Chandra. 2017. Nepali private schools and tolerated illegality: A Foucauldian analysis of privatisation of education in Nepal. *Policy Futures in Education* 15 (4): 537–549.

Sharma, Prayag Raj. 1977. Caste, social mobility and Sanskitization: A study of Nepal's old legal code. *Kailash* 4: 277–299.

Sharma, Sanjay, Pandey, Shibani, Pathak, Dinesh and Sijapati-Basnett, Bimbika. 2014. *State of Migration in Nepal*. Centre for the Study of Labour and Mobility, Kathmandu.

Shrestha, B. P. 1967. *The Economy of Nepal: A Study in the Problems and Processes of Industrialisation*. Vora Publishers.

Shrestha, N. R. 1990. *Landlessness and Migration in Nepal*. Westview Press.

Shrestha, N. R. and Velu, R. P. 1993. Frontier migration and upward mobility: The case of Nepal. *Economic Development and Cultural Change* 41 (4): 787–816.

Shrestha, Sabin 2017. *Report on Citizenship Law: Nepal*. European University Institute.

Sijapati, B. and Limbu, A. 2012. *Governing Labour Migration in Nepal: An Analysis of Existing Policies and Institutional Mechanisms*. Centre for the Study of Labour and Mobility and Himal Books.

Singh, K. S. 2007. Problematising proselytisation: A case study from West Nirmar. *Social Science Probings* 19: 105–148.

———. 2023. Moribund capital in tribal societies. *Seminar* 265: 47–51.

Singh, N. S. 1997. *Nepalese Economy and India*. Delhi: Anmol Publication Pvt Ltd.

Stiller, Ludwig F. 1975. The rise of the house of Gorkha (1768–1816). Ratna Pustak Bhandar.

Subedi, R. R. 2005. Historical entity of Vijayapur state. *Voice of History* 20 (1): 23–28.

Sugden, F. 2009. Neo-liberalism, markets and class structures on the Nepali lowlands: The political economy of agrarian change. *Geoforum* 40 (4): 634–644.

———. 2013. *Landlordism, Tenants and the Groundwater Sector: Lessons from the Terai-Madhesh of Nepal*. IWMI Research Report.

———. 2019. *Labour Migration, Capitalist Accumulation and Feudal Reproduction: A Historical Analysis from the Eastern Gangetic Plains*. Antipode.

Sugden, F., Seddon, D. and Raut, M. 2018. Mapping historical and contemporary agrarian transformations and capitalist infiltration in a complex upland environment: A case from Eastern Nepal. *Journal of Agrarian Change* 18 (2): 444–472.

Sugden, Fraser and Gurung, G. 2012. *Absentee Landlordism and Agrarian Stagnation in Nepal: A Case from the Eastern Tarai*. Nepal Institute of Development Studies.

Tamang, S. 2018. Ajako samrajyavada ra nepalabare Sitarama Tamanako lekha: Navaudaravadi khambako rupama visva vyapara sangathana. *Jugal News*. https://www.jugalnews.com/?p=3380 (accessed February 2025).

Tamrakar, Rabindra Man. 2012. A prospect of digital airborne photogrammetry approach for cadastral mapping in Nepal. *Journal on Geoinformatics, Nepal* 11: 1–6.

UNICEF. 2021. Overview of revenue mobilization: FY 2021/22, Nepal. Budget Brief Updates No. 2.
Upadhaya, R. 2020. *Cabals and Cartels: An Up Close Look at Nepal's Turbulent Transition and Disrupted Development*. Fine Print.
Vaidya, T. R. 2020. *Advanced History of Nepal: Expansion of the Gorkha State and the Political History from the First Battle of Nuwakot to Death of Bhimsen Thapa (1737AD to 1839 AD)*. Educational Publishing House.
Whelpton, J. 2005. *A History of Nepal*. Cambridge University Press.
Wickramasekara, Piyasiri. 2016. South Asian Gulf migration to the Gulf: A safety valve or a development strategy? *Migration and Development* 5 (1): 99–129.
World Bank. 2008. *World Development Report 2008: Agriculture for Development*. http://hdl.handle.net/10986/5990 (accessed June 2023).
———. 2019. Nepal trade. https://wits.worldbank.org/countrysnapshot/en/NPL.
Yadav, S. R. 1984. *Nepal: Feudalism and Rural Formation*. Cosmo Publications.
Zaman, M. A. 1973. *Evaluation of Land Reform in Nepal, Kathmandu*. Ministry of Land Reforms, Government Press.

4

Conceptualising the Agrarian Class Structure

The sub-Himalayan lowlands which make up the historic region of Morang have been shown to have a complex history, yet have emerged today with a clear geography of inequality. With waves of migration from the hills, the development of successful owner-cultivator communities to the north has been paralleled by the perpetuation of feudalism in the original Tarai-Madhesh settlements of the south – albeit with the rise of an absentee rather than local landlord class. However, even within the southern belt, which is the focus of this book, the peasantry is shown to be far from a unitary entity and is divided by land ownership status as well as a complex matrix of caste and ethnicity. These divisions are crucial to explore if one is to understand the contemporary interaction between the capitalist and pre-capitalist – and that is the focus of this chapter.

Before that, it is worth offering a bit more social and cultural context of the core field site and its diversity. The seven villages are located in the former Jhorahat, Bhaudaha and Thalaha VDCs, which in 2017 were merged into Gramthan and Katahari rural municipalities (see Figure 4.1). Travelling northeast from Biratnagar towards this cluster of villages on the recently widened road, the Singya Nadi river marks the northern boundaries of the built-up area. One passes some ribbon development, including new housing plots catering to urban dwellers, and a number of large agro-processing mills, and after 4 kilometres one reaches Jhorahat Bazaar (see Figure 4.2), the first settlement which is included in the study. This is one of five bazaars between Biratnagar and the foot of the hills to the north and forms the largest market in the field site. It hosts a large twice weekly *haatiya* (periodic market), has a number of shops and eateries, and a handful of cottage industries such as furniture workshops. Surrounding the bazaar and extending north along the canal is a tract of land which was once under forest, yet today is home

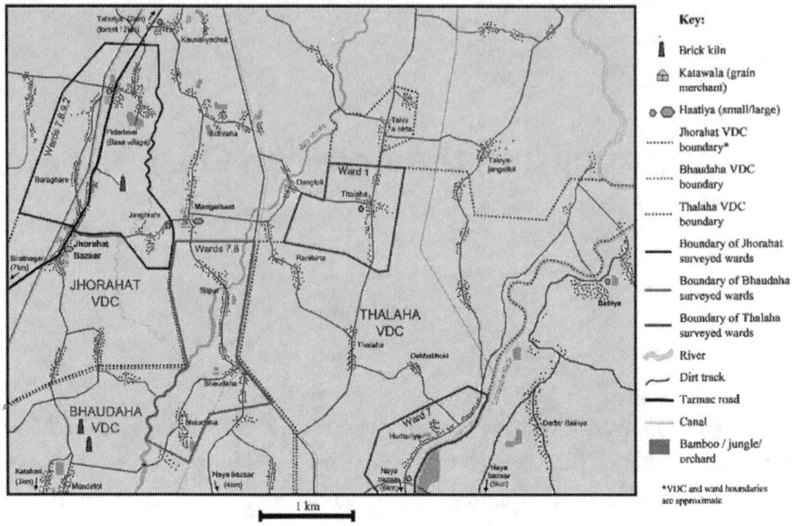

Figure 4.1 Map of field site, including the sampled wards

Source: Created by author.

Note: These wards were from the old VDC system which were key administrative units when the research started, although these have now been dissolved with VDCs merged to form rural municipalities.

Figure 4.2 Jhorahat Bazaar. This is the largest market in the field area, with a pitched road connecting it to the major urban centre of Biratnagar.

Source: Author.

mostly to Nepali-speaking hill Brahmins and Chettris who settled the land in the 1960s and 1970s, interspersed with Tharu and Rajbanshi homesteads. Many are medium-to-large owner-cultivators, although there are also tenant and marginal landowners, some of whom were escaping poverty and land degradation in the hills.

If one continues for a further 2 kilometres, one reaches the second village, Pidarboni, the largest village in the core study site, and the location where I was based during the fieldwork (see Figure 4.3). This community is predominantly Tharu, and is surrounded by fertile fields which are well irrigated by a branch canal bringing water from the Koshi river. There was historically an economically powerful Tharu landlord class here, although as discussed in Chapter 3, their power has greatly reduced in recent decades. The main village is composed of a network of lanes lined by drainage channels which radiate out from two main *chowk*s (road intersections), where tea stalls, shops and resting places form the centre of social and economic life in the community. The different *tol*s, or neighbourhoods, are interspersed with bamboo groves, fish ponds, wetlands and kitchen gardens. Unlike the caste stratified villages of Mithila with clear wealth divisions between neighbourhoods, in Pidarboni, the larger homesteads, outhouses and granaries of the better-off Tharu families, most of whom are medium and large owner-cultivators, sit adjacent to

Figure 4.3 Tharu homestead in Pidarboni in the old Jhorahat VDC

Source: Author.

the more modest dwellings of their poorer counterparts, many of whom work as tenant farmers. There is, however, a separate cluster of Rajbanshi households to the north of the settlement, while on the other side of the canal in the west there is a line of modest homesteads belonging to the Dalit Rishidev (Musahar) community, the majority of whom are landless or own quite small holdings, with limited engagement in cultivation. There is a small but growing bazaar area along the main road, with a cluster of shops, tea stalls and a school.

East of Pidarboni, one enters the former Bhaudaha VDC, where the cultural and economic character of the villages change significantly, as one leaves the Tharu heartland. The land is further from the main canal and is less well irrigated. The villages are smaller and more spread out, being mostly linear settlements along the network of earthen tracks. The clusters of shops around each *chowk*, or road intersection, are more modest than in the Tharu villages. It is here that vast tracts of land belong to the absentee landlords from Biratnagar. While most of the landlords are Nepali-speaking hill upper castes, the villages are home almost entirely to the indigenous Rajbanshi and Bantar communities, with smaller settlements of Munda, an Adivasi group who had migrated during the Rana period from central India. While electrification and motorable tracks have reached most settlements, concrete buildings are rare. In many parts of Nepal and South Asia, where neoliberalism as well as lucrative remittance flows have brought signs of prosperity and accumulation to a rural elite – particularly in housing stock. This does not appear to apply here.

One kilometre to the east of Pidarboni lies the Munda/Jhagar village of Jagharahi, the third village included in the core field site. East of Jagharahi, one reaches a fourth village, Sitpur, a Rajbanshi settlement, the vast majority of whom are tenants. The fifth village, known itself as Bhaudaha, is a densely clustered Bantar village. Most households here are also tenants, although there are a small number of medium-to-large owner-cultivators, most of whom belong to Maithili-speaking Madheshi middle castes. Moving further east one enters the old Thalaha VDC, which is also home primarily to the Bantar community, with some Tharu and Munda neighbourhoods, and, again, a predominance of absentee landlordism. This is home to the sixth community in the core fieldsite, Thalaha village, where there is a small market, and the seventh community, the large village of Hurhuriya, an isolated settlement which spreads out along the west bank of the Lohandra river.

In terms of the land ownership situation, there is a clear division between the old Jhorahat VDC on the one hand and the old Bhaudaha (see Figure 4.4) and Thalaha (see Figure 4.5) VDCs on the other. Table 4.1 shows that tenant

Figure 4.4 Bhaudaha village is home predominantly to the Bantar community. While there are some medium-sized farmers here, the majority of households are landless.

Source: Author.

Figure 4.5 Hurhuriya village of Thalaha is the most remote in the field site

Source: Author.

Table 4.1 Percentage breakdown of different land ownership categories by VDC and year

Land ownership category	Jhorahat		Baudhaha		Thalaha		Total	
	2007	2019	2007	2019	2007	2019	2007	2019
Landless*	34.43	31.15	52.38	35.71	67.50	52.50	48.95	38.46
Labourer	19.67	9.84	23.81	21.43	32.50	27.50	24.48	18.18
Tenant	14.75	21.31	28.57	14.29	35.00	25.00	24.48	20.28
< 0.5 ha	29.51	42.62	35.71	52.38	25.00	32.50	30.07	42.66
0.5–1 ha	4.92	9.84	2.38	2.38	0.00	7.50	2.80	6.99
1–2 ha	14.75	8.20	2.38	2.38	5.00	7.50	8.39	6.29
> 2ha	16.39	8.20	7.14	7.14	2.50	0.00	9.79	5.59

Source: Author.

Note: *Defined as households who own less than 0.05 hectare, which is why they are referred to in the text as 'functionally' landless. These households are classified as such because anything below 0.05 hectare would only be sufficient for one's homestead and not for any agricultural production.

farming is predominant in the sampled wards of Bhaudaha and Thalaha. Just over a third (35.71 per cent) of sampled households in Bhaudaha and over half (52.50 per cent) in Thalaha are functionally landless, a category which includes both those dependent only upon wage labour and those who are tenant farmers. Table 4.2 suggests that 65.54 per cent of the land owned or cultivated by the sampled households in Bhaudaha and 78.82 per cent in Thalaha is under tenancy. In the sampled wards of Jhorahat on the other hand, home mostly to Tharu and hill settler farmers, owner cultivation is more prevalent. Only 31.15 per cent are landless, with the remainder being small landowners. The lower prevalence of landlessness is unsurprising given the historical status and privilege the Brahmin/Chettri communities have held within the state apparatus and the Tharu's past role as a tax-collecting class in the Rana era. However, tenancy is still widespread, with just under half the land being under tenancy, at 49.73 per cent (see Table 4.2). Even among the owner-cultivators, the vast majority own less than 0.5 hectare, representing 40.98 per cent of the sample. There is, however, a notably larger class of medium-to-large landowners when compared with Bhaudaha and Thalaha.

There are few large landlords actually residing *within* the selected VDCs given the decline of Morang's traditional Tharu landowners, most of whom are today medium-to-large farmers. While half of larger landowners with more than 2 hectares do rent out plots, these large farmers form just 5.59 per cent of

Table 4.2 Status of land owned or cultivated by farmers in the sample (2019)

Land ownership		**Jhorahat**		**Bhaudaha**		**Thalaha**		**Total**	
Owner cultivated by local farmers		**area (ha)**	**% of total**	**area (ha)**	**% of total**	**area (ha)**	**% of total**	**area**	**% of total**
	Landless	0.17	0.35	0.30	0.52	0.06	0.16	0.53	0.37
Land owned and cultivated by sampled farmers (by land ownership category)	< 0.5 ha	6.26	13.01	5.67	9.78	3.23	8.83	15.16	10.62
	0.5–1 ha	3.34	6.94	1.01	1.74	1.84	5.03	6.19	4.34
	1–2 ha	5.20	10.81	1.68	2.90	3.36	9.18	10.24	7.18
	> 2 ha	9.21	19.15	9.28	16.00	0.00	0.00	18.49	12.96
	Total	**24.18**	**50.27**	**17.94**	**30.93**	**8.49**	**23.20**	**50.61**	**35.47**
Land rented from absentee landlords by sampled farmers		**8.46**	**17.59**	**34.68**	**59.79**	**18.99**	**51.89**	**62.13**	**43.54**
Land rented from local people by sampled farmers		**7.86**	**16.34**	**1.02**	**1.76**	**7.94**	**21.69**	**16.82**	**11.79**
Land rented out by sampled farmers		**7.60**	**15.80**	**4.36**	**7.52**	**1.18**	**3.22**	**13.14**	**9.21**
Total land		**48.10**	**100.00**	**58.00**	**100.00**	**36.60**	**100.00**	**142.70**	**100.00**

Source: Author.

the sample. Of all the land owned or cultivated by the sample, Table 4.2 shows that while 35.47 per cent is owner cultivated, only 9.21 per cent is owned by local farmers and rented out to others. Those who are renting out land locally do not therefore form a significant landlord class. The remainder of the land has been rented in by sampled farmers. While 11.79 per cent of the owned or cultivated land in the sample is rented from local farmers, 43.54 per cent of the total is rented from absentee landlords based predominantly in Kathmandu or Biratnagar. This includes members of the traditional landed elites such as *birta* recipients and those who have purchased the land more recently. In Bhaudaha and Thalaha, the control over land by absentee landlords is even more acute, whereby they own a substantial 59.79 per cent and 51.89 per cent respectively of the total land in the sample (see Table 4.2).

Analysing Agrarian 'Classes'

A starting point to better understand the mode of production in rural Morang is to identify the different strata within the peasantry – to both uncover internal divisions, including flows of surplus between them, but also, importantly, to shed light on how they relate to dominant classes outside the village such as landlords, as well as to merchant and industrial capital. Analysing agrarian 'classes' has long been fraught with controversy. In Nepali political discourse, peasant farmers, or *kishan*, traditionally were considered a 'class' or *bargiya* themselves – recognised as a vote bank by successive political parties, while also being organised politically under various grassroots *kishan* movements. As Dhakal (2018) notes though, the term should be used with caution given that it does not differentiate between landed and non-landed groups. A peasant federation leader who was interviewed acknowledged that in later years agricultural labourers and various other landless groups were recognised as a distinct grouping by political parties, but noted with frustration that political narratives around the peasantry often still did not account for the complex differences within the farming population. It is against the backdrop of this challenge that differentiating peasants between *sano* (small), *madhyam* (medium) and *thulo* (large) is becoming more common in government programmes.[1]

Exploring class differentiation within the peasantry in Nepal, however, is not only useful to identify categories for political action or the mobilisation of state support, but also offers an *analytical tool* to understand how differently situated farmers are affected by both landlordism and growing articulations with capitalism. Several methods were considered for this study to identify distinct groupings within the peasantry. The first was a 'surplus'-based criterion, and the second is based upon ownership of the means of production. Starting with the first, Athreya et al. (1987) identifies a methodology to measure the degree to which households retain a surplus. It seeks to identify whether or not farms yield a per capita grain and cash requirement above a set level which is deemed to constitute one's minimum subsistence needs. The challenge to this model is that the levels of surplus may depend on individual circumstances in a given year, and not every household has fixed food and cash requirements. Furthermore, the presence of distress sales or use of grain to repay loans could push a household below subsistence levels later in the year.

A study published during early fieldwork for this book (Sugden, 2009) also used a surplus-based criterion, and sought evidence of accumulation (investment in high-value assets) and distress (for example, dependence on menial labour). However, growing agrarian distress makes this methodology more challenging. Even some large owner-cultivators do not choose to reinvest profits in high-value assets and may divert them into luxury goods, processes described later. Similarly, in the context of monetisation and spiralling costs of living, even poorer farmers may make high-value cash investments far beyond their means such as payments for weddings or investment in luxury goods. Rather than being a sign of accumulation, such expenditures often push them further into indebtedness and financial insecurity.

This brings us to the second method – which is a more traditional Marxist approach based upon ownership of the means of production. Lenin's *Preliminary Draft Theses on the Agrarian Question* sought to define agrarian classes in the Russian peasantry during transition to capitalism, and put a particularly strong emphasis on land ownership as well as participation in the labour market (Lenin, 1951). He differentiated five main 'agrarian classes'. At the bottom are the landless agricultural proletariat or wage workers as well as a semi-proletariat, the small peasants who till small plots of land which provide part of the family subsistence, while labouring simultaneously for others to meet the remainder of their needs. The third category is the *small peasantry* who own or rent small plots of land enabling them to satisfy their family's minimum subsistence needs, without hiring outside labour or participating in the labour market. The fourth is the 'middle peasant', the small owner-cultivators who hold small plots which can potentially yield the family a surplus in good years, and who may sometimes hire labour. In the fifth category lies the big peasants, who have larger holdings and employ hired labour regularly on the land, renting out excess land. Finally, at the apex of the agrarian structure are the landlords, descended from feudal lords of the past, who do not labour on the land themselves, and exploit the labour of the proletariat/semi-proletariat, small and even middle peasants (Lenin, 1951).

This model presents the most useful means to understand classes within the peasantry, but comes with some caveats if applied to rural Morang, particularly in the absence of any nascent agrarian capitalism and the continued persistence of feudal landlordism. While the buying or selling of wage labour provides a useful measure to differentiate agrarian strata, in rural Morang, as in much of South Asia, surplus appropriation more often takes place through the rent burden. Furthermore, as will be discussed later, labour for others can occur as an 'exchange' of labour between households of the same economic status, something intricately tied to water and land management for paddy cultivation. Households may employ others to transplant their own land after applying water, and then may move on to labour on someone else's land for the same task. Given these nuances, it was decided to focus on households' relation to the primary means of production – land. From an analysis of the qualitative and quantitative data, it appears that one's socio-economic status, and indeed one's capacity to produce a surplus or accumulate, is intricately connected to the size of one's holdings, and whether they are owned or rented. Land ownership and tenancy status is also shown to be critical in shaping the type of surplus appropriation households are subject to.

Sukumbasi, *'Functionally Landless' and Labouring Households*

From an initial analysis of the farm survey data, it is clear that landlessness is widespread. The landless, as a conceptual category at the base of the agrarian structure, are classified as those with less than 0.05 hectare of land or no land at all, and they form 38.46 per cent of the overall sample, and over half of the sample in Bhaudaha and Thalaha (see Table 4.1). They are not a unitary group though. The first subgroup of landless households are those who own no fixed property at all – known in Nepal as *sukumbasi*. They are a distinct group, many of whom are effectively 'squatters' living on public land – and are associated with various political struggles for land rights,[2] although such mobilisation has been less prevalent in the Morang region. The second subgroup are those households who lack agricultural land but may still own their homestead or possibly a very small kitchen garden. They are often referred to using the more generic word *bhumihin* (landless) or *bhumihin kishan* (landless farmer), although a more technical term would be that of the 'functionally landless', who may own some land, yet not the primary means of subsistence.

The *sukumbasi* are the most marginalised, and a large share are from the Rishidev (also known as Musahar) community, who live on public land, particularly along the irrigation canals. They remain one of the most marginalised Tarai Dalit communities. Many face challenges accessing citizenship documents or loans due to the lack of fixed property. However, while the *sukumbasi* label has important political connotations, the difference with functionally landless households is of less significance when understanding the relations of production. Both subgroups participate in tenancy and farm/off-farm labour on similar terms. For this reason both categories of households will be referred to simply as 'landless' in the subsequent analysis.

Out of all of these landless households, the Rishidev form just a small share of the sample (7 per cent), while over three quarters are from the indigenous Bantar, Rajbanshi and Munda communities. These three communities historically played a less active role in the Rana-era tax collection bureaucracy in the core study area, when compared to their Tharu neighbours. They thus experienced feudal subordination to a greater extent than many other ethnic communities (see Figure 4.6). All other ethnic groups are also included in the landless stratum, albeit in low numbers. These include destitute migrants

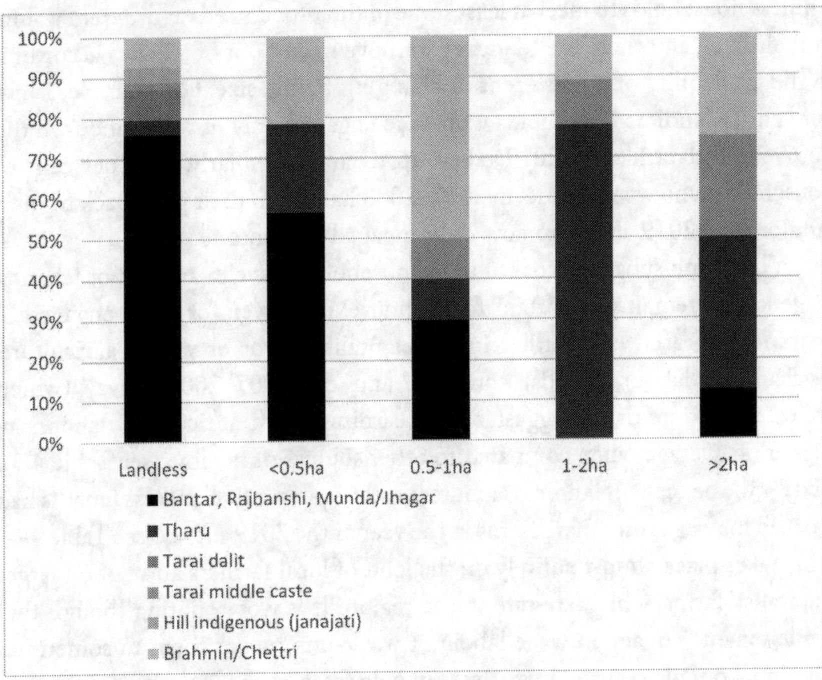

Figure 4.6 Ethnicity of different land ownership categories (2019)

Source: Author.

from the hills in Jhorahat (even those from upper castes), some of whom were driven out by ecological stress, and a small number of Tharu households.

Another distinction can be drawn within the landless group between those engaged in agriculture as a tenant and those who are engaged only in labour for others, including on other people's farm. Just under half of the group, and 18.18 per cent of the total sample, were landless labourers (*bumihin majdur*) who did not lease any land for farming (see Table 4.1) at the time of the survey, although this includes both *sukumbasi* and functionally landless households. Their engagement in agriculture is limited to livestock rearing and in some cases the cultivation of small kitchen gardens on homestead land, alongside fishing from the ponds, rivers and wetlands that span the landscape. The majority though derive their subsistence through labour alone. The other half of landless households are tenant farmers, representing 18.18 per cent of the sample overall, and are one of the main rent-paying groups.

While those engaged in tenancy are considered locally to be slightly better off than those who meet their food needs through wage work alone, there is considerable fluidity between these two landless groups, and they cannot be considered distinct agrarian classes. Tenancy tends to be important for all landless households to meet at least some of their food needs at different points in their lives, and there is a tendency to move in and out of tenancy according to the availability of land to rent or changing family size. For example, 14.54 per cent of landless households who were engaged only in wage labour in the 2007–2008 data had by 2019 taken up tenancy. Similarly, 10.9 per cent of households who were tenants in 2007–2008 had given their plots back to their landlords by 2019 and were now only engaged in labour.

While both subgroups of landless households move in and out of tenancy, wage labour remains important for all households, even for those engaged in farming on leased land, either in the capitalist sector or within agriculture. Agricultural labour is most common, and the 2007–2008 survey (which collected income data) suggested that earnings from agricultural labour are higher on average when compared to other sources of income (see Table 4.3). Sixty-nine per cent of landless labourers and 62 per cent of landless tenants had worked for wages on others' farms in the year of the 2019 survey (see Table 4.4). This takes place almost entirely on the land of local farmers and not on larger 'capitalist' farms, which are rare in the region. It is worth noting though that while tenants engage in wage labour, it was common for them to sometimes hire in labour also during busy times in a de facto 'exchange' with neighbours. Respondents stated that for a *bigha* (0.67 hectare) of land, an average-sized

Table 4.3 Average income sources over the last year by land ownership category (NPR), as of 2007–2008

Land ownership category	Average income in the last year (NPR) by employment type					
	Agricultural labour	**Factory work**	**Professional work**	**Semi-skilled employment**	**Agricultural income**	**Micro-enterprise income**
Landless	16,535	7,117	0	3,530	5,073	13,951
< 0.5 ha	5,640	10,125	5,277	5,709	12,373	6,346
0.5–1 ha	0	0	8,867	0	18,117	2,750
1–2 ha	1,892	2,600	20,031	1,313	13,680	6,786
> 2 ha	0	0	33,450	0	59,498	4,318
Total	8,807	6,916	11,708	3,631	15,074	8,197

household of six usually has no choice but to purchase up to 35 days of non-family labour for the planting and weeding of paddy, with additional labour costs during the harvest time. Households, after hiring in labour, would then go on to conduct a similar amount of labour for other farms. This was a monetised relationship, unlike in the hills where labour is exchanged through the *parma* system, or further west in the Mithila region where a non-monetised exchange persists, known locally as *sapati* or *paincho.* Nevertheless, an exchange without cash existed in the past, and even today, labour often takes place on a reciprocal basis amongst relatives or neighbours – although payment of a wage ensures fairness in the case that the provider of labour is unable to return the favour. The average expenditure on outside labour in the 2007–2008 dataset was just NPR 2,953 per *bigha*, and was notably lower than for larger land-owning farmers (see Table 4.5).

In terms of wages, agricultural labour is the lowest paid, and is often seasonal. As of 2007, wages were between NPR 52 and NPR 62, a value which included an 'in kind' payment in grain (see Table 4.6). Farm wages had risen considerably by the time of the 2019 survey and now vary from NPR 342 per day in Jhorahat to NPR 268 in Bhaudaha. For men it rises up to NPR 500 per day (see Table 4.5). This rise has in part been stimulated by labour migration to higher income regions, but importantly it is also in line with spiralling costs of living, and respondents expressed that if given a choice, a tenancy was far preferable to working as an agricultural labourer. Likewise, non-agricultural labour also offered much better wages than work on others' farms. Most landless households do therefore engage in wage labour in the

Table 4.4 Percentage engaging in different types of labour outside the households within the last year in 2007–2008 and 2019 respectively

Land ownership category	Agricultural labour		Factory labour		Casual unskilled labour		Casual semi-skilled labour (mostly construction)		Business		Professional	
	2007	**2019**	**2007**	**2019**	**2007**	**2019**	**2007**	**2019**	**2007**	**2019**	**2007**	**2019**
Landless	47.83	65.45	19.44	9.09	38.89	12.73	8.33	45.45	12.50	5.45	1.39	3.64
< 0.5 ha	15.91	23.81	20.45	20.63	13.64	14.29	13.64	26.98	13.64	6.35	6.82	17.46
0.5–1 ha	0.00	0.00	0.00	10.00	25.00	0.00	0.00	10.00	0.00	0.00	50.00	30.00
1–2 ha	16.67	0.00	16.67	11.11	0.00	0.00	8.33	22.22	8.33	0.00	25.00	11.11
> 2 ha	0.00	0.00	0.00	0.00	0.00	12.50	0.00	0.00	15.38	25.00	23.08	62.50
Total	29.58	35.17	17.24	13.79	24.14	7.59	8.97	31.03	12.41	6.21	8.28	15.17

Source: Author.

Table 4.5 Average cash spent on outside labour as of the 2007–2008 sample per *bigha* and total (NPR)

	Per *bigha* investment (NPR)	Total investment (NPR)
Landless	2,953	5,488
< 0.5 ha	3,772	8,983
0.5–1 ha	insufficient data	insufficient data
1–2 ha	4,164	7,191
> 2 ha	5,881	24,626

Source: Author.

Table 4.6 Average wages paid by respondents to agricultural workers by VDC

VDC	Average daily agricultural wage paid to men (inc. in-kind payments)** (NPR) 2007–2008	Average daily agricultural wage paid to men (inc. in-kind payments)** (NPR) 2019	Average daily agricultural wage paid to women* (inc. in-kind payments) (NPR), 2007–2008	Average daily agricultural wage paid to women* (inc. in-kind payments) (NPR), 2019
Jhorahat	Insufficient data	Insufficient data	62	342
Bhaudaha	109	500	56	298
Thalaha	106	Insufficient data	52	268

Source: Author.

Notes: *Men are generally paid considerably higher wages than women due to both a culturally established devaluation of women's labour power as well as the different tasks carried out by male labourers. Men generally engage in *halo jotne* (ploughing) or repairing and building dykes, while women primarily are involved in *ropai* (paddy transplantation) and weeding.

**In-kind payments constitute a fixed quantity of *chamal*, uncooked rice (normally 1.25 kilograms). The value was calculated from the average selling price reported in a survey of shops in the village.

capitalist sector also, although engagement in capitalist wage labour has been slower amongst the poorest of this group such as the Rishidev community. As of 2009 none of these households had taken up factory work, although some had worked in construction. A small number of the Rishidev depended only upon agricultural labour. Such households were forced into extreme poverty, pushing their subsistence needs down to the bare physiological minimum, working for households who are themselves in many cases being simultaneously exploited by landlords.

While the proportion of landless households engaged in industrial labour has declined to below 10 per cent, a trend which will be discussed in more detail later (see Table 4.4), there has been a rise in semi-skilled labour – at 45.45 per cent of both landless subgroups, particularly on construction sites in Biratnagar. It is higher paid, yet casual in nature. Industrial labour wages were on average NPR 564 per day, versus NPR 713 for semi-skilled labour at the time of the 2019 survey. Just under a quarter of landless households were also engaged in migration either to India, the Gulf countries or Malaysia – processes which will be discussed in Chapters 7 and 8 (see Table 4.7). While this has increased considerably from just 8.54 per cent in the 2007–2008 survey, amongst the poorest landless households overseas migration is less common due to the financial costs associated with migration.[3] Landless households also have some additional income from non-agricultural micro-enterprises such as handicraft production or the running of village tea shops, although monthly income is generally low.

Small Landowners

After the landless farmers, a significant share of the sample is made up of marginal producers who own a small plot of land for farming which is below 1 hectare. This group is also disproportionately made up of the Rajbanshi, Bantar and Munda communities, at just over half, but there are also

Table 4.7 Percentage of households with migrants

Land ownership category	Family member works abroad (2007–2008)	Family member works abroad (2019)	Domestic migrant (2019)*
Landless	8.54	25.45	1.82
< 0.5 ha	8.93	23.81	4.76
0.5–1 ha	20.00	40.00	10.00
1–2 ha	18.75	0.00	11.11
> 2 ha	14.29	0.00	37.50
Total	10.40	25.45	6.21

Source: Author.

Note: *2007–2008 data on domestic migrants not available.

significant shares from poorer Tharu households in Pidarboni and even some Brahmin and Chettri hill settlers in Jhorahat (see Figure 4.6). Importantly, 86 per cent of this group actually own less than 0.5 hectare, a subgroup which forms 42.66 per cent of the sample overall (see Table 4.1). Significantly, the land they own is far below what is required for a household to subsist and, therefore, just over half (53.23 per cent) of households with less than 0.5 hectare were engaged in tenancy as of the 2019 survey (see Table 4.8). For these poorest 'part-tenants', rented land is their primary source of food, with 82.11 per cent of their total farm on average being under tenancy. Like their landless counterparts, however, they move in and out of tenancy periodically, and for certain periods they may combine cultivation of their owned plot only, along with wage labour.

Like landless households, most small landowners with less than 0.5 hectare engage in wage work on the side and just under a quarter are engaged in agricultural labour (see Table 4.4). As they have the security of a plot of land, they are generally less dependent upon it for income, as shown by Table 4.3 where earnings (as of 2007–2008) were on average less than other income sources. However, again many participate in farm labour as part of an 'exchange' between similarly situated households, simultaneously 'buying in' labour for other farms at busy times – although like for landless farmers, the levels of investment in labour are not high (see Table 4.5). Labour in the capitalist sector is also widespread, with 20.63 per cent engaged in factory labour, 14.29 per cent in casual unskilled work, and 26.98 per cent in casual semi-skilled work (see Table 4.4).

Table 4.8 Engagement in tenancy by farmer category

Farmer category	% engaged in tenancy		Average % of cultivated land rented in (not including landless labourers)	
	2007–2008	2019	2007–2008	2019
Landless	48.61	46.43	98.14	94.68
< 0.5 ha	59.09	53.23	37.81	44.42
0.5–1 ha	25.00	40.00	13.33	16.55
1–2 ha	16.67	11.11	6.85	4.69
> 2 ha	46.15	0.00	13.04	0.00
Total	48.28	44.14	48.61	48.68

Source: Author.

The other subgroup of 'small' landowners, with between 0.5 and 1 hectare, form just 6.99 per cent of the total sample. Farmers suggested that this is still too small a holding to meet one's food security from the land, but they benefit from greater livelihood security when compared to their poorer counterparts. Only 40 per cent are engaged in tenancy (see Table 4.8), although they are also engaged in a wide range of unskilled and semi-skilled labour off the farm, which is still required for them to meet their minimum needs.[4]

The three groups – landless labourers, landless tenants and small farmers with less than 1 hectare of land, form the base of the agrarian structure in the region, and make up 88.12 per cent of the sample overall. In spite of this, only 15.33 per cent of the total land in the sample is under owner cultivation by these three groups combined (Table 4.2) – a reminder of the persistent concentration of land amongst absentee landlords.

Medium Landowners

The remaining share of the sample comprises of medium-to-large landowners, the vast majority of whom reside in the better-off villages of Jhorahat and Pidarboni. The medium landowners are defined as those with between 1 and 2 hectares of land (6.29 per cent of the sample). A substantial 78 per cent of this group are Tharu, although it also includes some Brahmin and Chettri as well as Maithili-speaking middle castes (see Figure 4.6). While there are variations according to fertility of the soil and irrigation, local farmers considered 1.50 *bigha*s (which is approximately 1 hectare) as generally a sufficient sized farm for a typical household of six to subsist.

This group can meet most of their food security needs from their land – and thus they in many ways represent the archetypical self-sufficient peasant farm, or the group that farmer leaders referred to as *madhyam kishan* (literally medium peasant). Some even produce a saleable surplus in a year with good rains and favourable production conditions. Evidence of the latter includes the fact that four out of the nine medium landowners captured in the sample had cultivated higher-value Basmati rice in the last year alongside other varieties. Basmati is primarily produced for the market with profit in mind, and while some smaller farmers have cultivated it to generate cash, the numbers are negligible (only one landless farmer had cultivated it). As Basmati is lower yielding than the dominant Kanchi and Mansuli varieties, it is usually only produced by farmers who already have achieved food security through cultivation of the latter.

Only 11.11 per cent of these medium farmers are engaged in tenancy. While some do agricultural labour, it is largely part of an exchange with others during busy times. Many of this group therefore hire in agricultural labour also, yet they do not have the cash to employ much more outside labour than they themselves sell on other farms (see Table 4.5). Given that they are engaged mostly in owner cultivation, and are largely in control of their own surplus, they could be classified as 'independent peasants' such as those on the hill settler belt further north, farming under a quite different mode of production when compared to their land-poor neighbours who depend largely on landlords. They are also engaged in off-farm labour, but as indicated by Table 4.3, they depend less on this than their poorer counterparts, and many have salaried or 'professional' jobs such as in government offices – particularly the Nepali-speaking Brahmin and Chettri communities in Jhorahat. Just over 10 per cent of households in this group have migrants overseas. A third of medium farmers have rented land out. However, this does not necessarily imply that they are using their excess land to generate surplus from poorer tenants. Discussions suggested that some medium-sized farmers who suffer from labour scarcity yet have alternative income sources, such as single women whose husbands are working abroad, may opt to rent their land out rather than cultivate it directly.

Large Landowners

There is a relatively small group of larger producers who potentially display signs of accumulation. For analysis purposes, these have been classified as those with more than 2 hectares of land, which for an average family is generally sufficient to yield a surplus. In the sample, only 5.59 per cent of the sample are from this group – representing only eight households, and thus data is not accurately representative of the group as a whole. Nevertheless, some insights can be gained through the data on these families, alongside qualitative interviews held with a much larger subset of richer farmers across the south Morang region. Two of the sampled larger landowners are Brahmin and Chettri farmers in Jhorahat Bazaar while four are Tharu farmers in Pidarboni. The latter includes some of the descendants of the former Tharu nobility, although their economic power is substantially weaker today. There are also two larger landowners from Maithili-speaking middle castes in the Bhaudaha region.

In terms of landholdings, the average size of plot amongst these eight households was 3.4 hectares, with the largest plot being just under 6 hectares.

While these holdings are by no means extensive (when compared to absentee landlord estates), the 27.54 hectares owned by this small group still accounts for 43.23 per cent of the land owned by sampled farmers (see Table 4.2). It is, however, just 21.04 per cent of the area cultivated by the sample, given that absentee landlords still control a disproportionate share of the land.

When compared to medium landowners, however, there are notable differences. These larger farmers are all producing a sizeable surplus which can be sold. For instance, five out of the eight households have produced Basmati rice. The 2007–2008 data suggested they had earned a profit of NPR 11,316 on average from crop sales over the last year after deducting costs – although this will be discussed in more detail in Chapter 6. This group can afford to employ a reasonable amount of non-farm labour while not selling their labour at all, and in the process they can yield a sizeable surplus. The 2007–2008 data, for instance, suggested they were spending NPR 24,626 on labour, including in-kind payments over the last year, compared to well below NPR 10,000 for medium and small landholders (see Table 4.5). With this outside labour they can cultivate a far greater area. They also employ more labour on a per hectare basis, pointing to slightly more labour-intensive production. If one looks at Jhorahat alone, where most large farmers are located and thus the most reliable comparison can be made, the few large farmers with more than 2 hectares are spending NPR 4,196 per hectare on average, whereas landless farmers are spending NPR 2,699 per hectare on labour, which is likely as part of an exchange.

While the high use of labour points to some 'accumulation', they are far from making the transition to becoming capitalist farmers. Data on labour use was not collected during the shorter 2019 survey, but anecdotal evidence in interviews suggested that it was becoming less common to hire in labour, and renting out land was a preferred option due to rising labour costs. As of 2019, half of these larger farmers were renting out plots of land on a sharecropping basis, thus extracting some additional surplus as rent from tenants. Although not included in the sample, a few richer Tharu farmers had reportedly even employed a *haruwa*, a bonded labourer who works for a whole year – in many ways a feudal relic from the period when there was a powerful indigenous landed nobility. A significant source of wealth amongst the larger farmers today appears to be not from agriculture, but from salaried employment. For example, numerous interactions with prosperous Brahmin and Chettri farmers around Jhorahat revealed that many have government jobs as well as other salaried positions such as teachers.

Absentee Landlords

The true apex of the agrarian structure is arguably the absentee landlords. There was not a local term for absentee landlord, and all big landowners with inherited wealth were referred to locally by the generic term *jamindar* or *jimindar*.[5] This is not to be confused with the Rana-era functionary position *jimidar* and is an important distinction. While both terms originate in Mughal India, the latter is derived from the Arabic 'jimmadar', or functionary, while the former is equivalent to *zamindar*, which referred to a colonial-era tax collecting landlord in India, and is a term widely used in both Nepal and India to refer to a landlord, including in the writings of the communist movement.[6] This is derived from the Persian word for land, *zaman* (Regmi, 1976).

Given the almost complete decline of the local Adivasi landed class (at least in the core study area), and the fact that few hill-origin landlords lived locally anymore (with many having never lived in the village), most references to *jamindar*s today were with regard to absentee landlords. Urban dwelling landlords own a substantial 48.45 per cent of the land cultivated by the sample, and 78.69 per cent of the rented land. It is difficult to gauge the actual size of landlords' estates, particularly when they are often spread between multiple family members. Gathering data on absentee landlords themselves was also challenging given that they lived in urban areas and could not be included in any surveys. Few tenants were aware of what their own landlords' total holdings were. In 2012, an effort was made through a focus group to compile information on eight landlords in the area. Of the five for whom respondents had some ideas as to the size of their holdings, the largest was reportedly around 50 *bigha*s (34 hectares) spread across a number of family members, while others had 35 *bigha*s (23.8 hectares), 32 *bigha*s (21.76 hectares), 40 *bigha*s (27.2 hectares) and 8.5 *bigha*s (5.78 hectares) respectively – there were rumours of some landlords with larger holdings of over 100 *bigha*s, but these are difficult to verify. The majority were from the Brahmin and Chettri communities of Biratnagar, given the legacy of historic land grants and speculative investments from urban dwellers. There was also land belonging to Newar and some plains upper and middle castes. As will be shown later though, the drain of surplus by absentee landlords remains a central element of the mode of production in rural southern Morang, and has a critical role in mediating the trajectory of change.

Landlordism: A Local or Regional Phenomenon?

It is useful to explore how widespread these patterns of landlord–tenant relations are within the larger Tarai-Madhesh and Eastern Gangetic Plains region.

Starting at a district level, the 2001 census offers some insights into the extent of landlessness within Morang district according to VDC, the old administrative unit (see Figure 4.7). Unfortunately, data on landlessness was not collected in the 2011 or 2021 censuses, but even this old data gives some insights into the patterns across the district. The map shows a clear concentration of landlessness across southern and western Morang, where the proportion of landless households is, with a few exceptions, above 40 per cent. Discussions with farmers in across this belt suggest that these are the locales where absentee landlordism is most widespread.[7]

The southernmost VDCs, where landlessness is highest, at 50 per cent or more of the population, are home to Rajbanshi, Bantar, Gangai, Munda and other smaller indigenous groups with a long history of subjugation. This includes the three focal VDCs of Thalaha and Bhaudaha. Closer to Biratnagar municipality, it rises further, likely due to the high levels of speculative investments in land as well as the presence of peri-urban non-agricultural settlements.

The region north of Biratnagar, including Jhorahat, is predominantly Tharu, and there one observes slightly lower levels of landlessness, which as noted earlier may be connected to the higher levels of owner cultivation amongst the Tharu and their historical links to Rana-era state power. The third belt within Morang includes the eastern and northern parts of the district. These localities were once extensively forested, and today are home predominantly to settlers from the hills. Absentee landlordism is less common (although there are some localised exceptions) and most farmers operate their land as owner-cultivators. The far north encompasses the hilly tract where, again, most farmers are owner-cultivators.

These severe inequalities in the distribution of land and the continued predominance of landlordism are not just a phenomenon localised to this part of eastern Nepal. Landlessness and tenancy is a phenomenon which is particularly prevalent across the Nepal Tarai – with the latest living standards measurement survey (2022–2023) for Nepal suggesting that 44.38 per cent of land in the sample is under tenancy, with 39.9 per cent of agricultural households owning no farmland (National Statistics Office, 2024). Two large random surveys on agriculture and livelihoods suggest that these agrarian relations are prevalent across the larger Eastern Gangetic Plains. The first survey (see Sugden et al., 2014) of 427 households was carried out in 2013 in Rakuwari and Bhupatti of Bihar's Madhubani district, Thadi Jijha and Ekrahi of Nepal's Dhanusha district, as well as in four of the Morang villages from this study, Sitpur, Bhaudaha, Pidarboni and Hurhuriya, albeit involving a different dataset of farmers.

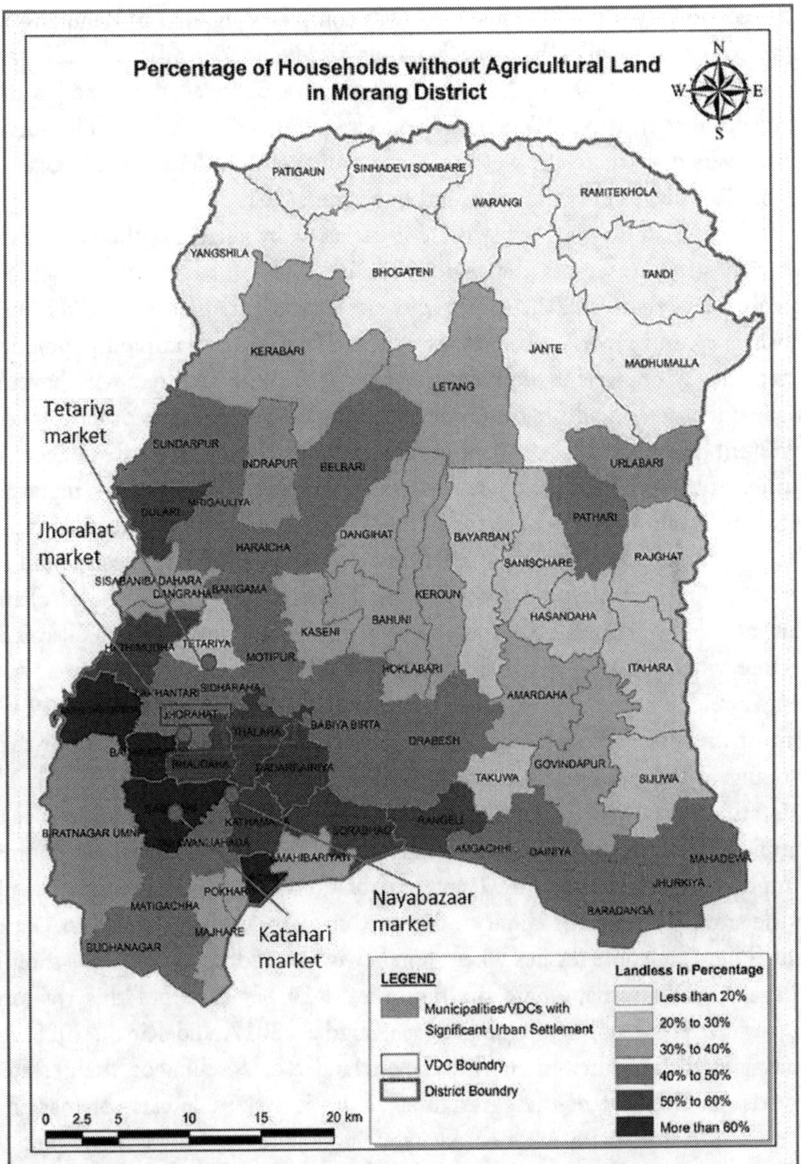

Figure 4.7 Percentage of households without agricultural land in Morang district by VDC as of 2001

Source: Central Bureau of Statistics (2001). Map adapted from original created by Pabitra Gurung at International Water Management Institute (IWMI), Kathmandu.

Note: The more recent censuses omitted the question on household-level land ownership.

The second survey of 809 households was completed in 2014 in Ragunathpur and Giddha of Nepal's Dhanusha, Korahiya and Nanour of Bihar's Madhubani, Dogachinagar and Damdaha of Bihar's Purnea district, and Simariya and Mahendranagar of Nepal's Sunsari district (Sugden et al., 2015). The survey thus covers districts to the west, southwest and south of Morang. An analysis of this 16-village study can be found in Sugden (2017).

Table 4.9 shows that while there is variation by village, at the base of the agrarian structure across the region is a large class of landless households (owning less than 0.05 hectare), who are dependent upon others for their subsistence and form between a quarter and half of the sampled population – and thus Morang is by no means atypical. Landless labourers who have no engagement in agriculture other than working on others' farms or pastoralism represent between 12.91 per cent in Dhanusha of Nepal and 33.82 per cent in Purnea of Bihar. The second landless group, the pure tenant farmers, represent between 10 and 17 per cent of the sample. There are, however, like in Morang, also a significant proportion of 'part-tenants', representing between 9 and 15 per cent of the sample, who both own small plots (at less than 0.5 hectare) and rent most of their land. The average size of the owned portion is small, at 0.34 hectare, while the rented area is on average 0.78 hectare.

Most illustrative are the levels of tenancy. In the total sample, 49.19 per cent of the land is under tenancy (see Table 4.10). While this is lower than Morang, which was 64.54 per cent in the 2019 survey used for this book, it is still substantial, and there is considerable variability. For example, in sample villages in neighbouring Sunsari, which has a similar socio-economic composition to Morang, 56.92 per cent of the land is under tenancy, while in the sites in Purnea of Bihar to the south of Morang, this lies at 46.12 per cent. There are some locales where tenancy is less widespread, such as sample villages in Dhanusha, where the figure is 31.14 per cent, but this was due in part to recent political changes (see Sugden, 2017, and Rinck, 2025, for analysis) which resulted in many in the old landed class selling off their estates.

Also at the base of the agrarian structure is a sizeable class of marginal owner-cultivators who are not engaged in tenancy yet own small plots – 18.3 per cent of the sample are small owner-cultivators with less than 0.5 hectare, and a further 12.31 per cent have between 0.5 and 1 hectares. There is a small class of medium farmers with between 1 and 2 hectares, yet this group is small, at just 11.58 per cent of the sample.

Large farmers with more than 2–5 hectares represent an even smaller proportion, at just 4.94 per cent. Those with more than 5 hectares, who could be considered 'landlords', represent just 0.6 per cent. Together, all of

Table 4.9 Concentration of land within the other district samples

District	Farmer land ownership category	% of sample	% total cultivated land belonging to each group	% total land owned by sample belonging to each group
Madhubani	landless labourer	24.80	0.58	0.68
	Landless tenant	15.36	0.16	0.18
	< 0.5 ha (part-tenant)	14.82	7.66	8.93
	< 0.5 ha (owner-cultivator)	21.56	10.03	11.69
	0.5–1 ha	8.63	11.08	12.91
	1–2 ha	10.78	27.79	32.39
	> 2 ha	4.04	28.50	33.21
	Total	100.00	85.79	100.00
Purnea	landless labourer	33.82	0.01	0.01
	tenant	17.39	0.00	0.00
	< 0.5 ha (part-tenant)	9.18	4.27	6.71
	< 0.5 ha (owner-cultivator)	8.70	2.35	3.69
	0.5–1 ha	10.63	7.49	11.76
	1–2 ha	12.08	18.31	28.75
	> 2 ha	7.25	31.25	49.08
	Total	100.00	63.68	100.00

(*Continued*)

Table 4.9 (*Continued*)

District	Farmer land ownership category	% of sample	% total cultivated land belonging to each group	% total land owned by sample belonging to each group
Dhanusha	landless labourer	12.91	0.28	0.33
	tenant	10.81	0.11	0.13
	< 0.5 ha (part-tenant)	15.32	7.15	8.40
	< 0.5 ha (owner-cultivator)	20.42	7.01	8.24
	0.5–1 ha	16.82	15.77	18.53
	1–2 ha	15.62	25.20	29.62
	> 2 ha	7.81	29.56	34.75
	Total	100.00	85.07	100.00
Sunsari	landless labourer	19.90	0.38	0.59
	tenant	13.93	0.06	0.09
	< 0.5 ha (part-tenant)	15.42	8.22	12.87
	< 0.5 ha (owner-cultivator)	20.90	7.78	12.18
	0.5–1 ha	13.43	12.28	19.24
	1–2 ha	9.95	16.83	26.37
	> 2 ha	4.48	18.30	28.67
	Total	100.00	63.84	100.00

(*Continued*)

Table 4.9 (*Continued*)

District	Farmer land ownership category	% of sample	% total cultivated land belonging to each group	% total land owned by sample belonging to each group
Total	landless labourer	22.67	0.30	0.43
	tenant	14.33	0.11	0.16
	< 0.5 ha (part-tenant)	14.74	6.76	9.73
	< 0.5 ha (owner-cultivator)	18.30	6.23	8.96
	0.5–1 ha	12.31	11.25	16.19
	1–2 ha	11.58	20.20	29.06
	> 2 ha	5.51	24.66	35.46

Source: Author.

Table 4.10 Total cultivated area under tenancy

District	Land rented in (ha)	Land rented out (ha)	Total land rented (ha)	Total land cultivated (ha)	% area rented in	% area rented out	% area under tenancy
Madhubani	53.00	24.27	77.27	202.21	26.21	12.00	38.21
Purnea	82.62	9.52	92.14	199.77	41.36	4.77	46.12
Dhanusha	64.05	26.65	90.70	244.23	26.23	10.91	37.14
Sunsari	70.59	12.56	83.15	146.08	48.32	8.60	56.92
Total	373.19	83.10	456.29	927.55	40.23	8.96	49.19

Source: Author.

those in the sample owning more than 1 hectare (the medium farmers, large farmers and landlords) constitute just over 17 per cent of the sample, yet own a substantial two-thirds of the land in this cross-regional sample, pointing to a considerably unequal distribution of holdings.

One difference with Morang and Sunsari when compared to Bihar and the Nepal Tarai districts west of the Koshi is that there is a larger local landlord class in the latter. This is reflected in Table 4.8 whereby, depite high levels of tenancy, the proportion of land owned by the upper strata of the sample is more modest in Sunsari when compared to Dhanusha, Purnea and Madhubani. This is because fewer of the large landowners were included in the sample in Sunsari, as they were not resident. The higher prevalence of 'local' landlords in districts such as Madhubani is linked to the ethnic and caste demographics of these districts, whereby the landed elite is primarily from the local Maithili-speaking upper castes, and one observes much more localised landlord–tenant relationships. This contrasts with Morang and Sunsari of Nepal whereby these relationships were mediated by state power and the distribution of land grants to elites from the hill upper castes. Nevertheless, earlier research from the larger region suggests that absentee landlordism is increasing, as local upper-caste landlords seek alternative employment in urban areas (Sugden, 2016, 2017). Regardless as to who the landlords are, the impacts on agricultural livelihoods which will be discussed in the pages ahead are similar.

In sum, there is evidence that marginal and landless farmers, particularly those with less than 1 hectare of land, make up a majority across this part of the Gangetic plains, where landlord–tenant relations are a fact of life. What appears particularly prevalent in Morang, however, is absentee landlordism – and most notably, the sheer volume of land held under tenancy, which represents just under a two-thirds of the total. While there is a small medium-to-large farmer class in Morang, they are by no means a 'dominant' class locally, with only a small portion of land rented out, and just some hiring in of labour. It has also been shown in this chapter that there is some overlap between land ownership, caste and ethnicity – with a clear gulf in wealth between the Nepali-speaking Brahmin and Chettri communities, the indigenous Tharu community, and smaller Adivasi groups such as the Rajbanshi and Bantar. How this distribution of resources shapes the patterns of surplus appropriation is explored in the next chapter.

Notes

1. See, for instance, efforts by the Gandaki state government to differentiate farmers according to spending capacity (small, medium and large) to support the roll out of agricultural interventions in the province (Rasas, 2020).
2. There has been a *sukumbasi*, or squatters, movement for a number of decades, including that associated with the spontaneous settlement on government land by destitute landless families from the hills in the Tarai-Madhesh during the 1960s–1980s clearing of forests. Their later eviction or denial of official papers by the government paved the way for a number of mass mobilisations in the 1980s (Kaplan and Shrestha, 1982), including in northern Morang (Seddon, 2018). More recently, the term has been associated with the urban landless poor who have also been politically organised (Tanaka, 2009).
3. None of the Rishidev (Musahar) community in the sample had migrants, and for the landless labouring subgroup, it was just 17 per cent (versus 30 per cent for landless tenants).
4. It is worth noting that there are some households within this group whose livelihood security is not directly linked to land ownership, such as a small number of Brahmin and Chettri households who have professional employment such as government jobs, yet who retain a small amount of land on the side.
5. Tenants themselves would sometimes refer to their landlord using the deferential *maalik*, literally 'owner/boss'.
6. For instance, *jamindar*s are mentioned several times in the first manifesto of the Communist Party of Nepal (Communist Party of Nepal, 1949).
7. While the study was focused on three VDCs, informal FGDs and interviews were carried out across 14 VDCs in southern Morang between 2006 and 2015 as part of the scoping out for field sites and to gain comparative perspective.

References

Athreya, V., Boklin, G., Djurfeldt, G. and Lindberg, S. 1987. Identification of agrarian classes: A methodological essay with empirical evidence from South India. *Journal of Peasant Studies* 14 (2): 147–190.

Central Bureau of Statistics. 2001. *Nepal Population Census 2001*. Government of Nepal.

Communist Party of Nepal. 1949. *Nepal kamyunist partiko pahilo ghoshanapatra (purnapatha)*. https://www.cpnmc.org.

Dhakal, S. 2018. Peasant as an anthropological category and ethnographic subject: A critical overview of peasantry and peasant politics. In *Peasant Studies in Nepal*, edited by Uprety, L. P., Dhakal, S. and Basnet, J. Vajra Books.

Kaplan, Paul F. and Shrestha, Nanda R. 1982. The Sukumbasi movement in Nepal: The fire from below. *Journal of Contemporary Asia* 12 (1): 75–88.

Lenin, Vladimir Il'ich. 1951. *Preliminary Draft of Theses on the Agrarian Question*. Current Book Distributors.

National Statistics Office. 2024. *Nepal Living Standards Survey IV 2022/23*. Government of Nepal.

Rasas. 2020. Kisanako vargikarana. *Nagarik*. 24 Shravan 2077 (8 August 2020).

Rinck, J. 2025. Marxist past to speculative futures: Migration, land markets, and political storytelling in Nepal's Tarai. *Journal of Peasant Studies* 52 (1): 157–177.

Seddon, D. 2018. Resistance, rebellion, revolt and revolution: A historical/anthropological consideration of peasant movements and other forms of rural unrest in Nepal. In *Peasant Studies in Nepal*, edited by Uprety, L., Dhakal, S. and Basnet, J. Vajra.

Sugden, F. 2016. Improving dry season irrigation for marginal and tenant farmers in the Eastern Gangetic Plains: Baseline socio-economic report. Unpublished project report, International Water Management Institute.

———. 2017. A mode of production flux: The transformation and reproduction of rural class relations in lowland Nepal and North Bihar. *Dialectical Anthropology* 41 (2): 129–161.

Sugden, F., Maskey, N., Clement, F., Ramesh, V., Philip, A. and Rai, A. 2014. Agrarian stress and climate change in the Eastern Gangetic Plains: Gendered vulnerability in a stratified social formation. *Global Environmental Change* 29 (November): 258–269.

Sugden, F., Silva, S. de, Saikia, P., Maskey, N. and Kumar, A. 2015. *Irrigation and Water Management Constraints for Marginal and Tenant Farmers in the Eastern Gangetic Plains*. Report compiled for project: Sustainable and Resilient Farming Systems Intensification.

Tanaka, Masako. 2009. From confrontation to collaboration: A decade in the work of the squatters' movement in Nepal. *Environment and Urbanization* 21 (1): 143–159.

5

Ground Rent, the Market and Debt

The Appropriation and Distribution of Agrarian Surplus

Paddy, or *dhan*, is the most important subsistence crop produced by farming households across Nepal's lowlands, regardless as to whether they are farming as tenants or as independent peasants (see Figure 5.1). Not only is it viewed as an essential food staple, but its production is central to the culture and way of life of the Tarai-Madhesh and the larger Eastern Gangetic Plains.

Figure 5.1 Fields of paddy near Pidarboni village during the monsoon. Rice is by far the most important crop across the Tarai-Madhesh.

Source: Author.

This, it should be noted, is a food culture in which Morang's Adivasi peasantry has been integrated into since the clearing of the forest frontier and their transition from forest-based shifting cultivation to sedentary agriculture. It is planted in the monsoon month of Ashadh (June–July), and *ropai*, or transplantation, is a time of peak labour demand – a process which entails extensive exchange of labour between households, albeit usually in a monetised form. During the mid-monsoon months, labour is limited to periodic weeding and irrigating in the run-up to harvest as the rains subside in the autumn.

After the paddy harvest with the onset of the cooler, drier months of winter known as the *rabi* season, the farmers plant a crop of *dhal*, mustard or more often wheat (see Figure 5.2), the flour of which is used to make *chapatti* (unleavened bread), a secondary staple. Wheat is harvested prior to the pre-monsoon storms in April. The severe heat and thunderstorms of the pre-monsoon months, known as the *pre-kharif*, mark a quiet period in the agricultural calendar nowadays. As of 2007, just under a third of households

Figure 5.2 Intercropped wheat and mustard in Jhorahat VDC during the dry winter. As wheat requires irrigation, the area of cultivated land is normally less than that for paddy.

Source: Author.

would produce a smaller harvest of spring rice, or *chaite dhan*, from April until July, although production had virtually stopped by the time of the follow-up survey in 2019, with only 1 per cent cultivating it. Jute, which was sown alongside paddy before the onset of the rains, has also declined substantially – as noted several times earlier. For most farmers today, land lies fallow during the pre-monsoon period.

Many farmers also own livestock, fruit trees and small vegetable gardens, the products of which further contribute to meeting their nutritional needs, although production is generally modest. The production priority for all but the wealthiest households is to meet basic food needs through the cultivation of the three main grain staples: rice, wheat and pulses. These staples are generally threshed in the village using cattle or, increasingly, hired threshing machines, before being husked at home or taken to one of the village rice mills. Grain is then kept in raised storehouses, or *mora*, to feed the family until the next harvest. However, for a large share of the rural population, a significant share of this grain is lost through multiple mechanisms of surplus appropriation, and it is to these we now turn.

Conceptualising Subsistence and Surplus in a Pre-capitalist Society

One of the primary differences between the land-poor farmers who produce grain staples primarily as tenants and the middle and large farmers who cultivate the land independently rests on their capacity to meet their minimum subsistence needs off the land. In other words, this refers to their ability to meet the needs of 'simple reproduction', and by extension their additional capacity to produce, and *retain*, a surplus, which can be used to improve their nutrition or living standards or be sold and reinvested on the land to expand production.

It is useful in this context to briefly examine Marx's understanding of surplus. According to Marx, under capitalism, individuals perform both 'necessary' and 'surplus' labour. The 'necessary labour' is the time required to produce a product that will meet the subsistence needs of the worker and his/her family. Once they have met these needs, additional work is known as 'surplus labour time', within which a 'surplus product' is generated (Marx, 1974, 208–209). Under capitalist relations of production, the worker who does not own the means of production and therefore has no control over the labour process is only remunerated for their necessary labour time. The capitalist thus extracts the product of the worker's surplus labour in value form (Marx, 1974).

However, at several points in *Capital*, particularly volume 3, Marx mobilises the concept of necessary and surplus labour (in non-value form) for the analysis of pre-capitalist modes of production. For example, with regard to 'communal' pre-capitalist modes of production, a distinction is drawn between

> that portion of labour whose product is directly consumed individually by the producers and their families – aside from the part which is productively consumed – that portion of labour which is invariably surplus labour, whose product serves to satisfy the general social needs no matter how this surplus product may be divided, and no matter who may function as a representative of these social needs. (Marx, 1974, 877)

This would indeed apply to many of the lineage-based Adivasi modes of production that likely prevailed in the Morang region prior to their subordination to feudalism.

In the context of the contemporary peasant farm in South Asia, similar principles apply, and the combined product of family labour beyond what is required for subsistence constitutes the surplus product. Athreya et al. (1987, 159) clarify the definition of 'surplus' for a peasant household as 'what is available for luxury consumption or for accumulation, once the requirements of simple reproduction have been met'. The needs of simple reproduction entail the reproduction of labour power through the provision of food, and the reproduction of the means of production[1] (for example, investment in inputs) which is a prerequisite to produce these subsistence goods (Athreya et al., 1987). One may also include cultural capital expenses such as weddings as part of the requirements of simple reproduction given that they are viewed as 'necessary' expenditures for many households. Therefore, in a peasant household, the aggregate household labour time in which the needs of simple reproduction are met within a set unit of time can be classified as the households' 'necessary labour'. 'Surplus labour' refers to the extra hours in which a surplus product can be produced.

What happens with any surplus produced by the peasantry is connected fundamentally to land ownership (Marx, 1967, 807). Starting with peasants who own their land, any excess production after they have met their minimum needs would be surplus, and this can be retained by the household. Such a household can in theory reinvest this surplus to purchase outside labour and invest in improved inputs, thus developing the forces of production.

The accumulation of profit as capital would eventually allow expanded reproduction, a first step in the transition towards a capitalist mode of production – a topic which will be explored at length later. However, a large share of the global peasantry is *not* able to generate a significant surplus, even when they own their land. The farmer, for instance, may simply not own a large enough area of land to meet their subsistence needs at current levels of productivity. This factor is particularly acute in this region of rural Morang, where absentee landlords have control over a large share of productive holdings. Unless the farmer can develop the forces of production to improve productivity, they may only be able to meet subsistence needs through an increase in the hours of work on the land. They may also reduce their levels of consumption, reducing necessary labour requirements, yet undermining the nutritional wellbeing of the household. To Kautsky (1988), this tendency towards overwork and under-consumption is a central feature of peasant production. However, this also has its limits, and in the context of opportunities to labour in the capitalist economy, farming households have another option. It is clear from the sample that most marginal farmers, even those with small plots of land, simultaneously work for wages off the farm to meet their simple reproductive needs. In such contexts they perform the remainder of their necessary labour and all of their surplus labour off their farms. They would thus have much of the product of the aggregate surplus labour of the household appropriated by off-farm employers, often in the capitalist mode of production.

The discussion here relates to peasants owning their land. However, there are further barriers faced by those who are tenants, due to the rent burden – and this is particularly critical in the Adivasi belt of southern Morang. What is notable is that small owner cultivators who are not engaged in tenancy in rural Morang often cannot meet their subsistence needs off the land due to the small size of plots, yet for tenants, plot sizes are generally larger. The average plot size of pure owner-cultivators with less than 0.5 hectare is 0.27 hectare, rising to 0.54 hectare for those with 0.5–1 hectares. However, by contrast, landless tenants operate on average 1.21 hectares, and part tenants owning less than 0.5 hectare or 0.5–1 hectares operate 1.59 hectares and 1.41 hectares on average respectively. As around 1.5 *bigha*s, or 1 hectare, was recognised as a suitable sized farm for a typical family of six to subsist, it is quite possible that a large share of these tenants *do* produce a surplus at the end of the harvest, or are at least have enough to feed their family. However, unlike their land-owning counterparts, they cannot *retain* this within the household for use or reinvestment, as this surplus is appropriated as ground rent by landlords.

This echoes the additional challenge facing the peasantry across the periphery today. As well as small and fragmented holdings undermining their ability to subsist, they face multiple mechanisms of surplus appropriation, and this occurs most commonly when the peasant does not own their land. As Marx (1974) notes:

> Capital has not invented surplus-labour. Wherever a part of society possesses the monopoly of the means of production, the labourer, free or not free, must add to the working-time necessary for his own maintenance an extra working-time in order to produce the means of subsistence for the owners of the means of production, whether this proprietor be the Athenian calos cagaqos [well-to-do man], Etruscan theocrat, civis Romanus [Roman citizen], Norman baron, American slave-owner, Wallachian Boyard, modern landlord or capitalist.

There are notably other mechanisms of surplus appropriation, most notably through the market, or through usury – which even those who own their means of production (that is, owner-cultivators) are vulnerable to. All of these mechanisms of surplus appropriation will now be explored in the context of the Morang field sites, starting with those linked to land and rent.

Landlord–tenant Relations and Rent

As noted earlier, ground rent is by far the most significant form of surplus appropriation, given the extent of tenancy in the region. There are two primary contract types. *Adhiya*, known sometimes as *baataiya*, is a form of sharecropping whereby 50 per cent of the harvest is given away as rent, and represents 38.96 per cent of rental contracts recorded by the sample in 2019, down slightly from 42.5 per cent in 2007–2008. The remaining tenancies are under *thekka*, a fixed-rent contract, whereby the farmer pays the landlord in kind, usually through a predetermined share of paddy or wheat (see Figure 5.3). *Thekka* has become more common over the last few decades as absentee landlords spend less time in the community, since it requires less oversight compared to *adhiya*, where the landlord needs to be present at the time of harvest to monitor the share of the crops. The amount of grain given via *thekka* rents varies according to the perceived fertility of the land and whether it has access to reliable canal irrigation. *Thekka* rates varied according to soil quality and canal irrigation access, but in general they were around 25 *maund*s of paddy (1 *maund* = 40 kilograms) per *bigha*, although some

Figure 5.3 Winnowing the paddy grain. Once the grain has been measured, either half must go to the landlord under an *adhiya* contract or a fixed amount must be measured under a *thekka* arrangement.

Source: Author.

combined a share of paddy and wheat. There was a consensus though that rates had been increasing in recent years. *Mohi*, or legally registered tenants who had benefitted from earlier land reform laws, paid only around 11 *maunds* per *bigha*, yet they were a tiny minority today. While some absentee landlords also sharecrop out their land under the *adhiya* system, it is more common amongst local big farmers, as it is easier for them to monitor production.

The appropriation of surplus through 'extra-economic' means that was central to feudal relations of production in the Rana era is less common today in the case study communities. There was little evidence, for example, of rents being forced up through coercion or debt bondage, or farmers being trapped into cycles of debt to the same landlord as in classical models of feudalism such as that described by Bhaduri (1977). This is likely due to the fact that the predominantly absentee landlords rarely visit their estates, and rent is often appropriated through a locally based agent, or *kamtiya*. In more recent years the *katawala*, or grain merchant, would also play an important intermediary role in processing rent payments for landlords. Coercive surplus appropriation, however, has been observed in the form of attached labour in other VDCs of Morang where there are more large locally based landlords (Hatlebakk, 2004), as well as in a similar village in the Koshi floodplain to the west, where unpaid labour is extracted from tenants (Sugden, 2016). In spite of this, rents remain high and represent a substantial drain for poor farmers, and while *adhiya* crop shares have remained unchanged over the 15 years in which data for this book was collected, there was evidence that *thekka* rents have increased, a topic which will be covered in Chapter 8.

For the majority of tenants, a significant share of the annual harvest is appropriated through rent. According to the 2007–2008 survey, the average grain output for households engaged in tenancy is 5,682 kilograms, but the amount actually retained after paying rent is only 3,827 kilograms, a share which varies according to the amount of their land under tenancy and the contract type. For sharecroppers, half of the harvest is given away as rent, while for landless tenants renting on fixed-rent *thekka* contracts, the total rent share retained by the households sits at 42 per cent on average as of 2007–2008, but in a bad year, such as following a drought, the rent can end up constituting a far larger share of the harvest. Recent increases in rents may mean that this share is even higher today. As noted in Chapter 3, *adhiya* and *thekka* rental contracts are primarily oral, often being arranged through historical family connections with landlords. As a result, tenancies are often insecure in addition to being extractive, and households can be evicted at any time, reducing tenants' bargaining power to negotiate rents and conditions.

There is also variability between farms according to their levels of investment in the land or due to localised crop failures. Six out of the 21 landless farmers on *thekka* contracts were giving away over half of their harvest, and for one household it was more than two-thirds. While *thekka* contracts have their advantages for farmers, as will be discussed later on, all the risk is borne by the tenant and they can experience a significant loss in a bad year. In fact, for three of this group who had experienced apparent crop failures, the data suggests their entire harvest would have been lost as rent. However, whether the landlord offered some leniency given the circumstances would need to be ascertained.

Farmers engaged in tenancy yet who also own small plots of land are slightly better-off given that they do not need to pay rent on the plots of their farm that they own. Nevertheless, the rented area is still much larger for this group than the owned area. As per the 2019 data, for farmers who own less than 0.5 hectare, who are also engaged in tenancy, the average farm size is 1.41 hectares, yet the average area that is owned and yields these farmers the full product of their labour is only 0.22 hectare. The average annual grain output for this group as of the 2007–2008 survey is 6,430 kilograms, while the grain retained after rent is just 4,509 kilograms.

Within the context of ground rent, and depending on individual household circumstances, it is quite feasible that the entire product of surplus labour is appropriated as rent – and it may even eat into a proportion of the product of the household's aggregate necessary labour (see Patnaik, 1983; Pearce, 1983). We return to the issue of what rent means for households subsistence needs in Chapter 6 – but it is important to note that rent is not the only mechanism of surplus appropriation in rural Morang, and the next section looks at how surplus is extracted through the market, particularly via merchant capital.

Market Participation and Distress Commerce

Most households must participate in the market to a small degree, and this is not new. Historical changes such as the breakdown of cottage industry because of imports from India and the monetisation of tax created a need for cash. This has likely encouraged some level of commodity production and a loose articulation between the peasant economy and capitalist sector since Rana times or earlier. Indeed, a cross-border trade of agricultural commodities from Morang was documented even in the early nineteenth century (Hamilton, 2007 [1819]). Importantly though, as in the past, participation in markets in Morang today is not antithetical to pre-capitalist relations of production on the ground. This section will explore how surplus is appropriated not at the stage of production, but through the sphere of circulation. While some surplus may be appropriated by the capitalist sector through unequal terms of exchange, as in the case of the 'petty commodity production' described by Harriss-White (2016) in Tamil Nadu, in Morang, it is surplus appropriation via merchant capital which is most significant. Merchant capital extracts an additional 'rent' via the pricing mechanism and interlinked contracts, and is feudal in character rather than capitalist.

In terms of commercial production, it is worth noting that there are very limited sales of traditional 'cash crops' in the study communities. While some farmers elsewhere in the lowlands have turned to commercial vegetable production, competition with highly productive regions of India makes commercialisation challenging, and Table 5.1, which looks at average income,

Table 5.1 Average income from crop sales (NPR) as per the 2007–2008 survey

Farmer category	Kanchi, Rada-12 and Mansuli paddy	*Chaite* (spring) paddy	Other paddy (Basmati Chanachur)	Wheat	Pulses	Vegetables	Jute	Livestock products	Total agricultural income	Total profit/loss
Landless	2,511	465	224	1,640	27	0	0	1,236	5,412	–1,349
< 0.5 ha	7,366	3,178	2,716	4,201	591	403	163	1,372	16,082	2,226
0.5–1 ha	8,690	6,656	1,313	3,196	1,205	300	140	1,550	19,259	4,028
1–2 ha	7,792	1,191	430	1,851	944	128	219	1,834	12,424	3,088
> 2 ha	39,697	5,531	1,394	7,811	2,806	811	1,061	3,681	61,100	11,316
Total	8,205	2,314	1,296	3,148	686	244	177	1,768	14,511	

Source: Author.

suggests sales are marginal compared to other crops. Even jute, which the region was once renowned for, has been in decline in recent decades. While Table 5.1 points to some jute income across farmer categories, only two large farmers with more than 2 hectares of land are producing it on a significant basis commercially.

What is notable from Table 5.1 though is that paddy and wheat dominate the agricultural market of rural southern Morang. Furthermore, a majority of sales are of the dominant rice varieties produced for *home* consumption, coarse-grained Kanchi and Rada-12, and medium-grained Mansuli. These improved varieties of paddy are today the dominant staple crop locally, and most local varieties have been long since abandoned. Income from these crops was on average NPR 8,205 at the time of the 2007–2008 survey. Fine-grained 'aromatic' varieties such as Basmati and Chanachur, which commonly are produced commercially for the urban middle-class market, form a small share of annual income (only NPR 1,296 on average). Farmers producing aromatic rice such as this need to compete with large-scale producers in India, which dominate the urban consumer market in Nepal (Pudasainee et al., 2018). There is, however, a large local market for Kanchi, Rada-12 and Mansuli, and medium- to coarse-grained paddy varieties such as this are the staple for farmers who are food insecure and for landless labourers. While import of coarse-grained rice is widespread, there is also a large quantity being produced, milled and sold locally. There are several reasons for the high sales of these crops. First, rather than investing resources in risky 'niche' commercial crops, farmers prefer to focus on the production of staples, with the aim of meeting their minimum food needs – yet they have the option of selling off some of their grain stock in order to meet urgent cash needs or if they have any surplus left at the end of the year. Second, the fact that the dominant commercially sold crop is also the dominant food crop sheds some light on the nature of market participation amongst the southern Morang peasantry – whereby a majority are not selling a 'surplus', but are selling some of their subsistence crop to meet urgent cash needs. As will be shown, their engagement in such trade is often on highly unequal terms – and paves the way for additional mechanisms of surplus appropriation.

To better understand how this takes place, it is useful to understand the structure of agricultural commerce in rural Morang (see Figure 5.4). There are essentially two parallel agricultural marketing systems. First, there is the informal marketing system via *haatiya*s, or periodic markets, whereby vegetables and fruits are sold by farmers directly to consumers. The system of rotation

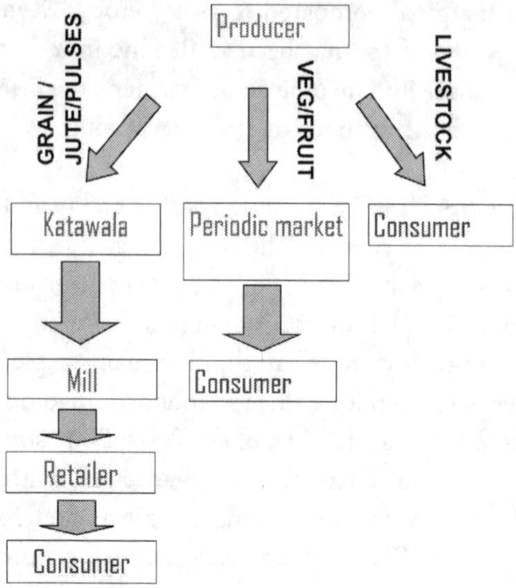

Figure 5.4 Commodity chain in rural Morang

Source: Author.

between villages ensures that most communities are within easy walking distance of a periodic market on any given day. They play an important social as well as economic role within the community, particularly for women who tend to sell their produce there – although the amounts sold and income are generally modest. Other than the *haatiyas*, livestock products are often sold door to door within the village. The informal trade via *haatiyas* and door-to-door sales represents part of the sphere of circulation which, although monetised, primarily entails exchange *between* pre-capitalist units of production. However, occasionally larger traders buy up crops in rural *haatiyas* and sell them to urban consumers in Biratnagar's two larger *haatiyas* or in Gudri Bazaar, the central vegetable market, providing relatively cheap wage foods for the urban working class.

The second and most important marketing system entails farmers selling their produce to *katawalas*, or grain merchants (see Figure 5.5). This is the primary marketing channel for the main commodities produced in rural Morang, namely paddy, wheat, jute and pulses. In the months following the harvest, male household members from throughout rural Morang rent bullock carts or rickshaws which are loaded with sacks of grain, and lead them to the *katawalas* in the most conveniently located bazaar (see Figure 5.6).

Figure 5.5 *Haatiya,* or periodic market. These take place once or twice a week in set locations and are the primary outlet for the sale of vegetables, fruit and handicrafts. They are also important sites of social interaction, particularly for women.

Source: Author.

In the merchants' yards, the paddy is weighed and purchased according to the daily market rates. Every few weeks, merchants go on to sell the grain or jute to larger traders or, more often, directly to the rice, wheat and jute mills to the east and north of Biratnagar. It is processed here before being transported to urban retailers across Nepal. The *katawala*s in this context act as intermediaries in the supply of commodities from the rural pre-capitalist to capitalist mode of production. As will be shown though, they also extract a share of surplus through interlinked contracts and forms of 'forced' or 'distress' commerce more commonly associated with feudal agrarian formations (Bhaduri, 1986).

There is only one group which appears to be yielding a significant profit from the market, and those are the large farmers owning more than 2 hectares of land, who operate mostly as owner-cultivators, including better-off hill settler and Tharu farmers – who had generated NPR 11,316 on average of profit at the time of the 2007–2008 survey (see Table 5.1), with the richest

Figure 5.6 *Katawala* – the merchant shops where grain is measured and sold

Source: Author.

earning up to NPR 88,387. This group could in theory make the transition to becoming 'capitalist' farmers. For many marginal (owning less than 1 hectare) and tenant farmers, however, engagement in the market is widespread, yet, critically, it does not represent a source of *accumulation*, but instead acts as a further 'drain' on already fragile livelihoods.

The sale of paddy and wheat is part of their day-to-day strategy through which they meet the monetised component of their subsistence needs to make up for what cannot be earned through wage labour.[2] For many households, market participation actually involves selling some of their annual Kanchi and Mansuli paddy harvest, only to have to buy this grain later on, often at considerable economic disadvantage. This is particularly pronounced amongst tenant farmers, who, as noted earlier, often fail to meet their minimum dietary needs in grain after paying rent. In fact, for many, sales fail to even cover the costs of inputs. Landless farmers had made an average loss of NPR 1,349 as of 2007–2008 (see Table 5.1). As for those owning less than 0.5 hectare of land, while there is a moderate 'profit' of NPR 6,544 after deducting input costs, this becomes meaningless when one considers that many of these households cannot meet their subsistence needs off the land (as will be discussed in detail later) and have to buy grain to compensate for what was sold.

There is a broad literature on these 'distress sales' whereby the farmer enters the market on conditions that are detrimental to one's economic wellbeing, with the short-term aim of meeting urgent cash needs or repaying loans, rather than a desire to yield a profit (Bhaduri, 1986; Bharadwaj, 1985; Harriss-White, 1996; Crow and Murshid, 1994).

The divergence between profit-oriented and 'distress' market engagement and the outcome for farmers is exemplified by the time of the year when grain is sold. The market price for grain fluctuates on a seasonal basis, being lowest immediately after the harvest while rising gradually in subsequent months as supply decreases, only to drop again at the next harvest. The price of coarse rice in the Nepali market increases by around 25 per cent between Ashwin (October–November) and Chaitra (March–April) (Paudel et al., 2017). Most farmers sell some grain immediately after the harvest and sell again at various stages later in the year. By storing grain and selling it in the season when prices are higher (see Figure 5.7), farmers can get a much better price. The small number of larger, more profit-oriented owner-cultivators store much of their

Figure 5.7 A raised grain larder, or *mora* (building on right). These are typical in Tharu and other Adivasi villages in the far-eastern plains and can be used to store grain until the market price is more favourable.

Source: Author.

surplus grain until the price is at its peak, giving them a greater net profit. One Tharu farmer who owned sufficient land to produce a surplus, like many larger producers, noted how he sells off any excess supply of paddy, yet explained how he prefers to keep hold of the grain for as long as possible to maximise the price received:

> If we need money then we sell it [the paddy] immediately otherwise we sell later on ... sometimes in Jestha or Ashadh[3] as we might get a better price. This year I sold it at 400 rupees during the [harvest] season while a few days ago I sold for 600 rupees.

Interviews with marginal and tenant farmers suggested that most sell a far greater proportion of their grain immediately after the harvest to meet urgent cash needs or repay loans taken to purchase inputs (a process discussed later), buying grain later at a higher price for consumption. This increases the likelihood that they will bear a financial loss at the end of the season.

Ekaadhikar: Price Manipulation and Surplus Appropriation through the Market

It is important to note, however, that while the seasonal fluctuation in prices disadvantage marginal farmers, the associated losses cannot on its own be read as a form of 'surplus appropriation' in the Marxian sense. However, this can be read as such when an additional 'rent' is extracted via the price mechanism. Bhaduri (1986) notes that in the context of distress sales by farmers under pre-capitalist modes of production, it is common for prices to be manipulated for reasons *other* than supply and demand. While Bhaduri primarily focused on 'sales' to landlords to repay loans, other studies (for example, Harriss-White, 1996) have shown how a separate intermediary class, that of merchant capital, can also extract an additional 'rent' through price manipulation. In a similar vein, in Morang, where the landlords play a limited role in money lending or marketing, the role of the *katawala*s, or grain merchants, comes to the fore and the evidence suggests they also play a role in appropriating surplus from the peasantry alongside absentee landlords.

Before looking at the exchange relations between farmers and *katawala*s, it is worth exploring how merchant capital fits within a complex social formation such as rural Morang home to parallel capitalist and pre-capitalist modes of production. To Marx (1974) the market, or 'sphere of circulation', is composed of several interconnected circuits of capital. It is in many ways an 'extension' of the mode of production given that it is necessary for the reproduction of the forces of production after each productive cycle – for example, to purchase agricultural inputs. It can also, however, lie 'between' modes of production, as a mechanism through which pre-capitalist and capitalist economic formations are articulated.

The circuit of merchant capital entails the purchase of commodities which are sold on at a higher price. Marx (1974, 155) denotes the circuit as M-C-M', whereby the merchant advances money (M) to purchase a commodity (C) which is sold on at a higher price (M') – what he terms 'commercial capital'. Merchant capital also includes an abridged circuit (M-M'), whereby money is lent (M) to be returned with interest (M'). Marx refers to this circuit of merchant capital as 'interest bearing capital', which will be discussed more later (Marx, 1967, 267). Both circuits are differentiated clearly from the circuit of 'productive capital', which is central to capitalist production, whereby a capitalist purchases inputs and labour to yield a commodity with profit. Marx (1956, 25) denotes this as M-C ... P ... C'-M'. The capitalist uses money (M) to buy the commodity (C). The process of circulation is interrupted while the commodity goes through the process of production (P) releasing a new commodity which embodies surplus value, or 'commodity capital' (C'). This is returned to the circuit being sold and yielding a profit, so money capital becomes M'. The renewal of the circuit allows reproduction of the mode of production and accumulation.

In rural Morang, the peasantry sell their grain to the *katawala*s, who in turn sell it to the processing industries, representing productive capital. Importantly, the *katawala*s also sell agricultural inputs to farmers, most of which are produced in the capitalist sector – albeit often from overseas. Crucially, many farmers also take loans from the *katawala*s to purchase inputs, only to repay them in crop sales at harvest time. This process of merchants making advance purchases of produce through loans to farmers already subjugated to feudal landlords appears to have a long history in this region, and Francis Buchanan-Hamilton reported that it was widespread over the border in Purnea even in the early nineteenth century (Regmi, 1978). It appears therefore that merchant capital, in both its interest-bearing and commercial forms, is an intermediary in the reproduction of both the pre-capitalist and capitalist mode of production in Morang.

Although Marx considers merchant capital 'unproductive', he believes its activities are necessary for the circulation of commodities and realisation of profit. Under idealised 'competitive' capitalist conditions, it is suggested that the share of surplus falling to these different capitals is included in the average rate of profit produced in an economy as a whole (Marx, 1967, 285–290). To Marx therefore, both the share of the surplus appropriated through interest rates on loans and the share taken by merchants for the buying and selling of commodities should be determined according to competitive market forces, fluctuating according to supply and demand. It should not therefore act as a 'constraint' to profitable production. Under pre-capitalist conditions, however, merchant capital can play a quite different role, whereby merchant profits are determined not by competitive market forces, but by extra-economic means driven by the principle of 'buying cheap and selling dear' (Nagatani, 2004).

This is highly relevant in the context of the southern Morang grain market whereby merchants are able to further manipulate the price of crops beyond the usual seasonal fluctuations. This is made possible by two forms of unequal market power between merchants and farmers. First, the fact that many farmers are entering the market on a distress basis reduces their bargaining power, as they have urgent cash needs to meet. However, second and most significantly, in the absence of sufficient competition between traders in a concentrated market, merchants are able to yield greater monopoly or monopsony power. Nagatani (2004, 73) argues that relations of exchange based upon 'buying cheap and selling dear' allow merchants to appropriate some of the products of surplus labour left behind after the subtraction of rent and other obligations, and like rent itself, can even eat into the product of necessary labour – pushing households into further food insecurity.

We now explore the processes through which this takes place. Farmers complained repeatedly of the lack of competition in the grain markets, and the capacity for a small number of *katawala*s to manipulate prices in their favour, yielding profit at the expense of sellers. They referred frequently in interviews to the merchants' *ekaadhikaar* – literally in Nepali or Hindi as a 'monopoly'. There was a perception that there was a highly concentrated market with few traders, who were well organised, with limited competition if they were unhappy with the price offered for their grain.

In economic terms this represents a form of monopsony (dominance of a single buyer) or, more accurately, oligopsony (dominance of a small group of buyers). Marx argues that under idealised capitalist conditions capital maintains full mobility, and if the rate of profit in the producing sector (for example, agriculture or industry) is greater than that of the commercial sector (those who buy and sell commodities – which includes merchant capital), capital will leave the commercial sector until profit rates are equalised (Marx, 1967, 202). The rate of profit to capital advanced in a set unit of time will therefore be the same for both productive and commercial capital. In conditions of capital immobility, however, which characterises many social formations that have yet to see the full development of capitalism (Friedman, 1980), concentrated markets emerge, and commercial capital has the power to absorb a much greater proportion of the surplus value realised by the producer (Marx, 1967, 308). This is because traders cannot easily move into the commercial sector and increase competition, and the 'necessary' function of merchant capital is superseded by its parasitic character, with little pressure to invest productively (Milonakis, 1995).

Measuring the potential for oligopsony in markets is a complex process, yet attempts have been made using the neo-classical structure-conduct-performance (SCP) paradigm (Bain, 1941, 1950, 1951; Caves, 1972; Dessalegn et al., 1998; Nyoro et al., 1999). While the approach can be criticised from a political-economic perspective, as will be done later, there are some useful elements of the paradigm that offer indications as to whether or not merchant capital is able to yield an oligopsony rent through price manipulation. The SCP framework suggests a relationship exists between market structure and the behaviour of actors or 'conduct', which affects market performance and price formation (Caves, 1972; Nyoro et al., 1999; Bain, 1950). Nyoro et al. (1999) and Dessalegn et al. (1998) have applied the SCP framework for analysing the structure of agricultural markets where farmers sell their goods in Kenya and Ethiopia respectively. Variables to determine the market *structure* typically include the entry conditions for a particular trade, which of course refer to the mobility of capital, the degree of seller and buyer concentration and the degree of product differentiation. Market *conduct* is measured by an examination of the behaviour of firms and the means through which they determine their buying or selling prices. Market *performance*, on the other hand, is measured by variables such as profit rates, evidence of competitive innovation and the relation between production and marketing costs (Dessalegn et al., 1998).

It is now useful to examine the market structure within the core study site, to further explore farmers' complaints, and assess the potential for price manipulation. To analyse of the *structure* of the rural markets in which farmers in Jhorahat, Bhaudaha and Thalaha sell their produce, a useful starting point is identifying the entry barriers to the trade, or, in line with a Marxian framework, the 'mobility' of capital. Interviews revealed that entry into new trades by the cultivating majority is not easy. Most agricultural buying and selling trades are dominated by certain ethnic communities such as the Marwaris and certain Maithili-speaking middle castes such as the Baniya[4] who have migrated to the region as the economy has become increasingly monetised and rural markets have expanded. Over the years, the close-knit community of *katawala*s have inherited expertise and market knowledge as well as valuable business connections further up the commodity chain which are essential for their mercantile operations.[5] Most of the local people who are predominantly from other ethnic groups do not have the same level of access to these networks or knowledges. In fact we only met three grain traders (out of the 35 who were surveyed) who were not either Marwari or Baniya. Most of the grain traders we spoke to had originally migrated to the area from elsewhere.

The second measure of market structure, which is likely to reflect these high entry barriers, is the level of market concentration, and it is this which facilitates price manipulation. A market characterised by high entry barriers is likely to be more concentrated with a smaller number of firms dominating a greater share of key activities. In these contexts one would expect more 'uncompetitive activity' such as collusion over prices. The most commonly used variable is the 4 firm concentration ratio (CR_4) representing the proportion of total trade within a particular market handled by the largest four traders (Caves, 1972; Dessalegn et al., 1998; Nyoro et al., 1999).[6] To calculate this ratio, the volume of total trade by each firm for a set period of time must be recorded so that firms can be rank ordered by total turnover. The level of market concentration can then be calculated using the following equation:

$$CR_4 = VT_4 / VT$$

VT_4 = the annual volume (kilograms) of total trade in a crop by the largest four traders in the sample.

VT = the annual volume (kilograms) of total trade in a crop by the entire population of the sample.

In the study area, there are two main marketing regions where farmers sell their produce. Farmers of the old Thalaha VDC and part of Bhaudaha VDC take their produce to the merchants in Naya Bazaar or Katahari to the east of Biratnagar. Farmers in the old Jhorahat VDC and western parts of Bhaudaha, meanwhile, generally sell to merchants in Jhorahat Bazaar and its surrounding settlements or the smaller market of Tetariya to the north.

To calculate the volume of trade by commodity, *katawala*s were asked to report the approximate net quantities of each crop they had purchased over the last year. Merchants generally calculated this in quintals (100 kilograms) according to the number of truckloads or tractor loads they had sent to the mill.

As they would only send a truck to the mill once completely full, and merchants knew the approximate capacity of the trucks or trailers they used, this appeared a suitably accurate measure. The survey was restricted to the three primary commodities sold by farmers, namely paddy, wheat and jute. Table 5.2 displays the data gathered and the 4 firm concentration ratio, calculated by the formula $CR_4 = VT_4 / VT$.

The results suggest that around 55 per cent of the paddy market in Naya Bazaar and Katahari and 60 per cent in Jhorahat and Katahari are controlled by the largest four *katawalas*. Similarly, 56 per cent and 59 per cent of the wheat market respectively, and 62 per cent and 72 per cent of the jute market are controlled by the largest four traders. Kohls and Uhl suggest that a four firm concentration ratio of less than 33 per cent indicates a competitive structure for agricultural markets, while above 50 per cent is indicative of concentrated oligopolistic conditions (cited in Dessalegn et al., 1998). It can thus be suggested that there is a significant level of concentration in the agricultural markets in which the peasantry sell their produce.

While the structure has been established, how does this translate into the conduct of traders when it comes to setting the price? Oral testimonies by farmers suggest they have little bargaining power with the merchants. If they complained about the price and went to a different merchant, they would generally be offered the same rate. A medium-sized Brahmin farmer recounted his experience of price negotiation in agricultural markets:

Table 5.2 Concentration of agricultural market for purchase of key commodities

Market region	Crop	Total no. of enterprises trading in each commodity	Total annual turnover (quintals)	Total annual turnover controlled by largest 4 firms* (quintals)	4 firm concentration ratio (CR_4)
Naya Bazaar and Katahari	Paddy	20	191,875	105,000	55%
	Wheat	17	62,200	35,000	56%
	Jute	17	59,218	36,875	62%
Jhorahat and Tetariya	Paddy	15	116,425	70,125	60%
	Wheat	14	29,075	17,175	59%
	Jute	11	7,975	5,750	72%

Source: Author.

Note: *Largest four firms in terms of the total volume of trade (in kilograms) in the commodity.

1 quintal = 100 kilograms.

> We take our crops to the *katawala* and ask them the price and they buy our crops at a rate which is fixed by them. There is no other alternative. We cannot fix the price ourselves. When we go to sell our crops to the *katawala*s they are the ones who fix the price. And when we need rice to buy from the mill then we also have to pay them in their price which is very high. We don't have a right to fix the price for our own crops.

Despite being part of the relatively more prosperous hill settler community in Jhorahat Bazaar, he still experienced a feeling of powerlessness during the process of selling his grain during years when he had a surplus as well as while purchasing paddy from the mill during years when there was a deficit.

One large farmer from a Maithili-speaking caste complained that for certain crops in particular, such as *chaite* paddy, the merchants have enhanced power to lower the price they offer the farmers. The farmer we spoke to suggested that as it is harvested in the monsoon and cannot be stored due to the damp climate, they are compelled to sell it immediately, even if the price is low:

> We grow *chaite* rice with so much hard work but when we harvest, we cannot receive a fair price. The *katawala*s fix the price themselves and we get a low rate. They fix the price, for example, at NPR 300, but as the *chaite* cannot be stored for a long time we are compelled to sell it.

The aforementioned testimonies suggest that farmers have limited bargaining power in the market and farmers frequently claimed there was collusion between traders to maximise their profits. It is argued in the SCP literature that profit rates increase in accordance with the level of market concentration due to the enhanced potential for collusion so that traders can buy low and sell high (Bain, 1941, 1951; Caves, 1972). This is of course in line with Marxian theories of merchant capital under pre-capitalist conditions, which assert that immobility of capital leads to unequal relations of exchange.

What therefore is the actual measured *performance* of the market in the study area? Do the profit rates suggest that merchants are yielding an 'oligopsony rent' through the pricing mechanism? The data in Table 5.3 records differences between the *katawala*s' reported price at which they buy from farmers and the price at which they sell to the mills for the commodities being bought and sold while the survey was underway in March 2008. The difference ranges from only 2.8 per cent to 4.6 per cent. When transport and brokerage costs are accounted for, one would expect only marginal rates of profit for each transaction.

Table 5.3 Average difference between reported buying price and selling price by commodity (NPR)

Market region	Crop	Average buying price (per quintal) (NPR)*	Average selling price (per quintal) (NPR)*	% difference between buying and selling price
Naya Bazaar and Katahari	Kanchi/Rada-12 paddy	1,423	1,469	3.1
	Mansuli paddy	1,611	1,655	2.7
	Basmati paddy	2,187	2,273	3.8
	Jute	1,798	1,866	3.7
Jhorahat and Tetariya	Kanchi/Rada-12 paddy	1,387	1,454	4.6
	Mansuli paddy	1,577	1,644	4.1
	Basmati paddy	2,023	2,116	4.3
	Jute	1,625	1,679	2.8

Source: Author.

Note: *Given the risk of bias in comparison due to price fluctuations, we endeavoured to complete all surveys with merchants within a two-week period from 15 March to 1 April. Fortunately there were no significant price fluctuations during this period.

Merchants themselves felt that competition had increased in recent years, and their profit margins had been pushed down as farmers had greater choice. It was reported that until the 1990s, merchants in Naya Bazaar and Katahari had control over the grain markets in Jhorahat also – although this had been undercut by the establishment of new *katawala* shops in these other villages, and over the last few years, by travelling traders buying direct from farmers. However, this likely only represents part of the story. Although the *katawalas*' reported buying and selling prices displayed in Table 5.3 suggest very low rates of profit, when one listens to farmers' testimonies and observes the prices they were given for their paddy, the data appears to suggest there are, in reality, huge divergences in the price offered to farmers.

Table 5.3 suggests that the buying price for paddy and jute is on average 5.5 per cent higher in Naya Bazaar and Katahari than in Jhorahat and Tetariya while the selling prices are 3.7 per cent higher – a difference claimed by merchants to be due to the prices offered by local mills. However, contradictions emerged when farmers were asked to report the highest and lowest prices they received for the main Kanchi[7] variety of paddy from the 2007 harvest, generating an 'average' figure. The results in Figure 5.8 suggest that although there is considerable variation in the prices received, and contrary to the data in Table 5.3, farmers selling Kanchi paddy in Naya Bazaar and Katahari actually report a *lower* average price than those who sold their crop in Jhorahat and Bhaudaha. The bottom quartile of recorded prices in Jhorahat and Tetariya ranged from NPR 6.75 to 8.75 per kilogram while the top quartile ranged from NPR 10.24 to 12.5 per kilogram. This contrasts with Naya Bazaar and Katahari where the bottom quartile in reported price ranges from NPR 6.25 to 7.19 while the top quartile only ranged from NPR 8.75 to 10.23. The difference between the average prices was 16 per cent.

During follow-up interviews, farmers were asked about why those who sell in Naya Bazaar and Katahari receive a lower price. There were some explanations which related to the perceived quality of paddy in Jhorahat and

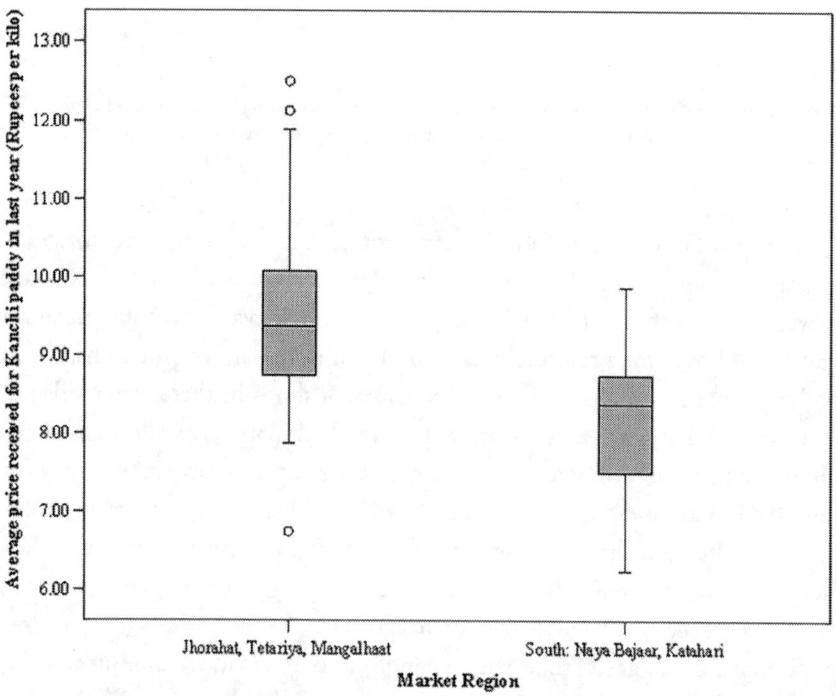

Figure 5.8 Reported prices offered for Kanchi paddy in Jhorahat, Bhaudaha and Thalaha

Source: Author.

Tetariya, while others pointed to the fact that the *katawala*s purportedly need to pay more tax in Naya Bazaar as it was closer to Biratnagar. A third reason for the divergence which was offered by farmers was that in spite of a recent increase in competition, the enterprises in Naya Bazaar and Katahari are larger, more organised and more close knit than in Jhorahat and Tetariya, where the traders moved in more recently. The Naya Bazaar and Katahari merchants were thus apparently better able to control prices in their favour.

However, this likely only gives part of the answer – and a more convincing reason for poorer prices in the Naya Bazaar and Katahari region is the weaker economic status of the selling farmers in this market area. Figure 4.8, the map which displays landlessness in Morang, shows that landlessness is notably higher in the VDCs surrounding Naya Bazaar and Katahari, unlike around Jhorahat and Tetariya where there are more landowning Tharu and hill settler farmers.

What is, however, particularly notable in Figure 5.8 is the significant variation in prices even within each marketing area. This implies that while many farmers appear to be offered an unfavourable price that is likely to yield the *katawala* a surplus profit, many also get a much higher and more competitive rate, likely to yield the *katawala* only a small profit.[8] The variations suggest that while the merchants may collude to fix some kind of 'maximum' selling price, there is significant variation around this rate, with some farmers receiving a far lower price and some obtaining a much higher price closer to what the merchants receive from the rice mills. Understanding these processes requires an analysis of individual exchange relations between farmers and merchants, and their links to the agrarian structure. It is on this note that Harriss-White (1996) criticises the SCP approach, arguing that the measures of market structure traditionally used are insufficient in explaining the process of price formation and the *specific* power relations between exchange partners in a highly stratified agrarian formation (Harriss-White, 1996). Bharadwaj (1985) adds that in much of rural South Asia, the terms of exchange between farmers and traders vary according to the type of market involvement, which in turn is rooted in their position in the rural class structure. Large cultivators who enter the market with the incentive to achieve a profit have a much greater capacity to set the conditions of exchange on their own terms when they sell their produce. Marginal producers, on the other hand, many of whom commercialise on a *distress* basis, are often compelled to participate in the market on highly unfavourable terms of exchange (Bharadwaj, 1985).

In the markets of Morang, this would suggest that while all farmers could potentially suffer to some extent from merchant price manipulations through collusion, poorer producers, many of whom are already facing the rent burden, suffer disproportionately. In other words, surplus appropriation via rent contributes to further surplus appropriation by merchant capital. A more informative picture of the role of one's position in the agrarian structure and their capacity to bargain in agricultural markets can be gained through an analysis of the price received by differently situated farmers. With regard to Kanchi paddy prices from the Jhorahat market area, evidence from the 2007–2008 survey suggests that a disproportionate share of those reporting lower average prices are landless or own less than 0.5 hectare of land, while higher prices are more commonly reported amongst those with more than 1 hectare of land, few of whom are engaged in tenancy. For example, the highest reported average[9] price for the medium and large farmers with more than 1 hectare was NPR 12.5 per kilogram, with an average of NPR 10.31. By contrast, for landless tenants the highest price was just NPR 10.6, and only NPR 9.8 on average. In the Katahari and Naya Bazaar market area, landless farmers on average received just NPR 9.2 with a maximum reported price of NPR 10.6 per kilogram. This was notably higher for small land holders with less than 1 hectare, at NPR 10.4 with a maximum of NPR 12.5, suggesting the security of a plot of land could have been beneficial. As there are only five farmers in the 1–2 hectares and less than 2 hectares categories in the Katahari and Naya Bazaar market region, there is insufficient data to analyse market prices for these two groups.

While further analysis is likely required using a larger dataset, the price data we have gives a tentative indication that one's position in the agrarian structure plays some role in shaping one's bargaining power. This is backed up by qualitative testimonies. In interviews carried out in 2008, respondents from marginal and tenant farming households frequently noted that while they were aware that the price was poor and was well below what was being offered by the mills to the merchants, they had no choice but to accept what was offered – particularly when they needed cash urgently. Even if they moved on to a different trader, poorer farmers remarked that they would probably still be offered the same low price.

In contrast, the small number of larger farmers who produce a large saleable surplus are generally viewed by *katawala*s as 'valuable' customers, given that they sell in large quantities each year, even out of season when business is scarce. It was even remarked that merchants come to the house of such producers to see if they have any commodities to sell. Wealthier producers can bargain with the merchants to a much greater extent, shifting the economic power back to the farmer and reducing the difference between the merchant's buying and selling prices. Similarly, many can also build up a long-term trust-based 'relationship', or *sambhanda*, with such producers, and some have been trading with the same merchant for generations.

A 'large farmer' we spoke to in Bhaudaha reported that although merchants in Naya Bazaar do collude to 'fix' the prices, exceptions can be made for those with whom they have a 'special' trading relationship.

> Actually all the *katawala*s offer the same price. There is no difference in the price on a given day between all the *katawala*s. Sometimes, however, if the relationship between the farmer and the *katawala* is good, then the *katawala* offers the farmer a better price … this is the secret of business.

He went on to state:

> If they [the *katawala*] have a good relationship with the farmers they give 10 rupees more [per *maund* (40 kilograms)] and they don't tell this to any other farmers with whom they do not share this relation. The farmers who have a good relationship sell again to the same *katawala*. In this way it is good for them [the *katawala*s], as with more business they can make more money. If they give 10 rupees more the farmers do not go to other *katawala*s.

The farmer in question had a reasonable holding of land and produced a safe saleable surplus each year. Such farmers who would reliably sell a large consignment of grain each year were considered valuable clients by the *katawala*s, and thus room for negotiation was enhanced. Platteau (1994) terms these trust-based rules as 'multilateral reputation mechanisms', used as actors seek to maintain their reputation in order to guarantee future transactions. However, as Bardhan (1989) argues, mutually beneficial institutional norms do not materialise if they reduce the control of surplus by a particular class.

Unlike the quoted large farmer, marginal and tenant farmers not only have more urgent cash needs, but generally sell in small amounts and are thus not viewed as 'valuable' customers. One respondent we spoke to argued that even if he sells paddy off-season when the price is highest, he still receives a rate below what many of the more prosperous farmers receive. Another farmer reported frankly that '…if we sell greater quantities, and on regular basis then we might get a better price but if we sell less we get lower price'. Oya (2001) observes similar processes in the Senegal groundnut sector, whereby traders discriminate in favour of producers with a high output when agreeing upon a price.

Price Manipulation, Interlinked Contracts and Debt

While it has been established that merchants can manipulate prices through collusive activity and take advantage of those with a weaker bargaining power, there are other more direct mechanisms through which this can occur, maximising the share of surplus which is appropriated. Friedman (1980) suggests that in pre-capitalist peasant economies, 'naked monopoly' by traders is difficult to enforce on its own in the long run and therefore debt can be used to enforce sales below market rate.

As was noted earlier, *katawala*s are not simply engaged in buying and selling commodities but are an important source of credit for farmers. This represents an interlinkage of commercial and 'interest bearing capital', better described as 'usury capital' under pre-capitalist conditions. While follow-up interviews with *katawala*s in 2019–2021 suggested that this practice had declined, the panel data points to a more complex picture. Back in 2007–2008 it was common for both larger and more marginal farmers to take loans from the merchants at the start of the season to buy inputs, then repaying them in cash. A notable 61.54 per cent of large farmers with less than 2 hectares had taken these loans in 2007–2008. However, the expansion of institutional credit in subsequent years meant that they no longer needed these loans, and loans taken by these same farmers had dropped to zero by 2019.

However, tenant farmers continue to regularly take these loans – and there is evidence that it is increasing. They lack savings from the previous years' sales to cover costs of inputs, and face greater challenges in accessing institutional credit due to limited collateral. Meanwhile, the cash which comes into the household from distress sales, remittances or wage labour is used primarily to cover food needs. As of 2019, 48 per cent of landless households engaged in cultivation had taken a loan from the *katawala* over the last year, a notable increase from just 35.29 per cent since 2007–2008 (see Table 5.4), a trend likely associated with the spiralling price of inputs and costs of production.

These landless farmers would often be trapped into a cycle of indebtedness, taking credit from the *katawala*s each season to purchase inputs, only to repay them in crop at the harvest time, on top of the share of rent expected from the landlords. As one interviewee from Jhorahat reported:

> The farmers who have little income have to take a loan. The loan is taken when the crop is planted and when the crop is ready we repay the loan. After paying the entire loan the farmers are empty handed, so they have to take a loan again and start farming.

Table 5.4 Percentage of farmers taking loans from *katawala*s by land ownership category

Land ownership category	% farmers taking loan from *katawala* (2007)	% farmers taking loan from *katawala* (2019)
Landless	35.29	48.00
< 0.5 ha	36.36	8.62
0.5–1 ha	25.00	28.57
1–2 ha	40.00	28.57
> 2 ha	61.54	0.00
Total	39.05	20.39

Source: Author.

It is worth exploring how these interlinked contracts impact the prices received by poorer farmers dependent upon these loans. There was evidence during the 2007–2008 study that farmers who have taken loans from *katawala*s receive a de facto lower price for their commodities when debt is settled through grain sales. First, given that interest accumulates each month the loan is outstanding, farmers who have taken loans must sell immediately after the harvest. They cannot therefore take advantage of seasonal variations in the price, as was discussed earlier. Second and most significantly, the interlinkage of interest-bearing and commercial capital give extra leverage for the *katawala* to manipulate prices.

Studies by Crow and Murshid (1994) in Bangladesh and Harriss-White (1996) in Tamil Nadu have examined the phenomena of interlinked contracts. Crow and Murshid (1994) demonstrate with regard to Bangladesh how by taking credit from merchants in advance, farmers are compelled to sell their produce to the same buyer at a price far below the competitive market rate. Similar processes are evident in rural Morang. During a discussion with a group of farmers in Bhaudaha they explained the situation in the Naya Bazaar market:

> If we have not taken a loan and have good quality crops, they [the *katawalas*] provide us a good price. However, if we have taken a loan, then we are not provided with a good price even if we have good quality goods.... We take loans in accordance to our needs, on average 5 to 6 thousand rupees for one bigha [0.67 hectare of land]. We borrow money from the merchants for fertilisers, pesticides and also labourers.

Those who have taken loans in the planting season must sell their grain to a particular merchant to repay an equivalent value in grain to what was borrowed in cash. A price for a borrower's crop is sometimes fixed in advance at the time the loan is taken (as in Crow and Murshid's study), but normally it is agreed upon after the harvest during repayment. Either way, the borrowing farmer's bargaining power remains low. Given their lack of choice, the price at which repayment in grain is calculated is often depressed to abnormally low levels on top of the deductions already made as interest on the loan. This process of price formation to Bhaduri (1973) represents an additional form of 'concealed' interest. A respondent from a larger owner-cultivating household in Bhaudaha explained this process:

> If you have taken a loan from the *katawala*, then you are compelled to sell to the same *katawala* as you have to repay the loan, even if the price is low. In this case the *katawala* has the power. However, if the farmer has not taken the loan, then he can sell the crops to a different *katawala* where he can get better price, so in this case the farmers will have the power.

While this quote was from a better-off producer, it still appears to be the tenant and marginal owner-cultivating households who suffer from the greatest price manipulations as loans generally comprise of a much larger share of their total agricultural sales, and on many occasions their only market involvement is to settle debts with the *katawala*s – a classic phenomenon during 'distress commercialisation'. For two-thirds of landless farmers who had taken loans in 2007–2008, loan repayment constituted more than half of their total sales in the last year (see Table 5.5), and for 42 per cent it absorbs their entire income from crop sales. This is notably lower for farmers with more than 1 hectare, for whom the acquisition of loans from *katawala*s was anyway rare by 2019.

Figure 5.9 displays the average reported price received for Kanchi paddy in the 2007–2008 season by those taking loans from the *katawala*s, but divides the results into quartiles according to the percentage of total agricultural income which constituted loan repayment over the last year (as used in Table 5.5). As one would expect, the lowest prices were reported by those for whom the loan constitutes more than three-quarters of their annual income – 90 per cent of whom were landless tenant farmers or those owning less than 0.5 hectares. For this bottom quartile, most if not all of their harvest *must* be sold to the same merchant. They had reported on average only NPR 9.36 per kilogram, with a maximum of NPR 11.38 per kilogram and a minimum of only NPR 7.5. On the other hand, the top quartile, for whom loan repayments comprise only 0.25 per cent of the total agricultural income, receive on average NPR 10.86 per kilogram for Kanchi paddy with a maximum of NPR 12.5.

Table 5.5 Percentage of households from different land ownership groups according to the share of agricultural income made up of loan repayments

Land ownership category	Loan is 0–25% of total agricultural income	Loan is 26–50% of total agricultural income	Loan is 51–75% of total agricultural income	Loan is 76–100% of total agricultural income
Landless	11.11	22.22	22.22	44.44
< 0.5 ha	33.33	26.67	13.33	26.67
0.5–1 ha	66.67	33.33	0.00	0.00
1–2 ha	66.67	33.33	0.00	0.00
> 2 ha	33.33	33.33	0.00	33.33
Total	33.33	27.27	12.12	27.27

Source: Author.

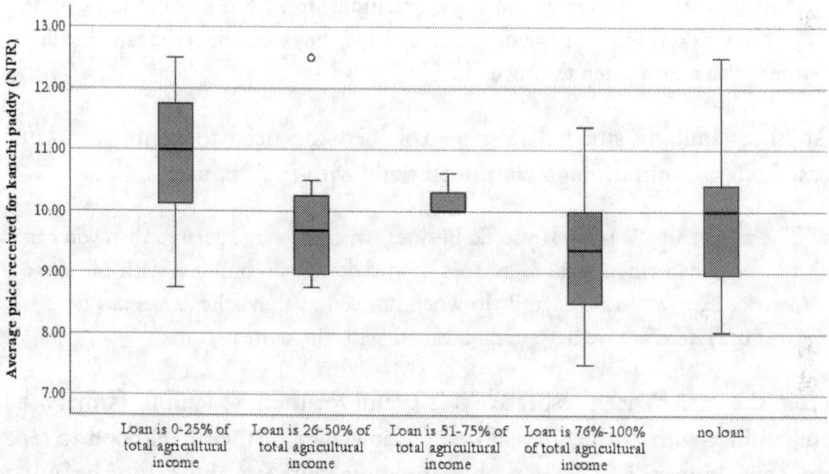

Figure 5.9 Average price received for Kanchi paddy in the last year according to percentage of agricultural income comprising of loan repayments

Source: Author.

For those who have taken no loans, which includes many other tenant farmers who have alternative means to pay for inputs including institutional or other private loans, there is still considerable variation. This is not surprising given the other compounding factors discussed earlier, such as bargaining power – and thus interlinked contracts is just one of several mechanisms through which merchants can squeeze additional surplus from farmers.

It is worth noting that many of those who would frequently take loans from *katawala*s during 2007–2008 would still sell their crops to the same merchant when cash was needed, even once the loan had been repaid. While in theory they could sell elsewhere and get a higher price, respondents stated that selling the remainder to the same merchant ensured they would be offered credit again next year. Harriss-White (1996) observes similar 'non-contractual' elements in interlinked credit and cotton markets in Tamil Nadu, whereby producers feel an obligation to sell the entire marketed surplus to the creditor to secure future contracts.

One tenant farmer who had taken large advance loans from *katawala*s to purchase inputs was asked whether he could sell any remaining paddy to a different merchant for a better price once the debt had been settled; he replied as follows:

> Yes, if we get a better price we can go to a different merchant but we normally don't do that so as to maintain a good relationship.... The relationship will be bad [if we don't sell to the same merchant] and they won't help the farmers next time with a loan when they need it.

Another similarly situated farmer explained the need to maintain a trust-based relationship through continued trade with the *katawala*s.

> The main thing is trust. If you do business with the same person, then you can ask for a loan when you are in need. If you do not do business with the same person, then you do not get help when in need as they [the *katawala*] do not trust us. Therefore we have to do business with the same person.

From the merchant's perspective it is useful for them to lend to farmers they are familiar with as they have a better knowledge of their likelihood to repay the loan. However, it appears that the merchants use the risk of default to justify threats that they will not give loans at all, even to farmers with a long history of trading with them. This in turn ensures the farmers sell them their entire crop, even at a depressed price, informally tying them into an unequal relation of exchange.[10] This dependence also explains why producers in parts of Thalaha and Bhaudaha who could just as easily travel to either market region have a tendency to prefer Naya Bazaar, even though reported prices are poorer. Naya Bazaar was famous for its *katawala*s, and this included the easy availability of credit – and it was reported that in the past farmers would travel from distant villages to sell their produce there. Even though the less organised merchants of Jhorahat tend to offer a more favourable price, landless or small landholding farmers are less likely to have a 'relationship' with them; the traders are smaller, and thus are less likely to offer credit.

Thus far the focus has been on how merchants can squeeze surplus from farmers through price manipulation – or so-called concealed interest. It is also important to remember that additional surplus is extracted via the actual interest which was agreed at the time of lending. As with prices for commodities, the farmers who borrow money from *katawala*s are subject to interest rates determined not by 'competitive' market forces but by power relations rooted once again in the unequal bargaining positions between market actors. Interest rates are usually around 3 per cent per month the loan is outstanding, although at times they can increase to 5 per cent. One merchant we interviewed admitted that if a farmer appears 'desperate' for cash, they will ask for a higher rate of interest, normally 5 per cent. The compulsion to take loans at higher interest is particularly acute for landless farmers who cannot even leave collateral such as land to guarantee credit.

However, if a *katawala* feels he has a 'good relationship' with a particular farmer, it was reported that they charge farmers a lower interest rate. In some cases they waive the interest altogether so long as the loan is repaid quickly, a process we observed while conducting participant observation in a *katawala*'s shop in Naya Bazaar. However, these special lending relationships, as with favourable prices, appeared to benefit primarily the wealthier producers whose patronage is valued by the merchants – and who today rarely take loans anymore. A large farmer from Bhaudaha who was producing a reasonable surplus and was a regular seller on a profit-oriented rather than distress basis explained how the interest rate depends upon the relationship one has with the merchant:

> The *katawala* sometimes even doesn't charge the interest to the old farmers who have good relationship and whom they trust, so when buying the crops they charge lower interest. However, when they have to lend to new farmers they charge 10 to 12 per cent interest.

Although 10–12 per cent appears to be an exaggerated monthly rate, the general trend is evident. When I asked how farmers are able to build such a relationship, the respondent replied:

> It's difficult. If you sell your crops this year and again next year to the same *katawala*, then the relationship starts. For small farmers who produce smaller quantities it is difficult to have a relationship with the *katawala*s.

High interest rates, however, are sometimes even charged to some of the merchant's 'special' clients if they need money urgently, as the following quote by another large surplus-producing farmer suggests:

> It [the interest rate] is 3 to 5 per cent. If the farmer has a good relationship, it is 3 per cent while others are charged 5 per cent. However, if farmers need money immediately, even the familiar farmers are charged 5 per cent.... If anyone is sick or if we need money, then we tell [the merchant] our problems. At that time the merchant tells us that he does not have money. He tells us that if we give him more interest than he will get the money from others and then lend to us. So in this way they increase the interest rate.

There were several other sources of private loans, including the local *byapari manche*, literally 'businessmen', and landlords, but these had become rare. Landlords in Morang had given out some loans as of the 2007–2008 survey at a staggering 60 per cent per year interest (NPR 5 per NPR 100/month in Bhaudaha). These loans which were taken independently from crop sales had emerged particularly in the context of overseas migration, which requires large upfront cash payments to recruitment agents. However, these loans were not recorded by the time of the 2019 survey, perhaps due to the expansion in institutional credit availability.

It seems then that at least in the immediate future, interest on loans and the 'concealed interest' imposed by *katawala*s through buying at a lower price from indebted farmers remain a regular feature of the agricultural cycle for the poorest landless cultivators already experiencing the rent burden, even if it is declining for the farmers with land. It thus represents an additional form of surplus appropriation in the context of a feudal mode of production.

Agro-processing and Price Formation: Unanswered Questions

It is worth noting that it may not only be merchant capital which can manipulate prices to receive high rates of profit at the expense of producers. In the relations of exchange between the mills and merchants, there is a chance that the mill owners could also use their control over markets for unprocessed grain to enforce sales of products below the prevailing market rate. This would further depresses the price already offered to farmers alongside the price manipulations on the grounds of individual bargaining power or tied contracts.

Merchants and farmers complained also of the price offered by the rice processing mills – suggesting that price manipulations (including hoarding) may also occur further up the commodity chain in the circuit of productive capital whereby mills purchase grain from the *katawala*s and sell it in processed form, often back to the same marginal farmers who made distress sales of grain in the first place, not to mention landless labourers. As one larger farmer complained:

> They buy the crops and then create an artificial shortage, then they fix a higher price and sell the rice back to the villagers. In this case farmers sell their crops at a cheap price but buy at a higher rate.

Collusion on prices in agricultural processing industries represents one mechanism through which capitalist firms can depress market buying rates for commodities (Palaskas and Harriss-White, 1993; Banerji, 2004). This would increase the profits for the capitalist agro-processing sector at the expense of the peasantry, representing a further transfer of surplus between capitalist and pre-capitalist modes of production, alongside the supply of peasant wage labour.

The process of price formation in the exchange between *katawala*s and the mills is, however, complex (see Figure 5.10) and concrete evidence is hard to come by. Merchants or *katawala*s who buy grain from the farmers and sell to the mills generally agree on a price through a broker. Merchants explained how they would call once or twice each day to enquire about different prices being offered by the mills, and the broker would finalise the deal between both parties in return for a small share of the profits. From our discussion with farmers and merchants, however, it was suggested that the negotiation process is not necessarily equal. Business organisations such as the Morang Byapaar Sangh produce daily recommended price lists for different products based upon current market conditions. However, there were many complaints by both farmers and traders that the prices offered to them were determined not just by external market forces but also by the personal collusion of the mill owners. It was alleged that agricultural mill owners operate in a *oligopsonistic* manner, colluding with each other to fix a maximum buying price below the competitive market rate. Some *katawala*s also reported cheating by the processing mills once the price had already been agreed. Mill operators would sometimes claim that the rice was of 'poor quality' or had 'dust' in it, and thus would subtract some kilograms from the total sale when calculating the payment.

Figure 5.10 Grain being loaded at a *katawala* shop en route to the mill. The price for a shipment, which can be of considerable value, is normally arranged through a broker.

Source: Author.

Of course, it is impossible to prove whether or not cartels and price manipulation do exist based purely upon oral testimonies by farmers and local businessmen. It also needs to be considered in the light of the broader challenges facing the industrial sector that have affected the price offered to *katawala*s or the retail price of processed grain, including spiralling costs and energy shortages – and the recent closure of rice mills due to competition from India (Joshi et al., 2020). Nevertheless, data for Morang and Sunsari districts suggest that the input market for food and beverage industries (a large share of which includes agricultural produce) is relatively concentrated amongst a few large firms. For example, seven food product industries in Morang have assets worth over NPR 10 crore (100 million) represent 10 per cent of the total (Central Bureau of Statistics, 2008), yet control 68 per cent of the market for inputs. In the neighbouring Sunsari district there are four units with assets worth over NPR 10 crore, representing 5 per cent of the total number of enterprises, who control 50 per cent of the market. This would point to the potential for some collusive activity.

Gautam's (2005) report for the Ministry of Local Development pointed out that 'anti-competitive' practices such as collusion over prices and cartels were widespread in Nepal, suggesting that they were facilitated by business and trade societies.[11] This problem stimulated the government to draft a 'Fair Competition Bill' in 2004. The problem of cartel formation in agricultural processing industries more specifically was raised in Nepal's 2004–2005 economic survey (Nepal Ministry of Finance, 2006), and, more recently, Joshi et al. (2020) cited the presence of cartels specifically with regard to the rice processing industry. With regard to the 'hoarding' of commodities, this was discussed in Nepal's post-conflict Three Year Interim Plan as one of the problems that must be dealt with by the new government (Nepal National Planning Commission, 2007), while a number of reports have noted that such practices are widespread (World Food Program, 2008; Gautam, 2005; Sedhain, 2005).[12] To fully uncover the process of price formation in the grain-processing sector, however, one would require a much more extensive study.

Parallel Axes of Exploitation

As noted at the start of this chapter, while the archetypical peasant in theory produces their own food and thus retains their own 'surplus' during the initial process of production, this surplus can subsequently be appropriated by dominant classes, and this reflects a challenge facing the entire global peasantry today. It is clear that for the land-poor and landless majority in rural southern Morang this surplus appropriation takes place most notably via absolute ground rent and the large shares of the harvest that must be paid to absentee landlords. For many farmers, the appropriation of rent extends beyond just absorbing any surplus produce, and can even eat into their minimum subsistence needs.

However, it is also clear from the discussions here that surplus appropriation does not stop at the farm. For those already vulnerable to exploitation via rent, a further share of grain or income is lost through the sphere of circulation – particularly via merchant capital in the context of widespread 'distress commercialisation'. Collusive activity in a relatively concentrated mercantile sector has allowed traders to collectively depress prices, particularly in the Naya Bazaar and Katahari market region. Furthermore, there are clear differences in the price received rooted in the bargaining power and class position of market actors. The manipulation of prices by merchants is made more acute through the interlinkage of commercial and interest-bearing capital in contracts. When farmers are in debt to the *katawala*, the traders have a greater power to depress prices as a form of 'concealed interest', on top of the additional interest extracted via loans. The exploitative inter-linkage of contracts appears to once again disproportionately affect landless and small landowning farmers due to their more restricted access to credit. Further price manipulations may also take place via the agro-processing sector, which are transmitted to the farmer – although this requires further research.

It is evident, therefore, that the peasantry – and particularly the marginal and tenant farmer majority – experience multiple *parallel* axes of exploitation. What this means for livelihoods and food security will be the focus of the next chapter.

Notes

1. Investment in the means of production entails the investment in inputs that maintain existing levels of productivity. Under capitalism, the reproduction of the means of production is paid for out of surplus value. However, as labour has not been separated from the means of production in pre-capitalist formations, investment in the inputs necessary to produce enough for the family to subsist must be paid for with the product of necessary labour time.
2. Even the poorest households, for example, have for generations had consumption expenses such as salt, cooking oil and utensils which must be bought from the capitalist sector. Furthermore, cultural capital investments such as dowry gifts are nowadays purchased from capitalist markets. There are also expenses associated with agricultural production itself (which in turn is necessary for households to produce grain staples), such as fertiliser and agricultural tools, or to pay for the labour power of those who help with *ropai* (rice transplantation) or renew their livestock from time to time. In general, cash needs have risen in recent years, a topic which will be discussed in Chapter 7.
3. Jestha (May–June) and Ashadh (June–July) are Nepalese months half a year after the rice harvest when the price is at its highest.
4. The Baniya are a caste traditionally engaged in business activities throughout rural northern India and the Nepal Tarai.
5. Harriss-White (1996, 2005) has written considerably on caste-based networks as an entry barrier to agricultural marketing activities.
6. Harriss-White's (1996) study of agrarian markets in Tamil Nadu also measures concentration by the control of assets and number of transactions (in this case by the top 1 per cent of traders rather than the top four firms).

Both these variables were considered, but in the post-conflict political context merchants would have been unlikely to reveal information about the value of their assets to strangers. Meanwhile, they were generally unable to recall the number of transactions in the last year or even month. Therefore we settled on the total volume of trade to measure concentration.

7. As noted earlier, Mansuli and Kanchi paddy (and the similar Rada-12 which sells for a similar price) are the main crop consumed and sold by farmers to *katawalas*, although Kanchi is the most widespread variety. Eighty-six per cent of the 76 households who have sold crops to the *katawalas* have included some Kanchi paddy. It represented 40 per cent of the total recorded grain sales in the 2007–2008 survey, as opposed to 18 per cent for wheat, 18 per cent for *chaite* paddy, 14 per cent for Mansuli paddy and 11 per cent for Basmati paddy. Its popularity means there is sufficient data on price variations for reliable data analysis.
8. Note that the prices reported by farmers in the survey will be lower than those reported by merchants as it represents current prices, while the prices reported by farmers are from the previous season, so unfortunately these cannot be compared.
9. This is the average sales from across the year, so the seasonality of sales does not affect the data.
10. The ability to secure credit was at times framed by farmers as a favour, although there are clear elements of a patron–client relationship which effectively disguises and reproduces an exploitative form of exchange (see Rankin, 2004).
11. This would parallel Harriss-White's (2005) findings that suggest elite business associations in Tamil Nadu can be used to increase rates of profit at the expense of small producers and labourers by colluding to fix prices and wages.
12. What is unclear though is whether or not this is practised by industries themselves or distribution companies. Sedhain (2005) suggests that a large supply of rice, flour, oils and sugar distribution in Nepal is controlled by a small number of powerful business houses. Sedhain points to the lack of an adequate competition law in Nepal.

References

Athreya, V., Boklin, G, Djurfeldt, G and Lindberg, S. 1987. Identification of agrarian classes: A methodological essay with empirical evidence from South India. *Journal of Peasant Studies* 14 (2): 147–190.

Bain, J. S. 1941. The profit rate as a measure of monopoly power. *Quarterly Journal of Economics* 55 (2): 271–293.

———. 1950. Workable competition in oligopoly: Theoretical considerations and some empirical evidence. *American Economic Review* 40 (2): 35–47.

———. 1951. Relation of profit rate to industry concentration: American manufacturing, 1936–1940. *Quarterly Journal of Economics* 65 (3): 193–324.
Banerji, A. 2004. Millers, commission agents and collusion in grain auction markets: Evidence from Basmati auctions in north India. Delhi School of Economics, Working Paper No. 129, Centre for Development Economics.
Bardhan, P. 1989. The new institutional economics and development theory: A brief critical assessment. *World Development* 17 (9): 1389–1395.
Bhaduri, A. 1973. A study in agricultural backwardness under semi-feudalism. *Economic Journal* 83 (329): 120–137.
Bhaduri, A. 1986. Forced commerce and agrarian growth. *World Development* 14 (2): 267–272.
Bharadwaj, K. 1985. A view on the commercialisation in Indian agriculture and the development of capitalism. *Journal of Peasant Studies* 12 (4): 7–25.
Caves, R. 1972. *American Industry: Structure, Conduct, Performance*. Prentice-Hall.
Central Bureau of Statistics. 2008. *Census of Manufacturing Establishments, Nepal, 2006/2007*. Central Bureau of Statistics, Kathmandu.
Crow, B. and Murshid, K. A. S. 1994. Economic returns to social power: Merchants' finance and interlinkage in the grain markets of Bangladesh. *World Development* 22 (7): 1011–1030.
Dessalegn, G., Jayne, T. S. and Shaffer, J. D. 1998. Market structure, conduct and performance: Constraints on performance of Ethiopian grain markets. Working paper 8, Grain Market Research Project, Ministry of Economic Development and Cooperation, Addid Ababa.
Friedman, H. 1980. Household production and the national economy: Concepts for the analysis of Agrarian formations. *Journal of Peasant Studies* 7 (2): 158–184.
Gautam, R. 2005. *Competition Policy and Law in Nepal.* Ministry of Local Development, Government of Nepal, Kathmandu.
Hamilton, F. B. 2007 [1819]. *An Account of the Kingdom of Nepal: And of the Territories Annexed to This Dominion by the House of Gorkha*. Rupa and Co.
Harriss-White, B. 1996. *A Political Economy of Agricultural Markets in South India: Masters of the Countryside*. Sage.
———. 2016. From analysing 'Filieres Vivrieres' to understanding capital and petty production in rural south India. *Journal of Agrarian Change* 16 (3): 478–500.
Hatlebakk, Magnus. 2004. Attached labor in Nepal: A field-study of landlord–labor relations that are misrepresented in the Nepal-LSMS data. Presented at 75 Years of Development Research conference at Cornell University, May.
Joshi, Krishna Dev, Upadhyay, Santosh, Chaudhary, Pashupati, Shrestha, Suchit, Bhattarai, Kamal and Tripathi, Bhaba Prasad. 2020. The rice processing industry in Nepal: Constraints and opportunities. *Agricultural Sciences* 11 (11): 1060–1080.
Kautsky, K. 1988. *The Agrarian Question*. Zwan Publications.

Marx, K. 1967. *Capital: A Critique of Political Economy (Volume 3)*. Progress Publishers.

———. 1974. *Capital: A Critical Analysis of Capitalist Production (Volume 1)*. Progress Publishers.

Milonakis, D. 1995. Commodity production and price formation before capitalism: A value theoretic approach. *Journal of Peasant Studies* 22 (2): 327–355.

Nagatani, K. 2004. Capitalist exploitation and the Law of Value. *Science and Society* 58 (1): 57–79.

Nepal Ministry of Finance. 2006. *Nepal Economic Survey: Fiscal Year 2005/06*. Government of Nepal, Kathmandu.

Nepal National Planning Commission. 2007. *Three Years Interim Plan*. Government of Nepal, Kathmandu.

Nyoro, J. K., Kiiru, M. W. and Jayne, T. S. 1999. *Evolution of Kenya's Maize Marketing Systems in the Post Liberalization Era*. Tegemo Institute of Agricultural Policy and Development, Nairobi.

Oya, C. 2001. Large- and middle-scale farmers in the groundnut sector in Senegal in the context of liberalization and structural adjustment. *Journal of Agrarian Change* 1 (1).

Palaskas, T. B. and Harriss-White, B. 1993. Testing market integration: New approaches with case material from West Bengal food economy. *Journal of Development Studies* 30 (1): 1–57.

Patnaik, U. 1983. Classical theories of rent and its application to India: Some preliminary thoughts on sharecropping. In *Sharecroppers and Sharecropping*, edited by Byres, T. J. Frank Cass and Co.

Paudel, S., Kafle, A. and Amgai, S. 2017. Rice marketing in Nepal. In *Rice Science and Technology in Nepal: A Historical, Socio-cultural and Technical Compendium*, edited by Paudel, M. N., Bhandari, D. R., Khanal, M. P., Joshi, B. K., Acharya, P. and Ghimire, K. H. Ministry of Agricultural Development and Agronomy Society of Nepal, Government of Nepal, Kathmandu.

Pearce, R. 1983. Sharecropping: Towards a Marxist view. In *Sharecropping and Sharecroppers*, edited by Byres, T. J. Frank Cass and Co.

Platteau, J. P. 1994. Behind the market stage where real societies exist – Part I: The role of public and private order institutions. *Journal of Development Studies* 30 (3): 533–577.

Pudasainee, A., Chaulagai, T. R., Ghimire, Y. N. and Chaulagain, B. P. 2018. Drivers of transition from export to import of rice in Nepal. *Nepalese Journal of Agricultural Sciences* 17: 208–216.

Rankin, K. N. 2004. *The Cultural Politics of Markets*. Pluto Press.

Regmi, Mahesh Chandra. 1978. *Thatched Huts and Stucco Palaces: Peasants and Landlords in 19th-century Nepal*. Vikas Publishing House.

Sedhain, G. K. 2005. Critical review of the design and strategies of the agriculture perspective plan (APP): Food and livelihood security perspective. *The Reconstruction – Punarnirman* 9: 5–10.

Sugden, F. 2016. Improving dry season irrigation for marginal and tenant farmers in the Eastern Gangetic Plains: Baseline socio-economic report. Unpublished project report, International Water Management Institute.

World Food Program. 2008. *Market and Price Impact Assessment Nepal: Final Report*. United Nations World Food Program and Nepal Development Research Institute.

6

Surplus Appropriation and Its Implications for Food Security and Productivity

It is clear thus far that rural poverty in southern Morang has complex roots. Unlike in many villages of the Eastern Gangetic Plains, there is not a local landlord class or a traditional caste-based land ownership hierarchy, where villages are divided into neighbourhoods by caste, with clear disparities of wealth in terms of housing and asset ownership. The region also does not experience the open political and ideological subjugation by a local dominant caste or landlord class at a local level, such as those which garnered support for the Naxalite struggle in Bihar in the 1980s and 1990s (Kunnath, 2017) or in the central Tarai-Madhesh during Nepal's People's War. However, the largely Adivasi peasantry experiences a silent drain of resources through a more complex and 'distant' network of feudal exploitation, with rents being appropriated in parallel by urban-based landlords and merchant capital.

It is important to now understand what this means for household livelihoods and the reproduction of rural poverty in southern Morang, as well as the long-term opportunities for 'accumulation' within the peasantry. The first section of this chapter explores the ability of households to meet their minimum subsistence needs or produce a surplus in the context of ground rent, distress commerce and usury. The second goes on to look at the implications of this drain of resource for investment on the land – in other words, it explores the constraining role played by the relations of production in developing the forces of production at a time of economic liberalisation and state-promoted commercialisation. Finally, this chapter synthesises what this means in terms of how one characterises the rural mode(s) of production in the southern Morang social formation.

The Drain of Surplus and Food Security

As indicated earlier, it appears likely that exploitative surplus appropriation, first via rent and second by merchant capital, means the landless and small landholding majority have little agricultural produce left to enhance nutrition or generate income – and for many households, rent and other axes of exploitation actually eat into basic subsistence needs. To better understand this phenomenon, this chapter begins with an analysis of the detailed agricultural production data collected during the 2007–2008 survey.

To gain a very approximate understanding of what is required for households to meet their minimum food needs and the impact of rent on food security from the land, it is useful to look at production and retention within the household of the two main crops – paddy and wheat. These two crops both make up the bulk of household diet, while also being the primary medium through which rent is paid via sharecropping or fixed-rent contracts. A first stage is to estimate the annual needs of households in terms of rice and wheat consumption. National data shows the average milled rice consumption per capita per year in rural Nepal is 142.9 kilograms, and wheat flour consumption is 24.4 kilograms (Central Bureau of Statistics, 2016). At a farm level this is equivalent to 200.06 kilograms of unprocessed paddy (accounting for the 40 per cent milling loss) and 30.5 kilograms of unprocessed wheat (accounting for 25 per cent milling loss), or 230.56 kilograms of unprocessed grain. Given that these are Nepal-wide statistics, including hilly domains where other crops such as maize and millet are important, one would expect minimum rice and wheat requirements to be much higher in Morang. For example, Bangladesh, which has a dietary and climatic pattern close to Morang, is estimated to have a per capita annual consumption of 206.61 kilograms of wheat and rice (Hossain and Yunus, 2016), equivalent to 288.01 kilograms of unprocessed grain.

Identifying a measure of the typical grain needs in rural southern Morang was challenging in the field sites given the degree of subjectivity to this question. Nevertheless, in focus groups and interviews respondents were asked what they felt was the minimum grain requirements. The response was invariably that one would need between 10 and 15 *maund*s (400–600 kilograms) of unprocessed paddy per family member per year for a family of six. Digging deeper it became apparent that farmers would calculate their grain needs as approximately 1 *maund* per person per month. They would also consume around 1 *maund* of wheat (40 kilograms) per family member in a year. This is a useful measure, bearing in mind that there will be individual

Table 6.1 Estimated per capita grain needs

Estimated per capita grain needs per year	Unprocessed grain	Processed (husked) grain
Paddy	12 *maunds*, or 480 kg	288 kg
Wheat	1 *maunds*, or 40 kg	30 kg
Total	13.5 *maunds*, or 540 kg	318 kg

Source: Author.

variations according to the age of the family members and other factors. In Table 6.1 this has been calculated as approximately 318 kilograms of unprocessed grain being required for each family member in a year, higher that the national consumption estimates, although this is likely due to the more limited production of other carbohydrate-rich crops such as maize and potatoes in the plains.

Regardless of the exact consumption needs, the survey results from 2007–2008[1] calculated the total grain output, as well as what was lost due to rent, distress sales and in-kind debt payments to *katawalas*, as well as modest in-kind payments that were used to pay for labourers or for threshing (mechanical thresher owners would take a small share of the paddy). Starting with landless tenant households, the average quantity of unprocessed paddy and wheat produced over the last agricultural year which is retained following these deductions is only 109.11 kilograms (see Table 6.2). This is well below the 318 kilograms per capita food security threshold suggested by farmers and is also significantly below the national average consumption of 230.56 kilograms per capita. Per capita grain retention increases to 252.61 kilograms for those with less than 0.5 hectares, although for the poorer of this group the figure is closer to the levels of grain retention by their landless counterparts.

For those with between 1 and 2 hectares of land, it increases substantially to 579.65 kilograms per capita and above. This is higher than the average consumption, as understood by farmers (and national estimates) – suggesting that during that year these medium farmers could meet their subsistence needs from the land with a small surplus. The farmers with more than 2 hectares, with the figure of 466.42 kilograms, retain less grain than the middle groups but still well above what is needed to subsist. The slightly lower figure should be viewed with caution due to the small number of farmers in this category, although it may be because they are more commercially oriented with just under half of their grain being sold (see Table 6.1). Some of this will have been

Table 6.2 Percentage use of grain (paddy and wheat) after harvest

Farmer category	Average % total grain output paid as rent	Average % total grain output used to pay for services and labour	Average % of total grain output sold (including debt repayments)	Average % of total grain output for home consumption	Average grain retained for household consumption per capita (kg)
Landless	39.55	10.13	16.15	35.64	109.11
< 0.5 ha	28.69	8.48	21.38	47.20	252.61
0.5–1 ha	3.48	7.54	25.51	63.47	365.02
1–2 ha	2.04	10.42	28.17	66.40	579.65
> 2 ha	9.75	12.80	48.18	29.27	466.42
Total	24.87	9.66	24.62	45.17	243.08

Source: Author.

to repay loans but a share is also sold for profit. As noted earlier, around two-thirds of this group also cultivate grains with a good market value yet lower yield such as Basmati rice.

Table 6.2 gives a breakdown of what happens to the grain harvest. For landless households engaged in agriculture, all of whom are tenants, what is striking from Table 6.1 data is that after they bring this grain to their courtyards for threshing, only 39.64 per cent of the grain harvest on average is actually retained by the family for home consumption. Some of this is lost due to necessary expenses such as in-kind payments for rental of threshing machines and labour, the latter of which is usually compensated for when the farmers work in turn for neighbours. Nevertheless, this forms only 10.13 per cent on average of the harvest. A substantial 39.55 per cent on average is lost as rent. As noted earlier, this is set at 50 per cent for sharecroppers, while for landless *thekka* (fixed-rent) farmers, rent formed 39.79 per cent on average of the harvest at the time of the survey, although, as noted earlier, rents have increased since this survey data was collected and a bad harvest may mean the share is notably higher. Furthermore, 16.15 per cent of the harvest was also lost due to sales, all of which can be assumed to be on a distress basis, given their shortfalls of grain for consumption.[2] While some may have been to meet urgent cash needs, it was often to pay off debts to the *katawala*s.

Even for land owners with less than 0.5 hectare, it appears that over half of the harvest is lost for this group. Losses to pay for services are also low at just 8.48 per cent on average, while the losses due to rent form on average 28.69 per cent of the annual grain harvest (as many simultaneously rent holdings). This is lower than landless tenants, given that this group own their own plots on the side which are not subject to the rent burden, yet nearly a quarter of the harvest is also lost through distress sales. In fact, if one excludes those engaged in tenancy, distress sales still make up 26.97 per cent of their total harvest. This may have declined somewhat in the most recent data given that households with land are taking fewer loans from *katawala*s compared to 2007–2008.

If one understands agricultural production for these groups in terms of surplus and necessary labour, it appears that a portion of the product of their aggregate necessary labour on the land and the entire product of their surplus labour is appropriated through rent, interest and distress sales. While some may have additional income from the sale of non-grain crops or livestock against which they can purchase grain, their ability to reproduce through agriculture alone is still severely constrained when one considers the additional cost burdens on households (for example, to buy spices, salt, tea, cooking oils and snacks) as well as other living costs (for example, electricity, taxes, mobile

Figure 6.1 In the Bantar villages of Bhaudaha, the vast majority of households work on the land of absentee landlords. Few can meet their subsistence needs off the land.

Source: Author.

credit, clothes and healthcare) (see Figure 6.1). Therefore, an intensification of family labour in the capitalist sector off the farm or reducing consumption is often the only choice for households if they are to meet their minimum needs – an issue which will be discussed at length in Chapter 8.

The Struggle to Develop the Forces of Production

In spite of the burden of rent and distress sales, the last few decades have seen a wave of technological change across Nepal with the introduction of various hybrid paddy varieties (Mishra et al., 2016), the use of mechanical threshers, rising tractor use and a range of new irrigation technologies (Biggs et al., 2011). There were a range of agricultural training programmes run by local NGOs during the fieldwork period, particularly in Jhorahat, and each village had its recognised 'leader farmers' – generally larger producers who were usually the first to try out new cropping systems, land management practices or technologies.

This raises further important questions relating to peasant livelihoods in rural Morang. The focus of this chapter has thus far been on understanding the *relations* of production – with emphasis on the ownership of land, and the mechanisms of surplus appropriation that go with it, and the implications for households in meeting their subsistence needs. However, the ability of households to meet their minimum needs is not shaped by only the size of holdings or the burden of surplus appropriation. Also important are farmers' capacities to raise levels of productivity through new technologies – in Marxian terms, their capacity to develop the 'forces of production'.

The primary question for this section is what farmers can do to improve yields on their land so that they can more easily meet their minimum needs or yield a small surplus, while they are simultaneously experiencing multiple parallel forms of surplus appropriation. Farmers can in theory raise productivity through *increasing* the hours of necessary labour on their land to increase cropping intensity while simultaneously embracing technological change. Investments in technology not only can allow more output to be produced for each unit of labour; they are themselves a perquisite for raising cropping intensity given the seasonality of rainfall. The first significant mechanism to develop the productive forces is to invest in irrigation, to increase the yields of paddy during the monsoon itself, while also allowing an intensified cultivation of dry season *rabi* or winter crops such as wheat and pulses, as well as *pre-kharif* (pre-monsoon) crops such as *chaite dhan*, or spring paddy. Development of the productive forces can, second, include investments in improved seeds and fertilisers and improved nutrient management, allowing increased yields across the seasons. By raising productivity, households can *decrease* the hours of necessary labour time, making it easier for them to meet their minimum needs at the end of the agricultural year, while for the bigger farms, they can more easily retain of a surplus after paying rent.[3]

The expansion of technology to support agricultural intensification and higher yields has been central to Nepal's agricultural strategy since the 1990s, and the 20-year Agricultural Perspective Plan (APROSC, 1995) and later Agricultural Development Strategy were heavily technology and input focused – with access to irrigation, seeds, fertiliser and mechanisation at the forefront. New technologies and cropping systems are generally introduced locally via junior technical assistants (local extension officers). However, extension services have for years been overstretched despite numerous committed local staff, and there were notable cutbacks following economic liberalisation. District agricultural staff complained of how the number of service centres had been cut by more than half, and the remaining village-level extension staff were overworked with low morale. Junior technical assistants were often responsible for a large number of villages and were under-resourced.

In interviews, only 31 per cent of respondents in Jhorahat and 9 per cent in Bhaudaha and Thalaha had participated in agricultural training in the last year. While half of large landowners had participated, only 8 per cent of tenants and 19 per cent of small landowners (less than 1 hectare) had done so.

The creation of rural municipalities and improved local budgets may improve the extension system in the future. Nevertheless, knowledge of technologies is only part of the problem; a more significant challenge is investment capacity – particularly for the technologies which could have a transformative impact on yields such as groundwater irrigation. As noted elsewhere (Sugden, 2009, 2014), while there is uptake amongst some better-off farmers, for the landless and land-poor majority across the region, the dual burden of rent and distress commerce impede their capacity to invest. In other words, the relations of production themselves are a constraining factor in developing the forces of production. We will now proceed to explore these constraints with regard to irrigation and fertiliser use.

Year-round irrigation provided by diesel pump sets (or electric pumps where infrastructure allows) reduces farmers' reliance upon unreliable canal irrigation. It improves yields of the main paddy and wheat harvests, and determines whether or not households can cultivate an additional crop of spring, or *chaite*, paddy. The Sunsari–Morang irrigation project has several canals which channel water from the Koshi and pass through the study area. This was built following the signing of the bilateral agreement with India to construct the Koshi flood barrage in the 1960s. In Jhorahat and Pidarboni, the canals offer plentiful water during the monsoon and usually allow some winter wheat cultivation – although for tenants, this additional productivity is reflected in elevated *thekka* rents. The water yields, however, have reportedly dropped considerably in recent years due to maintenance challenges following the 2008 Koshi flood (Bhandari and Ghimire, 2015), as well as siltation and weak management structures. Farmers also complained of poor enforcement of rules for upstream users regarding release times for water on the smaller sub-branches, resulting in reduced water availability downstream. While farmers are called together periodically to contribute to cleaning, larger repairs and more extensive desilting require an excavator. This can be costly, and recently farmers complained of work not being carried out due to a conflict with the contractors. In Bhaudaha and Thalaha, which only has access to smaller feeder canals, farmers felt the water was insufficient, particularly over the last few years.

It is set against this context that groundwater comes to the fore. Pump irrigation from shallow tube wells was deemed necessary to cultivate wheat, or even to support paddy cultivation during dry spells. As of 2006–2007 it is estimated that 726,000 hectares of land in the Tarai-Madhesh had 'good' potential for shallow aquifer development, while 305,000 hectares reportedly had 'marginal' potential (Ministry of Irrigation, 2012). Within this context shallow tubewell development has been a central priority of Nepal's irrigation strategy and is associated with ambitious targets to increase cropping intensity (Ministry of Agricultural Development, 2014).

However, unlike canals which are a public resource, groundwater irrigation requires private investment, and thus the capacity of marginal and tenant farmers to invest is limited by the expense. The costs of boring a well can be considerable, and vary according to the underlying hydro-geology and proximity to water bodies or rivers, although it generally ranges from NPR 10,000 to 20,000. During interviews in 2012 and 2013, tenant farmers argued that they have few incentives to bore wells on land which does not belong to them, particularly given the prevalence of informal word-of-mouth contracts. During a group discussion in Sitpur of Bhaudaha VDC, a Rajbanshi farmer who operated around 2 hectares from an absentee landlord on a sharecropping (*adhiya*) contract explained how only two-thirds of his land received water from the canal. He noted how even this was insufficient as he was at the tail end of the system. However, boring a well was too big a risk as the landlord could take back the land any time given the informal nature of the contract.

Even on land which is owned by the farmer, the costs are often prohibitive. Irrigation subsidies which had at one point been part of the 1996–2016 Agricultural Perspective Plan were removed following Asian Development Bank pressure as conditions attached to the 1998 Second Agricultural Program Loan (SAPL) (Deraniyagala et al., 2003). Since then there have been multiple programmes active at the time of research by the government to install shallow tube wells. Most involve the establishment of groundwater user groups, each with a minimum of three farmers, jointly cultivating a land area of at least 4 *bighas* (2.68 hectares). However, benefitting from such schemes as a tenant is challenging. To register a user group can apply for a well. First, an organised group of farmers needs to establish a committee and travel together to the government's Groundwater Resources Development Board regional office in Biratnagar. It is, however, the responsibility of the landowners in the command area of the proposed well to get the group together and fill in the paperwork – and there were few reports of landlords showing any interest in doing so. Even if the farmer does own a plot on which to bore a well, coordinating with the owners of adjacent plots to make up the 4 *bigha* minimum is challenging, particularly if some of the land belongs to absentee landlords. The plot they own may also be in a different location from the one they want to irrigate. Furthermore, government-led opportunities for subsidised installation of wells were not widely publicised and the paperwork was cumbersome. It was more often through local connections and social networks that user groups would receive support, as shown in a study from Amgachhi VDC to the south (McCarl, 2013).

It is also important to note that access to tube wells is not the only requirement for groundwater irrigation. An equally significant expense is the pumping equipment (see Figure 6.2). Diesel pump sets cost between NPR 35,000 and 40,000 as of 2012. However, given the high rent payments, few tenants yield a significant surplus that can be reinvested in such equipment. Only two landless farmers and two owning less than 1 hectare owned their own pump sets in the 2019 survey. Only one large farmer was reported to own a pump set, although this was because most large farmers lived in Jhorahat and Pidarboni and thus had access to canal irrigation. If one were to do a large study of richer farmers beyond the command of the canal, one would expect higher

Figure 6.2 Diesel pump set. While they can offset the risk of droughts and can increase cropping intensity during the dry months, they represent a significant expense.

Source: Author.

levels of pump set ownership. For instance, a 16-village study across the eastern Tarai-Madhesh and north Bihar in largely groundwater-dependent communities found that 29 per cent of those with between 1–2 hectares and 33 per cent of those with more than 2 hectares owned a pump set, whereas ownership was less than 10 per cent for those with less than 0.5 hectare, with negligible ownership amongst tenants (Sugden, 2017).

It is worth noting though that one's inability to invest in a pump set does not necessarily mean that they do not irrigate their land. It is clear from Figure 6.3 that there is not a notable difference between land ownership category and whether one irrigates using a pump, and farmers without pumps make up for this by renting equipment. In Bhaudaha and Thalaha, where there is limited canal irrigation, 43 per cent of landless farmers had rented a pump set, alongside 41 per cent of small landholders with less than 0.5 hectare. All three large landholders in Thalaha and Bhaudaha were renting pump sets. When deciding whether or not to rent a pumpset, the potential for increased yields is often balanced out by the considerable expense and risk it entails – not to mention the impracticalities on small and fragmented plots which were often located some distance apart. The rental fee for the pump set, including diesel, was as high as NPR 200–300 as of 2012, and has increased in subsequent years. This represents a 'rent' which

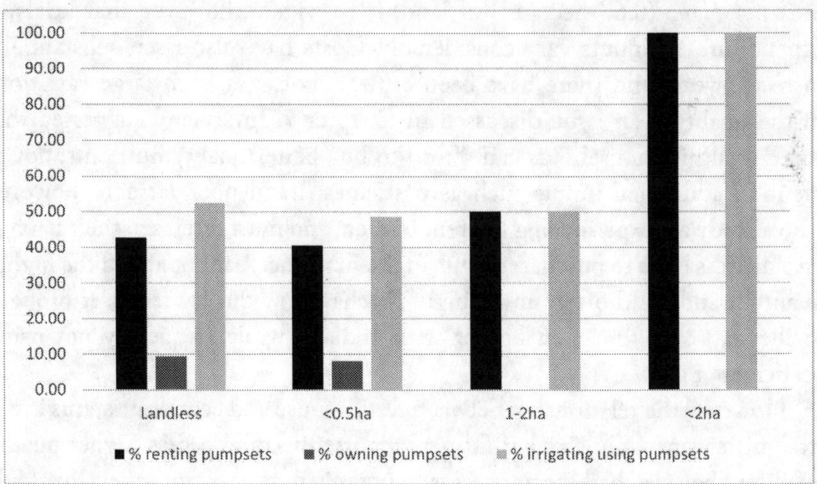

Figure 6.3 Groundwater irrigation status by farmer category 2019 in Bhaudaha and Thalaha

Source: Author.

is extracted by the (generally better-off) farmers who own the equipment. An earlier study from Morang and Dhanusha showed that pricing was arbitrary and dependent on one's bargaining power and the level of competition in the groundwater market (Sugden, 2014).

For the land-poor cultivators who do choose to rent pump sets, while this can increase yields, this group faces a far greater economic pressure, particularly when they are already giving a large share of their harvest away as rent. There is some evidence that as a result, the overall level of irrigation may be less. Out of those who had hired a pump set, the 2007–2008 survey suggested that small landholders (with less than 1 hectare) who had at least one plot of their own spent more over the last year (on average NPR 2,864 per hectare), than pure tenants who had spent on average just NPR 1,608.[4] This was likely linked to the fact that ownership of at least a plot of one's own land offers comparative economic security to justify additional investment, with less of the net harvest being taken by the landlord. One would expect even higher pump set use amongst larger farmers, although the group forms too small a part of the sample to draw conclusions.

Another investment which is important to maintain current yields or improve them is in nutrients. It was generally perceived by farmers in interviews that for a sufficient harvest, at least one *bora* (50 kilograms) was required of each of the main fertilisers, DAP (diammonium phosphate) and urea per *bigha* (0.67 hectares) of land. It is evident, however, that levels of expenditure on inputs vary considerably. Costs have also risen substantially in recent years and there have been critical shortages, with large variations in the quality – an issue discussed in Chapter 7. Interviews suggested that some wealthier households can afford to buy better quality nutrients, not to mention additional inputs such as pesticides. Land-poor farmers, however, who already are experiencing the rent burden, and must often sell their harvest on a distress basis to purchase inputs in the first place, cannot afford the higher quality brands, and often unwittingly purchase low quality fertiliser brought in illegally over the open border with India – while frequently not using pesticides at all.

However, the relationship between fertiliser use and economic status is not straightforward. While richer farmers reportedly could access higher quality fertiliser, they also had greater access to organic nutrients from their livestock. Most households acknowledged the need for an appropriate mix of organic fertiliser, composed primarily of dung, and chemical fertiliser to maintain soil quality. However, accessing *gobar*, or buffalo/cattle dung, is difficult given its additional use value as fuel. The villages far to the north of Jhorahat on the fringe of the vast Charkose jungle have access to forest resources (see Figure 6.5) which provide them not only a source of income through sale of forest products but also a ready supply of wood for cooking, or *daura*. However, those to the south around the field site are reliant upon what fuel can be collected from local common lands such as riversides or, most importantly, upon animal dung which is dried and burnt (see Figure 6.6). There is limited dung in the study site, therefore, for farmers to use on the land, particularly amongst poorer households who own less livestock. The average number of cattle or buffalo owned by landless households as of 2007–2008 was 1.6, rising to 2.1 for landowners with less than 1 hectare, 3.2 for those with 1–2 hectares, and 5.3 for larger landholders with over 2 hectares. Respondents from many land-poor households stressed that all the dung available from their farms is used as fuel and, as a result, many rely purely on chemical fertiliser. This has implications for soil quality but, critically, puts an extra financial burden upon such households – reproducing their dependence on *katawala*s for credit for fertiliser, and thus perpetuating the dual exploitation by merchant capital and landlords.

Larger land-owning farmers meanwhile keep more livestock, while some also had alternative sources of fuel such as wood purchased from the north or cooking gas – leaving them with sufficient organic nutrients for the land. Some were also producing *hariyo mal*, literally 'green fertiliser', produced from the leaf litter of the small tree Ipil-Ipil (Leucaena leucocephala), a known source of nutrients for paddy cultivation (see Abdullah and Hossain, 2007). One wealthy farmer in a border village from the prosperous Kushuwaha community, a Maithili-speaking caste with a strong tradition of commercial vegetable production, explained how he uses only organic manure and *hariyo mal*, while chemical fertiliser was applied in the same way as *achaar* (or chutney) was to a meal. However, he noted that its use depends upon access to enough land to grow it.

Based upon this discussion it is unsurprising that in Figure 6.4 there does not appear to be higher per hectare expenditure on nutrients amongst better-off farmers. In fact, the highest expenditure at the time of the 2007–2008 survey was amongst landless farmers – suggesting they face a greater financial burden than their richer counterparts, while in the long term, potentially having to face the negative ecological impact of fertiliser overuse. This may explain why the latter group had also applied 102 kilograms on average of

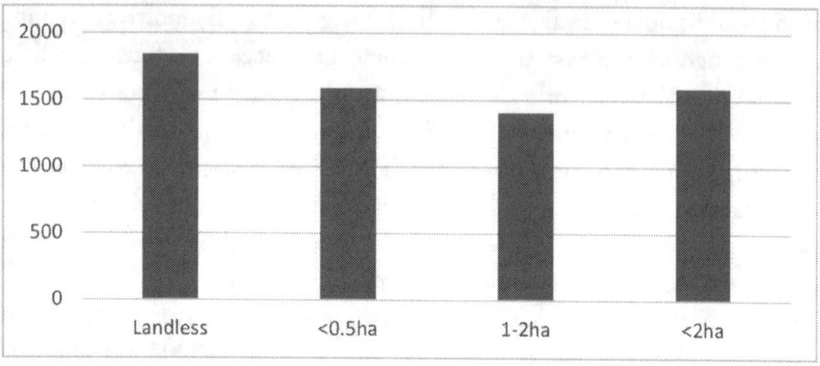

Figure 6.4 Average investment per hectare in fertiliser

Source: Author.

Figure 6.5 Collecting *daura* (firewood) from Charkose forest in Indrapur VDC, north of Jhorahat

Source: Author.

Figure 6.6 Dung drying on the banks of the Lohandra Nadi for use as fuel

Source: Author.

nutrients (a combination of DAP, urea and potash) per *bigha*, while other farmer categories had applied between 81 and 82 kilograms.

Agricultural Investment and Yields

Thus far, it appears that for land-poor farmers who form the majority in rural southern Morang, the economic burden posed by rent and further exploitation by merchant capital act as an absolute barrier to the development of the productive forces. It impedes their capacity to invest in irrigation – and for those who choose to 'rent' this equipment, it adds an additional cost, which further eats into what cash is available for subsistence. There are also complex outcomes in terms of productivity – for instance, landless and small landholders face a trade-off between energy security and nutrient management, and the use of dung for fuel means they are more likely to depend on chemical fertilisers – further increasing the costs of production and indebtedness, not to mention potential ecological impacts on the soil.

As one would expect, there is evidence that this impacts productivity amongst the land-poor and tenant farmers. There are an insufficient number of cases to support a statistically significant analysis of the role of land ownership category in influencing yields. However, given the critical constraint played by the rent burden and tenure insecurity in shaping production decision for tenants, it is worth exploring the role played by tenancy alone in shaping agricultural yields – and this opens up a much larger dataset for analysis. Table 6.3 looks at the monetary value of total annual agricultural output for each hectare of land, calculated on the basis of average prices for different crops which were received by farmers at the time of the 2007–2008 survey. This gives an overall indication into the levels of resources being allocated to the land each year and the associated returns, accounting for households who choose to invest in multiple harvests or higher value crops. The average value of output for households renting none or under half of their total land area is NPR 21,178, whereas for those renting more than half of their land it is NPR 16,132. On a similar note, annual paddy output per hectare varies from 2,697 kilograms for those renting more than half of their land to 3,640 kilograms for those operating more than half their land under owner cultivation. There is sufficient data to test these two measures statistically through a two sample T test.[5] With a p-value of 0.003 and 0.008 ($p < 0.05$) for value of output and annual paddy yield respectively, this difference is statistically significant. In other words, the constraints to developing the forces of production amongst those who farm mostly as tenants has an impact not only on the cost of production but also on the actual yields. Of course, this data may be distorted by the fact that there are fewer tenants in the Jhorahat region, which has better access to irrigation. However, separate data suggests there is still a notable difference if one looks at these two regions alone, although there are insufficient cases when broken down to test if these differences are statistically significant.[6]

It is also worth noting that the type of tenancy contract also has some influence over the levels of investment and yields. While absentee landlords tend to prefer fixed-rate, or *thekka*, contracts due to the convenience, many still rent out on *adhiya*, or sharecropping, contracts, which represent 38.96 per cent of rental contracts recorded by the sample in 2019, down slightly from 42.5 per cent in 2007–2008. *Adhiya* contracts in particular offer few incentives for tenant investment. This is because the benefit of any investment they make is shared with the landlord. This is in line with a well-established scholarship on sharecropping. Neoclassical theories such as those of Marshall state that on fixed-rent contracts the entire incremental product accrued from enhanced allocation of capital and labour will be retained by the tiller, while under sharecropping, for any additional increment in production, the landowner

Table 6.3 T tests for differences in mean of total value of annual agricultural output and paddy output per hectare of land according to percentage of land under tenancy

Measure of output	Tenancy status	No. of cases	Mean	Standard deviation	F value	T value	2 tail probability
Total value of agricultural output (NPR)	More than 50% operated land under tenancy	64	NPR 16,132	7,390	0.636	–3.033	0.003
	Less than 50% of land under tenancy	38	NPR 21,178	9,237			
Total paddy output per hectare (kg)	More than 50% operated land under tenancy	58	2,697 kg	1,458	1.535	–2.721	0.008
	Less than 50% of land under tenancy	46	3,640 kg	2,071			

Source: Author.

takes half – leading to a disincentive to maximise resource allocation (Marshall, 1907; Nabi, 1986).

One marginal farmer was interviewed who rented land through both systems of tenancy. He stated:

> *Thekka* is a better option. In *adhiya*, we have to take the crops to the landlords' home. To make them believe, we have to leave the crops in front of them. However, in *thekka*, after giving the agreed amount of paddy, we can do what we like with the remaining crops. Therefore, if we can get it, *thekka* is always better. We do not have our own land and that is why we are compelled to work as *adhiya* as well. If I have agreed to give them 22 *maund*s [880 kilograms] *dhan*, then it's done. We do not have to share any extra production such as Mushuri and Alash[7] with them … *adhiya* workers are not motivated like *thekka* workers. Whatever they grow, *adhiya* farmers have to share with their landlords. *Thekka* workers can do hard labour.

When asked about the livelihood security of *adhiya* farmers, the respondent went on to suggest:

> *Adhiya* is not sufficient to join hand to mouth. Some people are going to India, Bombay. And some people are doing extra work in a brick factory or elsewhere.

Most notable is the suggestion that there is limited motivation to produce under *adhiya* contracts – which suggests that if given a choice of allocating more family labour along with additional investment on the land or foregoing these investments and spending more time working in the capitalist sector, farmers choose the latter. For instance, after the monsoon, some farmers may forego an additional harvest of wheat or another dry season crop, with the associated irrigation costs, and focus on securing off-farm work, in spite of the poor returns – a topic which will be discussed in the next chapter.

This appears to be reflected in yields. In Table 6.4, the total annual agricultural output per hectare for households operating over half their land through *thekka* is valued at NPR 17,943. It is lower, at only NPR 13,843, for households who primarily operate their land through *adhiya* tenure. This is tested statistically through a two sample T test.[8] With a p-value of 0.03 ($p < 0.05$), it is clear that this difference is statistically significant. Similar findings have been identified across the Tarai-Madhesh and Bihar (Sugden, 2016).

It has been argued that differences in productivity can be reduced if the landlord provides half of the financial cost of inputs, therefore sharing some

Table 6.4 T test for differences in mean of total annual agricultural output per *bigha* of land according to primary rental contract

Tenancy status	No. of cases	Mean (NPR)	Standard deviation	F value	T value	2 tail probability
More than 50% operated land rented through fixed-rate contract (*tekkha*)	23	17,943	6,121	1.041	−2.218	0.03
More than 50% operated land rented through share contract (*adhiya*)	40	13,843	7,543			

Source: Author.

of the risk (Marshall, 1907; Nabi, 1986). Landlords renting out land as *adhiya* in the study villages normally contribute to the cost of inputs. However, it is usually restricted to paying half the price of fertiliser, and not labour, irrigation or other capital investments that can improve productivity. One may therefore assume that farmers renting land through the *adhiya* system still have less of an incentive to intensify resource allocation than *thekka* farmers.

It is worth remembering though that this is a mixed blessing. While *thekka* contracts increase the incentives for tenants to invest on the land, they still absorb much of their surplus product, and can even eat into their 'necessary' labour time. Further, as noted earlier, these contracts carry additional risks – the most notable of which is the potential to make significant losses in the event of a failed harvest – whereby regardless of the yield, the same rent must be paid to the landlords.

The Elusive 'Improving Landlord'

It appears that landless and small landholder farmers have very limited options to develop the forces of production, and when they do, such as through irrigation investments, it can drive greater financial hardship, trapping them into seasonal cycles of debt to the *katawalas*.

A final question associated with the relations of production is whether or not landlords can play any 'improving role', facilitating the development of the productive forces for tenants and helping them improve productivity while overcoming the financial hardship they face in paying for inputs on their farm, even to meet their minimum subsistence needs.

In the European agrarian transition there was evidence of landlords playing a 'progressive' role in promoting innovation to develop the productive forces and encourage capitalist development on their estates. For example in rural Aberdeenshire in early-eighteenth-century Scotland, landed property took a form which would promote capitalist development through the introduction of new cropping systems and improved technology (Carter, 1977)[9]. This echoes an observation by Regmi (1976) on the establishment of the Rana-era *jimidari* system in the Tarai-Madhesh in the nineteenth century. While the character of the regime was extractive, there was some belief amongst Rana administrators that a landlord class would play a role in encouraging investment and innovation in Tarai agriculture. This vision was never realised in reality, however, as the *jimidar*s remained a rent-seeking class largely unconcerned with rural development.

This raises the question as to whether anything has changed today, particularly at a time when the government has pursued a largely technology-led agricultural development strategy. Returning to the debate on tenancy, Nabi (1986) suggests that landlords can offer technical advice and supervision to tenants to compensate for the lack of incentives for farmers to increase labour and input allocation, something which applies in particular to sharecroppers. Newbery (1975) suggests that encouraging innovation is in the landlords interest as they are able to profit by increasing rents or adapting the conditions of the contract in their favour. Advice may include recommending and encouraging use of the most suitable inputs (Nabi, 1986). In addition landlords can offer general non-economic production advice such as advising farmers on new techniques as well as supervising production (Nabi, 1986).

Contrary to the aforementioned literature, however, the data from Jhorahat, Bhaudaha and Thalaha suggest that landlords play a negligible role in encouraging innovation or supervising production. In the 2007–2008 survey, 23 per cent of farmers who rented land stated that the landlord has made no visits to their land in the last year and their only interaction with them is through a *kamtiya*, a locally based agent who comes once a year to collect the crop. A substantial 54 per cent of farmers who were renting land stated that the landlord has made one or two visits in the last year, mostly with the sole purpose of collecting the rent. Meanwhile 55 per cent of farmers stated that landlords have never offered any agricultural advice, while 78 per cent claimed the landlords have not even had an influence in deciding what was to be produced. As of 2023, qualitative testimonies suggested that if anything, landlord engagement has declined even further. Some farmers said their interaction is only via the *katawala*s in markets such as Naya Bazaar. The farmers deposit the grain there, and the landlords collect it in cash or via bank transfer according to the market rate.

There were no reported instances encountered of landlords investing in fixed assets on the land, such as boring tubewells or investing in pump sets for use by the tenants. One respondent in Bhaudaha operated 2 *bigha*s (1.5 hectares) as *thekka*. He recalled asking his landlord if he could support him to purchase a pump. The landlord simply replied that if he wanted one, he could manage it himself, otherwise he should just leave the land so he could give it to someone else.

The lack of landlord interest in 'improving' agriculture on their estates is puzzling. Bhaduri (1977) suggests that under the semi-feudal conditions which characterise many parts of South Asia, landlords will actually block the introduction of technological improvements and innovations. As farmers are in perpetual indebtedness to landlords, usury or 'interest bearing' capital represents an important source of income alongside rent. Innovations may undermine this source of revenue by increasing the tenants' financial security. This reluctance results in an equilibrium situation, whereby landlords seek to keep technological development at a level that does not disturb the need for tenants to take consumption loans (Bhaduri, 1977). While the dependence of the peasantry upon landlords as a result of stagnation in industry has been established, Bhaduri's thesis does not seem a likely scenario in rural Morang. Bhaduri assumes that there is an inter-linkage of landlord and usury capital. However, the evidence outlined earlier in this chapter suggested that landlords play a marginal role in moneylending. Therefore, although most tenants are subject to surplus appropriation through usury, the moneylenders are from a separate class (in particular the *katawala*s) that takes advantage of the impoverishment arising from feudal tenancy.

There are therefore more complex explanations for landlords' lack of incentives to encourage investment and innovation. The predominance of absentee landlordism provides some answers. Indeed while the small number of local landlords visited their plots on average four times a year, the absentee landlords visited only once. Discussions in the village and in Biratnagar suggest that most of the landlords are not themselves farmers and often have little interest in agriculture today. Furthermore, the large size of many of the holdings and the distance of them from the landlords' place of residence would make supervision and the promotion of innovations impractical to the point that they outweigh the benefits of higher yields. This contrasts starkly with Nabi's (1986) study in Pakistan, where it is noted that 47 per cent of landlords, most of whom reside locally, visit their tenants at least every second day during the peak season while 22 per cent report weekly visits. As a result, Nabi (1986) concludes that landlord supervision and advice to sharecroppers encourage resource use comparable to that of owner-cultivators – a situation which clearly does not apply in Morang.

Low landlord engagement was aggravated during the 1996–2006 civil war, which made travel in rural areas risky. More recent unrest during the 2007, 2008 and 2015 Madhesh Andolans also deterred landlords from visiting the rural hinterland beyond the Biratnagar city boundary. While these risks are now low, this has contributed to a long term trend of landlord disengagement.

It is evident therefore that both the economic and non-economic costs of engagement with tenants by landlords outweigh the financial benefits. Interestingly, these perceived costs may have been lessened if land was the sole source of prosperity for the landlord's household. However, many already have secure income from professional employment and some are already in positions of wealth and privilege. Land is kept for cultural and speculative reasons which will be discussed later.

Feudalism Today: Understanding the Mode of Production

A glance at the rural social formation suggests that many of the characteristics of feudalism outlined earlier still apply – namely (*a*) the concentration of landed property, (*b*) surplus appropriation through absolute ground rent (at times using extra-economic coercion) and (*c*) use of surplus for consumption rather than productive reinvestment.

With regard to the first and second features, as of 2019 it is evident that land is still concentrated amongst a small class of landlords. Surplus is being appropriated, in kind, through absolute ground rent, payment of which means many farmers cannot meet even their basic subsistence needs, let alone make a profit, which one would expect if the transition to 'capitalist' ground rent had taken place. Surplus is also appropriated through the additional 'rent' extracted via sales to grain merchants through interest or price manipulation.

With regard to the role of extra-economic coercion, this is more complex today. Many of the extra-economic bonds between landlords and tenants that Marx (1932) describes with regard to European landlordism in the *Economic and Political Manuscripts* are much weaker today than they were during the

Rana and early Panchayat years – particularly given the prevalence of absentee landlordism. As indicated earlier, there is also no evidence of interlinked contracts, which bonded farmers to landlords via debt or labour relations, which were central to some definitions of feudalism in India's mode of production debate. The relationship between landlords and tenants in southern Morang is today a far more impersonal one, mediated through meetings a few times a year to collect rent at harvest time or through the *kamtiya* (landlords' agents) or even the *katawala* (grain merchant) who sometimes collects rent on the landlord's behalf. While this has removed the dependence of tenants upon a single 'overlord', it has also finally removed any 'productive' role that landlords could play locally, as their engagement with the land becomes entirely extractive – focused on generating rent, rather than investment.

Nevertheless, elements of the extra-economic relationship between landlords and tenants persist in other ways – albeit more indirectly. First, land is still loosely linked to political power. The state has long supported landed interest, and a number of landlords are themselves highly active in party politics. A number of high-level political leaders and bureaucrats reportedly own estates in the region, and some farmers reported patron–client relations with their tenants linked to electoral politics. One tenant, for example, reported that he and his son had both been offered jobs by their landlord, who was linked to a political leader, and as a result, they would support them during elections. However, while land ownership can help bolster one's political power as shown elsewhere in Nepal (Joshi and Mason, 2007), it is clear that the two are not as dependent upon each other as they were in the Rana years.

However, the legacy of the old link between land ownership and political power lingers on when reflecting upon social status, and the reasons why landlords hold on to their land and continue to extract rent, even when they have alternative sources of income via the bureaucracy or salaried employment. As Regmi (1976) and Stiller (1975) emphasise, land ownership in Nepal was historically utilised as a system through which state power was mobilised in rural areas. This was manifested in practices such as the assignment of *birta* grants to the political elite and *jirayat* holdings for tax collectors. Land ownership was thus more than just about material wealth, but was linked to questions of political authority and status.

Interviews with officials at the land revenue office (and one absentee landowner) suggest that status and emotional bonds to the family estate are a significant reason why urban-based landlords continue to hold on to their lands in the Morang countryside. As ownership of land in the countryside is favoured as much for cultural and status reasons as for economic gain, the inevitable outcome is a reluctance to sell one's estates, even in the context of economic change, in turn perpetuating the concentration of land ownership within this class across generations. This link between land and social status echoes Marx's (1932) observation of the deep bond of 'attachment' that landlords held to their estates under European feudalism:

> Likewise, the lord of an entailed estate, the first-born son, belongs to the land. It inherits him. Indeed, the dominion of private property begins with property in land – that is its basis. But in feudal landed property the lord at least *appears* as the king of the estate. Similarly, there still exists the semblance of a more intimate connection between the proprietor and the land than that of mere *material* wealth. The estate is individualized with its lord: it has his rank, is baronial or ducal with him, has his privileges, his jurisdiction, his political position, etc. It appears as the inorganic body of its lord.... For those belonging to it, the estate is more like their fatherland. It is a constricted sort of nationality.

While this strength of feeling has arguably dwindled in recent years amongst landowners in rural Morang, particularly as landlords rarely live locally and estates pass on to sons with even less engagement in rural life, the legacy of such sentiments may well shape landlord decisions with regard to the division or sale of their holdings. Furthermore, the rising prices of land in recent years brought about by infrastructural improvements also reduce any incentives for landowners to part from their holdings.

A third feature of feudalism is the diversion of surplus into consumption rather than productive reinvestment. It is clear from the discussion here that landlords have played a negligible role in encouraging the development of the productive forces through investment or advice to farmers, and their role in the mode of production appears limited to extracting rent. In theory, landlords could choose to 'invest' this surplus productively in the non-farm capitalist sector – casting doubt upon whether the mode of production is really 'feudal' in character.

Understanding landlord livelihoods and how they use their surplus is an extremely challenging task given that the group is dispersed and in cities, and would require a sustained project of 'studying up' to uncover the spending and investment patterns of this group. However, an overview of the employment status of landlords suggests that productive reinvestment of rent is highly unlikely. Most tenants had limited knowledge of what their landlords did, but information on 12 landlords was collected during interviews and focus groups carried out in 2012 and 2021–2023, giving some insight into their current or past occupation (many had retired). Some of these landlords were known to have owned the land from Rana times, but added more later, and others may have bought land more recently, but this information was not known. What the interviews did reveal was that within this group, one landlord had no reported alternative income – with the landlord's tenants reporting that they lived off the rent from their 50 *bigha*s of land, and lived in a large house in the city. Five landlords had positions in the bureaucracy or party apparatus – including high-level political appointments in Kathmandu. Two had jobs in banks, although whether these were private or government owned was not known. One landlord reportedly deals in urban real estate in Kathmandu as their primary source of income.

Importantly, there were no concrete reports of any landlords being engaged in 'capitalist' production. While more evidence is needed, this outcome would be unsurprising given that most manufacturing was in the hands of a quite separate industrial class. Many factory owners were Marwaris who had settled in Biratnagar several generations ago from India – who traditionally had limited role in agricultural production of any kind. Others were high-caste Nepali speakers, albeit often from a business background. A large share of landlords, by contrast, were from a bureaucratic and political background. They were more likely to have inter-generational connections to the historical feudal state and its rulers rather than to a national or even comprador bourgeoise under capitalism. There may be some fluidity, particularly when one considers urban dwellers who purchased land more recently. Three landlords out of twelve owned a business, although these were in the retail and the hotel sector, and were not in capitalist 'production'. While landlords may have unknown investments, interviews with tenants pointed to limited evidence that rent is 'reinvested' into capitalist production of any sort – and it is likely that a large share went into consumption. One interview suggested that the rent was used to meet the food needs of the landlords' family. It could be consumed as it is after milling, or could be sold, transformed into cash, and used to cover day-to-day costs, or contribute to accumulated savings, likely to purchase consumer goods. Another farmer reported that the landlord takes the higher quality Basmati share of the harvest for their home consumption, while selling off the Kanchi or Mansuli paddy which is the primary subsistence crop.

A remaining question is the role of merchant capital and its relation to feudal landlordism. Surplus appropriation by merchant capital is not directly part of the feudal mode of production as it exists primarily in the sphere of circulation. This is in contrast with Bhaduri's (1973) analysis of semi-feudalism in India, whereby merchants were also the landlords and used indebtedness to reproduce the relations of production. Landlords and merchants/moneylenders or *katawala*s in Morang, however, are from different caste communities and engage in quite different economic activities. While the *katawala*s increasingly play an intermediary role between landlords and tenants by operating as the medium through which landlords extract rent, they primarily operate as a separate class, who advance credit to farmers or purchase grain from farmers under duress, in the process absorbing their own share of the surplus via interest or the price mechanism. They also support the articulation between capitalist agro-processing enterprises and feudal agriculture. They supply grain from the farmers to the mills, some of which ends up back in the rural economy after processing, only to be purchased by farmers unable to reproduce through the land.

Like landlords, it is unlikely that the merchants play any 'productive' role in the rural economy through reinvestment of surplus, echoing Marx, who argued that merchant activities are predominantly 'parasitic'. Lengthy engagement and interviews with the *katawala*s where we got to know several traders well, didn't provide any evidence that they diversify out of agro-trading. The profits appeared to be traditionally used for consumption purposes and expanding their trade (and money lending) capabilities rather than for productive reinvestment in industrial ventures. It thus essentially represents a flow of surplus out of the agricultural sector that does not 'reappear' elsewhere in the economy.

It is important to note that while a feudal mode of production appears predominant, this has not subsumed the middle to large land-owning farmers to the same extent. The latter appear to be essentially part of an independent peasant mode of production grounded in production of their own surplus using their family labour, and some external labour. Their position is broadly similar to the settler farmers in northern Morang who almost entirely farm as owner-cultivators. However, unlike farmers in the north, they farm alongside other producers subject to feudal landlordism. This places a limit on their capacity to expand their holdings. However, the two modes of production also articulate at times. For instance, some medium farmers may move in and out of tenancy according to family needs. They may also at times be subject to exploitation by merchant-moneylenders, who could corner a share of the surplus – although, as the most recent data suggests (2019–2023), most have alternative sources of institutional credit as of 2023 (and thus do not depend on *katawala*s for loans) and tend to have a better bargaining power. While this group does have the potential to become part of a proto-capitalist farmer class, this appears unlikely in the short term, as will be discussed later on.

The presence of this class of middle farmers should not deflect from the fact that for the marginal and landless farmers who make up the vast majority of the rural population, the drain of surplus, first, via rent and, second, via merchant capital is central to the reproduction of rural poverty – impeding households from meeting their minimum needs on the land, and even eating into households' basic subsistence requirements. It is not only driving a cycle of perpetual food insecurity but also impeding their capacity to develop the forces of production. They are integrated into a mode of production that remains distinctly 'feudal' in character – with a concentration of land amongst a landed elite, appropriation of surplus through absolute ground rent, and diversion of surplus for consumption rather than productive reinvestment.

Notes

1. Note that while the survey started before the 2007 paddy harvest in the monsoon and finished in the winter, farmers interviewed after the harvest were asked to report on the *previous* agricultural year to ensure comparability. All farmers were thus referring to the paddy planted in the 2006 monsoon.
2. Had the household been retaining sufficient grain to meet the household subsistence needs as per the thresholds discussed here, one could surmise that sales may have been profit oriented. However, given that these households were retaining far less grain than what was required for subsistence, then it is highly likely that these sales were to meet urgent cash needs or to pay off loans, and the household would be required to buy grain later in the year.
3. To Marx, this would be the equivalent of a capitalist increasing productivity through capital investment, decreasing the hours of labour to produce a commodity and increasing the rate of 'relative' surplus value (rather than the 'absolute' surplus value which is produced through 'overwork') (Marx, 1974).
4. As most larger owner-cultivators lived in the command of the canals, it was not possible to compare expenditure with this group.
5. The first null hypothesis for this model thus states that those operating most of their land under tenancy do not produce a lower agricultural output per hectare than those operating most of their land under owner cultivation. The second states that share-contract tenants do not yield a lower total agricultural output per *bigha* than fixed-rate tenants.
6. For instance, those with more than half their land under tenancy in Bhaudaha and Thalaha produced an agricultural output valued at NPR 14,231 per hectare as compared to NPR 18,168 for those with more than half their land under owner cultivation. The difference for Jhorahat alone is NPR 19,761 and NPR 22,112 respectively.
7. Mushuri and Alash are varieties of pulse.

8. The first null hypothesis for this model thus states that share-contract tenants do not produce any less of the main autumn paddy harvest than fixed-rate tenants. The second states that share-contract tenants do not yield a lower total agricultural output per *bigha* than fixed-rate tenants.
9. The role of landlords in promoting capitalist development in the British Isles, of course, culminated in Marx's 'primitive accumulation', whereby capitalism was unleashed through the eviction of marginal peasants from the land to become wage labourers, while many landlords represented the new agrarian bourgeoisie. This path to agrarian capitalism, whereby a capitalist class emerges out of the feudal landed class rather than from within the peasantry itself, was known to Lenin as the 'Prussian' or 'Junker' path to capitalism, as discussed in Chapter 2.

References

Abdullah, M. R. and Hossain, K. L. 2007. Effects of urea-N fertilizer dosage supplemented with Ipil-Ipil tree litter on yield of rice and insect prevalence. *Journal of Forestry Research* 17: 335–338.

APROSC. 1995. *Agriculture Perspective Plan*. Agricultural Projects Services Centre (APROSC), Kathmandu.

Bhaduri, A. 1977. On the formation of usurious interest rates in backward agriculture. *Cambridge Journal of Economics* 1 (4): 341–352.

Bhandari, Binod and Ghimire, Madhav. 2015. Ageing Sunsari-Morang irrigation line in dire straits. *The Kathmandu Post*, 22 June. https://kathmandupost.com/money/2015/06/22/ageing-sunsari-morang-irrigation-line-in-dire-straits.

Biggs, Stephen, Justice, Scott and Lewis, David. 2011. Patterns of rural mechanisation, energy and employment in South Asia: Reopening the debate. *Economic and Political Weekly* 46 (9): 78–82.

Carter, I. 1977. Social differentiation in the Aberdeenshire peasantry, 1696–1870. *Journal of Peasant Studies* 5 (1): 48–68.

Central Bureau of Statistics. 2016. *Annual Household Survey 2015–2016: Major Findings*. Government of Nepal.

Deraniyagala, S., Katiwada, Y., Sharma, S., Roy, R. and Deshpande, A. 2003. *Pro-Poor Macro Policies in Nepal*. UNDP, Asia-Pacific Regional Programme on Macroeconomics of Poverty Reduction.

Hossain, M. and Yunus, M. 2016. Estimates of per capita consumption of food grains in Bangladesh. *Bangladesh Development Studies* 89 (1–2): 103–116.

Joshi, Madhav and Mason, T. David. 2007. Land tenure, democracy, and insurgency in Nepal: Peasant support for insurgency versus democracy. *Asian Survey* 47 (3): 393–414.

Kunnath, George, J. 2017. *Rebels from the Mud Houses: Dalits and the Making of the Maoist Revolution in Bihar*. Routledge.

Marshall, A. 1907. *Principles of Economics: Volume 1.* Progress Publishers.
Marx, K. 1932. *Economic and Political Manuscripts.* Progress Publishers.
———. 1974. *Capital: A Critical Analysis of Capitalist Production (Volume 1).* Progress Publishers.
Mccarl, B. 2013. From plump to pump: Land, wealth and inequality in Nepal's groundwater irrigation strategy. MSc thesis. International Water Management Institute (IWMI) Colombo, Sri Lanka, and University of Queensland, Australia.
Ministry of Agricultural Development. 2014. *Agricultural Development Strategy.* Government of Nepal.
Ministry of Irrigation. 2012. Groundwater Resources Development Board. http://www.gwrdb.gov.np/about_us.php.
Mishra, Ashok K., Kumar, Anjani, Joshi, Pramod K. and D'souza, Alwin. 2016. Impact of contracts in high yielding varieties seed production on profits and yield: The case of Nepal. *Food Policy* 62: 110–121.
Nabi, I. 1986. Contracts, resource use and productivity in sharecropping. *Journal of development Studies* 22 (2): 429–442.
Newbery, D. M. G. 1975. Tenurial obstacles to innovation. *Journal of development Studies* 11: 263–277.
Sugden, F. 2009. Neo-liberalism, markets and class structures on the Nepali lowlands: The political economy of agrarian change. *Geoforum* 40 (4): 634–644.
———. 2014a. *Landlordism, Tenants and the Groundwater Sector: Lessons from the Tarai-Madhesh, Nepal.* IWMI Research Report 162.
———. 2016. Improving dry season irrigation for marginal and tenant farmers in the Eastern Gangetic Plains: Baseline socio-economic report. Unpublished project report, International Water Management Institute.
———. 2017. A mode of production flux: The transformation and reproduction of rural class relations in lowland Nepal and North Bihar. *Dialectical Anthropology* 41 (2): 129–161.

7

Capitalist Expansion, Cash and Climate

A Brewing Agrarian Crisis

Thus far it is evident that the rural livelihoods in southern Morang are embedded within a deeply inequitable agrarian structure, with dual surplus appropriation by landlords and merchant capital. However, it is important to remember that feudalism, like capitalism itself, is not a static system, but is dynamic and subject to evolution and flux. While changes to the feudal system over the last few centuries were explored in Chapter 3, this chapter explores the contemporary trajectory of change. The last three decades in particular have marked a new era in Nepal's agrarian political economy. As noted earlier in this book, pre-capitalist inequalities have not been undermined, and these in part contributed to the 10-year civil war and waves of more recent ethnic unrest. However, at a national level, Nepal has also undergone significant economic change following neoliberal restructuring.

Within this context, capitalism is articulating with rural pre-capitalist economic formations like never before. A key argument is that there is growing 'agrarian stress' associated with climatic-ecological pressures, expanding capitalist markets with an associated wave of monetisation and cultural change. In its wake, farmers are becoming more dependent than ever before on off-farm labour in the capitalist sector both locally and overseas, to supplement the meagre returns gained from the land under feudal agriculture. This has intensified throughout the 17 years within which this research has taken place. We explore these changes in turn below.

Climate Change and Pressures on Yields

Over the last decade or so there have been rising perceptions of climatic stress amongst farmers. Assessing the dynamics of both historical and future climate change is a complex task given the regional variability within the Gangetic plains region, the lack of high resolution data, and the inherent unpredictability of climate change outcomes. It is not the intention of this section to chart the trajectory of climate change in this part of the lowlands, but, instead, to identify patterns of climate-related stress which farmers *perceive* have affected their agricultural livelihoods and, importantly, have shaped production and livelihood decisions.

The greatest challenge as perceived by farmers appeared to be the unpredictability of climatic patterns. There was awareness of an increase in extreme precipitation events over the last two to three decades. There were severe floods in the monsoon of 2017, whereby large areas of rural Morang were inundated. Analysis of weather patterns in the eastern Tarai-Madhesh between 1975 and 2005 (Practical Action, 2009) suggests that there has been an increase in rainfall from 1 to 2 millimetres per year in the pre-monsoon and post-monsoon periods and an increase of up to 10 millimetres during monsoon itself, with a marginal decline during winter in some regions. However, reports of extreme precipitation events in Nepal can be deceptive as they do not account for the increase in the variability of rainfall – in particular, a rising incidence of drought (Bartlett et al., 2010; Sharma, 2009). A study in Nepal by the Water and Energy Commission Secretariat (WECS) analysed meteorological data to suggest also that an increase in intense precipitation over recent decades has been paralleled by a lengthening of dry spells (WECS, 2011). Increased incidences of precipitation and drought extremes have also been identified in more recent studies (for example, Shrestha et al., 2021). For most respondents, however, periods of water scarcity did not necessarily manifest themselves as a weak monsoon or a seasonal shortage of rain, but an increased unpredictability, with rain often coming later than expected when compared to a generation ago. The decision over when to transplant paddy in particular was increasingly associated with risk, especially away from the canals, as a late onset of the rains or dry spells early in the season could be devastating for harvests.

A corollary of late monsoon rains was a perception that unseasonal rains, particularly large storms, during spring had increased. Increasing spring rain was also identified as a long-term trend in the Practical Action (2009) study. They could be particularly damaging to wheat cultivation, as storms damage the crop around harvest time, causing it to rot and lose its value, while high winds can flatten crops. During focus groups in 2012, farmers complained of significant losses due to rain and hailstorms for the second spring in a row – with one farmer claiming that he would not plant wheat in future years.

In fact, the survey suggests that the percentage of farmers who had cultivated wheat over the previous year had declined between 2007–2008 and 2019 from 68 per cent to 59 per cent.

Other changes reported by farmers include an increase in summer and monsoon temperatures which were reported in all three sites to have increased the levels of pest infestations of the rice, wheat and vegetable crop. This parallels analyses of climatic trends across India (bearing in mind local variations), whereby between 1901 and 2009, annual mean temperatures have been shown to have increased by 0.56°C, and have been above normal since 1990 (based upon period from 1961 to 1990) (Sharma, 2009). The study by Practical Action (2009) similarly suggested there had been an increase in mean maximum pre- and post-monsoon and monsoon temperatures across the Nepali plains from 0.02 to 0.04°C per year between 1976 and 2005.

The canals provide some respite, at least during the monsoon season, whereby they protect farmers from late rains, and in some locales they allow the cultivation of wheat in winter. However, canal water was insufficient for households beyond the relatively more prosperous villages of Pidarboni and Jhorahat and, as noted earlier, water yields have been declining in recent years due to siltation, poor maintenance and weak enforcement of water allocation rules.

The risks of a failed harvest are severe for landless and small landholders in Bhaudaha and Thalaha, particularly given that for the majority, a significant share of what is produced is appropriated via rent or by merchant capital. Rent and interest payments still need to be made regardless of the output from the land. One advantage for sharecropping tenants is that in the event of a failed harvest due to a delayed monsoon, flood or spring thunderstorm, they still need to pay rent, but the loss is 'shared' with the landlord. It is those paying rent on a *thekka* basis who are most vulnerable. While this contract type has its advantages, as outlined earlier, in the case of a lower than expected yield, the agreed share still needs to be paid. One tenant from the Bantar community recalled how he had been farming his land on a fixed-rent contract from an absentee landlord, who demanded a 20-*maund* (800-kilogram) share of paddy. Due to the late monsoon in 2012, the farmer reported that his rice harvest was itself just 20 *maund*s, all of which was given as rent. A season's labour and expenditure on the farm was wasted. He had already taken a loan to invest in fertiliser. At the time of research he was urgently seeking non-farm labour to repay the debt and provide food for his family.

When set against this risk, using tubewells and pump sets are even more important than before to cope with agrarian stress, particularly for farmers beyond the command of the canal. While this cannot protect farmers from the risks of floods or rising temperatures, it is crucial for them to reduce the risk of droughts or late monsoons by providing water 'on-demand'. Tubewell irrigation is also essential if one is to cultivate any land during the dry season for wheat. As noted in the previous chapter, around 43 per cent of landless farmers in Bhaudaha and Thalaha (the area beyond the command of the canal) had rented a pump set, as of 2019 alongside 41 per cent of small landholders with less than 1 hectare as of 2019. All three large landholders with more than 2 hectares had done so. Back in 2007–2008, however, only 23 per cent of landless farmers, 31 per cent of those with less than 1 hectare and two out of three landholders with more than 2 hectares reported pump rental expenses. This notable increase is likely to be due to the rising perception of water stress – and as noted in Chapter 6, this has contributed to a steadily increasing cost of production – particularly when an additional 'rent' for the equipment owner needs to be factored in. As Dhakal et al. (2016) note from a study from Rautahat further west in the lowlands, farmers are able to adapt to rainfall unpredictability and rising temperatures through greater investment in inputs such as irrigation or pesticides and shifting crop choices, although the benefits of higher or stable yields are offset by rising production costs. While purchasing one's own pump or installing a well could lower costs of production, as noted earlier, the vast majority of small landholders and landless farmers cannot afford to make investments themselves, and installation of tubewells is unfeasible due to tenure insecurity.

While payment to rent pumps may be a manageable cost for large and medium landholders, for the small and landless farmers, surplus appropriation through rent and usury means they are not only vulnerable in the first place to subtle changes in the climate on a year-by-year basis, but the available cash to invest in irrigation is also far more limited. When compelled to irrigate as an 'adaptation strategy', they are thus pushed into further financial distress.[1] When deciding whether to irrigate, therefore, tenants have difficult choices to make regarding the benefits of irrigation in terms of meeting their food security needs, rent and debt repayment obligations, set against the considerable financial cost.

Weakening Terms of Trade, Costs of Production and Spiralling Food Prices

The cost of tubewell irrigation is itself part of a much broader rise in production costs for the peasantry. Looking at national data from across the

Tarai-Madhesh, the cost of paddy production in Nepal was NPR 23,642 per hectare in 2007–2008, yet had increased 193 per cent in half a decade to NPR 69,289 per hectare by 2013–2014. Similarly, the production cost per quintal of paddy rose 205 per cent from NPR 523 in 2007–2008 to NPR 1,596 in 2013–2014 (Aryal and Bhandari, 2017). This was reflected frequently in interviews, particularly over the last five to six years.

These rising costs are partially linked to the rising costs of fuel, which is required for those renting-in diesel irrigation pumps. However, diesel and other petroleum products are also required for thresher and tractor hire, which are becoming more important in the context of rising male engagement in off-farm labour and associated labour shortages. The price of diesel increased by 352 per cent between 1995–1996 and 2009–2010 (Pant, 2011), and this was aggravated in Nepal due to dependence on India for a large share of imports.

In part connected to the rising price of fuel is the rising cost of fertiliser (Pant, 2011). This is a trend which has been underway for the last two to three decades. Data collected from the Morang Byapar Sangh (Morang Merchants' Association) suggested that there was a disproportionate rise in fertiliser prices compared to those of agricultural commodities between the early 1990s and 2008, in the run up to the first phase of research. Figure 7.1 outlines the official government-recommended price of fertiliser against the farm gate post-harvest price for the main grain products, as recorded by the Morang Byapar Sangh. This suggests that while the prices for the two main fertilisers, DAP and urea, rose considerably, only the price of wheat rose at the same rate. The prices of the main Kanchi and Mansuli paddy meanwhile had increased only modestly. Fertiliser prices have fluctuated considerably in subsequent years, with the general trend pointing to a susbstantial rise. While DAP and urea were just over NPR 25 per kilogram each in 2008, in Biratnagar, the price for DAP was NPR 44 per kilogram in 2022, while urea had dropped slightly to NPR 15 per kilogram (Krishi Samagri Company, 2022), although this locally available data does not account for later increases. In the context of the war in Ukraine, and a global shortage of fertiliser given the sanctions on Russia (a major producer of nutrients) and resultant restrictions on exports by another supplier (China),[2] prices continued to rise, and the government announced a further increase in the price of DAP to NPR 50 per kilogram and urea to NPR 25[3] in 2023 (*The Kathmandu Post*, 2023).

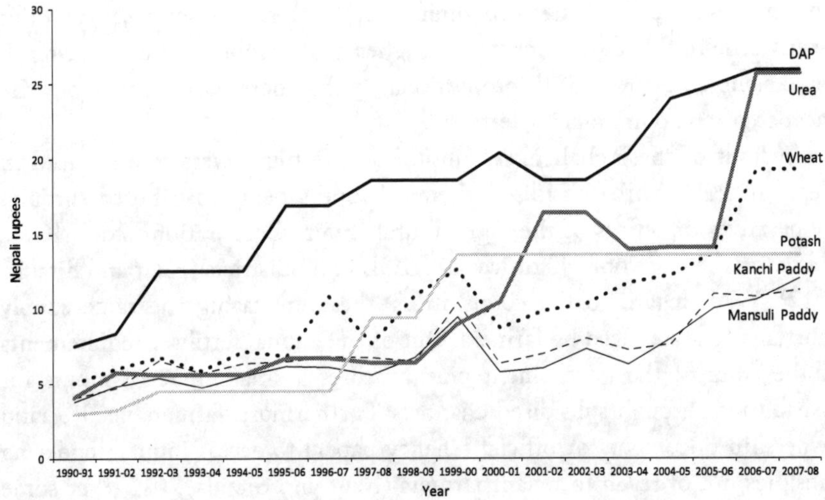

Figure 7.1 Official price of fertiliser* per kilogram against farm gate price of key grain crops** over the last 18 years in the Morang market

Source: Author.

Notes: *This represents the official recommended price for Biratnagar by the government's Agricultural Inputs Corporation which are fixed annually.

**These are the farm gate prices recorded in a daily survey of grain merchants by the Morang Byapar Sangh (Morang Merchants' Association). Unfortunately data was only available on a day-by-day basis and data sets were not digitised, making an annual average difficult to generate. I therefore took the daily price for the first of Kartik each year (around 22 October) at the peak rice harvest season. I am extremely grateful to both the Morang Merchants' Association and the Biratnagar branch of the Agricultural Inputs Corporation for the co-operation and time they offered me in reviewing their archival data.

For farmers in Morang, difficulties in accessing quality fertiliser at an affordable price have become more acute following the abolition of subsidies and scaling down of the government distribution of inputs under economic liberalisation in the 1990s. Aside from the higher prices, the unregulated flow of illegal fertiliser means farmers can no longer guarantee the quality of what they buy, a point raised by Sharma and Babu (2002). Referring to the withdrawal of subsidies and the end to state regulation, one farmer in Jhorahat in an interview in 2008 stated:

> The quality of fertiliser provided by Krishi (Agriculture) office was much better. They could provide it at a cheaper rate and in substantial amounts. If there are no subsidies then how can farmers access fertiliser at an affordable rate? That is why there is no benefit from doing agriculture in Nepal.

The enhanced 'choice' that economic liberalisation was supposed to offer means little to this farmer for whom higher quality inputs were out of reach – and as noted earlier, it is disproportionately the poorer farmers who buy the cheaper, often poorer quality, fertiliser.

In light of these challenges, subsidies on fertiliser were reintroduced in Nepal in 2009, with subsidised chemical inputs being distributed through cooperatives or offices of the Agricultural Inputs Corporation Ltd (AICL). However, there are only 40 offices of AICL in 39 districts (Raut and Sitaula, 2012). With regard to the cooperatives, these are facing the same supply shortfalls that are faced by farmers. Out of the annual fertiliser requirements of the country, the government only procures a small share of inputs for distribution through subsidised channels. Furthermore, farmers needed land ownership documents or official tenancy papers to access inputs, rendering subsidies out of reach to tenant farmers (Raut and Sitaula, 2012). For some time, Indian fertiliser that had been brought informally across the border was available in local markets, particularly further south, although the authorities had cracked down on this in the last few years. In this context, farmers still depend on poor-quality inputs from the private sector. The shortages have been further worsened in recent years in the context of the global shortages brought about by the war in Ukraine as well as the Covid-19 pandemic.[4] This agricultural inputs crisis has been aggravated by Nepal's negligible fertiliser production capacity. As with other industries, producers lack the economies of scale to develop the industry and are unable to compete with larger producers abroad.[5]

Rising costs, however, is relevant not only in the context of agricultural production. There are a number of broader changes that have increased household cash needs – the most notable of which is the rising cost of food. This was cited by farmers to be linked to consumer grain prices in particular. The prices of grain staples and vegetables in Nepal doubled between 2000 and 2010 in the years leading up to the first phase of fieldwork (Pant, 2011). The retail price of milled coarse grain paddy, which is the dominant consumption crop in rural Morang, rose from NPR 17.97 per kilogram in 2000 to NPR 36.55 per kilogram in 2010, and by 2014 this was NPR 42.83, an increase of 138 per cent in just 14 years (Aryal and Sapkota, 2017). Rice prices had risen even further by 2023, to between NPR 55 and INR 60 per kilogram.

Pant (2011) in part links the longer-term trends of rising food prices to oil prices, which influence the costs of diesel for irritation or ploughing, and fertiliser, as well as the costs of food processing (for example, rice milling). Also important is the diversion of farmland into commercial and residential developments in peri-urban areas, hoarding by traders and climate change itself, which has contributed to weakened harvests (Pant, 2011). Changing food habits in the hills (including the replacement of millet and maize with rice in diets) and urbanisation have also driven increases in the retail price, not to mention the Ukraine crisis, which is a global phenomenon (Arndt et al., 2023).

A corollary of rising food costs and expenses is that the poorest landless households, once dependent in part on agricultural labour, are no longer able to subsist on the wages that they accepted in the past. While women continue to be engaged extensively in agricultural labour for other households, and the proportion engaged in farm labour has actually increased between 2007–2008 and 2011 (see Table 4.3), male household members in particular are increasingly seeking work outside of the sector, a topic which will be dealt with in more detail later. In this context, labour-employing farmers can no longer find labourers willing to work on their land at previous wage rates – particularly male labourers, for tasks such as land preparation. Wages have also become monetised. In-kind wages were commonplace in 2007, whereby some rice would be given alongside a small payment of cash. In 2019 none of the surveyed farmers had received these wages, and most farmers were paid a *sukka* (literally 'dry') wage, with cash only.

Higher labour costs impact not only richer large and medium landholders but also smaller landholders and tenants who are dealing with a worker shortage during busy times of the year. The 2019 data suggested that 14 per cent of landless farmers, for instance, still need to hire a ploughman, particularly if costs or availability make the use of a tractor unfeasible. The following quotation by one small landowner from the Tharu community outlines some of the challenges posed by rising costs of labour and inputs:

> The farmers used to hire a person for ploughing the field and do the remaining work themselves but now the ploughman has to be paid two thousand rupees. He also has a problem in his house and he has to look after his children. If we give him food also then it costs us four thousand per month. Now it costs about 17 to 18 thousand rupees to buy our own bulls. Farmers also need to buy the fertilisers which are also expensive. So farmers are facing problems.... Even larger farmers have left farming. The farmers take a loan for everything, for *patuwa* (jute), fish and other cultivation, but still, the return is not good. You have seen the returns for rice also. The farmers have to pay loan repayments

> and wages for the workers. DAP costs 28 rupees per kilo, urea costs 20 rupees but if we use it twice [in a year] it costs 100 rupees per kilo! The fertilisers are expensive now. Now you can imagine how the farmers are suffering.

The farmer's empathy with the ploughman and his need for higher wages reflects the shared class consciousness the marginal farmer feels with his worker – and is a reminder that the circumstances where farmers use outside labour is very much dependent upon their own position in the agrarian structure. Unlike the small number of larger landholders who may use outside workers to accumulate and yield a profit, many small and landless producers employ labour due to family circumstance or lack of assets (for example, an absence of draught animals), while simultaneously working for other households at other times in the year. Rising costs of living and rising wages have thus disrupted the long established 'exchange' of labour between marginal farming households.

Just as these patterns of agrarian stress have pushed many landless and tenant farmers into further food insecurity or financial stress, they have also impacted the larger surplus-producing farmers, including both Tharu and Brahmin–Chettri owner-cultivators, who could potentially make the transition towards 'capitalist' farming. First, in spite of recent rises in the price of grain, for larger farmers who could potentially yield a surplus, this is offset by the rising costs of production – even if they can make some savings through ownership of their own irrigation and farm equipment. According to Aryal and Bhandari (2017), the net profit per hectare of paddy production across the Tarai-Madhesh is estimated to have declined by more than half from NPR 25,385 per hectare in 2007–2008 to NPR 11,793 in 2013–2014. In spite of a 205 per cent increase in production costs per quintal, the farm gate price of paddy has increased by only 79 per cent, from NPR 11.15 per kilogram in 2007–2008 to NPR 19.93 per kilogram by 2013–2014 (Aryal and Bhandari, 2017, 628). In this context some paddy varieties such as *chaite* (spring rice) have been abandoned almost entirely by bigger farmers. In 2007–2008, 54 per cent of large landholders with more than 2 hectares and 42 per cent of medium landholders with between 1 and 2 hectares cultivated *chaite* paddy in the pre-monsoon – it was a popular choice for those with the capital to meet the high irrigation costs. As of the 2019 survey, none of the farmers had reported cultivating the crop over the previous year, with land increasingly left fallow during the *pre-kharif* (pre-monsoon) season (see Figures 7.2 and 7.3).

A second challenge to profitability relates to the price received. While not affecting larger landholding farmers to the same extent as landless and small landholding farmers, price manipulation by merchant capital is a concern.

Figure 7.2 Pre-monsoon fields near Thalaha in late May. Other than some early rice seedlings, most of the land lies fallow due to the prohibitive costs of irrigation and poor returns for spring, or *chaite*, paddy.

Source: Author.

However, even the competitive market price can fail to offer an acceptable return, particularly in the context of the open border with India. Discounting manipulations by merchant capital, the 'competitive' market price for rice, wheat and jute sold to local *katawala*s is determined by the wholesale and retail prices for processed grain in Biratnagar, which is the site of both legal and illegal imports of agricultural commodities across the border. The quantities of rice imported from India have increased exponentially over the last decade. In 2008–2009, 104,151,350 kilograms were imported, increasing to 590,015,393 kilograms in 2016–2017 (Pudasainee et al., 2018).

To give one example, the paddy variety with the greatest market value is fine-grained aromatic rice such as Basmati. This is increasingly the primary form of rice favoured by urban consumers in Nepal (Paudel et al., 2017) and in the field area is the main crop produced by larger farmers seeking to sell for profit (rather than on a distress basis). Two-thirds of large landholders produced Basmati as of 2019, up from just 15 per cent in 2007–2008.

Figure 7.3 Fields being irrigated to plant *chaite* paddy near Rangeli in March 2013. Given that this is the dry season, it is an expensive investment due to the irrigation cost and as of 2023, only a small minority of farmers plant it.

Source: Author.

However, despite its much higher market price, local farmers in Morang find it difficult to compete with imports from India, and this was brought up repeatedly in interviews with farmers, local government officials and *katawalas*. Larger producers felt they could simply not give away their crop at the rates the Indian grain was selling for and yield a profit to facilitate 'accumulation', particularly when considering the enhanced subsidy regime in India and lower cost of production. When comparing the market prices for fertiliser in Bihar and the Nepali lowlands, the price of urea is 68 per cent more expensive in Nepal, the price of DAP is 41 per cent higher, while potash is 48 per cent higher (Nepal Rastra Bank, 2008).

Only a temporary ban on non-Basmati rice exports in India in 2008 as a result of grain shortages caused some relief for local farmers. Conversely, occasional 'import surges' from India cause severe distress for farmers selling their grain. For example, in 2000 imports rose by 800 per cent during a de-stocking of public grain reserves by the Food Corporation of India (Action Aid, 2008), causing a 17 per cent drop in grain prices in the Tarai-Madhesh districts to the disadvantage of local farmers. As well as Basmati, there are also considerable imports of non-Basmati rice, which directly impacts the price received by both marginal and tenant farmers selling on a distress basis in Morang. In 2018–2019, 2,874,000 kilograms of Basmati were imported from India, alongside 438,628,000 kilograms of non-Basmati grain (Hussain and Sinha, 2019). Only *chuira*, or beaten rice, derived from poorer quality grains such as *chaite* (spring paddy), was produced and sold within Nepal, with 95 per cent deriving from domestically produced paddy (Pudasainee et al., 2018), although as noted earlier, *chaite* is an increasingly unfeasible crop given the high cost of irrigation.

It is not only rice cultivation that is affected by the open border. Jute cultivation had all but ceased due to competition from India – not to mention the high costs of irrigation and labour. While 15 per cent of large landholder with more than 2 hectares had cultivated Jute in 2007–2008, only one large landholder was cultivating jute today, along with a single small landholder. One large owner-cultivating farmer who had once grown large areas of jute on his surplus land described how production had declined in recent years:

> People stopped growing jute as the investment requirements are higher than the income. The price farmers get is very low in the market while the effort the farmers have to put in is high. For that reason jute now is imported from Bihar, although jute can be grown in Nepal.... It is cheaper in India because the government provides the subsidies.

The poor returns on sales mean that some richer farmers noted a preference to lease out rather than invest on the land and employ labour, so that tenants 'bear the risk'. For example, one hot day in May during the final phase of fieldwork, in the aftermath of a major thunderstorm, a better-off farmer spoke in dismay about the damage the storms were doing to his wheat crop. As well as complaining about the price received, he explained his decision that next year he would just cultivate enough land to meet his family's food needs and the rest he would give away as *adhiya* (to sharecroppers). He already had some salaried employment income, and felt that by giving his land to tenants, he would at least get something from the land and would not have to worry about making a loss on his investments. It is difficult though, given the small number of large farmers in the sample, to assess how widespread this is, and the data suggests that the number of large farmers with more than 2 hectares renting out land has declined, although it has increased for those with between 1 and 2 hectares.

Another phenomenon through which larger farmers could generate income from agriculture beyond farming the land itself was to invest in agricultural equipment to rent out. Tractors and threshers were an increasingly

Figure 7.4 Mechanical thresher in Thalaha. This saves time, and wealthier farmers who own a thresher generally rent them out to other villagers who pay in kind.

Source: Author.

secure source of income as more and more farmers used them due to rising labour costs (see Figure 7.4). While these investments offered better-off farmers the opportunity to accumulate, they do so via the rent offered by the equipment, and not so much through expanding productivity on or increasing the size of their own farms. On the whole, though, interviews and the survey data (see Table 4.3) suggested that income from salaried employment by family members was as significant for the accumulation of wealth as were investments in agriculture.

Consumerism, Privatisation and the Cost of Living

In order to fully understand the patterns of stress facing agricultural livelihoods, it is important to look beyond just the agricultural and food economy, and explore other ways in which neoliberal capitalism is infiltrating lives and livelihoods in the southern Morang plains, and translating into rising demand for cash. A first driver of change has been the privatisation of public services which has swept Nepal since the 1990s. After education was opened to the private sector, a two-tiered schooling system has emerged in Nepal. With the quality of education in government schools deteriorating (see Figure 7.5), now 14 per cent of primary school students and 15 per cent of secondary school students attend private schools, the majority of whom are from the middle and upper classes, while the rural poor still predominantly attend government schools (Subedi et al., 2014). A majority of landless and small landholder farmers continue to send their children to local government schools in the village where fees are negligible. However, it is increasingly popular amongst better-off farming families to also send their children to the private school in Jhorahat Bazaar or in some cases even in Biratnagar. This was common amongst medium-to-large farmers from the Tharu community in Pidarboni or the Brahmin–Chettri community in Jhorahat Bazaar, and represented a significant monthly expense.

However, it is with regard to healthcare where the impact of privatisation on household finances becomes most apparent across all land ownership groups. While the government hospital in Biratnagar is often the first point of call during illnesses or accidents, in the case of serious or complex conditions, households often have no choice but to go to better equipped but expensive private hospitals – and at times patients must be transported to Kathmandu

Figure 7.5 School children returning from a government school. Education in state-run schools is being undercut by a burgeoning private school sector which is attracting children from medium-to-large farming households.

Source: Author.

by air or to India. As is evident from the data in Table 7.1, 22 per cent of households in the 2007–2008 sample had a large healthcare expenditure in the previous year, with an average expenditure of NPR 29,184. While the extremely high figures of more than NPR 200,000 reported by one middle and one large landowning household may be due to their ability to pay for private facilities, even landless and small landholders had borne significant expenses, with one having paid NPR 65,000. As well as paying for admission to private facilities, Adivasi households also reported (as of 2007) spending money on the services of *dhamis*, or faith healers. In terms of the proportion of one's cash expenditure which is absorbed by health expenses, Table 7.2 explores some of the major expenditures by households over the previous year (excluding day-to-day food and living costs which are hard to estimate). Out of these, 16.43 per cent of the expenditure for large landholders was on healthcare, while for landless farmers it was similar, at 15.40 per cent. Notably for the larger farmers, healthcare expenditure was at a similar level to what was spent on their farms in agricultural inputs or investments in equipment or livestock.

For better-off producers, healthcare costs can undermine their capacity to invest productively on the land with a view to maximising output and yielding a profit. For the landless and small landholding farmers already suffering from the rent burden, these costs can drive further distress commerce which eats into their grain needs for subsistence. Alternatively, they may consume what little savings are left from wage labour which could have otherwise been used productively.

Another cause of rising non-agricultural expenses is spiralling expenditure on consumer goods. This process has taken place over several stages. Throughout the second half of the twentieth century, the import of Indian made commodities

Table 7.1 Health expenditures in the previous year (2007–2008) by land ownership category

Land ownership category	% who had made large heath expense in previous year	Minimum reported expenditure (NPR)	Maximum reported expenditure (NPR)
Landless	18	2,000	25,000
< 1 ha	31	3,000	65,000
1–2 ha	13	65,000	200,000
> 2 ha	14	15,000	350,000
Total	22	2,000	350,000

Source: Author.

Table 7.2 Total allocation of selected expenditure by land ownership category over previous year (2007–2008)

Land ownership category		Weddings, religious, and lifecycle ceremonies	Healthcare	Household maintenance	Other	Luxury goods	Agricultural equipment or livestock	Recurring farm inputs (nutrients, irrigation and labour)
Landless	Total (NPR)	445,500	152,500	12,000	12,000	68,500	20,000	279,672
	%	44.99	15.40	1.21	1.21	2.02	6.92	28.24
< 1 ha	Total (NPR)	558,000	309,000	150,000	243,000	332,500	9,000	391,541
	%	28.00	15.50	7.53	12.19	0.45	16.68	19.65
1–2 ha	Total (NPR)	547,000	265,000	0	0	43,500	0	105,083
	%	56.94	27.59	0.00	0.00	0.00	4.53	10.94
> 2 ha	Total (NPR)	1,377,500	382,500	91,000	31,000	298,000	16,500	131,907
	%	59.16	16.43	3.91	1.33	0.71	12.80	5.67
	Total (NPR)	2,928,000	1,109,000	253,000	286,000	742,500	45,500	908,203
Total	%	46.68	17.68	4.03	4.56	0.73	11.84	14.48

Source: Author.

had undermined local cottage industries across Nepal (Blaikie et al., 2001). As many of these locally produced goods had been exchanged for grain through the *jajmani* exchange between castes, the need to purchase goods once these exchanges collapsed meant that a process of monetisation took place, whereby households required more cash than in previous generations. This process continues to this day in the hills, driven by the expansion of roads (Sugden et al., 2018). In Dhanusha in the central Tarai-Madhesh, *jajmani* exchange continued up until the 1970s and 1980s, after which the market economy took over (Sugden, 2019). Further east in Morang itself, non-cash exchange systems likely ended earlier given the long history of market integration. Furthermore, given the predominance of Adivasi groups, the role of caste in driving exchange was likely less significant.

Nevertheless, many traditional cottage industries still persist, albeit in monetised form, such as the production of terracotta and copper vessels (see Figure 7.6) and metal tools. However, the market for such goods is declining with surging imports of more expensive consumables.

Figure 7.6 Terracotta vessels for sale during a *haatiya* (weekly market). There is growing competition for expensive imported plastic or metal vessels which is undermining traditional artisanal trades.

Source: Author.

Most significant, though, is that Morang is also in the midst of a second wave of monetisation and rising cash demands, driven now not so much by demand for manufactured essential goods such as cookware, tools or clothes, but instead by the demand for luxuries. These include more expensive imported clothes, but most significantly technology such as televisions and smartphones. The latter has only really taken off in the last six–seven years,[6] and with many young people using social media, the cost of data is a significant additional expense. While rising consumption of 'luxuries' is less prevalent amongst the poorer farmers, particularly in Bhaudaha and Thalaha, it appears to be disproportionately taking place amongst medium-to-large landholders in the Tharu and Brahmin–Chettri communities.

While Table 7.2 points to relatively low expenditure on luxury goods, expenditure was likely underestimated as the interviewees were focusing their attention on 'household' costs, whereas many luxuries would be bought as one-off purchases by individuals. Furthermore, many luxury goods were acquired via gift exchange in the context of marriages, which will be described later. Most importantly, this was based upon 2007–2008 data (the 2019 survey did not capture expenditure on luxuries), and qualitative interviews suggested that expenditure had risen considerably in the 15 years since the original survey. Changing consumption patterns are particularly evident if one looks at the changes in Pidarboni, one of the villages with a large number of medium-to-large landholders. During the early fieldwork in 2007–2008, there were just two–three small *kirana* stores selling basic goods such as rice, oil, salt and tobacco, and occasionally some locally made snacks or biscuits (see Figure 7.7). However, over the last five years, a number of larger specialised shops have been established, selling clothes and household essentials imported from India and China, while local *kirana* stores sold a wide range of domestic processed foodstuffs, beer and imported and local liquor (see Figure 7.8). This contrasts with 2007 when fieldwork started, when one had to travel 2 kilometres to Jhorahat Bazaar, or in most cases to Biratnagar, to procure these goods. By 2023, there was even a small bazaar developing near the main *chowk* (intersection with main road) (see Figure 7.9) with a line of new shops. When asked about this change within a decade, respondents simply noted that people 'spend more' nowadays and the demand is higher, and that there is a greater circulation of cash. It echoes changes across Nepal which took off in Kathmandu in the 1990s (see Liechty, 2003), which today have spread beyond urban areas to the upper strata of the peasantry who increasingly aspire towards middle-class consumption patterns. Further driving these changes today is the improved

Figure 7.7 The operation of traditional village *kirana* stores are an important source of supplementary income for farmers. However, these are now facing growing competition from larger, more well-stocked enterprises along the newly improved roads.

Source: Author.

Figure 7.8 Changing face of retail: a liquor store in 2022. At the time when fieldwork started in 2007, factory-made alcoholic and non-alcoholic beverages were not available in the village.

Source: Author.

Figure 7.9 The main *chowk* (intersection) in Pidarboni in 2008 (*top*) and again in 2023 (*below*). By 2023 the grassy verge once used for informal trade had been replaced with a row of permanent concrete shops along the side of the newly upgraded highway.

Source: Author.

transportation and availability of goods, greater mobility within Nepal and abroad via migration, as well as rural people's integration into globalised media landscapes via the internet and global television networks.

However, perhaps more significant than day-to-day consumption of luxuries in influencing household finances, is the spiralling cost of weddings and other ritual events (see Figure 7.10). This has a significant, albeit more complex, relationship with capitalist expansion in a neoliberal economy. Just under half of the average expenditure listed in Table 7.2 is for weddings, religious and lifecycle ceremonies. Out of these expenditures, weddings are by far the most important, and the costs are not only associated with the ceremony itself (such as hiring the cook, priest and vehicle) but the gift and financial exchange associated with the union. In Tharu marriages in particular, although gifts are given to the family of the bride (bride price), it is gifts to the groom – which often includes financial payments or dowry – that represent the most significant expense. Studies from the Tharu elsewhere suggest that bride price was more common in the past (Krauskopff, 2003), although it is likely that this has changed in Morang over the decades. This echoes a shift across South Asia whereby many indigenous communities have made a transition from bride price to dowry as class stratification increases (Randeria

Figure 7.10 Tharu wedding band. As in many parts of South Asia, weddings and other life-cycle ceremonies represent a considerable non-agricultural expense most households must bear.

Source: Author.

and Visaria, 1984; Anderson, 2007),[7] given the importance of dowry for the reproduction of class status – a topic dealt with later.

The fact that all social groups invest extensively in lifecycle events – and that these costs are rising – deserves some discussion. It is incorrect to simply dismiss investments in lifecycle events as an 'irrational' use of resources, given that for the families involved these are considered crucial investments to generate alliances, access new social networks and reproduce social or class status. Dowry payments in particular, which rises according to the wealth of the groom's family, ensure that one's daughter marries into a family with similar (or better) economic prospects (Anderson, 2007),[8] while also securing robust social networks with such families. Nevertheless, what has changed is that payments for weddings, dowry and associated gift exchanges are putting greater financial stress on households in the context of a neoliberal market economy and rising culture of consumerism. As a result, not only has the cost of gifts and weddings increased in line with the rising cost of living, but also their real value has risen. For instance, the exchange of livestock was widespread in the past, a manageable cost given that animals were likely raised on one's own farm. Today, however, there is a strong social expectation that families offer luxury consumer goods as gifts.

The costs are quite significant for the poorest households. During the 2007–2008 survey, landless households had collectively spent NPR 445,500 (approx. USD 3,300) on weddings and religious or lifecycle ceremonies (see Table 7.2). Out of the major expenses over the year captured in Table 7.2, it represents a substantial 44.99 per cent of expenditure across the landless household group, considerably more than the 35.16 per cent allocated to recurring farm expenses and investment in equipment or livestock. It is similarly high for small landholders, at 28 per cent. It is actually amongst the medium-to-large landholders, however, where the burden of these expenses is most significant. In spite of the falling profitability for agriculture amongst larger landholders, the cost of weddings, religious and other events has continued to rise. For large landholders with more than 2 hectares, expenditure is NPR 91,833 on average, with one household having spent up to NPR 300,000 (approx. USD 2,500) on a wedding – and bearing in mind that this was 2007–2008 data, these prices are notably higher today. They represent 59.16 per cent of major expenditures documented for large landholders in Table 7.2 – substantially more than the 12.8 per cent spent on agricultural equipment or livestock and the 5.67 per cent spent on recurring farm inputs.

Interestingly, it appears to be the Tharu who are spending the most. Out of large landholders (more than 2 hectares) from the Tharu community, the average expenditure was NPR 209,166. For Brahmin and Chettri larger landholders, the average expenditure was just NPR 59,071, in spite of the fact that they have traditionally been more economically powerful while also having alternative professional income sources.

One can shed some light on the heavy cultural capital requirements for wealthier Tharu households by investigating the agrarian relations of the past. The Tharu held some of the largest wedding ceremonies in the cluster of study villages, with feasts where large sections of the community would be invited, as well as organising various *pujas* (religious ceremonies) and other community ritual activities. A number of anthropological studies in Nepal (largely from the hills) have shown how in Adivasi modes of production in Nepal, prior to their subordination to feudalism, social obligation rather than maximisation of profit would influence what happens to surplus (Dahal, 1981; Macfarlane, 1976). In this context, ritual events were one means through which surplus could be redistributed, particularly from the household of the headman or other traditional leader to the wider clan unit, as shown amongst the Rai (McDougal, 1973; Dahal, 1981), for instance. It is probable that this also applied to the Tharu at a time when the Adivasi mode of production predominated, but following the transition to feudalism, and the Tharu leaders' emergence as a surplus-*appropriating* class, these expenditures arguably played an opposite function, to reproduce the social status of the landed elite. For example, funding community rituals and lavish wedding feasts increased one's social status and strengthened patron–client relations between the landed Adivasi elite and the many tenants and small farmers from within the Tharu community who worked for them. Similarly, dowry payments to secure marital alliances with other landed families evolved to become an important means through which to ensure the reproduction of the family's elevated social standing.

Today, however, the Tharu landed elite's political and economic power has dissipated, with absentee landlords replacing them at the apex of the agrarian structure. Nevertheless, the cultural pressure to spend lavishly on religious ceremonies, weddings and dowry remains unchanged – even as the costs have increased alongside a wave of neoliberal consumerism. With respect to dowry, the former nobility are still expected to make high payments to ensure they access a groom from another 'high status' family,[9] even if both households' actual material wealth has declined significantly. Today, wealthy Tharu households are expected to purchase a motorbike for the grooms' family when their daughters marry, alongside expensive imported electronic goods and other luxuries. Even guests are also expected to spend considerable amounts on gifts. One Tharu farmer in Pidarboni was asked about the greatest expenses associated with marriages:

> It's in the dowry. Many people spend money on home appliances and other things. Motorbikes are normal nowadays. As the people don't have cash they even sell their land. Dhani Ram [pseudonym] spent a lot during his daughters' marriage as he is one of the rich men!

In one discussion, we were informed of a Tharu household in a nearby village whose ancestors were *patuwari*s (clerks in the tax administration) and who once had considerable wealth, but had lost a lot of land supposedly due to wedding expenses. The respondent we spoke to, who was himself a larger landholder but not a descendent of the Rana-era functionary class, initially spoke with disdain of the circumstances of the former *patuwari*'s family. However, he went on to admit that even relatively more prosperous Tharu households who did not hail from 'landed' backgrounds felt compelled to copy the spending habits of these neighbours if they were to maintain their cultural status in the community – even if this ate into their agricultural income. He even displayed some anger that this former elite were 'distorting our customs', and compelling the rest of the community to copy.

Rankin (2004) cites similar processes occurring amongst the Newar merchant castes of the Kathmandu valley in the 1990s, whereby cultural capital requirements had increased while real incomes had declined, weakening their economic power. Ironically, the lower castes are not faced with the same obligations, leading to reduced inter-caste inequalities. These contradictions echo Althusser's (1969) assertion that although political-ideological systems, or the 'superstructure', emerge in the context of particular modes of production, they still have their own logic, and can persist as 'survivals', even in the context of economic change and new ideologies, such as those of neoliberalism. It is clear in this context that the emergence of large farmer households as a capitalist class (and differentiation) is being hindered by the persistence of ideological 'survivals' of an earlier economic formation. These cultural capital investments both increase levels of indebtedness for larger Tharu landholders and further decrease the chance that they would emerge into a 'capitalist' class.

With regard to the Brahmin and Chettri settlers in the core field area, who do not appear to have the same cultural capital expenses, this remains a puzzle. It may be connected to their very different history of settlement.

While many absentee landlords often hail from the Brahmin and Chettri castes, those who reside in Jhorahat are from quite different backgrounds. Most migrated to the village as enterprising settlers from the hills around 60 years ago. Although their economic status is arguably the most secure of all the ethnic communities, with many holding government jobs and caste privilege, not all are from prosperous or landlord backgrounds – and weddings were often more modest affairs.

Debt and the Rise of Microfinance Banks

The rising cost of inputs, labour and food, combined with a rising culture of consumerism and spiralling costs of weddings and associated events, has intensified indebtedness. While *katawala*s remain an important source of credit for agricultural inputs for land-poor and tenant farmers, a large share of the debt burden is today associated with institutional finance.

There has been a mushrooming of microfinance banks in rural Morang since the 1990s, echoing trends across low- and middle-income countries. The enhanced supply of credit was another 'priority input' of Nepal's Agricultural Perspective Plan (APROSC, 1995) and later Agricultural Development Strategy (Ministry of Agricultural Development, 2014). It was envisaged that loans could be used, for instance, to purchase chemical fertiliser or shallow tube wells and to develop animal husbandry and high value crop production, or make investments in tractors or other agricultural equipment.

Microfinance has been interpreted as an integral part of capitalist expansion and neoliberalism, whereby poverty alleviation is framed in terms of individual autonomy and entrepreneurship, rather than provision of social and political rights (Kamat, 2004; Mayer and Rankin, 2002; Rankin, 2004). A broad body of literature has, however, shown how microfinance in low- and middle-income countries does not necessarily create 'rational entrepreneurs', but instead has contributed to indebtedness, given that a large share of loans are diverted into basic necessities or health bills, being repaid often not through enterprise but via capitalist sector wages (Green and Estes, 2019; Rankin, 2001; Rankin and Shakya, 2007). For instance, over-lending and mass default on loans contributed to a crisis in the sector in India's Andhra Pradesh in 2010, with loans being taken not by farmers seeking 'opportunities' but due to agrarian distress amongst smaller landholders (Taylor, 2012). This quite aptly captures the situation in Morang over the last two to three decades. While microfinance has been present in Nepal since the 1970s, it took off following economic liberalisation and the introduction of the Grameen Bank model in the early 1990s. Today there are 63 different microfinance institutions in Nepal, with 3,750 branches, with a large number represented in the Biratnagar region (Jain, 2020).

There were several primary sources of credit as of 2023. The first is the *sahakari*, or 'cooperative', which raises funds from member deposits, with the size of loan being proportionate to the shares held. Loans were available of up to NPR 100,000 collateral free, but loans of up to NPR 10,000,000 were available with collateral. Interest rates as of 2023 were around 15 per cent. The second source were the actual microfinance banks themselves, which could give much larger loans, but usually at slightly higher interest rates of up to 20 per cent. However, again, the larger loans required collateral. Third, farmers could take loans from so-called development banks such as the state-run Agricultural Development Bank, which was popular with larger farmers, and, rarely, commercial banks. Such farmers could take much larger loans with collateral which could be used to invest in higher-value assets such as agricultural equipment. Poorer farmers and tenants tended to take loans from smaller microfinance banks and cooperatives.

As of the 2007–2008 survey, widespread borrowing from these multiple banks and cooperatives was a relatively recent phenomenon, but this appears to have increased substantially by the time of the 2019 survey. As of 2007–2008, 28.32 per cent of households had taken loans from a microfinance bank or cooperative in the last one year, including just over a third of all landless households, and 46.24 per cent had taken loans in the last five years, including half of all landless households (see Table 7.3). Loans from the Agricultural Development Bank and commercial institutions were below 10 per cent for small and medium landholders, but were up to 20 per cent for large landholders with more than 2 hectares. These loans were harder to come by and required farmers to be more financially secure, as well as also requiring collateral.

In the 2019 survey (see Table 7.4), respondents recorded their outstanding debts to different financial institutions. A substantial 61.69 per cent on average had recorded debts to microfinance banks and cooperatives, including 82.82 per cent of landless farmers. While this uses a different measure from the earlier survey, this is considerably higher than the proportion of those who had recorded loans in the last five years in 2007–2008, pointing to a substantial increase in lending activity, particularly amongst the poorest households. The average outstanding debt for landless households is a substantial NPR 34,627 – and it almost doubles for medium landholders who are eligible for larger

Table 7.3 Loans taken from microfinance banks as of the 2007–2008 survey

Land ownership category	Microfinance bank or cooperative				Agricultural Development Bank (and commercial)			
	Has taken loan in last 5 years	Average amount borrowed in last 5 years	Has taken loan in last 1 year	Average amount borrowed in last year	Has taken loan in last 5 years	Average amount borrowed in last 5 years	Has taken loan in last 1 year	Average amount of loans taken in last year
Landless	52.44	23,683	36.59	11,683	10.98	28,667	3.66	13,667
< 1 ha	48.33	361,154	23.33	16,429	21.67	45,038	6.67	22,375
1–2 ha	31.25	73,300	18.75	26,000	43.75	42,643	6.25	20,000
> 2 ha	20.00	122,500	13.33	5,000	40.00	55,000	20.00	18,333
Total	46.24	147,933	28.32	13,643	20.23	42,057	6.36	18,682

Source: Author.

Table 7.4 Outstanding debt from microfinance banks as of the 2019 survey

Land ownership category	Microfinance bank			Agricultural Development Bank (and other)		
	Has outstanding debt	Average initially borrowed (only those who were in debt)	outstanding debt (total)	Has outstanding debt	Average initially borrowed (only those who were in debt)	Average outstanding debt
Landless	81.82	82,045	34,627	3.64	insufficient data	insufficient data
< 1 ha	56.16	168,625	62,417	12.33	447,222	21,404
1–2 ha	22.22	200,000	22,222	22.22	400,000	76,667
> 2 ha	0.00	NA	0	50.00	600,000	165,313
Total	60.69	125,058	45,823	11.72	456,765	29,621

Source: Author.

loans. For larger landholders it is the Agricultural Development Bank and larger commercial banks which are offering loans, and the levels of debt are also very high – with some having taken loans of up to NPR 600,000. Debt thus affects both marginal and larger landholders.

Importantly, there is evidence that it is not only the number taking loans but also the average size of loan which has risen. In 2007–2008, for those who had taken loans the average amount borrowed from the NGO-led banks over a year was NPR 13,643, and from landless households it was NPR 11,683. As of 2019, when asked about the loans they are currently repaying, the total amount borrowed by those in debt was NPR 125,058 on average, and for landless households it was NPR 82,045 on average. This is higher even than the NPR 23,683 that landless farmers had borrowed over a five-year period back in 2007–2008. For other loans such as those from the Agricultural Development Bank, the average borrowed amount by larger landholders for outstanding debts was NPR 600,000 – far less even than what had been borrowed over a five-year period as of 2007–2008. While rising costs of living and inflation will contribute to this, it does point to a rising frequency and quantity of loans.

Interviews revealed that while some farmers use this profusion of loans for productive ventures, they are commonly used for day-to-day consumption, particularly for one-off expenses to cover healthcare or other urgent needs. They were also used to support the costs paid to so-called manpower agents to send family members overseas, with payments of up to USD 2,000 commonplace to secure employment in the Gulf or Malaysia – an issue discussed later. Furthermore, they were frequently used to cover the rising costs of weddings and other lifecycle events. Rankin and Shakya (2008) have suggested that easily available microfinance in Nepal have encouraged a culture of borrowing for consumption purposes. During a focus group discussion in Bhaudaha, one participant joked about the impact of bank loans on spending habits and economic security:

> In our community we have land but no other source of income. We don't have a brain. All of us keep the land as collateral and take the loan. We enjoy with that loan and when we can't pay the loan then we sell our land.

The upside to the expansion of microfinance institutions, even when they are used for 'non-productive' purposes, is that farmers are less dependent upon private money lenders for one-off consumption loans, a practice which is widespread in the Mithila belt of the Tarai-Madhesh where the expansion of microfinance has been more limited (Sugden, 2017).

One woman farmer who ran a rotating savings and credit scheme explained the benefits to group members of taking loans from their programme over the private moneylenders, back in 2008 as the sector was starting its expansion:

> We can use that money when we need it. If we go to businessman or rich people then they hesitate to give loan even in 2 per cent. They make us pay 4 per cent or 5 per cent which is calculated at 24 per cent annually, so now we don't go to them. At banks we don't have to pay that much interest. If there will be more money in our account then we can even reduce it to 1 per cent which is 12 per cent per year. No one can stop us within society as it's our group and money. We don't need any permission to use that money. If the secretary and chairman sign a cheque then it [the money] can be easily withdrawn from the bank.

While these sentiments reflect growing economic empowerment, particularly for women, as shown in a study from neighbouring Sunsari district (Karn et al., 2020), what is concerning are the intensifying cycles of debt to the microfinance banks themselves. The levels of outstanding debt as of 2019 were substantial. The average debt still to be repaid amongst surveyed farmers in 2019 was NPR 125,058 (approx. USD 1,050), with the poorest group, the landless households, having an outstanding debt averaging at NPR 82,045 (see Table 7.4). Even as early as the 2007–2008 study, seven farmers who were interviewed had taken new loans to repay outstanding debts that they were unable to repay from other microfinance banks. The rise in debt suggests that taking multiple loans had increased as of 2019. This practice, which is termed 'loan swapping', was also observed in Rankin and Shakya's (2008) village-level study of microfinance in Nepal and Vietnam. Taylor (2012) also highlighted the phenomenon of multiple borrowing in the Andhra Pradesh study. Such practices can be used to extend the duration of loans and meet the necessary repayment deadlines.

The rise in debt to microfinance banks puts considerable financial pressure on households, particularly for the women who increasingly shoulder the burden of loans from the smaller banks and cooperatives. Loans are often given through groups of women, and payments are made at fortnightly meetings. As many of these smaller loans are collateral free, they depend on peer pressure amongst group members to prevent borrowers from defaulting. If one member fails to pay the required instalment, it must be paid by the rest of the group. Furthermore, farmers complained of the lack of flexibility, and one respondent argued that the Agricultural Development Bank was out to 'extort' poor farmers, adding:

If a loan is taken from the local people then even if we can't repay it within one year then we can pay the interest for that year and then the next year we can repay the loan along with the interest. But with the bank what happens is that if we can't repay the loan within the stated time then the interest increases until it is higher than the villager's [village moneylender] rate! In the bank we have to repay within 6 months.

Pressures to repay mean that farmers even turn to private lenders to repay microfinance loans. As another respondent complained:

Once a bank releases 10,000 rupees, it is usually wasted on a celebration. People are happy to receive money! They also use them to buy cattle or big one-off expenses. Although these are necessary expenses, they will not yield instant returns to repay the 10,000. For that reason, people turn to the Marwaris to repay their bank loans. Eventually people may be compelled to sell their house or something to repay the loan. Banks have made things a little easier though, as people are not totally dependent upon Marwaris.[10]

This highlights a broader issue in that despite rising debt to banks, many farmers are still unable to use institutional credit to meet agricultural needs. Several farmers also complained that the money from banks is not available when required – particularly for the purchase of agricultural inputs, which requires a large investment in inputs twice a year for paddy and wheat respectively. Farmers complained that microfinance loans are not available this frequently, with the latter usually reserved for 'one-off' big expenses. Farmers also struggle to keep up with the periodic repayment schedules that these microfinance loans usually require, as cash only becomes available in the household after the harvest. If repayment schedules are not met, then the interest increases to the point that it is often higher than the rates charged by local moneylenders. For many poorer farmers, therefore, the *katawala* remains an important source of credit to purchase inputs.

Respondents also stressed that the bureaucracy for securing institutional loans is time consuming. These constraints are particularly acute for households seeking urgent cash loans, due, for example, to having to pay for medical treatment. A small farmer from the largely landless Rajbanshi community of Sitpur in Bhaudaha emphasises the convenience of accessing loans from *katawala*:

We take loans from the merchant because we can get loans easily, only with the words! For the process of taking loans from Bank, we have to show them a

> lot of formal paperwork and collateral, as well as a recommendation from the VDC office.

It is in the context of these challenges that land-poor farming households are *still* taking high-interest loans from *katawalas* to purchase agricultural inputs. They therefore face a dual debt burden, whereby they are repaying loans to banks while repaying loans (with usurious interest rates) to merchants.

Ironically, it was suggested by farmers that some wealthier villagers and moneylenders even take out loans from the microfinance banks and then lend them out again to their poorer counterparts at higher rates of interest, as one farmer in the largely landless village of Bhaudaha described:

> Farmer: The interest rate is 3 per cent for the farmers. We do not have to show the collateral and show them [the moneylender] our assets. When they give [the credit] in Ashad and Jestha then they will be repaid in Kartik.[11] The money does not stay with them long as they have also borrowed from others.
>
> Interviewer: So it is not their own money?
>
> Farmer: They borrow from various businessmen and from the banks. They do business in that way. If they have built a house which is of 10 lakh rupees, then they borrow 20 lakh rupees and they do their business. Here the poor are suffering.

However, whether this practice is still widespread is not known, given that the respondent appeared to be referring to private lenders rather than the *katawalas* who tend to offer most non-institutional loans today.

Off-farm Labour and Migration

Set against this context of dwindling yields, but also the rising demand for cash and spiralling debt, it was clear in interviews between 2008 and 2023 that households are adapting their livelihoods by *increasing* the engagement of male household members in wage labour in the capitalist sector – both locally and via migration. While this is a long-established pattern, it has increased notably in the last decade or so – with this articulation between capitalist and pre-capitalist being an increasingly entrenched feature of the larger social formation. This is evident in the 12 years between the 2007–2008 and 2019 surveys. As indicated in Table 4.4, agricultural labour on other farms has increased amongst small and landless households – perhaps a product of dwindling holdings. However, Figure 7.11 also points to a rise in households whose family members engage in labour in jobs associated with the capitalist sector – that is, factories or construction. While the change is not notable for small or landless households who have always been in part dependent upon work in the capitalist sector due to the rent burden, it has notably also increased for small (with less than 1 hectare) and even medium (with 1–2 hectares) landowners.

Most farmers who cannot meet their subsistence needs at current levels of productivity appear to prefer *not* to risk investments to increase productivity, but, instead, consciously choose to split their labour time between the farm and the capitalist sector. In a Marxian sense, they perform a portion of their 'necessary' labour (to meet their minimum needs) both on their farm and outside, while the product of their 'surplus' labour time is shared between both landlords and external employers. Many respondents stated that they preferred a combination of non-agricultural labour and tenant farming at a time of rising agrarian stress and costs of living – and thus a dual livelihood strategy is pursued.

In order, however, to better understand this shift, it is useful to explore in more detail the changes in the nature of engagement with capitalism. It is worth noting that an overall increase in farmers' dependence on off-farm

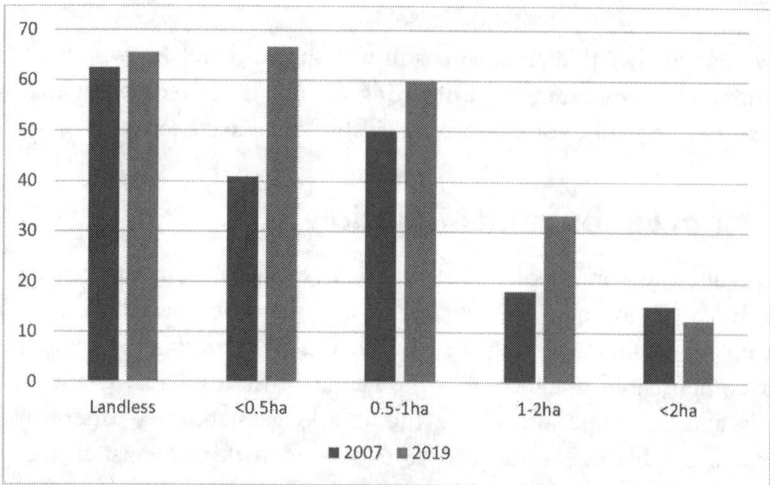

Figure 7.11 Percentage of households engaged in off-farm unskilled or semi-skilled labour in the capitalist sector in 2007–2008 and 2019

Source: Author.

labour has gone alongside a shift in the type of employment – and this also reflects larger changes in the post-liberalisation political economy. Up until the 2000s, factories were still one of the major employers. However, with the sector under increased stress in Nepal's import-dependent economy, the proportion of households in the sample engaged in factory labour has actually dropped between 2007–2008 and 2019 from 17.24 per cent to 13.79 per cent, with a particularly notable decline amongst landless households (see Table 4.4).

However, as noted in Chapter 3, the decline in industrial employment has occurred alongside the rapid expansion of the service sector over the last two decades in Nepal. Growth in this sector has been driven in part by rising prosperity amongst segments of the urban middle and upper classs, and the expansion of services such as banks, hospitality, healthcare, education and retail trade – all of which have benefitted from the wave of rural monetisation, privatisation and consumerism discussed earlier. As noted in Chapter 2, service industries have limited capacity to 'absorb' labour (Harriss-White and Gooptu, 2009). For instance, looking across the eastern Tarai-Madhesh as a whole, the 2011 census suggests that important service subsectors make up just a small share of the non-industrial employment share in the region. For example, healthcare accounts for 2.07 per cent, with finance at 1.47 per cent, hotels and restaurants at 2.77 per cent, real estate at 0.19 per cent (Central Bureau of Statistics, 2017).

The one segment of the service sector which does appear to have grown notably is construction. While this forms just 8.96 per cent of recorded non-agricultural employment in the 2011 census for the whole eastern Tarai-Madhesh (Central Bureau of Statistics, 2011), it was reported in interviews to be of growing importance in Morang given the proximity to Biratnagar. The rise of households engaged in casual semi-skilled labour (most of which is in construction) in the panel data in Table 4.3, from 8.97 per cent in 2007–2008 to 31.03 per cent, reflects this change – with work as a mason, or *mistry*, being most common. A substantial 45.45 per cent of landless households are engaged in such work, and it is particularly widespread amongst the Bantar community of Thalaha. An expansion in construction employment is itself stimulated by growth in the real estate sector in Biratnagar, as well as shopping complexes and hotels. Construction was also in part stimulated by the expansion of the bureaucracy, following the declaration of Biratnagar as the capital of Koshi Province, which encompasses much of eastern Nepal. Along with the establishment of new larger local units and the abolition of the old VDC system, there has been rising demand for labour to construct new government offices in the provincial capital, including the imminent provincial assembly hall, not to mention construction of offices in the new rural municipality centres.

The drop in households engaged in casual unskilled labour from 24.14 per cent to 7.59 per cent between the two surveys is largely due to the replacement of cycle rickshaws with e-rickshaws, which has resulted in a lost income-generation opportunity for the poorest households, although this has been compensated for by the rise in construction work. Some household members remain engaged in unskilled casual work in the town such as working as cleaners in hospitals or businesses. There has also been a rise in salaried 'professional' employment from 8.28 per cent to 15.17 per cent as one would expect given a burgeoning service sector. However, this has been driven by richer farmers who can afford to send their children to better schools. Nearly two-thirds of those with more than 2 hectares of land now derive income from professional employment.

Importantly, given the limited capacity for the local capitalist economy to fully absorb a rural labour force, one of the most significant changes in the context of rising cash needs has been the rise in labour migration overseas. Migration to the Gulf states and Malaysia appears to have increased substantially between 2007–2008 and 2019 when observing the panel data. Table 4.6 suggests that only 10.4 per cent of households had migrant family members overseas in 2007–2008, but this had risen to 25.45 per cent by 2019. A similar rate of increase is evident for both landless and small landholders, although, curiously, overseas migration appears to have declined amongst middle-to-large farmers. This requires further research, but the sample is too small to make concrete comparisons, and it may be due to their ability to secure professional employment. The levels of migration are still low compared to other parts of Nepal. For instance, a recent study from Dhanusha and Bhojpur (Gupta et al., 2022) placed the figures at 45 per cent and 69 per cent – but this is likely due to the fact that, unlike the latter two districts, which are relatively remote and agricultural, there are local sites of capitalist wage labour in Morang, although the nature of the articulation with capitalism is the same.

Today migration to India is low, with just one migrant reported, down from an already low number of four in 2007–2008, most of whom were members of the Rishidev community who migrated to Kashmir to pick apples during summer. Internal migration is also limited at just 6 per cent of households. The proximity of Biratnagar to the village means there is limited benefit in migrating beyond the district with the extra costs it involves. Most cases of internal migrants are for those with salaried or professional jobs who are posted outside and who send some savings back to the community – yet these are restricted to better-off households. This explains why over a third of the richer farmers have internal migrants, with negligible levels for marginal and landless farmers (see Table 4.6).

Feminisation and the Growing Work Burden

The increasing dependence on men working in the capitalist sector, particularly in the case of migrant labour, has contributed in some ways to existing agrarian stress – particularly with regard to labour shortages for work on the farm. This disproportionately affects women, who in the context of the Nepal Tarai-Madhesh, rarely migrate themselves and increasingly manage the farm after the departure of male family members. Only one woman had migrated in the entire sample for 2019. In a set of interviews with women in 2012–2013, the labour burden was raised repeatedly as a primary challenge facing their livelihoods in a post-migration context.

Even prior to the recent rise in migration, women already performed a disproportionate share of total household labour.[12] This stems in particular from their responsibilities to perform both *productive* and *reproductive* labour, such as tasks within the household. However, despite additional responsibilities, their remuneration remains the same or even less, as frequently theorised from a Marxist-feminist perspective (Benholtd-Thomson, 1982; Gibson-Graham, 1996; Folbre, 1982). For all ethnic communities in the southern Morang region, women performed the most labour-intensive agricultural tasks such as rice transplanting and weeding, while also being responsible for most essential household reproductive tasks. Men, meanwhile, would take responsibility primarily for land preparation, irrigation and general 'supervision'.

In the context of male out-migration, but also men's increased engagement with off-farm labour, women's productive work burden on the farm has risen further – even if men are contributing 'productively' to the household livelihood through work outside. Female respondents noted how they have to look after all the household works such as child rearing and established agricultural tasks such as paddy transplantation and harvesting, while taking on new agricultural tasks that were previously the domain of males such as hiring and supervising labourers, or negotiating the rental of a pump set or thresher. Some tasks such as ploughing are rarely done by women, and thus labourers have to be employed, which, as noted earlier, can put added financial stress on women, particularly as the rates for male farm labour increase (see Figure 7.12).

It is only in the better-off households that one may expect the women to cope without the same added work burden. As already noted in Table 4.4, large landowners had spent substantially more on labour not only in terms of the total area (due to their larger farms) but also in terms of the labour investment per *bigha*. Employing labour can offset labour shortages associated with men working outside, even while it adds to the financial burdens of these larger farms.

While there were few better-off households with migrants as of 2019 in the sample, there were several encountered in other villages outside of the core study area who were interviewed. Women at home can compensate for a decrease in male labour availability by hiring workers from other households. In this context women's primary role outside reproductive work is to supervise the labourers but not actually labour themselves. Some households with larger land holdings where men have migrated even give the land out to tenants,

Figure 7.12 Ploughman preparing paddy fields. Ploughing using an ox is one of the few jobs restricted to male household members – although this job is increasingly being replaced by tractors.

Source: Author.

so the women left behind can subsist on the rent and do not even need to supervise the farm production. One example was a Tharu woman several kilometres north of the field area, whose husband was in Qatar, and who owned 5 *bigha*s (3.35 hectare) of land – a relatively large holding. Production had declined, they had no tube well, and the harvest had suffered from the erratic weather of 2012. In this context, she gave the land to sharecroppers – passing on the risk – and invested in a chicken farm using the money from her husband's remittances, offering a more secure source of income. Her husband had a semi-skilled job in a factory in Qatar and was earning NPR 35,000 a month. A similar process was evident with regard to several women from larger Brahmin and Chettri landholders in Jhorahat whose husbands had government jobs in the town, who were also adapting through greater use of outside labour. By contrast, small landholders and tenants do not have sufficient cash income to hire workers to compensate for male engagement in the capitalist sector, causing the labour burden to fall on women.

The rental of tractors and threshers (see Figure 7.4) offers one option for women to cope with migration-induced labour scarcity, at least for the traditionally male tasks such as land preparation or manual threshing. However, given that only a small number of richer farmers own their own machinery, tractors and threshers need to be rented-in, adding to the costs of production – as noted earlier. Threshers were commonly used alongside traditional threshing (see Figure 7.13) although the latter is in decline. It is with tractors where one notices a significant change. Table 7.5 shows, for instance, that while in 2007–2008 tractor use was prevalent amongst less than half of all households, and their use was more widespread amongst landowning farmers, it appears that it has risen substantially by 2019, with over three quarters of farmers using tractors, regardless of wealth. While both tractors and threshers save time, they represent a considerable additional agricultural expense, particularly given the high fuel costs.

Women whose husbands had migrated faced further challenges beyond workload – particularly when it comes to investments on the land to renew or develop the productive forces. For example, accessing remittance cash to mobilise on the farm or in the home can sometimes be challenging. This was raised not only in interviews in Morang in 2012 but also in a parallel study in Dhanusha (Sugden et al., 2014), whereby overseas migrants must transfer the money through the banking system. In some instances the money is collected and controlled by the in-laws, who collect money on behalf of the household. There were also barriers in accessing agricultural knowledge. A women in

Figure 7.13 Traditional method of threshing using buffalo or cattle. This is a time-consuming task, which often falls into the male domain and is increasingly being replaced with mechanical threshers.

Source: Author.

Table 7.5 Percentage of farmers using tractors in 2007–2009 and 2019

Land ownership category	Use of tractor (2007–2008)	Use of tractor (2019)
Landless	21.74	74.07
< 1 ha	41.38	93.65
1–2 ha	20.00	88.89
> 2 ha	41.67	100.00
Total	30.77	81.20

Source: Author.

Haraicha of Morang who was interviewed noted how rising temperatures meant crop diseases had increased compared to the past, mainly for rice and wheat. She recalled how her husband used to deal with crop disease control when he was here, and she had limited knowledge of the right chemicals to use.

She complained of how productivity had decreased by 20 *maunds* (800 kilograms) on her 1.5 *bighas* of land that year.

Women, but also men, have even less time to participate in agricultural trainings in the context of a rising work burden due to the diversion of male labour to work in the capitalist sector. Interviews back in 2007–2008 discussed training for the innovative SRI (System of Rice Transplantation), which can potentially increase yields with limited additional inputs due to a changed transplanting technique (Uprety, 2006). One of the prime explanations given for women's lack of participation in farmer groups and training programs was simply that they could not take time off their household and farm responsibilities to participate in programmes, many of which may take several days.

This does not only affect women but also non-migrant men from landless and small landholder households, who are juggling both work in the capitalist sector and work on the farm. One Tharu farmer who had participated in a training programme through a farmer group explained how the time constraints combined with the lack of perceived immediate results led him to quit the training after just a day:

> I went for one day and left.... This time what happened was I was planting rice when the training was going on so could not participate. When I had gone there, they taught us how to use certain fertilisers but I do not think it worked well so I just left the training. I thought it was useless.

In another interview, we asked the leader of a farmer group in Jhorahat what was constraining participation of more marginal farmers. He responded by raising the challenges for these households to manage both agricultural and capitalist sector work, particularly given the time it takes to travel to and from Biratnagar each day.

> Many people are working in factories and furniture making, so they leave for work early in the morning and come back only in the evening, that is why many people don't get information about the training programmes. Many people from this VDC are working in Biratnagar, in factories, in furniture making, etc.

The relationship between agricultural education and 'free time' was in fact discussed in Kautsky's (1988) *The Agrarian Question*. Writing about nineteenth-century Europe, he observes that the 'overwork' smaller farms are compelled to engage in draws a greater amount of young people's labour into agricultural activities. This prevents them from developing their agricultural knowledge through formal training and education, with implications for the household's future. While Kautsky was referring most likely to formal education, even local-level agricultural training opportunities were, in the context of rural Morang, out of reach to the most marginal farming households, whose members are extending the working day simultaneously on the farm and in the capitalist sector.

Agrarian Stress and Articulation of Modes of Production

The last few decades have seen rising urban prosperity and a burgeoning middle class in cities such as Biratnagar, yet in the countryside, feudal landlordism remains entrenched. Nevertheless, it is clear from this chapter that the mode of production is not static, but is subject to considerable flux in the context of agro-ecological and economic change. The agricultural resource base is itself experiencing the stresses associated with a global climate emergency and increasingly unpredictable precipitation patterns. The risk of failed harvests further undermines the capacity of marginal farmers to meet their minimum subsistence needs on the land, particularly when already shouldered with the rent burden. They are thus obliged to invest in costly tube well irrigation, leave land fallow during the dry months, or risk a considerable loss. However, as well as the costs of irrigation, farmers are facing further financial pressures as Nepal's integration with the global capitalist market intensifies. The cost of agricultural inputs has risen along with spiralling prices of food. While the cost of farm labour has risen in sync with rising living costs, this has placed further burden on those households who depend on hiring workers for key tasks such as ploughing.

This chapter has shown that the economic pressures associated with neoliberal globalisation are associated not only with rising costs of production and food but also the rising expenditure associated with privatised healthcare and education. Capitalist expansion also has a cultural component, with the ideologies of urban middle-class consumerism rapidly infiltrating Morang's rural hinterland. The latter in particular is shaping the consumption patterns of the better-off farmers, amongst whom there is not only a rising demand for imported luxuries but also spiralling costs associated with weddings and religious and lifecycle events – which have particularly affected remnants of the Tharu landed class. The latter are also retreating from many forms of commercial production, such as jute, due to the same market and climatic pressures facing their poorer counterparts.

The overall outcome of these changes is a spiralling demand for cash. This has had two consequences. First, households are increasingly facing a rise in indebtedness, but not only to the *katawala*s, which represent archetypical merchant capital under feudalism, but also to microfinance and other banks which have mushroomed over the last 20 years in the wake of economic liberalisation.

Second, households are more than ever before dependent upon off-farm labour for their subsistence, alongside agriculture. The last decade in particular has entrenched the articulation between the pre-capitalist and capitalist modes of production both through work in the construction or manufacturing sector locally and via migration to the Gulf states and Malaysia. It is the capitalist sector which provides households their cash needs, while the agrarian economy, even under a feudal mode of production, meets households' food needs. Even the richer farmers are increasingly becoming dependent on salaried employment to meet rising cash needs rather than via investment on the land and commercial crop sales. This articulation drives further stresses and, in particular, overwork, both on and off the farm, which disproportionately harm women from small landholder and tenant households – the latter experience a loss not only of leisure time but also of time to devote to learning and engagement in agricultural training and other activities.

Notes

1. While electric pumps are generally considerably lower cost to run, they lack the flexibility of diesel pumps, which can be moved anywhere via bullock cart or tractor, and depend on fixed electrification infrastructure which is costly to install and unfeasible for tenants.
2. An International Food Policy Research Institute (IFPRI) study also found that fertiliser prices rose to historic highs globally in 2022 due to restrictions on imports from Russia and Belarus, which are major world suppliers. While they declined in 2023, domestic price inflation meant prices remained very high in many low-income countries (Hebebrand and Glauber, 2023).
3. See article in the *Kathmandu Post* (2023) which records how the government hiked the official fertiliser prices to reduce the subsidy bill.
4. Imports of fertilisers from India were restricted due to the pandemic (*Nepali Times*, 2020).
5. See, for instance, report on the fertiliser crisis (*Nepali Times*, 2020).
6. At the time when the fieldwork began in 2007, there was not even a reliable mobile network in the core study site village.

7. Although even amongst societies still practising bride price, monetisation and rising costs are still significant. Singh (2023) notes with reference to the Bhil of Madhya Pradesh how monetisation of ritual events (particularly bride price) is part of the long process through which Adivasi social formations are subordinated to capitalism, particularly via wage labour.
8. Dowry is also argued to be important in societies where females have fewer agricultural work responsibilities and therefore are not valued on an economic level for their labour participation (Anderson, 2007). Although in the study villages as a whole, women bear responsibility for the greatest proportion of labour, the greater wealth of many Tharu in the past would have meant that women had far fewer labouring commitments and were therefore valued less for their economic contribution, offering some possible insights into the development of dowry.
9. Marital alliances were often between former members of the Rana-era landed Tharu nobility from across the Morang–Sunsari region.
10. By Marwari, they are referring to the ethnicity of many of the *katawalas* and other merchants.
11. Ashad (mid-June to mid-July) and Jestha (mid-May to mid-June) are the Nepali calendar months in which the rice is planted. Kartik (October–November) is the month in which the rice harvest begins.
12. While children may also consume more value relative to what they produce, this will often be equalised over the lifecycle of family members as the younger generation will 'repay' their parents through contributing to family income later in their lives and supporting them in old age. However, the proportion of value consumed by female family members relative to what is produced often remains unequal throughout a lifecycle (Folbre, 1982).

References

Action Aid. 2008. *Impact of Agro-Import Surges in Developing Countries*. Action Aid International.

Althusser, L. 1969. *For Marx*. London: Verso.

Anderson, S. 2007. The economics of dowry and brideprice. *Journal of Economic Perspectives* 21: 151–174.

APROSC. 1995. *Agriculture Perspective Plan*. Agricultural Projects Services Centre.

Arndt, C., Diao, X., Dorosh, P., Pauw, K. and Thurlow, J. 2023. The Ukraine war and rising commodity prices: Implications for developing countries. *Global Food Security* 36: 100680. https://www.sciencedirect.com/science/article/pii/S221191242300010X.

Aryal, M. and Bhandari, N. 2017. Benefit cost analysis of paddy in different ecological zones of Nepal. In *Rice Science and Technology in Nepal: A Historical,*

Socio-cultural and Technical Compendium, edited by Paudel, M. N., Bhandari, D. R., Khanal, M. P., Joshi, B. K., Acharya, P. and Ghimire, K. H. Ministry of Agricultural Development and Agronomy Society of Nepal.

Aryal, M. and Sapkota, B. 2017. Market price of paddy in Nepal: A time series analysis, 1966–2017. In *Rice Science and Technology in Nepal: A Historical, Socio-cultural and Technical Compendium*, edited by Paudel, M. N., Bhandari, D. R., Khanal, M. P., Joshi, B. K., Acharya, P. and Ghimire, K. H.. Ministry of Agricultural Development and Agronomy Society of Nepal.

Bartlett, R., Bharati, L., Pant, D., Hosterman, H. and Mccornick, P. G. 2010. *Climate Change Impacts and Adaptation in Nepal*. IWMI.

Benholtd-Thomson, V. 1982. Subsistence production and extended reproduction: A contribution to the discussions of modes of production. *Journal of Peasant Studies* 9 (4): 241–254.

Blaikie, P., Cameron, J. and Seddon, D. 2001. *Nepal in Crisis: Growth and Stagnation at the Periphery*, revised and enlarged edition. Adroit Publishers.

Central Bureau of Statistics. 2017. *Nepal Statistical Yearbook 2017*. Government of Nepal.

———. 2011. *Nepal Population Census 2011*. Government of Nepal.

Dahal, D. R. 1981. The concept of economy in a peasant society: A case study of the Athpahariya Rais in east Nepal. *Contributions to Nepalese Studies* 8: 55–71.

Dhakal, S., Sedhain, G. K. and Dhakal, S. C. 2016. Climate change impact and adaptation practices in agriculture: A case study of Rautahat District, Nepal. *Climate* 4 (63).

Folbre, N. 1982. Exploitation comes home: A critique of the Marxian theory of family labour. *Cambridge Journal of Economics* 6 (4): 317–329.

Gibson-Graham, J. K. 1996. *The End of Capitalism (as We Knew It)*. Blackwell.

Green, W. N. and Estes, J. 2019. Precarious debt: Microfinance subjects and intergenerational dependency in Cambodia. *Antipode* 51 (1): 129–147.

Gupta, S., Kharel, A. and Sugden, F. 2022. *Migration and Agricultural Change in Nepal – AGRUMIG Final Report*. CESLAM and University of Birmingham.

Harriss-White, B. and Gooptu, N. 2009. Mapping India's world of unorganized labour. *Socialist Register* 37: 89–118.

Hebebrand, C. and Glauber, J. 2023. *The Russia-Ukraine War after a Year: Impacts on Fertilizer Production, Prices, and Trade Flows*. International Food Policy Research Institute (IFPRI). https://www.ifpri.org/blog/russia-ukraine-war-after-year-impacts-fertilizer-production-prices-and-trade-flows#:~:text=Russia's%202022%20invasion%20of%20Ukraine,%2D%20and%20mid%2Dincome%20countries.

Hussain, A. and Sinha, R. 2019. *The Political Economy of Rice Trade Between Bangladesh, India and Nepal*. The Asia Foundation.

Jain, B. K. 2020. Microfinance services and women empowerment in Biratnagar metropolitan, Nepal. *Journal of Underrepresented and Minority Progress* 4 (2): 251–270.

Kamat, S. 2004. The privatisation of public interest: Theorizing NGO discourse in a neo-liberal era. *Review of International Political Economy* 11 (1): 156–176.

Karn, S., Sugden, F. , Clement, F., Sah, K., Maharjan, J. and Sah, T. N. 2020. *Shifting Gender Relations in Agriculture and Irrigation in the Nepal Tarai-Madhesh*. CGIAR programme for Water, Land and Ecosystems, Research for Development (R4D) Learning Series 10, Colombo.

Kautsky, K. 1988. *The Agrarian Question*. Zwan Publications.

Krauskopff, G. 2003. An 'indigenous minority' in a border area: Tharu ethnic associations, NGOs, and the Nepalese state. In *Resistance and the State: Nepalese Experiences,* edited by David N. Gellner. Berghahn Books.

Krishi Samagri Company. 2022. *Retail Price of Fertilizers 2073/74*. Krishi Samagri Company.

Liechty, M. 2003. *Suitably Modern: Making Middle-class Culture in a New Consumer Society*. Princeton University Press.

Macfarlane, A. 1976. *Resources and Population: A Study of the Gurungs of Nepal*. Cambridge University Press.

Mayer, M. and Rankin, K. N. 2002. Social capital and (community) development: A North–South perspective. *Antipode* 34 (4): 804–808.

Mcdougal, C. 1973. Structure and division in Kulunge Rai society. *Kailash* 1: 205–224.

Ministry of Agricultural Development. 2014. *Agricultural Development Strategy*. Government of Nepal.

Nepal Rastra Bank. 2008. Monthly inflation data. https://www.nrb.org.np/.

Nepali Times. 2020. Corruption and Nepal's chronic fertiliser crisis. 24 September.

Pant, B. 2011. *Soaring Food Prices in Nepal: Causes and Consequences*. Institute for Integrated Development Studies.

Paudel, S., Kafle, A. and Amgai, S. 2017. Rice marketing in Nepal. In *Rice Science and Technology in Nepal: A Historical, Socio-cultural and Technical Compendium*, edited by Paudel, M. N., Bhandari, D. R., Khanal, M. P., Joshi, B. K., Acharya, P. and Ghimire, K. H. Ministry of Agricultural Development and Agronomy Society of Nepal.

Practical Action. 2009. Temporal and spatial variability of climate change over Nepal. Practical Action Nepal Office.

Pudasainee, A., Chaulagai, T., Ghimire, Y. and Chaulagain, B. 2018. Drivers of transition from export to import of rice in Nepal. *Nepalese Journal of Agricultural Sciences 2018* 17: 208.

Randeria, S. and Visaria, L. 1984. Sociology of bride-price and dowry. *Economic and Political Weekly* 19 (15): 648–652.

Rankin, K. and Shakya, Y. B. 2008. Politics of subversion in development practice: Microfinance in Nepal and Vietnam. *Journal of development Studies* 44 (8): 1214–1235

Rankin, K. N. 2001. Governing development: Neoliberalism, microcredit and rational economic women. *Economy and Society* 30 (1): 18–37.

———. 2004. *The Cultural Politics of Markets*. Pluto Press.
Rankin, K. N. and Shakya, Y. B. 2007. Neoliberalizing the grassroots? Microfinance and the politics of development in Nepal. In *Neoliberalization: Networks, States and Peoples*, edited by England, K. and Ward, K. Oxford: Blackwell.
Raut, N. and Sitaula, B. K. 2012. Assessment of fertilizer policy, farmers' perceptions and implications for future agricultural development in Nepal. *Sustainable Agriculture Research* 1 (2).
Sharma, K. P. 2009. Climate change trends and impacts on livelihood of people. Jalrsort Vikas Santha (Nepal Water Partnership), Kathmandu.
Sharma, S. and Babu, S. 2002. Food security in Nepal. In *Economic Reforms and Food Security – The Role of Trade and Technology*, edited by ICRIER-ICAR-IFPRI, S. A. I.
Shrestha, D., Sharma, S., Hamal, K., Jadoon, U. K. and Dawadi, B. 2021. Spatial distribution of extreme precipitation events and its trend in Nepal. *Environmental Sciences* 9(1): 58–66.
Subedi, G., Shrestha M. G. and Suvedi, M. 2014. Dimensions and implications of privatisation of education in Nepal: The case of primary and secondary schools. In *Education, Privatisation and Social Justice: Case Studies from Africa, South Asia and South East Asia*. Symposium Books.
Sugden, F. 2017. A mode of production flux: the transformation and reproduction of rural class relations in lowland Nepal and North Bihar. *Dialectical Anthropology* 41 (2): 129–161.
———. 2019. *Labour Migration, Capitalist Accumulation and Feudal Reproduction: A Historical Analysis from The Eastern Gangetic Plains*. Antipode.
Sugden, F., Maskey, N., Clement, F., Ramesh, V., Philip, A. and Rai, A. 2014. Agrarian stress and climate change in the Eastern Gangetic Plains: Gendered vulnerability in a stratified social formation. *Global Environmental Change* 29: 258–269.
Sugden, F., Seddon, D. and Raut, M. 2018. Mapping historical and contemporary agrarian transformations and capitalist infiltration in a complex upland environment: A case from Eastern Nepal. *Journal of Agrarian Change* 18 (2): 444–472.
Taylor, M. 2012. The antinomies of 'financial inclusion': Debt, distress and the workings of Indian microfinance. *Journal of Agrarian Change* 12 (4): 601–610.
The Kathmandu Post. 2023. Nepal hikes chemical fertiliser prices to curb subsidies. 13 March. https://kathmandupost.com/money/2023/03/13/nepal-hikes-chemical-fertiliser-prices-to-curb-subsidies.
Uprety, R. 2006. SRI takes root in Nepal. *Leisa Magazine* 22 (4): 25–27.

8

Revisiting Agrarian Transition in Morang

There is a widespread academic acknowledgement, much of which was covered in Chapter 2, that the classical 'semi-feudalism' which was the focus of Indian debates in the 1970s and 1980s is of limited relevance in the twenty-first century due to market expansion, labour migration and the subdivision of landlord estates (see Lerche, 2013). Even Nepali leftist commentators have suggested that the declining power of landlords and monetisation of wages mean that agrarian relations are now 'capitalist' rather than 'feudal' with the exception of a few pockets (see, for example, Sharma, 2019). However, a critical finding of this book is that landlordism has remained remarkably resilient through decades of change, which have included land reforms, the expansion of industry and a state-led modernisation agenda. While the old Tharu landlords' economic power may have declined in the ways documented in some other parts of South Asia, the absentee landed elite retain considerable control over its holdings, and rent and usury continue to act as the so-called depressor (Harriss, 2013) – constraining the development of the productive forces and pushing households into extreme food insecurity.

Nevertheless, intensifying articulations with the capitalist sector in the wake of economic liberalisation, and rising dependence upon wage labour, on a theoretical level could undermine dependency on tenancy or merchant capital amongst the landless and small landholders. Expanding capitalist markets could also simultaneously open up new avenues for capital investment amongst the urban and rural elite, reducing the incentive for landlords to hold on to their estates.

This chapter explores some preconditions for the peasantry which could bring forth the dissolution of the feudal economy. The first perquisite would be them gaining access to the land market; the second would entail a downward pressure on rents; while the third relates to the feasibility for 'exit' from agriculture in the context of new capitalist labour opportunities. Having established that neither of these preconditions has been met on the ground in rural southern Morang, the chapter goes on to explore what this means at the scale of the wider social formation – raising deeper questions around the relative stability through which the pre-capitalist co-exists with capitalism in an era of neoliberal globalisation. Of interest are the class relations at play, including the sharing of surplus between modes of production, and the degree to which these materialise as concrete class alliances. This raises fundamental political questions at a time of great political flux.

The Land Market and Dependence on Tenancy

A first process which could undermine feudal relations of production would be the acquisition of land by tenants – particularly through the land market, but also via inheritance. The injection of cash from migration and wage labour in particular could facilitate access to the land market, as shown elsewhere in the far-eastern plains (Gartaula et al., 2012; Sunam, 2015).[1] The diversification of landlords' incomes in a liberalised economy may also increase incentives for them to sell off their estates, as shown in Dhanusha to the west (Sugden, 2017). Through increasing one's access to land, marginal farmers can more easily meet their subsistence needs, or even retain a sizeable surplus, reduce their dependency on tenancies in the long run and accumulate.

A review of the panel data suggests the scope for this is limited. A first observation is that there has been a drop in the size of farms over the last 12 years, with an overall decline in the cultivated area by sampled farmers – of both rented *and* owned land. Table 8.1 suggests that the area cultivated drops from 166.9 hectares in 2007 to 130.05 hectares in 2019. The amount of land owned by farmers in the sample has declined by around 10 hectares from 73.86 hectares to 63.49 hectares (see Table 8.2). The average size of owner-cultivated holdings in 2019 was 0.48 hectare, down substantially from 0.71 hectare in the 2007–2008 survey (see Table 8.3). This suggests that far from increasing their economic security via land investments, ownership of the means of production is further dwindling. Part of this is down to land being sold off, and Figure 8.1 shows that the sampled farmers have sold a total of 7.96 hectares via 13 transactions. Interviews suggested that most were 'distress sales', usually linked to debt or to pay for a marriage or other expenses, as discussed earlier.

Table 8.1 Area of land rented or owned by year and locality (ha)

VDC	Jhorahat		Bhaudaha		Thalaha		Total	
Year	2007	2019	2007	2019	2007	2019	2007	2019
Owned land (ha)	45.64	31.77	17.79	22.26	10.44	9.46	73.86	63.49
Rented in land (ha)	32.75	16.29	39.16	35.78	37.32	27.13	101.15	79.20
Owner cultivated land (ha)	39.65	24.56	17.13	17.84	9.11	8.44	65.89	50.85
Owned and rented out land (ha)	6.06	7.21	0.67	4.42	1.34	1.02	8.07	12.65
Total land rented (ha)	38.8	23.49	39.8	40.20	38.7	28.15	109.2	91.85
Total land cultivated	72.3	40.84	56.3	53.63	46.4	35.58	166.9	130.05
Total land	84.5	48.1	57.6	58.0	49.1	36.6	183.1	142.7
% land under tenancy	45.96	48.89	69.13	69.26	78.74	76.93	59.66	64.37

Source: Author.

Table 8.2 Concentration of land

Land ownership category	% of sample		ha land owned		% land owned	
	2007	**2019**	**2007**	**2019**	**2007**	**2019**
Landless*	41.42	38.46	0.60	0.52	0.82	0.82
< 0.5 ha	26.04	42.66	13.81	15.89	18.70	24.95
0.5–1 ha	2.37	6.99	2.90	6.85	3.92	10.75
1–2 ha	7.10	6.29	15.78	12.90	21.36	20.25
> 2 ha	7.69	5.59	40.77	27.54	55.20	43.23
Total	100.00	100.00	73.86	63.70	100.00	100.00

Source: Author.

Note: *Some households own small plots for the homestead and possibly a small kitchen garden but are functionally landless, with no land for cultivation. The landless are thus classified as those owning less than 0.05 hectare.

Table 8.3 Average plot size

Mean	**land owned**		**land rented in**		**landowner cultivated**	
Land ownership category	**2007–2008**	**2019**	**2007–2008**	**2019**	**2007–2008**	**2019**
Landless	0.01	0.03	1.31	1.14	0.03	0.05
< 0.5 ha	0.31	0.26	1.66	1.43	0.31	0.26
0.5–1 ha	0.72	0.69	1.34	0.68	0.73	0.69
1–2 ha	1.31	1.43	0.84	1.01	1.31	1.28
> 2 ha	3.14	3.44	1.55	NA	2.73	2.64
Total	0.52	0.44	1.45	1.25	0.71	0.48

Source: Author.

However, distress sales cannot alone explain the dwindling holdings, as a greater amount (10.56 hectares) has actually been bought over the same period through 34, mostly small transactions, which will be discussed later. What is also causing a decline in the cultivated and owned land area is the division of land within the family, particularly amongst sons. These new family units were not included in the follow up sample – and thus the data shows that the total area of owned land has declined. The subdivision of farmland into smaller parcels is a challenge facing the peasantry across South Asia, whereby there are population rises alongside limited 'exit' opportunities from agriculture (Niroula and Thapa, 2005). Figure 8.1 shows that 15.23 hectares of land has been lost as families split.[2] While one son usually remains with parents, it is common for other sons to separate in their adult years, receiving a separate share of the family land in the process. Of course, these sons (and occasionally daughters) also inherit new land following the passing away of an elder. While 3.84 hectares of land has been inherited, this is far smaller than what has been lost when families split. With rising population and insufficient employment to draw farmers out of agriculture, one is observing a decline in the area of land owned with increasingly smaller holdings – and it is thus unsurprising that even amongst those with land, tenancy continues to fill the gap. For example, the households who were categorised as small owner-cultivators, with less than 0.5 hectare as of 2007–2008, account for 21 per cent of land sale transactions and 28 per cent of the land lost due to family splitting by the time of the 2019 survey (see Table 8.5). The average proportion of these smallest owners' farms which are under tenancy also appears to have increased, from 37.81 per cent

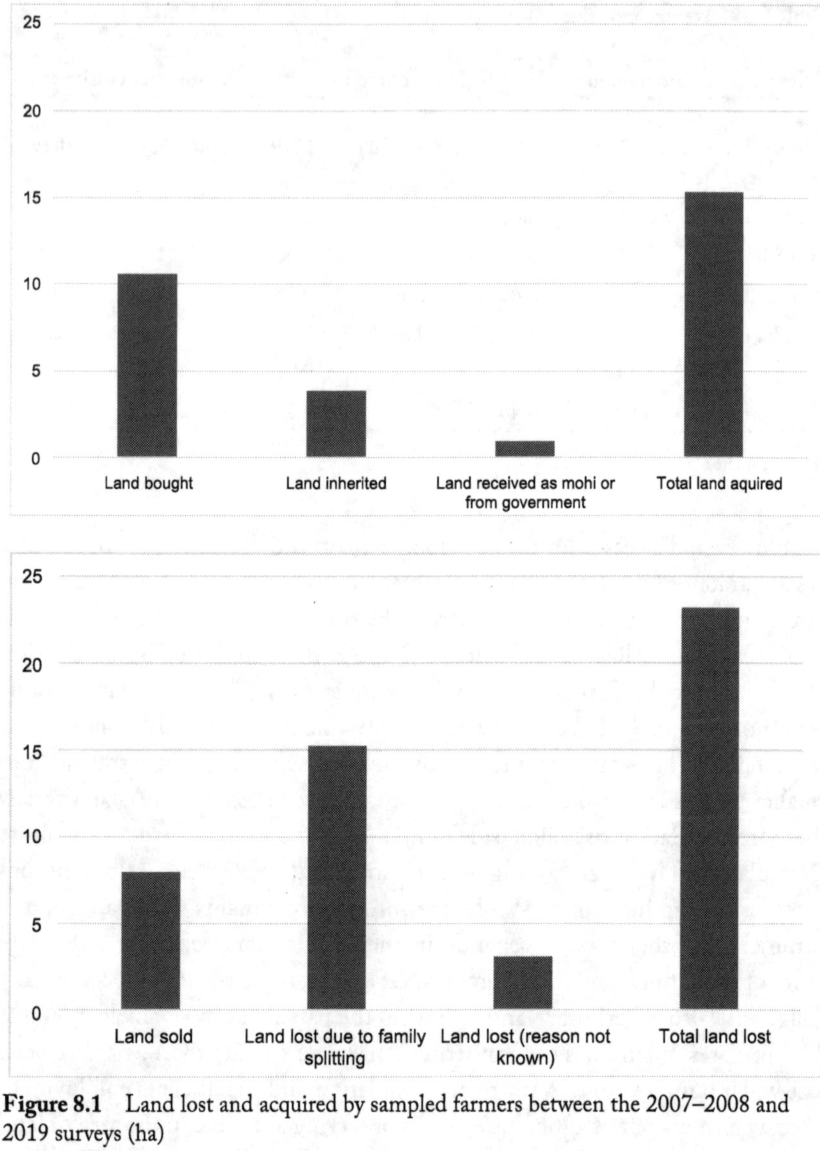

Figure 8.1 Land lost and acquired by sampled farmers between the 2007–2008 and 2019 surveys (ha)

Source: Author.

to 44.42 per cent. This suggests they are becoming more (not less) dependent upon landlords for access to the means of production (see Table 4.8).

An additional challenge associated with the dwindling size of holdings due to subdivision is the growing fragmentation of farms. Larger plots are being split, and later purchases (or acquisition by inheritance) of land are often in a different location – making irrigation and land preparation more challenging. In the Land Use Regulations of 2022 which sought to classify land into different categories and develop land use rules, Paragraph 4 prohibits the subdivision of holdings classified as agricultural to an area of below 0.0675 hectare (Government of Nepal, 2022). However, this limit is extremely small and will not reverse the existing fragmentation of holdings. It is also uncertain how successful the implementation will be given the considerable resources required for its implementation.[3]

There is also a similar drop in the size of rented plots. The area of land rented-in by farmers has dropped from 101.15 hectares in 2007–2008 to 79.20 hectares in 2019 (see Table 8.1). However, this does not appear to be driven by more farmers owning land (Table 8.2). There has been only a very small drop in the percentage of farmers engaged in tenancy from 46 per cent to 44.14 per cent (see Table 4.8) and the overall proportion of land under tenancy has actually increased during this same period, from 59.9 per cent in 2007 to 64.37 per cent in 2019, as can be seen in Table 8.1. This echoes a Tarai-wide trend, with the 2022–2023 national living standards survey suggesting that the area under the tenancy in the Tarai sample had risen from 19.93 per cent in 1995–1996 to 26.8 per cent in 2022–2023 (National Statistics Office, 2024).

Importantly, the average size of rented-in plots has also dropped from 1.45 hectares to 1.25 hectares (see Table 8.3). What this suggests is that, as with owned land, rented plots are also getting smaller as families split. Other reasons may include growing demand for tenancy to compensate for dwindling owned holdings or land being repurposed by landlords for residential 'plotting' and taken out of cultivation. At present, the creation of residential plots for sale is localised to a few roadside locations between Biratnagar and Jhorahat. The 2022 Land Use Regulations (Government of Nepal, 2022) included a clause that restricted the conversion of agricultural land for residential plotting without approval from the local land use commission. However, under pressure from the real estate sector, there were already amendments to the regulations in 2023[4] – and thus this is likely to be a persisting issue in the years to come.

The second observation is that there has been negligible change in the area of land owned by absentee landlords – and thus their position at the apex of the agrarian structure remains unchanged. The proportion of rented-in land which belonged to absentee, urban-based landlords was 78.85 per cent in 2007–2008 and had dropped only marginally to 77.58 per cent in 2019. There were a few sales of land to local farmers by this class, but they represented only 8.91 per cent of the total land area bought by sampled farmers since 2007–2008 (just 1.01 hectares in total) and thus by no means suggests that landless and small landholder farmers can 'buy' their way out of tenancy (see Table 8.4).

Table 8.4 Status of land transactions between the 2007–2008 and 2019 surveys

Buyer or seller category	Land bought from different landowner (ha)	% land bought from different landowner	Land sold to different landowner (ha)	% land sold to different landowners
Local	9.70	86.02	5.23	72.22
City person	1.01	8.91	2.01	27.78
Buyer not known	0.57	5.05	0.00	0.00
Total	11.27	100	7.24	100.00

Source: Author.

Absentee landlords had actually bought more land from sampled farmers than the other way around, and new purchases of land by city dwellers represented 29 per cent of the land area 'sold' by farmers in this 12-year period, although the amounts are small. Data from Dhanusha district west of the Koshi suggests that landlords, most of whom were local Maithili-speaking upper castes, have been selling off their estates, a trend largely driven by political unrest during the People's War, fear of land reform, as well as the younger generation aspiring to relocate to the cities (Sugden, 2017; Rinck, 2025). However, there is limited evidence of this happening in rural Morang, possibly due to the considerably higher value of land in Morang and the landlords' political power, which has allowed them to bypass land reforms in the past.

Interestingly, the Morang land revenue office suggested that they had been dealing with a large number of transactions by absentee landlords in the Thalaha area as of late 2008. However, the lack of any evidence of significant change via the longitudinal data suggests that these may have been in villages outside the sampled wards, or within different sections of the absentee landlord class. These could have included, for example, the old landlord class selling off portions of their estate to smaller absentee landowners, such as successful migrants who have returned from overseas and settled in the city. These transactions are described by one farmer in Thalaha:

> If people had sold 10 Kata in highway side, they can buy 3 Bigha in this area [in Thalaha]. Some people from the hilly area and some people who returned from abroad bought the land. To buy land, either they have to go abroad or they should have good employment. However, local farmers are facing many troubles. They have to pay back their loans for fertilizers. That's why they really cannot buy land.

What this points to is a continuation of the diversification of the landlord class described by Regmi (1976) during the Panchayat era, whereby the old 'ascriptive' landed elite from the Rana era are being joined by the 'non-ascriptive' landlords who were purchasing land through the market. Speculative investments by successful migrants were also mentioned in the quote, a phenomenon Sunam (2020) identifies in neighbouring Sunsari district, and Rinck (2024) highlights with regard to Dhanusha, further west. It is, however, difficult to gauge how widespread these changes are, and either way, the relations of production and associated surplus appropriation on the ground remain unchanged.

A third observation is that while there has been a decline in 'landlessness' from 48.95 per cent in 2007–2008 to 38.46 per cent in 2019 (see Table 4.1), this is not taking place on levels which undermine the importance of tenancy to livelihoods. Those who were landless in 2007–2008 and had now bought land had on average purchased just 0.27 hectares. While access to a small plot provides households with the security of some fixed assets, these amounts do not result in a transformation in one's ability to meet their subsistence needs. Most in the smallest landholder category with less than 0.5 hectare still depend heavily on tenancy or off-farm labour to subsist. In fact, even out of those who were landless in 2007–2008, some respondents had bought land, only for a portion to be sold again later – with these households moving from the landless group to the small land-owning group and then back to the landless group within a 12-year period. The national trend in fact points to a rise in landlessness, and the national living standards survey suggests that across the Tarai, the share of agricultural households without land has risen from 24.41 per cent in 1995–1996 to 39.9 per cent in 2022–2023 (National Statistics Office, 2024).

Given that absentee landlords retain their control over their estates, localised changes in rates of landlessness are linked to land transactions *within* the peasantry. The data suggests that almost all purchases of land by farmers were from other local farmers. This may be amongst farmers who have left the area and sold their plots. Indeed, four of the households from the original 2007–2008 sample had left at the time of the 2019 restudy. However, it appears likely that some land was bought from other local farmers in financial distress – and may have been associated with small farmers using saved remittance cash to buy up the land of neighbours who were of a similar economic status (see Table 8.5). Distress sales due to debt or to meet urgent cash needs have taken place across land ownership groups – with sales taking place both to landless farmers and to medium-to-large farmers.

Table 8.5 Percentage of land sold and bought by different land ownership groups between the 2007–2008 and 2019 surveys

Land ownership category (at time of 2007–2008 survey)	% land bought	% land sold	% land purchase transactions	% land sale transactions
Landless	45.60	17.26	48.78	14.29
< 0.5 ha	27.60	4.63	39.02	21.43
0.5–1 ha	0.48	7.16	4.88	14.29
1–2 ha	5.08	24.63	2.44	28.57
> 2 ha	21.25	46.32	4.88	21.43

Source: Author.

In sum, there is no evidence of farmers being able to gain a foothold in the land market in a way which would undermine the concentration of ownership amongst landlords, and, if anything, the need to rent in land has been amplified when one considers the subdivision of plots amongst sons, and even of rented plots, suggesting that competition for tenancies remains high. This may explain why the proportion of farmers engaged in agricultural labour, work which was previously considered the most undesirable, has increased, both for landless groups and those with less than 0.5 hectares of land (see Table 4.3). For the former, the number of households engaged in labour on others' farms has risen substantially from 47.83 per cent to 65.45 per cent between 2007–2008 and 2019.

While it is clear that land-poor farmers are highly unlikely to access the land market and absentee landlords retain control over their estates, could the medium-to-large landowners potentially accumulate and in the future challenge the local control over the means of production by absentee landlords? For this to happen there would need to be clear evidence of accumulation and differentiation within the farming population.

There are some instances of richer farmers with more than 2 hectares buying up land from poorer cultivators in a classic form of differentiation, and this pattern represented 21.25 per cent of purchases (see Table 8.5). The average farm size for households with more than 2 hectares has also increased marginally between 2007–2008 and 2019 from 2.14 hectares to 3.44 hectares (see Table 8.3). For example, one richer and more commercially oriented farmer had reportedly bought up land from two other households who were in debt to them. However, these tendencies appear restricted to just a few households. The medium and large landholder group with 1–2 hectares and more than 2 hectares had also lost land like their smaller landholder counterparts, particularly amongst the Tharu community. Table 8.5 suggests that a half of land 'sales' were actually amongst medium and large landowners themselves. 'Large' landholders have only purchased 2.24 hectares of land in the period between the two surveys, yet have actually sold 3.69 hectares due to distress, and have lost a further 4.12 hectares due to families splitting, with no land being inherited in the same period. Out of those medium farmers with 1–2 hectares of land, while the proportion of land owned remains much the same, more land has been sold than bought. Only 1.1 hectares have been inherited, while 4.27 hectares have been lost with families splitting. As a result, the proportion of large farmers in the panel data has actually declined in size from 7.69 per cent of the sample to 5.59 per cent of the sample between the 2007–2008 and 2019 surveys, and even the share of middle farmers with 1–2 hectares has declined in size by a few percentage points (see Table 4.1).

It is important to recall that, as noted earlier, middle and large farmers are themselves experiencing the same challenges of agrarian stress outlined earlier, such as climate fluctuations, spiralling costs of inputs and rising cultural expenditure and consumerism, and this is likely influencing any potential shift towards profit-oriented production and accumulation. While for marginal and tenant farmers, this stress translates into food insecurity and an inability to meet the needs of simple reproduction, for middle-to-large farmers this means low levels of profitability and a reduced ability for any 'expanded reproduction' with the expansion of one's assets and accumulation. It is in this context that some prefer to rent out their land to others.

There are of course a small number of better-off farmers who are able to remain profitable and who are actively investing in the land. However, given that there is limited evidence of absentee landlords being willing to sell off their estates, this sets a ceiling beyond which the larger farmers cannot expand their holdings any further. At most they may emerge in the future as a profitable class of commercially oriented peasants displaying some capitalist tendencies, which would operate in parallel to the existing farms cultivating under feudal conditions, yet these farmers would by no means 'replace' absentee landlords at the apex of the agrarian structure.

The overall message is that there has been relatively limited change in the distribution of land, aside from some low-level buying and selling within the local farming population. Absentee landlords appear to retain considerable control over the means of production in rural southern Morang – and thus far are not displaying any tendency to be selling off their land – and with rising land prices (and the growing speculative investment of land for real estate, particularly close to the road), this appears equally unlikely in the years ahead. There is therefore a very limited likelihood that landlordism could be undermined through local farmers, either large or small, gaining a foothold in the land market.

A Reduction in Rent? 'Profitable' Tenancy or Class Struggle

A second process which could undermine feudal relations of production is a drop in the value or level of rent. This would allow farmers to yield a profit while still paying rent and could even allow households to purchase land from urban landlords, facilitating accumulation within the peasantry. As noted in Chapter 2 when discussing Marx's differentiation between ground rent under feudalism and capitalism, it was noted that the emergence of farmers that are able to obtain a profit beyond what is taken as rent can undermine feudal landlordism. These farmers can go on to hire labourers, invest in the land and accumulate, and can shift the system towards profitable commodity production and eventual capitalist development. There are a number of circumstances that can facilitate such a process. For example, producers yielding a differential rent as a result of a natural endowment or rising commodity prices may begin making a profit and encourage other farmers to compete (Marx, 1967, 801–802). The differentiation of tenants could eventually occur, whereby profit-oriented tenants replace their more marginal counterparts, releasing a labour force and intensifying the process of capitalisation. However, Marx's analysis assumes that landlords are compelled to maintain rents at levels which are *profitable* to emerging capitalist farmers if they are to find tenants. Eventually rent, where it persists, would move from constituting the normal form of surplus appropriation to representing simply an 'excess' of the surplus product over that which is retained by the farmer as a profit, which is equivalent to the economy-wide average (Marx, 1967, 800). Only after these circumstances are met could the transition from pre-capitalist to capitalist ground rent be said to be complete.

In the context of southern Morang, one would assume that a sizeable section of tenants would have to develop into profit-oriented peasants by retaining a reasonable surplus in order to 'compel' landlords to lower rents.[5]

At present, however, it is clear that for many households, the current relations of production, including surplus appropriation through rent, debt and distress sales, act as an *absolute* barrier to even meeting the needs of simple reproduction, let alone producing a profitable surplus. While investments to develop the forces of production (particularly through irrigation) could potentially support the production of a surplus amongst landless and small landholder farmers, this is also highly unlikely given the indebtedness and financial barriers to investment (worsened by the rent burden itself), as noted in Chapter 6.

In theory, richer farmers could accumulate wealth through renting land and producing commercially. Patnaik (1983), in an example from Gujarat, noted how a class of improving farmers were able to break down landlord–tenant relations in a context where profit-oriented surplus-producing tenant farming emerged. This was because technical changes allowed some farmers the ability to increase yields, so only a portion of the product of surplus labour was appropriated as rent, leaving a profit for the farmer. However, in Morang, only the 'large farmer' households consistently produce a surplus, and only a small proportion rent-in land. Given that even richer farmers are experiencing agrarian stress, any downward pressure they place on rents will be negligible, particularly when this group is so small. The majority of households taking on tenancies are landless and marginal landowners and are competing for tenancies, no matter how insecure and exploitative those are.

One outstanding question is whether localised class struggle or collective mobilisation amongst tenants could have obliged landlords to lower rents. Research from the eastern hills north of Morang suggested that during the People's War, the local cadre of the Communist Party of Nepal (Maoist), or CPN (M), were successful in lowering rents amongst tenants to a third of the crop. While rents returned to 50 per cent after the war ended, this represented a significant challenge to landlord–tenant relations (Sugden et al., 2018). In Morang, there were few reports of rent reductions during the war, although there were reports of direct action by the Maoist cadre from the eastern parts of the district, such as land and harvest seizures from large landlords. However, land seizures were quickly reversed once the Maoists entered the political mainstream. On the whole, the level of Maoist mobilisation was more limited in southern Morang, likely in part due to the proximity to Biratnagar, which was a centre of state power during the insurgency, and on a practical level this limited their influence in the rural hinterland. There was an increase in labour activism through Maoist-affiliated unions (see Tulachan and Felver, 2019) in the factories surrounding Biratnagar, particularly after the 2006 ceasefire, but this did not appear to filter down to a village level and encourage collective mobilisation over rents. Thus, it appeared that the People's War had a limited impact in rural Morang in terms of the political assertiveness of marginalised groups, when compared to the Maoist heartlands in mid-west Nepal where there was notable political and economic transformation on the ground (Zharkevich, 2019). After the war, various left factions continued to be influential locally, including the CPN (M) after it joined parliamentary politics – although their 'radical' character dissipated in subsequent years – particularly after the short-lived merger with the mainstream Communist Party of Nepal (Unified Marxist–Leninist), or CPN (UML). In spite of occasional populist slogans relating to land, there was nothing close to the level of grassroots tenant mobilisation which characterised rural West Bengal during the 1970s land reforms.

The ethnic mobilisation which swept the Tarai-Madhesh between 2007 and 2016 garnered significant grassroots support amongst Dalit and Adivasi tenants in the field site, particularly amongst the Bantar community. While mobilisation was primarily directed against historic neglect by the state, lack of political mobilisation and limited upward mobility amongst youth from Tarai castes and ethnic groups, it failed to directly engage with issues of economic inequalities or challenge landlord power at a local level.

In the absence of any form of collective struggle amongst tenants who continue to compete for tenancies, it appears highly unlikely in the near term that 'negotiations' by tenants would allow a drop in the rate of rent – particularly so long as landlords hold on to their estates.

Semi-colonial Social Formation, Industrial Stagnation and the Persistence of Tenancy

A final process that could potentially undermine semi-feudal landlord–tenant relations would be linked to the development of capitalism in parallel to the peasant economy, which may draw tenants away from agriculture – even if landlords retain control over the land. While it is clear from the last chapter that peasant farmers increasingly depend on wages from the capitalist sector to meet their minimum cash needs, could capitalist wages or levels of employment rise to the point that farmers would no longer depend on tenancy or loans? Against such a context, larger landlords would perhaps be compelled to lower rents. They could also in theory hire more tenants as direct labourers, along with intensification of production through capital investment, so landlords and rich farmers could pay farm wages equivalent to what is available in the capitalist sector and extract 'relative' surplus value.

However, as noted thus far, there are no signs of the capitalist sector showing any ability to 'absorb' the peasantry. Patnaik (1983) suggests that in many parts of India, the perpetuation of inflated pre-capitalist ground rent is intensified by the high levels of under-employment and a large class of destitute agricultural labourers. This means farmers are willing to accept rents which even eat into their minimum subsistence needs (Patnaik, 1983; Pearce, 1983). The implication is that when there is insufficient capitalist employment to meet the subsistence needs of the peasantry, landlords need not be concerned with finding profit-orientated farmers willing to rent their land. There is a vast impoverished base to the agrarian structure willing to operate the land under any circumstances. There are thus no incentives for them to lower rents. Indeed, during India's mode of production debate, an important observation was how 'semi-feudalism' was strongly embedded within a larger semi-colonial social formation. Chandra (1974), Sau (1975) and Gupta (1977) asserted that imperialism had impeded the organic development of domestic capitalism, and thus capitalist employment has not risen above a threshold whereby landlord power is undermined. As noted in Chapter 3, Nepal has followed this same semi-colonial trajectory of development to an even greater extent than India (Blaikie et al., 2001), with industrial growth stifled by imports from India itself (and today also from China), a lack of forward and backward linkages for the sector, and dependence on foreign capital.

To better understand what this means for the peasantry in southern Morang and the role of tenancy in livelihoods, it is useful to review the range of capitalist wage labour options available. It is shown that in spite of the growing engagement in the capitalist sector via migration or local wage labour, the levels of cash they bring into the household are not sufficient to draw them away from exploitative tenant farming.

The first wage labour option is manufacturing. This is significant as in classical models of capitalist development, it is the growth of manufacturing which has the greatest potential to draw farmers from the countryside and undermine feudal relations of production – and Morang itself is a key node in Nepal's industrial development. In the study site, factory work was the most favoured source of employment, primarily because it offered a regular monthly salary. For instance, Morang Chamber of Industries (2021) data indicates that 78 per cent of workers in large industries in the Morang–Sunsari industrial belt were on a monthly salary, with the remainder on daily wages, while for medium-sized industries the figure is 62 per cent. Furthermore, 90 per cent of large and 64 per cent of medium industries are affiliated with a social security fund. Sixty-three per cent and 27 per cent of large and medium industries respectively report 'trade union formation' (Morang Chamber of Industry, 2021), although how widespread this is amongst workers in these industries is not clear. This is not to say that workers do not experience precarity – and this has been discussed at length in Hoffman's (2018) study on Tharu factory workers in the western Tarai-Madhesh. Smaller industries in Morang also (in particular, brick kilns) often have poorer working conditions and greater casualisation.

What is most important, though, is that even in spite of the study site lying in proximity to a large manufacturing belt, the sector appears to have had limited success in absorbing the surplus labour force and drawing farmers out of tenant agriculture. As noted earlier, while farmers are increasingly depending upon wage labour to subsist in the context of rampant monetisation and rising living costs, the actual proportion of households engaged in factory employment is low. As of 2007–2008, landless households as a group earned on average just NPR 7,116 from employment in manufacturing enterprises, with income representing only 18 per cent of the total annual cash earnings of this group. The poorest landholders with less than 0.5 hectares meanwhile earned on average NPR 10,125, representing 35 per cent of their total earnings (see Table 4.3). However, this share is likely to have fallen today. As noted earlier (see Table 4.4), the percentage of households with any income from factory employment has dropped from 17.24 per cent in 2007–2008 to 13.79 per cent, with the sector in decline. The struggles of local manufacturing which were discussed at length in Chapter 3 were documented during the period of research. For instance, a factory processing betel nut or *paan* was established near Pidarboni after the first phase of fieldwork in 2008. The factory itself employed a handful of local workers, but by the time of the 2019 restudy it had already closed down – with its warehouses and processing units lying vacant.

There is high competition for the few factory jobs available. The Morang–Sunsari industrial belt employs 26,963 workers according to their 2021 survey, with 77 per cent of the labourers coming from these two districts. Given that the eight municipalities which make up the core industrial belt where 85 per cent of the industries are located (Morang Chamber of Industry, 2021) are home to 800,592 people, these figures are modest. Even then, only 63 per cent of the jobs in 'large' industries in the Morang–Sunsari corridor were semi-skilled or unskilled roles, such as machine operator, with the remaining jobs being higher-level roles such as foremen, engineers or technicians which were out of reach for many workers from marginal farming households. Interviews suggested that it is difficult for workers from outside the immediate vicinity of factories to find employment (see Figure 8.2). Farmers in a focus group in Thalaha in 2022 suggested that you need a 'source' or connection to get a job there. For instance, the Morang–Sunsari industrial belt 2021 survey suggests that 77 per cent of workers are recruited word of mouth through current employees – meaning that jobs are more likely within certain villages which have established links to the factory in question, whereby workers are able to bring in neighbours and family members (Morang Chamber of Industry, 2021).

Furthermore, gender ideologies often exclude women from factory work, with options restricted primarily to the work in the brick kilns (see Figure 8.3) on the clay rich soils between Bhaudaha and Katahari. Work in the kilns is more menial, lower paid than other manufacturing work, and seasonal.

Figure 8.2 Rice processing factory near north of Biratnagar. Factories such as this offer more regular employment, although there are very few jobs relative to the large population in their vicinity.

Source: Author.

Figure 8.3 Labourers in a brick kiln near Jhorahat. This work is generally casual and seasonal in nature.

Source: Author.

Similarly, caste-based exclusion reportedly occurs, with few members of Dalit communities such as the Rishidev (Musahar) securing factory employment.

Notwithstanding the difficulties of finding work in the first place, the potential for manufacturing to 'pull' farmers out of tenant farming even for those who have successfully secured jobs is very limited. Factory work is favoured as it is regular and year-round. Alongside other perks, the wages – which were NPR 564 on average in the 2019 survey (see Table 8.6) – were notably higher than the NPR 125 reported in 2007–2008. However, this has gone alongside a significant rise in the cost of living – and only the smallest families were able to subsist from factory wages alone – and thus the capitalist industrial sector is still largely dependent upon agriculture, even under feudal conditions, to 'subsidise' wages.

The second labour option is the construction sector. As noted earlier, workers in factories were likely to be on a payroll and would receive a fixed monthly salary, offering regular income in spite of the lower daily wage. Construction work, by contrast, which today has eclipsed factory work as

Table 8.6 Average reported monthly or daily incomes by labour type (2019)

Labour type	Daily wages (Nepali rupees)	Monthly salary (Nepali rupees)
Factory	564	16,000
Casual unskilled	650	16,900
Casual semi-skilled (mostly construction)	713	17,200
Professional	NA	32,567
Labour elsewhere in Nepal (cash sent home)	NA	26,500
Labour overseas (average monthly remittances)	NA	32,032

Source: Author.

an income source (see Table 4.4), is far more likely to be wage based, un-unionised and casual, without any of the added perks – even for semi-skilled work such as that of a *mistry*, or mason. Some farmers in the 2019 survey estimated an average monthly income. The average wages reported for semi-skilled work in 2019 (NPR 713) was higher than factory work (NPR 564), yet the income was less regular given its casual nature, with only a minority of households receiving a fixed monthly salary for such work. On top of the day's labour, workers from villages such as Thalaha require a two-hour round trip by bicycle to reach Biratnagar town where most jobs are located (see Figure 8.4). As with factories, the sector does not create the levels of employment to draw farmers out of agriculture, and there are few jobs for females.

Unskilled casual jobs are even more precarious – with some, such as rickshaw pulling, being rapidly undercut by improvements in road infrastructure and the introduction of electric rickshaws. The latter emerged only over the last seven–eight years, and while six farmers in the 2019 sample were now engaged as electric rickshaw drivers, they require a large investment – which means that shifting from cycle to electric rickshaws is not an easy transition.

Aside from casual labour, a number of households also operate small businesses in the informal sector. These include buying and selling of agricultural produce in markets, small tea stalls or small shops adjoining their homes. These have been supported in part by the expansion of micro-credit. As of 2007–2008 only a small number of households ran enterprises, and they provided just 10 per cent of the total recorded non-farm income – and thus their potential to reduce households' dependence on tenancies is unlikely to be significant. By 2019 the proportion of households running these enterprises had dropped further.

Figure 8.4 People from the rural hinterland cycling into Biratnagar to trade and work

Source: Author.

This may be connected with the improvements in transport infrastructure, expanding markets and the competition with larger businesses in bazaars such as Jhorahat and the emerging market in Pidarboni. These have undercut some of the traditional village shops (see Figure 7.7), which were the main local source of foodstuffs and other essentials as of 2007–2008.

The only opportunities which could potentially draw households out of semi-feudal relations of production are 'white collar' jobs in the capitalist sector, which generally require a secondary education, such as work in offices and schools. For instance, in Jhorahat there are a few Brahmin and Chettri households who own only small plots of land or even rent out their holdings, yet gain most income from the salaried employment of family members. There has been an expansion in salaried jobs alongside the growth in the service sector in companies such as banks, travel agents, retail and hotels. Added to this is the burgeoning bureaucracy, which has grown further with the emergence of Biratnagar as the provincial capital and the expansion of new office positions.

However, the opportunities posed by an expansion of white-collar jobs has a limited impact in the rural hinterland around Biratnagar. As noted in the introduction to this book, Biratnagar itself has an unusual position within the local political economy. It has emerged in recent decades as a major economic and political hub with close links to Kathmandu,[6] while its links to the countryside is largely extractive. This takes the form of the extraction of rent by absentee landlords and the mobilisation of the vast surplus labour pool from the land-poor peasantry for the low-paid jobs associated with capitalist industry and the service sector, as well as the bureaucracy. There are few professional employment opportunities for the peasantry. Only 8.97 per cent of farmers have skilled, salaried jobs, and as one would expect these jobs are held by just 3.64 per cent of landless households, with two-thirds of larger landowner households (owning more than 2 hectares) holding such jobs – in large part due to the need for a higher-level education. This includes those who are resident in the village as well as family members who live outside for professional work and give money to the family.

However, there are also more complex constraints rooted in caste and ethnicity. Not insignificantly, half of the households reporting professional salaried income are Brahmin and Chettri, in spite of this group representing just 18 per cent of the sample. While 44 per cent of this community have family members with professional jobs, mostly with the government, for the Tharu and Bantar communities, 26 per cent and 5 per cent respectively have professional salaried jobs, and these are mostly lower-paid clerical jobs or work as teachers in local schools. Nobody from Rajbanshi, Munda or Musahar households have recorded any professional salaried work as of the 2019, survey. The more coveted employment opportunities are closely linked not only to higher levels of education but also to improved social networks, which, historically, the Nepali-speaking upper castes have benefited from. The latter have also benefitted in the employment market from speaking Nepali as their mother tongue (Mathema, 2011). The Brahmin and Chettri communities have long dominated government jobs, with 60 per cent of public service jobs being held by these two castes (and 70 per cent of those who joined in 2011–2012 alone), in spite of them forming under just 30 per cent of the population (Paudel, 2016). The perceived lack of representation in government jobs, alongside the limited opportunities for upward mobility amongst youth from Madheshi (but also from Tharu and other indigenous communities), was an important driver of the ethno-regionalist Madhesh movement (Gupta and Hajariya, 2012).

The fact that far fewer Tharu, Rajbanshi or other ethnic groups reside in Biratnagar city, where they can tap into networks and opportunities, may also shed light on their limited employment prospects in the urban service or government sector. While Biratnagar, where most jobs are located, is ethnically diverse, the largest group are the Nepali-speaking Brahmin and Chettri who not only form 29 per cent of the population but also form a large share of the urban middle class. The Tharu, who form the majority in the rural hinterland, represent just 3 per cent of the urban population, with Rajbanshi forming just 2.17 per cent and Bantar only 0.1 per cent (Central Bureau of Statistics, 2011). While some better-off Tharu families had relocated to Biratnagar during the time of research, for most the cost of land was a considerable disincentive.[7]

The Impact of the Remittance Economy

It seems likely from the discussion earlier that a small increase in capitalist sector jobs will not succeed in undermining landlord–tenant relations unless competition for jobs is substantially reduced to the point that wages begin to rise significantly. This process appears highly unlikely in the context of sectorally disarticulated industrial growth and the dominance of a service sector which offers only temporary construction jobs and a small number of high-paid jobs to the educated urban middle class. A final remaining question therefore is whether the rise in out-migration for work in the capitalist sector overseas, in India or elsewhere in Nepal, has any potential to undermine landlord–tenant relations. The rise in overseas migration in particular has been one of the most significant changes in Nepal over the last two decades.

During interviews it was discussed how overseas migration was considered one among several options to meet the households' minimum cash needs and make up shortfalls from the land, alongside casual or factory labour. However, importantly, in spite of notably higher earnings, it was rarely considered an opportunity to 'accumulate' wealth and assets. Only 25 per cent of landless farming households and 24 per cent of marginal (owning less than 0.5 hectare) farming households had overseas migrants at the time of the 2019 survey. The average monthly earnings for migrants in the Gulf or Malaysia which were reportedly sent home is NPR 33,570. While this is equivalent to what is earned by those gaining professional employment (see Table 8.6), this does not account for the significant expenses associated with migration. As noted earlier, most migrants must pay fees to middlemen, known locally as 'manpower agents', a sector with a reputation for opaque practices and deception (Taylor-Nicholson et al., 2014). Payments are usually around NPR 150,000 (USD 1,500), often far beyond the actual costs of tickets and visa processing, and are a major cause of indebtedness to banks. Sunam and McCarthy (2016) note also that poorer groups are more likely to be overcharged by recruitment agencies. It was common for migrants to spend the first year or two after migrating repaying debts which were incurred to fund the migration process.

There is also considerable variation in the levels of remittances. For example, one household had reported monthly remittances of up to NPR 60,000, yet just over a quarter of households with migrants were receiving less than NPR 25,000 per month. There are several reasons for the variation. While elsewhere in Nepal, certain more lucrative destinations such as South Korea or Japan yield higher earnings (Sugden et al., 2022), there were no respondents in the sample migrating to such countries, which generally require significant investment. A more likely reason for the divergence is variation in remittances according to the type of work, and the most menial jobs, usually in construction, pay only marginally more than what one could earn at home as a semi-skilled labourer. For example, the minimum wage in Qatar as of 2019 was Qatari riyal (QAR) 750, which was equivalent to NPR 25,000 – as compared to NPR 17,500 for semi-skilled labour in Nepal itself (see Figure 8.6) – with the primary advantage of the former being that it represents a guaranteed income for a period of two to three years. Past studies on migration from Nepal have suggested there is a link between one's economic and caste position and the type of work received overseas due to lower qualifications and weaker social networks (Sijapati et al., 2017).

Research in Nepal's eastern hills (Sugden et al., 2018) and the Maithili belt west of the Koshi (Sugden et al., 2016; Sugden, 2019) point to notably lower remittance flows for marginal and tenant farmers. It was more challenging to assess these differences in this study as overseas migration was less common amongst middle or large farmer households.[8] Nevertheless, this may be of some relevance here when one considers that landless farmers, whose livelihoods are by far the most precarious, had received on average NPR 29,250 in remittances, as compared to NPR 34,041 for the relatively better-off marginal and small landowners with less than 1 hectare of land.

Another challenge with overseas migration is that there is no guarantee that households at home will receive the same amount every month. The lower figures reported for some households (one received only NPR 9,000 per month) was due usually to remittances being sent sporadically – for instance, if the worker has other in-country costs to manage. There were also numerous reports of workers being underpaid or deceived by employers. Migration itself is highly precarious, and jobs can be lost at short notice due to company collapse, leading to deportation or a loss of investment. This came to the fore during the Covid-19 crisis in 2020, which saw a number of workers in the Gulf states from Nepal being made redundant, while putting a temporary pause on migration overseas (Nicol et al., 2020).

For the majority, migration, like local wage labour, just contributes to households meeting their basic subsistence needs – in other words, part of their 'necessary' labour time. Remittance cash was used by a majority of farmers to cover basic food needs, as shown in numerous studies in Nepal (Adhikari and Hobley, 2011; Sugden et al., 2018; Sijapati et al., 2017), including Sunam's study from neighbouring Sunsari (Sunam, 2020), with some at times diverted into house improvements, or imported luxuries such as televisions or mobile phones, and cultural capital expenses. While there were some reported instances of remittances being invested in land or high-value assets, it seems highly unlikely that they are sufficient to draw farmers away from tenancy, particularly given the difficulties in accessing the land market, as discussed earlier.

Stability of Landlord–tenant Relations and Competition for Tenancy

Given the high competition for land, absence of profit-orientated production, and the distorted development of Nepal's capitalist sector, farmers remain dependent upon landlords for a large part of their subsistence. Even the rise in migration has had limited impact on prevailing livelihood strategies. Migration and the rising articulation with capitalism via off-farm labour instead simply echoes a global trend whereby households are moving towards a *dual* livelihood, where peasant farming is combined with labour in the capitalist sector of cities or overseas, often to provide households access to cash in the face of rising living costs and agrarian stress, while the land provides households with their food needs (Shah and Lerche, 2020; Sehgal, 2005; Sugden, 2019).

The evidence from rural southern Morang suggests that large segments of the Adivasi peasantry depend on both agriculture and capitalist sector labour, yet cannot strengthen their economic position through either. The majority seek to combine tenancy and small-scale owner-cultivation with wage labour, representing a stable articulation of modes of production. Respondents acknowledged that renting land would at least guarantee the household *some* of their minimum grain needs, even if the high rent would still oblige many to supplement this with outside income. Within this context it is unsurprising that in the 12 years between 2007 and 2019 when the study took place, farmer testimonies reported no drop in rents, and demand for tenancies amongst the peasantry and control of the means of production by absentee landlords appear to remain high. In fact, interviews suggested that *thekka* rents (which are becoming more common than *adhiya*) were increasing. For instance, focus groups in 2022 in Bhaudaha suggested that due to the appreciation in the value of their holdings, landlords had increased the rates over the last decade from around 18–20 *maund*s to 25–30 *maund*s per *bigha*. On good quality land it could even increase to 40 *maunds*. In Thalaha interviewees reported that they had increased from 20–25 *maund*s to 30 *maund*s. While some farmers dropped their tenancy to focus on off-farm labour, this was rare, and most had little choice but to accept the new rates.

There is evidence that the availability of land to lease likely outstrips demand, and this is evident in Bhaudaha village, where it was revealed in a discussion in 2008 that six or seven households are farming as sub-tenants. A few 'enterprising' individuals have used their social networks to rent out some land and then sub-let it to those not fortunate enough to have the necessary contacts, taking 5 *maund*s (200 kilograms) as payment. Poor farmers were willing to take up sub-tenancies at inflated rates of rent given the high unemployment and landlessness and the tendency for tenants – as stated by one respondent – to be 'satisfied with whatever they can earn', echoing Marx's assertion that farmers under pre-capitalist conditions are willing to force their subsistence needs down to the physical minimum.

Articulation of Modes of Production and the Sharing of Surplus

It is clear that there is a stable articulation between the pre-capitalist economy of rural southern Morang and the larger capitalist economy – in part through distress commerce, but in particular through wage labour. There is no evidence that greater engagement with the capitalist sector has 'undermined' exploitation by landlords or merchant capital. It is important to ask, however, how capitalism benefits from this relationship.

As noted in Chapter 2, the articulation between pre-capitalist modes of production and capitalism via the supply of peasant wage labour (migrant or local) can provide exceptional profits for the capitalist sector. On a conceptual level this is applicable to rural Morang. Adivasi wage workers in the Biratnagar industrial or construction sector, or in labour destinations overseas, receive a wage that is insufficient to support a family on its own. The only reason though that these wage regimes remain in place is the fact that food produced from the land can make up for shortfalls in income. This allows capitalist employers to increase the surplus value generated from workers, and represents an indirect transfer of surplus between the peasant farm and capitalism.

In the classic analyses by Meillassoux (1980) and Wolpe (1982) discussed in Chapter 2, it is the cost of 'labour reproduction', or the costs of maintaining the labour force over time, which is provided by the peasant farm in these contexts, while capitalist wages only cover the cost of 'labour power' – that is, what is needed to cover the subsistence costs of the worker. In Morang, workers are paid a basic wage which may be sufficient to cover the basic needs of the worker or the nominal cash needs of the household for the temporary period in which they are employed. However, it is feminised agriculture (even under feudal conditions with constrained productivity) which offers households longer-term livelihood stability and supports the costs of labour reproduction.

Agriculture provides, first, the food needs of the wider family, including the non-productive family members such as children, who will go on to be future wage workers. Second, agriculture covers the food needs of the worker during periods when he is not in employment – considering that many local capitalist sector jobs are casual in basis. For instance, 40 per cent of industries in the Morang–Sunsari industrial belt closed during the pandemic (Morang Chamber of Industry, 2021) and much construction work also stopped. In this context, agriculture filled in the gap.

Even in the case of overseas migrant destinations such as the Gulf or Malaysia, there are long spells when the migrant is not in employment. A degree of temporariness is ensured through the provision of fixed-term work permits and strict employment regulations (Chalcraft, 2010; Hanieh, 2010), which means that workers will return after a few years and migrate again, often on a new contract in another country. This is akin to the migrants from West Africa in post-war Europe documented by Meillsassoux (1981), who were restricted by short-term contracts, ensuring that the village economy would support them when they returned home. The third and final role for agriculture is to support workers in their retirement. It is a particular age group engaged in local and migrant wage labour – namely men generally between 18 and 50 – and agriculture is there to support them when they are no longer 'productive', that is, when they reach retirement age. As noted earlier, the value of these labour reproduction 'costs' provided by the pre-capitalist sector are transferred to capitalism as a 'rent' which, alongside surplus value already extracted by workers, supports the generation of profits that are far above the societal average.

Importantly, the reproduction costs of labour are also provided by the pre-capitalist sector during times of stress, as exemplified by the Covid-19 lockdown which, as noted earlier, led to the short-term cessation of capitalist labour. Hundreds of thousands of Nepali migrants were stranded in the Gulf states awaiting repatriation, while quarantine centres filled up across the country as returnees from India or overseas flooded back. Meanwhile many of those who were working in the local capitalist sector such as in Morang remained at home, and returned to the daily routine of life on the farm. This temporary rupture illustrated the fundamental role played by the peasantry in the global capitalist economy more broadly. Agriculture is the safety net that will, in the long term, cover the reproductive cost of labour, generating substantial profits for capitalism in the process. Importantly, it allows labour to remain flexible and 'disposable' at times of crisis or changing demand.

What is different in Morang is the added layer of complexity posed by the presence of simultaneous surplus appropriation by a pre-capitalist landlord and moneylending class. This raises the question over how 'super-profits' for capitalism are generated when a portion of the surplus is extracted by landlords and merchant capital. This is a distinctive feature of the larger Eastern Gangetic Plains region, which until now has received limited analysis (Sugden, 2019).[9]

It appears that for this dual exploitation to take place, the tendency for overwork has increased – as noted in Chapter 7. There has been a further reduction in the families' aggregate leisure time or time for training and education, as farmers depend more and more on both wage labour *and* agriculture.[10] As noted earlier, 'overwork', as Katusky (1988) terms it, has long been a feature of peasant livelihoods. He cites the example of the commercialised small farm competing with their larger capitalist counterparts in the market. In the context of rural Morang (where there is only limited production for the market), overwork is not to 'compete' with other producers, but to meet the needs of simple reproduction when faced with dual surplus appropriation through capitalist and pre-capitalist modes of production, alongside rising costs of living driven by expanding capitalist markets.

This overwork is manifested through several changes. First, men appear to have increased their contribution to the aggregate family labour time by working for longer hours in the capitalist sector both at home and abroad. One tenant farmer in Thalaha was asked why households choose to combine agricultural and factory employment. She responded by suggesting:

> If people have agricultural land, family members can work on the land in their leisure periods. Females cannot work in factories easily. Males can work in factories. Therefore, if farmers have both things, it is supportive.

The respondent states that during free time household members can work on their own farm and the rest of the time they can work in factories. Working during what is traditionally leisure time represents a classic situation of 'extension of the working day', as Marx described with reference to capitalist exploitation. This quote also alludes to a second manifestation of 'overwork' under the dual livelihood strategy – the feminisation of agriculture, as discussed in Chapter 7. Male labour contributions have declined in agriculture due to their growing engagement in wage labour (including as migrants), sectors whereby gender ideologies restrict jobs to men. With limited change to the cropping intensity, the additional labour burden on the farm has been passed on to women, who are simultaneously responsible for household reproductive roles such as cooking, cleaning and childcare (see Figure 8.5). The quote implies that women are working the land during times they would otherwise be resting.

Figure 8.5 Wheat harvest. With increased engagement of men in wage labour in the local capitalist sector or overseas migration, the burden of agricultural labour is more than ever before falling into the female domain.

Source: Author.

Within this context of overwork, a portion of 'necessary' labour time is performed in the capitalist and pre-capitalist sectors to cover cash and food needs respectively, and the surplus labour time is in effect 'shared' between landlords, merchants/moneylenders and capitalist employers.

Structural Power and Political Alliances

What has yet to be analysed in the discussion so far, however, are the political alliances that support these articulations between feudal agriculture and capitalism. It is clear that the parallel forms of surplus appropriation are by no means 'functional' parts of a larger system of exploitation. However, at the same time, the presence of these multiple class interests does not imply that power is 'fluid and dispersed' as Glassman (2003) notes in his critique of the 'post-structural' Marxist position discussed in Chapter 2.[11] In other words, this study would stop short of considering the multiple class relationships (for example, between landlord and tenant or between factory worker and capitalist employer) as independent unconnected axes of exploitation. Likewise, the sharing of surplus between the capitalist and non-capitalist modes of production cannot be considered purely coincidental.

To better understand the structural power that ties the seemingly unrelated flows of surplus between the peasantry of southern Morang on the one hand and disparate classes of capitalist employers and feudal landlords on the other, it is worth exploring whether there is a convergence (or divergence) of class interests which are at play when these two modes of production interact, and its political manifestation. It appears that the diverse capitalist employers in Biratnagar and even overseas are drawing substantial profits from the labour provided by the largely Adivasi peasantry of Morang, yet their interests are not necessarily in conflict with those of landed classes, and they could even be argued to align. In *Economic and Political Manuscripts*, Marx himself noted with regard to Europe how the feudal landlord's interests were in general opposed to the expansion of capitalism, which threatened their monopoly over landed property, yet they did have a vested interest in capitalist exploitation – for instance, in keeping wages low (so farmers were not drawn away from the land) (Marx, 1932, 58).

Thus far, it has been suggested that control over land by absentee landlords constrains farmers' from meeting their subsistence needs through farming due to their inability to access the land market, the rent burden, and the reduced capacity of tenants to develop the productive forces. This in turn drives farmers to simultaneously 'compete' for work in the non-agricultural sector. Demand for work in the capitalist sector both at home and overseas means they are willing to receive wages that do not (on their own) cover the entire cost of family subsistence and labour reproduction – and this is made possible by their continued ties to the land. Furthermore, levels of employment and wages in the capitalist sector at home or abroad remain at levels that ensure competition for tenancies and loans does not drop with an influx of off-farm wages or remittances, favouring landlords. This articulation thus clearly benefits both landlords and capitalist employers – and the net surplus is in this context 'shared' between these two groups.

However, this convergence of interests can be considered neither an active 'strategy' of capital and landlords nor a coincidental alignment of class interests. Instead, this more likely represents both groups 'seizing' an opportunity for surplus appropriation at a given historical juncture. The loose nature of these alliances is all the more apparent when one observes the migration economy. The acceptance of thousands of Nepali workers whose reproduction costs are covered by the pre-capitalist sector is an 'opportunity' seized by the Gulf states and other overseas migrant destination economies, yet they have no direct stake in policies within Nepal which favour landed interests, or those of a comprador class which benefit from Nepal's sectorally disarticulated industrial development. At a national level one can perhaps observe a closer alignment of interests between landlords and capitalism. The comprador bourgeoise which dominates the capitalist sector in Nepal arguably benefits from the low wages that emerge in the context of the impoverishment of the peasantry due to landlordism in the countryside. At the same time, it is in the interest of this group to maintain the current sectorally disarticulated industrial structure to protect their own investments in both industry and commerce (for example, importation of consumables). Similarly, it would be in the interests of landlords to not only maintain their holdings, but to favour the perpetutation of the underdeveloped industrial economy, given that limited employment opportunities and low wages ensure competition for tenancies (and rents) remains high. Similarly, for both landlords and the capitalist sector, the rising expenditure associated with consumerism continues to drive economic stress, the imperative for households to compete for tenancies or wage labour employment, while simultaneously bolstering the comprador import-based economy.

However, these processes are not necessarily manifested through active collusion and 'alliances' amongst different segments of the dominant class, and more likely take place via a reluctance to support transformative change. The crystallisation of class interests on a political level most likely takes place through the bureaucracy, the policies and practices of which serve to reproduce this articulation of modes of production. As argued in Chapter 2 with regard to India (Gupta, 1977; Sau, 1975), imperialism was argued to have impeded the organic development of capitalist industry, undermining the capacity for the latter to draw farmers out of agriculture, thus perpetuating landlord power in rural areas. It was further argued that this paved the way for an accommodation between historically divergent interests of landed elites who appropriate surplus from the peasantry and a capitalist class (Lin, 1980), with the interests of both groups reproduced through the political apparatus of the state (Ghosh, 1988). As touched upon in Chapter 3, this conceptualisation can also be applied to Nepal. Dependence on imports due to weaker development of the productive forces within Nepali industry, and a dominance of foreign capital in the limited domestic manufacturing sector in Biratnagar, have impeded the organic development of domestic capitalism. The People's War, a new constitution and the emergence of federalism have done little to transform the structure of the economy – notwithstanding localised achievements at the grassroots in terms of the political empowerment of marginalised groups.

This lack of change can be better understood if one considers that the bureaucracy in Nepal and even the interests served by the mainstream political parties have changed little in spite of frequent changes of government. This role of the bureaucracy in perpetuating landed interests is evident most prominently in the persistent failure to implement long-promised land reforms (Alden-Wily et al., 2008). State support for landlords has been a common theme in research on land policy in Nepal (Adhikari, 2006; Alden-Wily et al., 2008) – a phenomenon which is a direct legacy of the centralised-state-sanctioned feudalism of the Rana era (Blaikie et al., 2001). Land reform proposals have been persistently delayed or mothballed in spite of it being a key rallying cry of the 1996–2006 People's War and the subsequent integration of the Maoists into the ruling government. A frequent phenomenon over the last few decades was that land reform would be brought up to garner popular support, yet there would be limited commitment to follow it through. One policy maker in Kathmandu with a background in land, when asked about the prospect of land reform, stated:

> It [land reform] is a very sensitive issue. It is directly linked with the power structure of important families and power interests... and the donor's themselves off and on they send some mission to look into the land issue.... Their main mandate is poverty, and ending deprivation, but no one dares raise the land issue.... The [land reform] commission submits the report to the government and then the government changes, and nothing happens. And there were several land reform commissions. Each comes out with a grand master plan, a land reform plan. There is no political commitment to change.

Absentee landlords such as those who own much of the land in rural southern Morang are themselves well represented within the same bureaucracy implementing reforms, and this itself has been blamed for limited incentives for the state to follow up on promises (Alden-Wily et al., 2008).

By 2023 redistributive land reform had largely dropped from the political agenda. While 'scientific land reform', or *vaijnaanika bhumi sudhaara*, was mentioned in the Constitution of Nepal 2015 (Law Commission of Nepal, 2015, 50, e), which enshrines access to land for all and includes clauses to 'discourage' absentee landlordism and ending dual land ownership, the actual mechanisms through which to achieve this, including redistributive justice, are absent. The 2019 Land Use Act and 2022 Land Use Regulations were largely focused on the classification of land. Meanwhile, more fundamental issues such as tenancy reforms or ceilings on land are now rare in mainstream political discourse. The 2022 election manifestos of the mainstream CPN (UML) (2022) and Nepali Congress (2022), for instance, place a considerable emphasis on agricultural transformation yet there is only a brief reference to land, and even then, this is largely through the reference to the implementation of land use regulations and so-called land banks. This involves landowners depositing their fallow land in a 'bank' which can be then leased out to others. Government-owned wasteland or riverbanks can also be leased out through the bank. This, however, as argued by Community Self Reliance Centre (CSRC) (2021), represents a reversal of the pro-tiller agenda associated with redistributive reforms, as it essentially protects the landowners' property rights.

The land bank idea also echoes the 'market assisted land reform' which was pushed by the World Bank in the 2000s as it sought a solution to the Maoist insurgency (Bhandari, 2006). Just as donors had supported redistributive land reforms in the context of the Cold War, these ideas have evolved in line with neoliberal orthodoxy, which protects private property.

A peasant federation leader (affiliation withheld for anonymity) interviewed in Kathmandu expressed his frustration at the lack of willpower of political leaders to implement real land reforms:

> We have raised this issue [land reform] very aggressively before the current government as well.... We hope that if there is a new government, it implements it. A commission has been formed to solve land-related issues. It has started some works, and that is better than no progress, so we welcome it. But, instead of that, an implementing unit for scientific land reform should be formed which would study the reports of all three land reform commissions, and create a synthesised work plan, programme, and come up with the statistics of the number of landless throughout the country, and the amount of land available for distribution as I said before, and how much land can be given to each farmer based on the local factors. If we could have prepared these matters in these three years, we would have been able to solve the problem of landlessness at once. But the government has not been able to do that.... We have been raising the issue of limiting land ownership from the start. But this issue has not been coming up significantly now, a wide national agreement is needed for it.

The leader in question, who was in favour of nationalisation of land and its distribution to peasants – which he understood as 'scientific land reform' – was also strongly opposed to the so-called land bank, which he viewed as a ploy to avoid actual redistribution of property.

> The actual concept of Land Bank is that land reform should not be implemented, farmers should not be given land for free, the land that they have taken should be made like a collateral, and they should be made to pay the money in instalments, at 0 per cent or 1–2 per cent interest. The concept of Land Bank brought in Nepal is described as providing fallow land at a lease. Irrespective of what they are saying now, there is a danger that in the future it may be implemented.... So, we do not want this, we want scientific land reform.

There was also a fear amongst peasant activists such as this, that the bank would pave the way for corporate agriculture to seize large areas of land for plantation-type farming, a risk also raised by CSRC (2021).

While landed interests are likely well represented by the bureaucracy and political party apparatus, what does this mean for other sectors of the economy? The role of the state in perpetuating a 'semi-colonial' economy led by a comprador bourgeoise has been widely acknowledged over the decades (Blaikie et al., 2001; Bhattarai, 2003). In more recent years, there has been limited research on the relationship between the state on the one hand and the 'comprador' interests – namely industries dependent on foreign capital and the local merchant capitalists engaged in the import of commodities – on the other. As discussed in Chapter 3, imports of manufactured consumables or component parts for local factories still play an important role in raising revenue for the state. State-sanctioned economic restructuring itself has allowed Nepal's domestic comprador bourgeoisie to intensify the accumulation of profit through the expansion of imports, both from India and competing powers such as China, further undermining local production while local consumption costs rise (see also Sugden et al., 2018). Similarly, the strong links between the bureaucracy and businesses more broadly has generated increasing interest, including the important mediating role played by political parties in allowing trade to take place (Shakya, 2013).

While more research is needed on how the convergence between landed and industrial interests plays out in reality, it is entirely plausible that the interests of both groups are reproduced through the political apparatus of the state. It is also worth noting that the one cannot simply talk of state support for a singular 'comprador class' alone at the apex of the Nepali national economy. There are multiple actors beyond those engaged in manufacturing or importing and distributing commodities. For instance, the service sector which includes privatised healthcare and education retains strong political patronage, and also plays its part in perpetuating economic insecurity amongst the peasantry. Added to this is a shadow rent-seeking economy of middlemen, including the overseas labour recruitment agencies (Kern and Müller-Böker, 2015) and politically affiliated contractors for public works projects (Shrestha, 2007) – which appears from testimonies in the field site to play a significant role in the rural economy, yet has received limited research. The latter in particular has been hugely significant since local-level restructuring whereby new rural municipalities have significantly enhanced budgets for public works programmes, and many local leaders were also becoming contractors. The shadow 'rent-seeking' economy itself represents a further drain of surplus – within the sphere of circulation, with patterns of wealth accumulation not dissimilar to the feudal mode of production on the ground. This is a significant area for further study.

An Uncertain Political Future

It is clear that the overall structure of the social formation both within Morang and at a national level has achieved some stability over time. While the trajectory of agrarian change over the last few decades is dynamic, it is not 'transformative'. In spite of intensifying articulations with capitalism via wage labour and growing monetisation, the prevailing relations of production remain in place, and remain feudal in character – with a convergence of interests between the multiple segments of the dominant class.

The paradox of the current conjuncture in Nepal is the dominance of various supposedly 'communist' and social democratic factions on the political scene since the 1990s. Achieving structural transformation which will replace a semi-colonial and feudal economy was a central rallying cry of the 1996–2006 People's War, while a wave of subsequent indigenous movements after the 2010s sought to transform the historically unequal state–Adivasi relationship which underlie many of the feudal inequalities in rural Morang. However, in spite of successive waves of rhetoric supporting 'socialistic' transformation, this has not been translated into any concrete structural change at the grassroots for the Adivasi peasantry in Morang, or elsewhere in Nepal. Any short-term change is unlikely so long as landed and comprador interests remain embedded within the upper echelons of the bureaucracy and political party apparatus.

A recent shift has been the global wave of right-wing populism which has been bolstered by the inequalities brought about by neoliberalism, yet has overridden class concerns with calls for majoritarian religious or ethno-national solidarity (Edelman, 2020). This shift has not spared Nepal, as observed by Rai and Shneiderman (2019). In spite of apparently left-wing credentials, most of the mainstream 'national' political parties (including those with the 'communist' label) have openly courted ethno-nationalist sentiments rooted in Nepali language, national 'unity' and the veneration of the same Gorkhali empire which conquered and brought feudalism to the eastern Tarai in the 1700s. Individuals (predominantly men) from hill upper castes continue to make up much of the leadership, and the main support base for these parties is in the hills and amongst hill settlers in the Tarai-Madhesh, while the regionalist parties with strong support in the lowlands are increasingly small and fragmented (Mørch, 2023). As during the Panchayat era, anti-India nationalism has been a strong rallying cry, although, paradoxically, other than efforts to open-up more trade with China which could undermine Indian monopoly in trade, Nepal's import-dependent comprador economy remains firmly intact with the trade deficit and remittance dependence continuing to rise.

In many ways the current political establishment represents the paradox of contemporary populism in the periphery, whereby neoliberal economic policies sit alongside tokenistic social policy interventions which fail to challenge the status quo, all set within the framework of an exclusionary ethnic agenda and calls for national 'unity' (Gudavarthy and Vijay, 2020; Fischer, 2020). For example, the Nepal Communist Party election victory in 2017 following a short-lived merger between the former Maoists, the CPN(M) and mainstream CPN (UML) led to the introduction of some popular social policy programmes such as a social security scheme. However, the political narrative shifted from questions of social or redistributive justice to *samriddhi*, or 'prosperity', sometimes combined with ultra-nationalism. This trend has largely continued with subsequent governments. Priorities have focused on market expansion, with a heavy emphasis on infrastructure. While some initiatives, such as efforts to develop the hydropower sector (Zou et al., 2022), are of course beneficial to the national economy, other large scale projects are surplus to Nepal's needs. These include a spate of often unnecessary highways (Shrestha, 2023) (see Figure 8.6) and airport building projects – including two international airports in Bhairawa and Pokhara with negligible international traffic, and the notorious Nijgadh international airport[12] project in the central Tarai (Geschewski and Islar, 2022).

Throughout the last decade, there has been a seemingly conscious effort to shift public discourse away from redistributive equality such as via land reform, not to mention questions of historical injustices against the Adivasi and Madheshi communities, the grievances of which remain unaddressed despite waves of ethno-regionalist sentiment since the mid-2000s (Mørch, 2023).

Figure 8.6 The deserted four-lane highway from Biratnagar to Biratchowk which passes through both Jhorahat and Pidarboni epitomises the post-2015 political context. Since the establishment of the federal system, there has been a surge of investment in infrastructure by the local, federal and national governments, including the so-called white elephant projects – alongside a worsening condition of the peasantry. The redundancy of this highway is notable when one considers the presence of a parallel six-lane highway from Biratnagar to Itahari just a few kilometres further west.

Source: Author.

The focus of most political actors has been creating the social stability and 'unity' needed for neoliberal economic growth.

In southern Morang, one observes a fusion between the twin tensions of ethnic autonomy and redistributive justice – and the rationale for land reforms in this region is all the more contentious given the clear link between alienation from land and historical state–Adivasi relations. Furthermore, the new constitution continues to place restrictions on one of the primary routes to land ownership security – access to citizenship papers, in part fuelled by populist conspiracy theories over an India-engineered demographic influx in the Tarai-Madhesh (Mørch, 2023).

However, active political mobilisation for political-economic reform is elusive. While interviews with farmer leaders suggested that there is popular support for redistributive land reform in lower echelons of political parties, these sentiments are not shared by those in leadership positions. At the same time, the indigenous movement in Nepal has been largely dissipated and divided by factionalism as well as the new federal boundaries which maintain hill upper-caste political dominance in all but one province (Mørch, 2023). There have been some recent political efforts to unite Nepal's ethnic minorities – it is largely under the leadership of Madheshi middle castes yet maintains support amongst the Tharu and hill *janajati* communities (Basnet, 2019).[13] However, there is still limited evidence that the wave of regionalist and ethnicity-based movements in Nepal have achieved systematic mobilisation around the issue of access to land and resources, given the focus on political representation and ethnic autonomy. Thus, for the meantime, any hopes for radical political mobilisation for structural change remain highly optimistic – with lessons for the wider Gangetic plains region.

Notes

1. Sunam (2020) in a study from Sunsari (the neighbouring district to Morang) notes that remittances allow some peasants to buy up land, although this is often for speculative purposes. Rinck (2024) also highlights this phenomenon with regard to Dhanusha, noting that land is of greater value for its speculative potential rather than its potential to yield surplus. It is notable, though, that agricultural productivity is notably lower in Dhanusha when compared to Morang and further research would be needed to compare the two districts.
2. For an additional 3.08 hectares, the reason for the change in land ownership between the first and the last survey was not stated or known by the

respondent (sometimes was the case if the household head had changed) – but it is expected that is due to either sale or family splits.

3. This challenge was identified by Community Self Reliance Centre (CSRC) with reference to the earlier Land Use Act (CSRC, 2019). As of 2023, only 161 (out of 753) local units had completed the classification, 10 months after the implementation of regulations, resulting in the government actually pausing the process to revive the real estate and financial sector, given that land could not be used as collateral on loans until the classification was complete (Fiscal Nepal, 2023).
4. This included decreasing the size of unit which can be divided as residential plots in the Kathmandu valley (*The Annapurna Express*, 2023).
5. This would be especially likely given that rent has a limited influence on commodity prices, which are influenced by the supply and demand factors in the broader cross-border economy into which Morang district is integrated.
6. Biratnagar has over 20 flights a day to the capital, an extraordinary level of connectivity for a town of just over 200,000 people equivalent to what one would observe between major Indian metropolises, and is a reminder of the intricately close link the city has with Kathmandu.
7. Other reasons for the limited migration of better-off Tharu households to the town include the strong social institutions and continued social status that they can benefit from in the village when compared to urban areas (Mørch, 2023).
8. In the study in Dhanusha, by contrast (Sugden et al., 2018), even family members from wealthier farmer households had migrated, albeit for higher paid work.
9. While wages in the capitalist sector (including migrant labour receiving countries) are already low, marginal and tenant farmers are unlikely to be able to accept lower-paid employment given that levels of food consumption are already close to the physiological minimum for many tenant households. Even for those with relative food security, cash needs are rising, a process itself fuelled by expanding capitalist markets and the associated process of monetisation and rising dependence on imported manufactured commodities. Thus, it is through increasing the hours of labour extracted from the peasantry that the capitalist sector continues to yield a substantial profit.
10. This is a similar process to that described by Marx, whereby the capitalist increases 'absolute surplus value' by extending the working day of labourers and reducing leisure time (Marx, 1974).
11. As Glassman (2003, 681) notes with regards to capitalism:

> Capitalists do not just dominate workers as one group of persons dominating another. Rather, the ability of capitalists to collectively dominate workers – which is always contested and in need of

> re-creation – resides in their capacity to exploit workers through control over investment decisions upon which workers and others in society are dependent, a capacity that is inscribed in legal structures, customary practices, institutions of repressive force, and networks of social relations.

12. The proposed Nijgadh airport is to be constructed in the Tarai-Madhesh to the south of Kathmandu, and will be the largest airport in South Asia (in terms of area) if completed. However, it has been heavily critiqued not only for the ecological impact, but because it is considered surplus to the country's needs.
13. Political factions representing the Tharu, Madheshi and hill *janajati* communities formed the Federal Socialist Forum in 2015, which acted as a counterweight to the hill upper-caste majoritarianism of the centre, with Basnet (2019) drawing parallels with middle-caste mobilisation in Bihar – this party went on to merge with two other parties to form the People's Socialist Party as of 2020. The general trend since the Madhesh Andolan II was of splits and in-fighting within regionalist parties, which has contributed to a weakening support base (Bashyal and Bashyal, 2023).

References

Adhikari, J. 2006. *Land Reform in Nepal: Problems and Prospects.* Nepal Institute of Development Studies.

Adhikari, Jagannath and Hobley, Mary. 2011. Everyone is leaving – who will sow our fields? The effects of migration from Khotang district to the Gulf and Malaysia. Nepal Institute of Development Studies (NIDS), Kathmandu.

Alden-Wily, L., Chapgain, D. and Sharma, S. 2008. *Land Reform in Nepal: Where Is It Coming from and Where Is It Going?* DFID.

Bashyal, Lalita Kaundinya and Bashyal, Keshav. 2023. The Madhesh Movement in Nepal: At the crossroad. In *Migration, Regional Autonomy, and Conflicts in Eastern South Asia: Searching for a Home(land),* edited by Ranjan, Amit and Chattoraj, Diotima. Springer.

Basnet, Chudamani. 2019. The federal socialist forum: Incipient middle caste politics in Nepal? *Studies in Nepali History and Society* 24 (2): 355–380.

Bhandari, Ravi. 2006. Searching for a weapon of mass production in Nepal: Can market-assisted land reforms live up to their promise? *Journal of Developing Societies* 22 (2): 111–143.

Blaikie, P., Cameron, J. and Seddon, D. 2001. *Nepal in Crisis: Growth and Stagnation at the Periphery*, revised and enlarged edition. Adroit Publishers.

Central Bureau of Statistics. 2011. *Nepal Population Census 2011.* Government of Nepal.

Chalcraft, John. 2010. Monarchy, migration and hegemony in the Arabian Peninsula. Research paper, Kuwait Programme on Development, Governance and Globalization in the Gulf States.

Chandra, Nirmal K. 1974. Farm efficiency under semi-feudalism: A critique of marginalist theories and some Marxist formulations. *Economic and Political Weekly* 9 (32/34): 1309–1332.

CPN (UML). 2022. *Pratinidhisabha tatha pradesasabha nirvacana-2079 Nepala Kamyunista Parti (Emale): Ghosanapatra*. Communist Party of Nepal (United Marxist-Leninist).

CSRC. 2019. Federal parliament passes the Land Use Act. 13 July. https://csrcnepal.org/federal-parliament-passes-the-land-use-act/#:~:text=The%20Act%20prohibits%20constructing%20new,have%20to%20demolish%20the%20house.

———. 2021. Land bank in Nepal: Is it relevant? Is it required? A position paper. Community Self Reliance Centre.

Edelman, Marc. 2020. From 'populist moment' to authoritarian era: Challenges, dangers, possibilities. *Journal of Peasant Studies* 47 (7): 1418–1444.

Fiscal Nepal. 2023. Government relaxes restrictions on land fragmentation. *Fiscal Nepal,* 19 April. https://www.fiscalnepal.com/2023/04/19/12378/government-relaxes-restrictions-on-land-fragmentation/.

Fischer, Andrew M. 2020. The dark sides of social policy: From neoliberalism to resurgent right-wing populism. *Development and Change* 51 (2): 371–397.

Gartaula, Hom, Niehof, Anke and Visser, Leontine. 2012. Shifting perceptions of food security and land in the context of labour out-migration in rural Nepal. *Food Security* 4: 181–194.

Geschewski, Hanna and Islar, Mine. 2022. A political ecology of aviation and development: An analysis of relations of power and justice in the (de)construction of Nepal's second international airport. *Journal of Political Ecology* 29 (1): 51–75.

Ghosh, S. K. 1988. Indian bourgeoisie and imperialism. *Economic and Political Weekly* 23 (45–47): 2445–2447, 2449–2458.

Glassman, J. 2003. Rethinking overdetermination, structural power, and social change: A critique of Gibson-Graham, Resnick and Wolff. *Antipode* 35 (4): 678–698.

Government of Nepal. 2022 *Bhu upayoga niyamavali 2079* (Land Use Regulations, 2079). Ministry of Land Management, Cooperatives and Poverty Alleviation.

Gudavarthy, Ajay and Vijay, G. 2020. Social policy and political mobilization in India: Producing hierarchical fraternity and polarized differences. *Development and Change* 51 (2): 463–484.

Gupta, N. Sen. 1977. Further on the mode of production in agriculture. *Economic and Political Weekly* 12 (26): A55–A63.

Gupta, S. and Hajariya, A. 2012. The youth of Madhesh: An overall national assessment. In *The Landscape of Madhesh: Politics, Society and Economy of the Plains*, edited by Tewari, R. and Sah, A. P. Nepal Madhesh Foundation.

Hanieh, Adam. 2010. Temporary migrant labour and the spatial structuring of class in the gulf cooperation council. *Spectrum: Journal of Global Studies* 1 (1): 67–88.

Hoffmann, Michael Peter. 2018. From bonded to industrial labour: Precarity, Maoism, and ethnicity in a modern industrial factory in western Nepal. *Modern Asian Studies* 52 (6): 1917–1937.

Kern, Alice and Müller-Böker, Ulrike. 2015. The middle space of migration: A case study on brokerage and recruitment agencies in Nepal. *Geoforum* 65: 158–169.

Law Commission of Nepal. 2015. *Constitution of Nepal 2015*. Translation by Nepal Law Commission. https://lawcommission.gov.np/en/wp-content/uploads/2021/01/Constitution-of-Nepal.pdf.

Lerche, Jens. 2013. The agrarian question in neoliberal India: Agrarian transition bypassed? *Journal of Agrarian Change* 13 (3): 382–404.

Lin, Sharat, G. 1980. Theory of a dual mode of production in post-colonial India. *Economic and Political Weekly* 15 (10): 516–529.

Marx, K. 1932. *Economic and Political Manuscripts*. Progress Publishers.

———. 1967. *Capital: A Critique of Political Economy (Volume 3)*. Progress Publishers.

———. 1974. *Capital: A Critical Analysis of Capitalist Production (Volume 1)*. Progress Publishers.

Mathema, K. B. 2011. *Madheshi Uprising: The Resurgence of Ethnicity*. Mandala Book Point.

Meillassoux, C. 1981. *Maidens, Meal and Money: Capitalism and the Domestic Community*. Cambridge University Press.

Morang Chamber of Industry. 2021. *Industrial Survey 2078: Sunsari Morang Industrial Corridor*. Biratnagar.

Mørch, M. 2023. *Plains of Discontent: A Political History of Nepal's Tarai (1743–2019)*. Fine Print Books.

National Statistics Office. 2024. *Nepal Living Standards Survey IV 2022/23*. Government of Nepal.

Nepali Congress. 2022. *Resolution of Nepali Congress: House of Representatives and State Assembly Election 2079*.

Nicol, Alan, Abdoubaetova, Aigoul, Wolters, Alexander, Kharel, Arjun, Murzakolova, Asel, Gebreyesus, Ataklti, Lucasenco, Eugenia, Chen, Fengbo, Sugden, Fraser and Sterly, Harald. 2020. Between a rock and a hard place: Early experience of migration challenges under the Covid-19 pandemic. International Water Management Institute Working Paper 195.

Niroula, Gajendra S. and Thapa, Gopal B. 2005. Impacts and causes of land fragmentation, and lessons learned from land consolidation in South Asia. *Land Use Policy* 22 (4): 358–372.

Patnaik, U. 1983. Classical theories of rent and its application to India: Some preliminary thoughts on sharecropping. In *Sharecroppers and Sharecropping*, edited by Byres, T. J. Frank Cass and Co.

Paudel, Narendra Raj. 2016. Inclusive governance: A case study of civil service in Nepal. *South Asian Journal of Social Sciences* 2 (1): 19–40.

Pearce, R. 1983. Sharecropping: Towards a Marxist view. In *Sharecropping and Sharecroppers*, edited by Byres, T. J. Frank Cass and Co.

Rai, Janak and Shneiderman, Sara. 2019. Identity, society, and state: Citizenship and inclusion in Nepal over time. In *The Politics of Change: Reflections on Contemporary Nepal*, edited by Thapa, D. Social Science Baha and Himal Books.

Regmi, M. 1976. *Landownership in Nepal.* Adroit Publishers.

Rinck, J. 2025. Marxist past to speculative futures: Migration, land markets, and political storytelling in Nepal's Tarai. *The Journal of Peasant Studies* 52 (1): 157–177.

Sau, R. 1975. Farm efficiency under semi-Feudalism: A critique of marginalist theories and some Marxist formulations: A comment. *Economic and Political Weekly* 9 (32/34): 18–21.

Sehgal, Rakhi. 2005. Social reproduction of third world labour in the era of globalisation: State, market and the household. *Economic and Political 40* (22/23): 2286–2294.

Shah, Alpa and Lerche, Jens. 2020. Migration and the invisible economies of care: Production, social reproduction and seasonal migrant labour in India. *Transactions of the Institute of British Geographers.* DOI: 10.1111/tran.12401.

Shakya, Sujeev. 2013. *Unleashing Nepal.* Penguin UK.

Sharma, R. 2019. Nepala ardha-samanti desa rahena, samajavadi krantika nimti upayukta vastugata adhara tayara. *E-Rato Khabar*, 26 December.

Shrestha, C. B. 2023. On the fast lane to expressways. *Nepali Times*, 29 January.

Shrestha, Purusottam Man. 2007. *Corruption in Infrastructure Provision and Service Delivery at the Municipal Level in Nepal.* Loughborough University.

Sijapati, B., Lama, A. S., Baniya, J., Rinck, J., Jha, K. and Gurung, A. 2017. *Labour Migration and the Remittance Economy: The Socio-political Impact.* The Centre for the Study of Labour and Mobility.

Sugden, F. 2017. A mode of production flux: The transformation and reproduction of rural class relations in lowland Nepal and North Bihar. *Dialectical Anthropology* 41 (2): 129–161.

———. 2019. *Labour Migration, Capitalist Accumulation and Feudal Reproduction: A Historical Analysis from the Eastern Gangetic Plains.* Antipode.

Sugden, F., Saikia, P., Maskey, N. and Pokharel, P. 2016. Gender, agricultural investment and productivity in an era of out-migration: A case study from

Nepal and Bihar. In *The Ganges River Basin: Status and Challenges in Water, Environment and Livelihoods*, edited by Bharati, L., Sharma, B. R., Smakhtin, V. and Mandal, A. S. Earthscan.

Sugden, F., Seddon, D. and Raut, M. 2018. Mapping historical and contemporary agrarian transformations and capitalist infiltration in a complex upland environment: A case from Eastern Nepal. *Journal of Agrarian Change* 18 (2): 444–472.

Sugden, Fraser, Nigussie, Likimyelesh, Debevec, Liza and Nijbroek, Ravic. 2022. Migration, environmental change and agrarian transition in upland regions: Learning from Ethiopia, Kenya and Nepal. *Journal of Peasant Studies* 49 (5): 1101–1131.

Sunam, Ramesh. 2015. The significance of foreign labour migration and land for poverty reduction in Nepal. In *Poverty Reduction Policies and Practices in Developing Asia*, edited by Heshmati, Almas, Maasoumi, Esfandiar and Wan, Guanghua. Springer and ADB.

———. 2020. *Transnational Labour Migration, Livelihoods and Agrarian Change in Nepal: The Remittance Village*. Routledge.

Sunam, Ramesh, K. and McCarthy, John F. 2016. Reconsidering the links between poverty, international labour migration, and agrarian change: Critical insights from Nepal. *Journal of Peasant Studies* 43 (5): 39–63.

Taylor-Nicholson, E., Paoletti, S., Sijapati, B. and Farbenblum, B. 2014. Risky business: Accountability of manpower agencies in Nepal. Centre for the Study of Labour and Mobility, Policy brief 3.

The Annapurna Express. 2023. Government reopens land plotting after 10 months. 20 April. https://theannapurnaexpress.com/news/government-reopens-land-plotting-after-10-months-41215.

Tulachan, Bojindra Prasad and Felver, Troy B. 2019. The evolution of industrial relations in Nepal: A biological evolutionary perspective. *Labor History* 60 (2): 126–143.

Zharkevich, Ina. 2019. *Maoist People's War and the Revolution of Everyday Life in Nepal*. Cambridge University Press.

Zou, Xiaolong, Pradhan, Sheela and Mukhia, Anmol. 2022. Nepal's hydropower development: Predicament and dilemma in policy-making. Natural Resources Forum, Wiley Online Library, 60–72.

9

Capitalism, the Pre-capitalist and the Peasantry

Looking Forward

The story of agrarian transition in southern Morang in many ways epitomises the larger crisis facing the global peasantry and its relationship with capitalism in the early decades of the twenty-first century. Capitalism is expanding into the most peripheral corners of the world, and the peasantry, particularly those at the base of the agrarian structure – who are facing rising costs and agroecological stress – are increasingly drawn into capitalist labour markets via migration and local off-farm labour. It is these articulations between the capitalist and pre-capitalist which are increasingly central to peasant livelihoods.

Recognition of this process of agrarian transition whereby capitalism and peasant farming co-exist, with the former providing substantial profits to the latter, is of course not new and, as noted at the start of this book, these phenomena are generating renewed academic interest (Shah and Lerche, 2020; Zhan and Scully, 2018; Sehgal, 2005). However, what has received far less attention is the added complexity posed by additional axes of exploitation on the farm which long predate the peasantries' integration into capitalist labour markets. This is a gap which this book has sought to address with a focus on the additional layers of livelihood stress when the economic and cultural burdens of neoliberal capitalism intersect with the legacy and persistence of landlordism and rent-seeking merchant capital. In doing so, this book offers a more nuanced analysis of the 'pre-capitalist' itself and its symbiotic (rather than subordinate) relationship with capitalism.

The case study from the plains of southeast Nepal has also broken from dominant narratives of agrarian change in South Asia – in particular, debates over feudalism and landlordism. The preceding chapters have sought to move away from 'capitalocentric' worldviews, which consider feudal landlordism as a relic of limited relevance when set against unprecedented expansion of neoliberal capitalism. It has, however, also cast doubt upon older and economistic models of 'feudalism' which imply a closed and static system. Importantly, the research has broken new ground in demonstrating how the growing articulations between the peasantry and capitalism via wage labour and expanding markets do not represent a functional relationship. The relationship is instead mediated by older feudal class relations in rural areas – including landlordism itself, but also merchant capital, which plays an intermediary role. It has shown how the pre-capitalist and capitalist can in fact operate in synergy, and both economic formations can support each other by jointly creating the economic, political and cultural conditions whereby surplus can be 'drained' from the peasantry.

This articulation of modes of production has achieved stability within a larger 'semi-colonial' social formation, whereby a skewed pattern of industrial development has limited the pathways out of agriculture. The articulation has also been mediated by a range of political-ideological processes. This includes, in particular, a problematic relationship between land, ethno-caste authority and political power which has epitomised state–Adivasi relations since the nineteenth century. Together, this has paved the way for a unique yet complex matrix of exploitation – with lessons for both political action and agricultural policy.

This book started by exploring the evolution of rural feudalism over the last two centuries in the Morang region, beginning with the subjugation of Adivasi communities by the Gorkha conquest and the subsequent Rana regime. An older, more redistributive mode of production grounded in shifting cultivation was subordinated to centralised feudalism by a combination of taxation, creation of internal hierarchy within Adivasi society, and the clearing of the forest frontier. A further wave of change took place as ethnic-political loyalties were further reconfigured under the royalist *panchayat* system. The old indigenous tax collectors were slowly disenfranchised through economic and political processes, while the largely Brahmin and Chettri landed class with links to the bureaucracy emerged into powerful absentee landlords. While industries were established during this period, manufacturing remained sectorally disarticulated, and the economy was increasingly import dependent. Morang's once burgeoning industries have failed to see significant growth and have been eclipsed by the service sector in the wake of economic liberalisation, which was rolled out alongside the introduction of parliamentary democracy in the 1990s.

Combined with limited 'escape' options from agriculture, the book has shown how these economic and political processes paved the way for the landlord–tenant relations that appear to dominate the agrarian landscape today, which were explored in Chapter 4. 'Independent peasant' production oriented around self-sufficient owner-cultivating farms is restricted primarily to settlers from the hills, while encompassing some descendants of the old Tharu landed class in the south. The vast majority of the peasantry in the south Morang field site is composed of landless or marginal landholders with less than 1 hectare of land – with absentee landlords at the apex of the agrarian structure. Tenancy is widespread, and even those owning plots rent a significant share of land from absentee landlords. Caste and ethnicity remain an important marker of economic status given the long association with historic political power, with the majority of the landless households belonging to the indigenous Bantar, Rajbanshi and poorer members of the Tharu communities. While landlordism such as this is applicable across the region including in north Bihar and the Mithila belt of the Tarai-Madhesh further west, absentee landlordism appears to be a particularly important sub-type which is prevalent in Morang, which will likely become more common over time elsewhere in the region as landlord families make the transition to an urban lifestyle.

Within the context of landlord–tenant relations in rural Morang, Chapter 5 showed how there are multiple forms of surplus appropriation, the most important of which is ground rent, with farmers paying either half the harvest or a pre-arranged share to landlords. Rent often goes beyond just absorbing surplus which could otherwise be accumulated, but also eats into the subsistence needs of farmers, depending on the annual yield, the size of plot or whether a portion of the holding is owned. An important observation, though, is that rent is not the only mechanism of surplus appropriation, and merchant capital plays an important role in the rural countryside in extending credit to farmers while also offering an outlet for poor farmers to free up cash at times of urgent need by buying up grain which they would have otherwise consumed. One thus observes classic forms of 'distress commerce'. How this translates into surplus appropriation is complex, but there is evidence of price manipulation in a concentrated grain market, as well as an interlinkage between interest-bearing and merchant capital. Landless farmers, who are already experiencing economic distress due to the rent burden, take loans to buy agricultural inputs, only to repay them at harvest with interest as well as additional 'disguised interest' via price manipulations. While merchant capital has similarities with feudal rent seeking via tenancy, it also plays an intermediate role between the pre-capitalist agricultural sector and Biratnagar's capitalist grain-processing sector.

In terms of the day-to-day lives of the southern Morang peasantry, this drain of surplus, primarily via rent and merchant capital, was shown in Chapter 6 to be central to the reproduction of rural poverty. Critically, it has contributed to a cycle of perpetual food insecurity, with few households retaining sufficient grain to cover their minimum needs. Furthermore, it has constrained farmers from taking up opportunities to develop the productive forces through investment in inputs or new technologies, casting doubt upon a succession of ambitious agricultural policies and plans by the Government of Nepal as well as international donors. However, the outcomes on investments are complex, with some landless and small landholder farmers paradoxically spending more on inputs because they need to rent equipment or us more chemical fertiliser due to an energy–nutrient trade-off. These constraints translate into lower yields for tenants, especially those on sharecropping contracts.

It is evident that the dominant mode of production, while having evolved since Rana times, remains feudal in character, with a concentration of land, appropriation of surplus through absolute ground rent, and diversion of surplus for consumption rather than productive reinvestment. The medium-to-large farmer class who retain control over their own land and surplus as 'independent peasants' represent a small minority. However, a further wave of agrarian stress is actively sweeping the region – and this increasingly extends across the peasantry, including all strata of the rural population. First, climate change has added further pressure to yields while also contributing to rising costs of production, with farmers spending even more money on tubewell rental. Once lucrative crops such as *chaite* (spring) paddy are being abandoned, leading to a drop in cropping intensity. Second, the deepening of Nepal's integration into global markets under economic liberalisation is itself also reshaping agricultural livelihoods for both landless and small landholding farmers dependent on tenancy and the more prosperous farmers – by unleashing a wave of monetisation. The cost of inputs, such as fertiliser and diesel for pumping, has risen considerably, along with a rise in the retail price for food. For larger owner-cultivating farmers cultivating as independent peasants, particularly from the Tharu and hill settler communities, any potential for long-term accumulation is undercut – with rising food costs translating into higher labour costs, set against dwindling farm gate prices for grain in the context of an open border with India.

However, the wave of monetisation which impacts farmers cultivating under feudal and independent 'peasant' relations of production is not restricted to the farm economy. Of note is the rising cost of education and healthcare, with the latter in particular representing a significant financial burden for the most marginal producers. Furthermore, while neoliberalism and the rise in the service sector have seen growing middle-class prosperity in cities such as Biratnagar, this wealth is not trickling down into the increasingly stressed rural hinterland. However, on a cultural level, the patterns of consumption associated with rising urban wealth *have* successfully reached the villages of rural Morang. The peasantry are spending considerable sums on consumer goods, and this is most evident with regard to the commodification and monetisation of gift exchanges and dowry during weddings. These patterns of investment are deeply rooted in middle-class aspirations, however removed these are from day-to-day realities of agricultural livelihoods. For the former Tharu landed class, the need to reproduce markers of social status from an earlier era through lavish expenditure, in spite of their dwindling economic power, epitomises the contradictions which arise when neoliberal capitalism comes into contact with a largely pre-capitalist agrarian economy.

The consequence of these multi-fold changes for the southern Morang peasantry is a spiralling demand for cash, which has two outcomes. The first is debt. While the long-established dependence on merchant capital for credit to purchase inputs at usurious rates remains entrenched, at least amongst landless farmers, there is now also growing indebtedness to microfinance institutions. While emblematic of the neoliberal notion of poverty alleviation through entrepreneurship, it appears that the primary function of the banks for many farmers is to cover large, one-off expenses such as weddings or to meet temporary shortages in cash inflows for day-to-day consumption as households manage the rent burden and rising costs. In other words, the banks paradoxically are taking on a role akin to the archetypical village moneylender under classical South Asian feudalism. As a result, households are often in cycles of debt to multiple banks.

The second and most important consequence of rising cash needs and monetisation is an intensifying articulation with the capitalist sector through wage labour. While reliable year-round factory labour is declining, it is being replaced by casualised but higher-paying semi-skilled work in construction as well as a substantial rise in labour migration to the Gulf states and Malaysia. A stable articulation has thus emerged whereby capitalism meets farmers' cash needs while the agrarian economy, even under feudal relations of production (with the associated rent burden), covers the food needs. Even larger owner-cultivators farming as independent peasants depend in part on off-farm income, although they often seek salaried employment from the service sector in the town or in the bureaucracy. For landless and small landholders, however, the rising dependence on casual and unreliable off-farm and migrant labour for part of one's livelihood has generated new cycles of vulnerability, which came to the fore during 'crises' in capitalism, such as in the wake of the Covid-19 pandemic.

A lingering puzzle, though, is why in spite of these growing articulations with capitalism, surplus appropriation via feudal landlordism and merchant capital is not being undercut. Concrete panel data suggests that absentee landlords retain their hold over land, with few of the land transactions being between local farmers – and, if anything, dependence on rented land is rising as owned plots are subdivided amongst sons. Control over land by landlords acts as a ceiling even for medium-to-large owner-cultivators, who are in a state of increased stress and show limited evidence of accumulation. Rents meanwhile appear to be rising, not helped by the lack of any collective mobilisation or widespread profit orientation which could oblige landlords to negotiate.

Dependence on tenancy and persisting high rent has increased, despite rising household participation in wage labour. It is increasingly clear that capitalist wages do not 'replace' sustenance from the land, but instead simply cover the escalating cash needs of households in the wake of expanding capitalist markets and the associated cycle of debt. A by-product of this dual livelihood strategy is a growing tendency for overwork, which takes on a distinctly feminised form as women take on much of the agricultural labour burden while men increase their engagement in the capitalist sector. This continues to generate substantial profits for capitalism, with a 'sharing' of surplus between landlords/merchant capital on the one hand and the capitalist sector on the other. Landlords arguably benefit from the distorted trajectory of industrial growth, which fails to draw the peasantry away from the land, while the capitalist sector benefits from the continued distress faced by the rent-paying south Morang peasantry, which reproduces the surplus labour pool.

In spite of what appears to be a convergence of interests, however opportunistic, there is limited evidence of a formal class 'alliance'. However, both the interests of the comprador bourgeoise, which has prospered from a sectorally disarticulated industrial sector and import-focused economy, on the one hand, and landed classes, on the other, appear to be upheld to some extent by the bureaucracy. In recent decades there has been limited political will for transformative change by the state *or* political parties. The political upheavals between the 1990s and 2010s, including a People's War, followed by implementation of republicanism and federalism, has had limited impact on the economic structure of the larger social formation which remains semi-colonial in character. At the same time, discussions of redistributive land reform have been shelved. Similarly, questions of ethnic inclusion, which shaped the post-conflict conjuncture, have been sidelined and a wave of ultra-nationalism and majoritarianism risk further perpetuating some of the unequal state–Adivasi relations that sustained feudalism at the grassroots during the Rana and Panchayat periods. This is set against a displacement of larger questions of social justice by narratives of 'development' and 'prosperity'.

The complex diversity of the surplus appropriation class, the often-loose connections between different 'elites' and the complex intersection of class, caste and ethnicity raise important questions about how one understands power in complex social formations at the frontier of capitalist globalisation. This includes important dilemmas around political action for social justice. The resultant agrarian and financial distress facing the Morang peasantry with its deep structural roots cannot be simply addressed via grassroots or national 'policy interventions' to improve agricultural productivity through technology or efforts to strengthen non-farm livelihoods via enterprise development. In the short term, 'technocratic' interventions such as improved access to low-cost and subsidised agricultural equipment such as tubewells, pump sets and tillage technology will indeed have some impact on yields, allowing a greater share of surplus to remain in the household. However, in the long term, the burden of rent and exploitative merchant capital will continue to act as a drain on resources, and improving yields will not offset the worsening labour burden and rising financial stress facing the peasantry. A far more radical transformation is necessary, and in many ways Nepal could offer a new pathway for peripheral nations.

A first field of intervention is in the non-farm sector, whereby labour opportunities are menial and the profusion of credit has not unleashed the predicted wave of rural entrepreneurship. Dialogue is necessary amongst state and political actors for a renewed industrial vision which will promote organic and grassroots-led industrial development which can draw labour from an increasingly distressed peasantry – as Nepal finds its place within a rapidly expanding global capitalist mode of production. This could include, for instance, the promotion and *protection* of niche production spheres in both agro-processing and the once-vibrant cottage industry sector, as well as a radical rethink of the Nepal–India economic relationship beyond symbolic patriotism.

This would extend to include equitable trade regimes with both emerging powers in the sub-imperium such as China as well as the established powers of the core. The strategy must chart an independent and sustainable pathway to industrial progress, oriented around supplying the home market (with forward and backward linkages) while identifying high-value niche exports and breaking import dependence and the dominance of comprador merchant capital in the national economy. Radical new strategies to overcome scale constraints to industrial production could be explored, including the establishment of collectively run enterprises.

While further discussions over industrial development pathways are beyond the scope of this book, what does become apparent from the earlier chapters is an agenda for the agricultural sector itself. With the Tarai-Madhesh peasantry in regions such as Morang reeling under the burden of landlordism, alongside large tracts of the Eastern Gangetic Plains, any new agrarian vision must have redistributive land reform at its core. This could go alongside radical ways or organising land and labour such as through a reinvigorated model of collective farming grounded in small scale, democratic units, with land and resources pooled amongst a handful of households. These have shown some successes in overcoming scale constraints to productivity, particularly in India (Agarwal, 2010; Sugden et al., 2020). However, redistributive land reform appears unlikely so long as landed interests remain entrenched in the bureaucracy (Adhikari, 2006; Alden-Wily et al., 2008). The kind of grassroots mobilisation which made reforms possible in 1970s West Bengal (Banerjee et al., 2002) appears overly optimistic in the case of Nepal.

Nevertheless, the legacy of multiple people's movements over the last two decades in Nepal, widespread politicisation and exposure to new ideas from cyclical overseas migration mean that this may be an opportune moment for transformative mobilisation amongst the peasantry over issues of rent, land distribution and the absence of meaningful employment. Given the complex matrix of inequality outlined in this book, political action in the years ahead needs to come from below and will likely entail multiple alliances across a broad spectrum of the multi-ethnic peasantry, urban working class and the many who sit between these two modes of production in the quest for a more equitable social formation.

References

Adhikari, J. 2006. *Land Reform in Nepal: Problems and Prospects.* Nepal Institute of Development Studies.

Agarwal, Bina 2010. Rethinking agricultural production collectivities. *Economic and Political Weekly* 45 (9): 64–78.

Alden-Wily, L., Chapgain, D. and Sharma, S. 2008. *Land Reform in Nepal: Where Is It Coming from and Where Is It Going?* DFID.

Banerjee, Abhijit V., Gertler, Paul J. and Ghatak, Maitreesh. 2002. Empowerment and efficiency: tenancy reform in West Bengal. *Journal of Political Economy* 110 (2): 239–280.

Sehgal, Rakhi 2005. Social reproduction of third world labour in the era of globalisation: State, market and the household. *Economic and Political Weekly* 40 (22–23): 2286–2294.

Shah, Alpa and Lerche, Jens. 2020. Migration and the invisible economies of care: production, social reproduction and seasonal migrant labour in India. *Transactions of the Institute of British Geographers*. DOI: 10.1111/tran.12401.

Sugden, Fraser, Agarwal, Bina, Leder, Stephanie, Saikia, Panchali, Raut, Manita, Kumar, Anoj and Ray, Dhananjay. 2021. Experiments in farmer collectives in eastern India and Nepal: Process, benefits and challenges. *Journal of Agrarian Change* 21 (1): 90–121.

Zhan, Shaohua and Scully, Ben. 2018. From South Africa to China: Land, migrant labor and the semi-proletarian thesis revisited. *Journal of Peasant Studies* 45 (5–6): 1018–1038.

Glossary

Adivasi	a term used to refer to indigenous or 'tribal' communities across South Asia
Agricultural Development Bank (ADB)	the main government-run microfinance bank in Nepal
ADS	Agricultural Development Strategy, the Government of Nepal's agricultural plan which succeeded the Agricultural Perspective Plan in 2015
APP	Agriculture Perspective Plan, the Government of Nepal's flagship agricultural plan which ran from 1995–2015
Ashadh	monsoon month in the Hindu calendar between June and July when rice is planted
Bantar	an indigenous Tarai community residing in the Morang region
bazaar	a market area
bigha	the predominant measure of land common in the Nepal Tarai and India; 1 *bigha* = 0.67 hectares
birta	a form of tax-free land tenure offered to members of the Rana ruling elite during the late nineteenth and early twentieth centuries, often as a form of salary
Chaitra	the month of spring in the Hindu calendar between April and May

chaudhari	a tax-collection role in the Tarai from before the Rana era which was often drawn from the local Adivasi community
godown	warehouse
haat bazaar or *haatiya*	Nepali term for a periodic market; each rural locality usually holds one once or twice a week in a set location
jagir	land given to an individual in lieu of salary during the eighteenth and nineteenth centuries
jamindar, often spelt *zamindar*	colonial era tax collector in India, although used today as a general term to refer to a big landlord throughout many parts of South Asia
Jhagar	a community residing in the Morang region; considered an Adivasi (indigenous) group in Nepal and South Asia, although the community in Nepal migrated originally from the Chotanagpur plateau in central India
jimidar	person given revenue-collection rights in the Tarai-Madhesh by the Rana rulers, and is derived from the Arabic term *jimmadar*, or functionary, and is not to be confused with *jamindar*, sometimes spelt *zamindar* (see above) – the latter comes from the Persian word for land, *zamin*, and is the same as the colonial and Mughal-era term *zamindar*, which translates as landlord; to add to the confusion, some farmers use the term *jamindar* as a generic term for a big landlord
katawala	a retailer specialising in the purchase of grain from farmers; *kata* refers to the scales used to weigh the grain
Khas	a collective term for the Nepali-speaking caste Hindus who trace their origins to western Nepal and today include the dominant hill Brahmin and Chettri communities and the erstwhile Shah dynasty
khudra	same as *katawala*

Kushuwaha	Maithili-speaking caste who are traditionally vegetable producers; also known as Koiri
Madhesh	the lowlands of Nepal which Morang is part of, also known as Tarai; the term 'Madhesh' has stronger political connotations, while 'Tarai' is the more neutral term to refer to the agro-ecological zone – many scholars thus refer to it as Tarai-Madhesh
Madheshi	a collective term which generally refers to the plains communities with cultural and linguistic affinity to communities on the Bihar and Uttar Pradesh side of the Indo-Nepal border. They include caste Hindus and Muslim communities who speak the language of their neighbours in India, namely Maithili in the east, Bhopuri in the central plains and Awadhi in the west.
Maithili	an Indo-European language spoken in the historical region of Mithila, on the plains of northeast Bihar, India, and the eastern Nepal Tarai – Morang is on the fringes of this region; the Maithili speakers have a rich culture and complex caste system
Marwari	an industrial and business community originally from India, who own many industries in Nepal
maund	a common measurement for crop weights, with 1 *maund* being equivalent to 40 kilograms
Musahar	Dalit community residing across the Nepal Tarai and the Indian state of Bihar, also known locally in Morang (more respectfully) by their surname, Rishidev.
NPR	Nepali rupees; USD 1 = approximately NPR 139 today, but at the time of the 2007–2008 research, it was around NPR 70
Pahadi	a generic term for a hill person in Nepal, not to be confused with Khas, which refers

	specifically to the Nepali-speaking Hindu castes
Ranas	a series of hereditary prime ministers who ruled Nepal from 1846 to 1950
Rajbanshi	an indigenous community who inhabit the Tarai plains from Morang to West Bengal, India
rupee or Rs	Nepali currency; see NPR
Santhal	a community residing in the Morang region; considered an Adivasi (indigenous) group in Nepal and South Asia, like the Santhal, although the community in Nepal migrated originally from the Chotanagpur plateau in central India, like the Jhagar
Tarai	the geographical strip of lowlands which skirts the Nepal and parts of the Indian Himalaya; see also Madhesh
tol	neighbourhood of a village or town, or sometimes a small settlement itself
Tharu	largest indigenous community of the Tarai; they were the main group in the Tarai-Madhesh prior to deforestation but now live a sedentary life
Tarai-Madhesh	see Madhesh
VDC	Village Development Committee – a division of local governance in Nepal; each district is divided into a number of VDCs

Index